HARDPRESS.NET
HOME OF HARD-TO-FIND BOOKS

Na Motu
by Edward T. Perkins

Copyright © 2019 by HardPress

Address:
HardPress
8345 NW 66TH ST #2561
MIAMI FL 33166-2626
USA
Email: info@hardpress.net

Na Motu

Edward T. Perkins

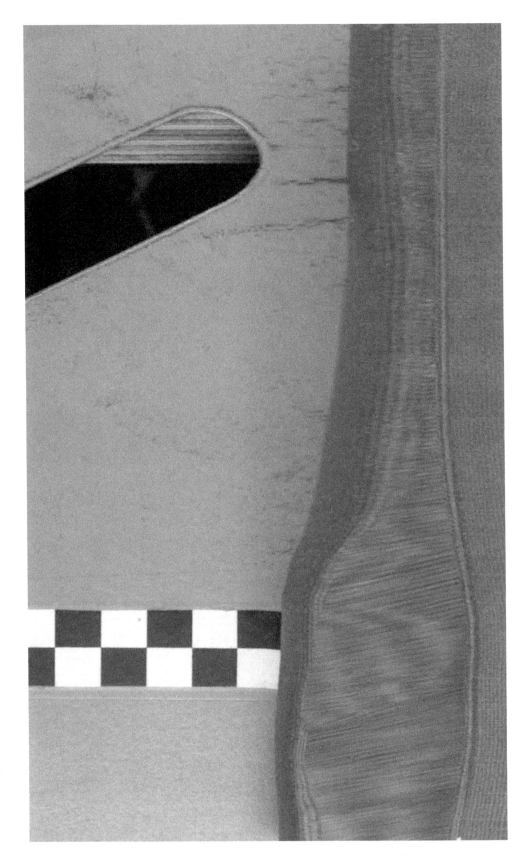

HAMOTU
OR
Reef Rovings
in the
SOUTH SEAS.

NA MOTU:

OR,

REEF-ROVINGS IN THE SOUTH SEAS.

A Narrative of Adventures

AT THE

HAWAIIAN, GEORGIAN AND SOCIETY ISLANDS;

WITH MAPS,

TWELVE ORIGINAL ILLUSTRATIONS,

AND

An Appendix

RELATING TO THE RESOURCES, SOCIAL AND POLITICAL CONDITION OF
POLYNESIA, AND SUBJECTS OF INTEREST IN THE PACIFIC OCEAN.

BY EDWARD T. PERKINS.

NEW-YORK:

PUDNEY & RUSSELL, PUBLISHERS,
No. 79 JOHN-STREET.

. . . .

1854.

TO

JARVIS M. ANDREWS. M. D.,

OF NEW-YORK,

As a Pledge of Friendship

THIS VOLUME IS INSCRIBED,

BY

THE AUTHOR

PREFACE.

NEARLY six years have elapsed since the writer of these sketches was numbered among the crew of an American whaler, and but little more than six months since he was passenger on board an English brig, voyaging in the South Pacific. Through sheer necessity recourse was had to writing, to beguile the monotony of an existence between sky and ocean, and the delineation of scenes and scenery has been attempted in the unpoetic confines of a state-room. The subject selected, a momentary consideration was involved as to the manner of treating it. A geographic, historic, and descriptive account of the various localities visited at first suggested itself, but the absence of either library or work of reference precluded its adoption, and at the hazard of the imputation of egotism, a narrative of personal adventures was concluded upon.

Though fugitive selections may awaken a momentary interest, these sketches profess to impart nothing new, save the recital of recent occurrences, which may possibly be deemed of political worth; the adventures are merely the experiences of a thousand others in this ocean, who, instead of publishing, retain them for an inexhaustible fund of future reminiscence. As an early schoolmate, Ik Marvel, has expressed it, " mine have been tossed from me in the shape of a book;" but in the endeavor to avoid prolixity, it is feared that points of incident and description which so materially enhance the interest of a cursory narrative, have been too hastily dealt with.

Unlike the Old World, Polynesia boasts of no monuments of antiquity : the ruins of *Heiáu* and *Maráe* are but the relics of a few generations that have passed away—beyond that resting-point we look into obscurity. Though we discover no hieroglyphics of mystic import to conjure up gloomy reveries, we are ever opening a new page in the Book of Nature, fresh and glowing with the intelligible symbols of beauty and sublimity. We are wont to associate with these miniature gardens the reveries of romance—the brightest conceptions of poetic imagery ; but reflection will impress us with realities of deeper interest, and the ideal will be forgotten as we link the present to the shadowy future. For a moment, we revert to the period when islands rose from liquid depths, put forth their fires, and hill and valley bloomed amid varied phenomena, unseen by other than the eye of their Creator. Again, we view them as in majesty and power they stand forth Nature's giant sarcophagi of a slumbering element—emeralds upon a field of blue, the home of millions basking in perennial sunshine, but covered with intellectual darkness. Centuries roll round ; science and enterprise hand in hand reveal but the relic of a once numerous race, for "the strong men have bowed themselves," and though religion has bestowed its precious boon, and benevolence and philanthropy have gratuitously scattered their gifts, they have failed to rescue a people hastening to oblivion.

At no period of our national existence have American in-terests been so prominently manifest in the great Western

Ocean. Laws, literature, and commerce are results of an enterprise that has established States and successfully combated a national antipathy. The recent opening of Japanese ports is an additional evidence of our characteristic policy; without a cannon-shot to shatter the barrier of hereditary prejudice, a noble conquest has been peacefully achieved. Invidious comparisons are not sought—they are unnecessary; a candid observer who surveys the broad track of American enterprise in this ocean, will seek in vain for beacons of selfish cupidity or ambition. It will be discovered that our victories, whether spiritual or political, have been marked by intellectual growth and commercial prosperity; to kingdoms and tribes we have bequeathed indelible impressions of our national worth and disinterested philanthropy.

The present subject embraces but a small proportion of the island nebulæ Oceanicæ, though including the two most prominent groups of the Polynesian Archipelago. But little more than ten years ago, both were native principalities: to one has been accorded the fellowship of nations; the other, the brightest gem of the Southern Ocean, after a protracted struggle for existence, has bowed to a conqueror, and its hills and valleys are bristling with European cannon. The commerce of kingdoms and colonies combined in this ocean is trifling in comparison with our own, yet the powers of the Old World have greedily coveted and seized upon independent soil,—independent by every principle of justice and equity, as if national greatness were to be promoted by hostile aggression, sanctioned by neither moral requirement nor commercial interests. The English and French in the South Pacific, and the Dutch in the Indian Archipelago, have appropriated most of the available

lands or prominent groups; and at the present rate of territorial absorption, an observer who surveys this broad field at
the expiration of ten years, will discover but few evidences of
original possession or primitive freedom.

The incidents narrated are comprised by the years '48 and '53.
The words "NA MOTU" signify in the Hawaiian and Tahitian
dialects "*The Islands.*" For various reasons, the present subject
has been confined to those two groups alone, namely, the
Hawaiian or Sandwich, Georgian and Society Islands. As a
prefatory link, it has been ventured to introduce "The Whale
Ship," but in doing so, the hackneyed routine of ship-duty has
been studiously avoided, and a combination of nautical incidents, grave and humorous, has been substituted, to relieve
the otherwise sombre shadows of the forecastle. It remains
but to be said, that if in idle moments a persual of these
sketches affords a moiety of the gratification experienced in
writing them, their object will have been attained; for to
please, if not to instruct, will ever be the wish of

THE AUTHOR.

NEW-YORK, *July*, 1854.

CONTENTS

PART I.

THE WHALE-SHIP.

SEQUEL TO THE FOREGOING.

PART II.

HAWAIIAN ISLANDS.

CHAPTER X.

CHAPTER XI.

CHAPTER XII.

CHAPTER XIII.

CHAPTER XIV.

CHAPTER XV.

CHAPTER XVI.

CHAPTER XVII.

CHAPTER XVIII.

PART III.
GEORGIAN AND SOCIETY ISLANDS.

CHAPTER XIX.

CHAPTER XX.

CHAPTER XXI.

CHAPTER XXII.

CHAPTER XXIII.

CHAPTER XXIV.

CHAPTER XXV.

CHAPTER XXVI.

APPENDIX I.

A GLANCE AT THE PRESENT CONDITION OF POLYNESIA.

APPENDIX II.

THE ISLAND KINGDOM OF THE NORTH PACIFIC.

APPENDIX III.

THE FRENCH IN THE PACIFIC.

APPENDIX IV.

AMERICAN WHALING INTERESTS IN THE PACIFIC.

THE WHALE-SHIP.

CHAPTER I.

WE SHAPE OUR COURSE.

To an observer from the shore, there is something imposing in the sight of a noble ship, with her masts looming loftily, and her taper spars standing forth in graceful relief against the clear sky, while a cloud of snowy canvas, like extended wings, is urging her onward through the liquid .element. If perchance a jet of flame leaps from her dark side, and a booming sound like distant thunder comes echoing across the water and reverberating among the hills, emotions of sublimity are awakened. But there is something indescribably ludicrous in the appearance of eighteen or twenty recruits lumbering the deck of a whaler, some of them leaning languidly against the try-works, with their orbs rolled deprecatingly up, and others grouped about the windlass in accidental postures of despair.

Without venturing upon undue familiarity, let me beg courteous readers to accompany me for a brief interval to my floating home, suggesting, however, to such as are ultra-fastidious, to wrap their garments carefully about them to avoid contamination. No gilded saloons nor decorated panels meet the eye; but there is a matter-of-fact appearance about everything that seems to imply, we have done with the frivolities, and now for the realities of life. I believe it will be mutually agreeable when I refrain from a disquisition on "dog watches" and "seven bells;" for ropes and marlinspikes have become stale, and meditations over tar buckets grown insipid.

2

Forecastles, like friendships, improve on acquaintance; and though diversified with the odds and ends of humanity, a careful study of the emotions and passions that have been hatched and brooded within their narrow precincts would afford no ignoble theme for the pages of philosophy. They are frequently the last jumping-off place for renegade pettifoggers and professional gentlemen of other denominations, whose fortunes have become desperate, and who exchange their ventilated insignia for duck trowsers and guernsey frocks. Here they abandon theories for realities, forsaking the comforts for the hardships of life; and if they be of meditative turn, they hamper themselves with the brighter incidents of retrospection, having ample opportunity to reflect upon the consequences of their indiscretion.

We were a motley assemblage of Americans, English, Irish, Scotch, French, and Portuguese; besides, we could boast of every shade of complexion, from the fair Saxon to the sable African; and, as might be supposed, there was a diversity of disposition among us, the consequence of personal habit or national characteristic. The blunt frankness of Bull and Jonathan was in striking contrast to the intriguing disposition of the swarthy Portuguese, while the volubility of the Hibernian harmonized with the enthusiasm of the merry Gaul. But there were never those feelings of odd-fellowship among us which usually characterize the crew of a merchantman: some feud existed, some score to be wiped out, precluding all possibility of a permanent reconciliation between the adverse parties, although a general treaty was sometimes agreed upon. Above every consideration, an hereditary warfare was perpetually waged against the greenhorns.

Without attempting an essay upon sleep, I conceive that fancy may invest the imagination with as pleasing imagery, though its possessor be inclosed between rough boards and immersed in the coarse fabric of Leeds, as it could do though surrounded by gorgeous tapestry and luxuriating amid the fine linen of Egypt. Nevertheless, it was a bone of contention to see who should secure the lower bunks, for the obvious reason that in warm weather, when the decks were washed down, a number of briny streams might be seen filtering through the oakum into the upper tier.

The " Planet's" forecastle had perhaps nothing to distinguish it from similar sub-residences. I descended the rough ladder with the feelings of a novice who for the first time ventures into the shaft of a coal-mine. Its form was of course triangular, and its sides lined with parallel rows of narrow bunks, some of which made a flaunting display of calico curtains, being otherwise decorated with amorous lithographic designs, while others made a modest display of the coarse blankets from the slop-chest. From some of them, diminutive shelves jutted out, for the purpose of securing a lamp when the occupant was disposed to devote a few moments of his watch below to reading. The floor was covered with chests of every description, from the old family trunk, bestowed by the doting mamma upon her adventurous boy, to the capacious receptacle of the professional Jack.

Rarely, if ever, is a forecastle silent, except during the night watches : yarns are spun and reeled, and loved ditties sung, chiefly on the chromatic scale ; some play fox and geese, or " old sledge," if the moral scruples of the skipper will permit. You will occasionally hear the unavailing regrets of some home-sick " verdant," who is continually tantalizing himself with visions of domestic bliss, hoping to elicit a sypmpathizing word from the older seamen, but which usually result in the protrusion of sundry heads from the blankets, accompanied by unmistakable growls and demonstrations, invariably producing the effect intended.

As regards dining utensils, it was sheath-knives and tin-pans *versus* silver forks and porcelain. Though the iron hoops of the pine coffee-bucket had grown rusty, and the interior of the vessel become saturated and discolored with a suspicious *debris*, yet it would have been a fastidious stomach that would not have yearned for its contents on a frosty morning when Weasle came staggering forward with it, almost enveloped in a cloud of savory steam.

With becoming reverence, I turn my attention to the quarter-deck, to look upon those who have so often reminded us that the Planet was to be our home for the next four years, and that we had " signed articles to do our duty by day and by night." Captain Peter Smith Buck was a man of medium height, broad-shouldered, having a well-knit frame ; yet there was nothing classical in his proportions. for they tended rather to corpulency than otherwise. He was an able, weather-beaten seaman, possessing at times generous impulses ; but on ordinary occasions his feelings were as callous as his features.

But how shall I attempt to describe Mr. Grasper—Mr. O. C. Grasper—our first officer, that champion of the lance and short warp, who has so often carried death to great leviathan beneath a burning sun and amid icy seas! He, too, in point of dimension, possessed extraordinary breadth of beam, that savored more of Bacchus than Apollo. His arm ! that brawny, muscular appendage, if incased in a leaden gauntlet, might have hurled terror into the arena of Olympia ; but, fortunately, its prowess was reserved for labors conducive to the wants of man. Between its flexors and inflexors a tacit understanding appeared to exist, so that digits and patronymic had a strong affinity for each other ; their incessant grasping propensity obtained for them the appellation of " grappling irons," and woe to the victim who felt their embrace !

That tall man issuing orders respecting the waist-boat, and clothed with blue trowsers and shirt, subscribes himself to a ship's articles as Hezekiah Gurrie, Jr. He is our second officer, a good seaman, and an industrious man. There are certain quadrupeds that intimate their disposition by a premonitory growl. Mr. Gurrie resembled one of these ; and although he always turned an evil eye upon me, I will frankly award him the praise his due, for it was what he considered an infringement of his rights and duties as an able seaman, by Captain Buck, that led to the rupture which subsequently occurred.

Mr. Short, our third officer, was in every respect of inferior calibre. Should this ever meet his eye, I hope he will remember that hypocrisy is an ungrateful return for favors bestowed. He was a hardy, weather-beaten sailor, and always at his post in case of emergency.

Mr. Easy, our fourth officer, was a young man, expert in his profession, and usually prompt in the performance of his duty. In his intercourse with his inferiors, I do not think he was ever guilty of personal violence ; and I am happy to add that with him I have passed many a pleasant hour.

Next in grade comes the steerage, a kind of stepping-stone for

Jack in the way of promotion : here lived the cooper, boat-steerers, and carpenter. Gouty old cooper ! How much I owe you for your kindness ! Perhaps you consider the debt cancelled in a measure by the soothing remedies I have so often applied to your rheumatic shoulders, not .forgetting instances of warm decoctions and "soft tack" prepared by special request. If the top-gallantmast required slushing, or the dead-eyes needed scraping, the cooper always wanted some one about that time to hold on to his staves, or help him make bungs ; and no one was "half so handy at it as the Doctor." Thus I was spared the annoyance of many a disagreeable job, while on such occasions he would entertain me with famous long yarns about the "heathen savages of the Feejees," with heads as large as half-bushels, and yellow eyeballs.

Our boat-steerers were, every one of them, good fellows, with ready hands, and, I hope, honest hearts ; one of them, "Old John," as we used to call him, was a most inveterate growl. Many were his sarcastic allusions to the old "gurry box," which on ordinary occasions was "too much by the head," and otherwise "out of ballast trim." A want of precision in trimming the yards, and the necessity of making or reducing sail, afforded him favorite themes for censure ; and as his views on these points never coincided with those of the officer of the watch, he was condescending enough to attribute the oversights or deficiency to that gentleman's error in judgment. But John had one treasure which he prized above all others, and that was an old Epitome, published, I imagine, when the science of navigation was in embyro. This was the oracle he invariably consulted when the topic in dispute happened to be nautical : with reference to latitude and longitude, any discrepancies that might exist between the observations of Cook, Wilkes, or the Spanish navigator, whose motto was, "Primus me circumdedit," John would happily adjust by reference to his medium.

It would, perhaps, be inappropriate to particularize all my companions, but I will endeavor to present brief delineations of character, as occasion may require. I made a companion of a fellow named Josh, a down-east Yankee, whose straight flaxen hair hung like thatch around his ruddy cheeks, who had some nautical experience, and was not to be intimidated by anything like bombast.

Josh had a sweetheart at home, and he showed me a parting souvenir she had bestowed—a lock of hair. Another individual, named Folger, who occupied the bunk above me, came from somewhere in Ohio. When I first met him at the rendezvous, he sported what had once been a white linen shirt-collar, and a *drap d'ete*, " shad-belly," and was commenting somewhat freely upon the contemplated arrangements. From various expressions, I inferred that he was drawing a marked line of distinction between himself and those around him. I subsequently learned something of this gentleman's history:—he was once a Democrat, but for three years had been a staunch Whig, and, I trust, a valuable acquisition to his party ; he had several times been an assistant delegate to some of our great Conventions, and on one occasion he condescended to accept the proffered hand of his political foe, Martin Van Buren. I had my fears at first lest his radical views might prompt him to set on foot some plot to overturn the established dynasty, and institute a sort of Marine Provisional Government ; but whatever might have been his prospective arrangements, his embryo aspirations forever vanished after the first night in the Gulf Stream.

Among our number was one we called Weasle, a tall, slim fellow, with a hatchet face, who had never before seen salt water. Being somewhat whimsical, he had forsaken his domestic vocations in the backwoods, and strolling through South Street, was picked up by some of the sharks, who persuaded him to ship on the Planet, alleging that the sea air was bracing to weak nerves. · There are some who, fashion them as you will, can never be modelled into sailors ; there is something about the " cut of their jibs" that in the eye of an old salt marks them as landsmen abroad. Weasle was one of these, and during the six months he was with us he acquired nothing pertaining to seamanship but what he was absolutely compelled to ; however, he had some redeeming traits, for as soon as his tribute to Neptune had ceased, he fell naturally into the routine of drudgery that had to be performed about the ship. Whether the vocation of tending swine revived pleasing reminiscences or not, he was faithful in the performance of that duty ; and it was pleasant to observe the sympathy for each other that sprung up between guardian and brute. Weasle, in his striped guernsey frock, could hardly cross the deck, in proximity to his proteges, without a grunt of recognition, and I believe the happiest moments he passed were those devoted to feeding them. Although no sailor, he was spared the jeers of his shipmates, for the duties instinctively performed by him spared them the necessity of many a disagreeable job. I wish I could add as much in behalf of the officers ; but it was an evil moment when Mr. Grasper conceived his first impressions of him, for I have seen him seize the unfortunate Weasle by the nape of the neck, and spin him around like a top. All these humiliations and indignities were meekly borne ; he held on the tenor of his way, patiently tending his swine, who looked upon him as an emblem of peace and love.

Before closing this chapter I will modestly venture a bit of egotism ; though, with reference to introducing myself to the reader in the poetic apparel of duck trowsers and hickory shirt, I would merely observe, that it is pleasanter to contemplate results than to investigate causes : what I wish to explain is, how I acquired the title of Doctor. I had taken the precaution to provide myself with a few medicines, and was indebted to the kindness of a professional gentleman for a couple of old forceps and a case of " dressing instruments," and who at the same time hinted " I might as well get my hand in." Though possessing a venerable edition of Wood and Bache, besides retaining a few recollections of cliniques, I would have blushed to rank myself among professed disciples of Hippocrates. Nevertheless, the evidences I possessed were sufficient to entitle me M. D. of the ship's company, and having grown wise by experience, my humble advice to all young gentlemen of the profession, who do not live in the cabin with recognized privileges, and whose propensities may tempt them to a more intimate acquaintance with the cetacean branch of comparative anatomy, or perhaps mammalia in general, is to conceal every indication of their craft, and to look indignant at the smell of drugs. In support of it, let me cite one or two instances of the annoyances to which I was frequently subjected. Perhaps I am seizing a "scotchman" on to the main swifter, and am just engaged in the most interesting portion of it, when I hear a prolonged cry of " Doc—t—o—r," issuing from the forecastle like the smothered cry of a victim in a subterranean dungeon. "Wanted down below there," echo several of the watch on deck. On such occasions, if I had an irksome job, I suited my convenience, and when I saw my patient, my diagnosis was usually brief. If an ordinary case, and it happened to occur on "duff day," I at once affirmed that he had been overloading his stomach with that approximation to pastry, and I was always supported in my opinion by some half dozen voices issuing from the blankets. One would "swear that he had seen him eat three quarts of bean soup for dinner ;" while another composedly declared that he "had stolen his ' soft tack' from the galley while he was standing mast-head." Half a dozen other charges would be preferred against the victim, while I prescribed, which would generally be Epsom salts and warm water, watching carefully meanwhile my patient's countenance as the surest symptom on which to base a subsequent diagnosis. One would hardly credit it, but during the cold weather, off Cape Horn, I have known a confirmed *phthisis* in Folger, together with general debility, to relapse into a severe headache and soon-get-better feeling, which miraculous change I would fain attribute to my prescription, approved by Mr. Grasper ; and that was a pint of warm salts and water, three times a day, and after the first day, if no relief was experienced, a black bolus, and a plaster of Spanish flies to the pit of the stomach. On these occasions Folger would give me a beseeching look.

Sometimes, on taking my position at mast-head, I would lean comfortably upon the royal yard, and instead of looking out for either "blows" or "flukes," would peer down from my eyrie to watch the manifold evolutions on deck. While listening to those sounds that afford an inspiriting theme for statesmen, the noise of the cooper, the ringing of the anvil, and the carpenter's hammer, and indulging a pleasing revery on the comparative qualities of lions and eagles, some one roars out, "Old Bill's dying with the colic !"

" On deck, there ! Hang Old Bill and his colic !"

" Descend from that crow's nest, you leech, and administer to the wants of suffering humanity," shouts Mr. Grasper from the quarter-deck.

Of course I had but one alternative, and while complying with the requirement, I have thought that had humanity ever been properly classified, I should have been puzzled to assign to " Old Bill" his appropriate genus.

CHAPTER II.

ELUCIDATIONS OF THE PRECEDING, HAVING REFERENCE TO NAUTICAL ECONOMY.

THE daily routine of a whaler is vastly different from that of a merchantman. In connection with the duties of the latter, there is always an amount of necessary work on hand which serves as a basis for extra labor, if such be the wish of the officer in command. After six months' experience, I cannot particularize every odd job, but this I recollect most distinctly, that the old forge sent forth its blasts as regularly as that of a village blacksmith ; while the cooper had exhausted all his spare material before doubling Cape Horn. I have seen the carpenter throw his cap on deck, and his hammer into the lee scuppers, while he poured forth a volley of abuse upon every one who burnt oil. The boat-steerers, too ; it seemed that they would never rig their boats to suit themselves ; and during the intervals of that occupation they sharpened their irons (harpoons) and lances, whose number constituted a formidable display of projectiles. Between boat-steerers and artificers in wood and iron, the grindstone was made to perform incessant revolutions. The foremost hands had their duties to accomplish, and I would have risked the rigging of the Planet in competition with that of any other whaler that floated. She was, as Chips facetiously remarked, " a floating workshop ;" and I have since learned that our duties were not so much from necessity as from the skipper's solicitude for our health, he having satisfied himself by long experience that incessant labor was, like Irish potatoes, an excellent antiscorbutic.

The most serious obstacle the recruits had to encounter was

" learning the ropes." Some of us, realizing that it must be done, applied ourselves to the task until we had mastered it ; but there were a few laggards for whom the rest of us bore no sympathy, and I would be the last to censure an officer for *striking* manifestations of his displeasure towards a soger, particularly if he is green. Mr. Folger, I regret to say, was dilatory in his acquirements, and this, together with other circumstances, resulted in his becoming one of the butts of the company. Two weeks passed by, and, with others, he was still as ignorant of the names of some of the most important ropes as the day he came on board ; it therefore became necessary that some decisive course should be pursued to bring the laggards to a sense of their duty. Accordingly, three or four of them were called aft, where they were informed by the captain that if in three days they were not perfectly familiar with the " running rigging," they should be deprived of their watch below until they were. At the expiration of the appointed time the culprits were summoned to the main hatch, where the examination took place, which was as interesting as that of a boarding-school, although no premiums were to be awarded. The captain commenced :—

" Folger, I want you to show me the main-topsail sheets."

Folger thought a moment, then went to the mainmast and laid his hand upon them.

" Very good, sir. Well, now I want you to tell me where I can find the fore-spencer vangs."

This was a poser ; he looked aloft despairingly at the net-work of black and white ropes, then most inquiringly at the crew, but he was rewarded by no answering hint ; for though some of us pitied him, the lynx-eye of Mr. Grasper, who enjoyed his perplexity, was watching every movement. With desperate resolve, he went forward, and laid his hand at random upon the top-gallant bunt-line.

" There, sir, that'll do for you. Cook ! the next time you make duff, I want you to tie that man's share on to the fore-spencer vangs. Go forward, sir, and don't you dare to go below until you've learned what I told you ; it's nothing but sheer stupidity. I'm afraid I shall have to give you some practical lessons, young man, before the voyage is up. Who have we got next ? What's that man's name there leaning aginst the try-works, with his hands in gaskets ?"

" That ? Why that's Weasle," said Mr. Grasper : " he's always got one eye clewed up and the other sheeted home."

" Come up here, Weasle ; hold up your head like a man, and take your hands out of your pockets ; I aint going to strike you, I only want to see whether you've learned the lesson I gave you ; I want every man to do his duty, and all share alike."

Weasle, who supposed he was about to confront some sea monster, was taken rather aback at the captain's friendly address, although he did not entirely recover his self-possession.

" Show me the main-brace," said Captain Buck, wishing to encourage him by mentioning one of the most conspicuous ropes.

Weasle laid his hand upon it very promptly.

" Show me the foretopsail haulyards." After a little study, this was found.

" Now, Weasle, my boy, I want you to give a small pull on the larboard foretopsail brace, and haul taut the weather bowline."

Weasle's head dropped as suddenly as if it had been perforated by a bullet, while his hands mechanically sought the before-mentioned gaskets.

" Come, sir, start !"

He at once bolted off towards the starboard quarter.

" Come back, here ; don't you know the difference yet between larboard and starboard ?"

" Yes, sir," drawled Weasle : "starboard means the weather side, I guess."

" The hell it does !" roared the captain. " *You* guess ! Well, *I* guess that starboard means right, and larboard means left ; now do you know ?"

" Yes, sir."

" Well, have you learned the difference yet between a duff-kid and a pot of lob-scouse ?"

" I don't know, sir, but I guess I can."

" You *guess* you can ! Well, how many arms do you guess you've got ?"

" Two."

" Which is the larboard one ?"

Weasle deliberately poked out the right one.

" O murder!" exclaimed the captain, whirling about, at the same time laughing contemptuously. " *Was* I ever so green! No, I swear I wasn't. For heavens, Mr. Grasper, take charge of those sea-goats, and never let me get my hands upon them ; if I do, I shall seize them up to the mizzen rigging and give them a dozen every morning before breakfast."

I once heard of a witty skipper who sailed from port with an unusual complement of greenhorns, and encountering rough weather in the Gulf Stream, he was seriously embarrassed, owing to the ignorance of his recruits, but which he obviated by a happy thought. A pack of cards was distributed among the rigging oftenest in requisition, and each card properly secured to a rope ; if a squall was approaching, and the officer of the watch thought it necessary to reduce a top-gallant-sail, he would call out " Stand by there, boys, to let go your diamonds and haul away on the queen of hearts."

Having touched upon the subject, it would perhaps be as well to mention a few items of daily routine, to avoid the necessity of any explanation hereafter ; but as this is not intended for a seaman's manual, I shall spare the reader the old story of " seven bells," and the manner of " splicing the main-brace." The crew were divided into two watches, the second officer heading the starboard, and the third officer the larboard watch, alternately relieving each other every four hours, except during the dog-watches, when it was all hands. The first summons to duty of the morning watch is, " draw water ;" and this being anything but a favorite pastime, especially in cold weather, it frequently became a matter of dispute as to whose turn it was to rig and man the whip, and sometimes the discussion grew so animated that the interference of an officer was required.

" Come, come, what argument's that going on ? If there's any dispute to be settled, there's where I live. Bill, you and Josh rig the whip, and be quick about it ; the rest of you fleet aft, and get your scrub-brooms."

Such was the observation of Mr. Gurrie one morning, when Old

Bill replied that "he'd rather be relieved, because he'd got a lame back, and the doctor was going to give him a plas——"

"O, to the devil with your lame back, and the doctor, too! If I don't see that whip rigged to the main swifter in just two minutes and a half, I'll prepare the way for a plaster with the bight of the first rope I can lay my hands on."

The whip is a spar about twelve feet long, with a shive-hole at one end; through this is rove a rope, one end secured to a large bucket, while the other is free for hoisting. The spar is then elevated a few feet above the bulwarks, and fastened to the main swifter, with one of the ends projecting a convenient distance over the water, and the other resting upon deck. If the bucket is small, the job of drawing is not very disagreeable; but ours was as large as a half barrel, and the weight, so disproportioned to purchase and power, rendered it one of the most impressive illustrations of the pulley I ever met with. Two men usually perform the duty, while one sits astride of the rail to receive the buckets. I can distinctly recollect remonstrating with the cooper at the time I saw him hammering away at the tub. "Can't help it," said he; "must obey orders."

Our scrub-brooms, too, are worthy of consideration. Manufactured by sheath-knives from pickled blocks of seasoned oak, they possessed about as much flexibility as could be expected, and their action upon the pine sheathing I can compare to nothing else than the probable effect of rubbing a stiff brush briskly over a bald head.

Scrubbing finished, trowsers turned down, and mast-heads stationed, we turned on to any job we were ordered to, until seven bells or breakfast-time. This was announced to us by the captain's saying, "Give 'em their breakfast, Mr. Grasper."

"Aye, aye, sir. Give 'em their breakfasts, there, cook."

"Aye, aye, sir. Breakfast for'a-r-d!" which is echoed by several hungry "aye, ayes;" and if they did manifest any reluctance about manning the whip, their alacrity on this occasion was conspicuous, for several volunteers would spring to their feet, expressing a willingness to carry either the beef-kid or coffee-bucket.

I shall not attempt to describe the thousand and one odd jobs, besides the regular work; we took our turns at mast-head, which lasted two hours, also each his trick at the wheel. The difference between standing look-out at the main and foremast heads is this : the boat-steerers are the privileged characters in the first instance, and after reaching the topmast cross-trees, they have a " Jacob's ladder" by which they can ascend to the " crow's nest" direct, and in a cross sea they are less affected by the motion of the vessel than we of the fore, where at times we were compelled to give the royal-mast an affectionate embrace with both arms, and not unfrequently I noticed the recurrence of nauseating symptoms to the consternation of all who delight in clean canvas. This post was only reached by " shinning" up the top-gallant stays, and our instructions on these occasions were to "look sharp for blows, flukes, or white water," and he who first raised a whale from which we could secure a " blanket piece," should be rewarded with five pounds of " Mrs. G. B. Miller's fine cut," and a new pair of duck trowsers. Of course, with so brilliant a prize in perspective, we were a parcel of ambitious competitors, and each ascended with the determination of raising something, at least a breeze.

Although the work, as a general rule, ceased after four o'clock, the mast-heads were continued until sunset, and during this interval we amused ourselves as best we could without encroaching on the rights of privilege. The decks having been swept down, and the tools removed from the carpenter's bench, we would assemble around to listen with respectful attention to the opinions of the boat-steerers as to the probable chances and result of the voyage. The possible contingency of a depreciation in the value of oil, was discussed with as much gravity as a falling off from the last quotation of stocks would be in a chamber of commerce. Some read, some danced, and others sung. I have seen our Vulcan, " a merry wight," from Canada, perched upon the night-heads and roaring away with might and main at an old French ballad. If the weather was fine, John would bring his Epitome on deck, which he would peruse most seriously, while some of the uninitiated looked upon him as a prodigy—a master navigator in disguise. O'Connor, a son of the Emerald Isle, and a fellow of fair acquirements, would occasionally give us the latest steps of the Polka, while, for want of an instrument, Chips and I whistled the Carlotta Grisi.

From this outline it must not be inferred that the harmony of social intercourse continued uninterrupted. The enjoyment derived from an interchange of sentiment or favor among all classes might in most instances be traced to selfishness rather than to any feeling of personal regard. As wolves band together for mutual convenience, so our intercourse with each other was characterized by a smooth, deceptive surface, while an under-current of hidden meaning whirled tumultuously beneath, and thus it continued until subsequent events occurred to obscure the horizon of our hopes by gathering clouds

CHAPTER III.

A GLIMPSE AT THE SPIRIT-LAND.

" If there be a messenger with him, an interpreter, one among a thousand, to shew unto man his uprightness."

THERE are moments in life when the wing of the destroying angel flits between us and the sunshine of existence, and beneath its dark shadow pleasures fade and hope withereth ; and when with hearts despairing we hear the last sigh, or watch the last throb of departing life, we feel that the silver cord which unites us to earth has been loosened and, with hope and fear " see through a glass darkly"—into eternity. Again, when we witness the final struggle, we no longer tremble, but contemplate with mingled joy and sadness the transit of the soul to the spirit-land ; looking steadily up to a glittering edifice, spiritual or ideal, erected by faith in the zenith of human hopes.

It was a Sabbath morning, and the sun shone with unclouded splendor upon the Atlantic, where the trade-winds blew freshly, curling many a wave into foam, as it dashed harmlessly against the dark hull of the Planet. The sounds of daily labor were hushed ; and save the sighing of the wind, and the monotonous plash of the waves, as we glided steadily on over the heaving ocean—fitting sym-

bol of eternity—all was still ; for the destroyer was there to thrust
in his sickle while the harvest was yet ripe.   It was the mysterious
agent whose foot is upon the sea as well as upon the land ; who
waves his dark wand over the fields of summer, causing them to
glow for a moment with golden hues of autumn, only to perish beneath the chill mantle of winter.

Little Henry was a native of Raratonga, one of the Friendly Isles
of the South Pacific.   His delicate frame was not proof against the
hardship and exposure incident to a voyage to the United States ;
and the seeds of disease, that had already begun to germinate, received a genial impulse in the colder climate of the North : that
unsparing emissary of death, pulmonary consumption, had already
fastened itself upon the delicate boy.   He had come on board with
a faint hope of once more beholding his sea-girt home ; but that
fragile form was destined for a final resting-place in the blue ocean,
where, though storms sweep o'er its surface, he slumbers securely,
deep in its still bosom.   Day by day he continued to droop, until he
could no longer sit upon deck to enjoy the bright sunshine, or watch
the wild flight of the sea-bird ; and he was carried below to his
state-room, never more to leave it in life.   Whatever the ship could
afford towards mitigating the sufferings of the dying boy was freely
bestowed, and through the brief period of his illness, the captain
and officers were unremitting in their attentions to him.   I was
almost constantly at his bedside ; and once, when nearly overcome
by his emotion, he gave me to understand that he had a mother and
sister who would await his return.   I have seen him take from a
small bag, which he usually kept near him, gifts of affection for his
mother, a bunch of ribbons and beads for his sister, together with a
few trifling presents for his friends, and after looking at them sor-
rowfully, replace them again with a sigh, while the tears stole down
his emaciated cheeks.

But Henry had one source of consolation that lighted up the
shadow of death, and that was his Bible and a few tracts printed
in his native tongue ; when he was not reading, they were always
near him.   In them he found a soothing balm that enabled him to
endure patiently his afflictions, discovering, as he drank deeply from
the fountain of living waters, new sources of enjoyment, spiritual in

their nature. I verily believe that no death-bed was ever hallowed with brighter inspirations of Christian faith than was that of this poor boy. Hope was to him a beacon that grew brighter and brighter as he neared the goal of his aspirations, and he spoke with cheerfulness of the hour when it should please his heavenly Father to relieve him from his sufferings. I have heard his feeble voice in prayer, and, although to me in an unknown tongue, have bowed my head with reverence, and so has the hardy sailor watching at his bedside; for it was solemn, deeply solemn: it was the low converse of a spirit with its Creator. I would that the Christian and skeptic could have looked upon that bed of death: to the one, it would have been a bright example of faith; to the other, a solemn warning.

About eight o'clock, the steward informed me that Henry was dying. I was at his bedside in a moment, and beheld at a glance that the destroying angel was there. Though speechless, he was sensible of my approach. His Bible was by his side; but he no longer needed its consolations, for he was already at the threshold of that house his faith had built. Death came not to him amid the groves of his native isle, where the drooping plumes of the palm rustle in the breeze like the whispered converse of spirits, and where, amid the harmonies of nature, he might breathe a last farewell to weeping friends; but in his narrow room, where the rays of light through the cabin window shone faintly upon the bulkhead, and surrounded by hardy seamen, in whose feeling hearts his suffering touched a chord of sympathizing response. I sat beside him, and, raising his attenuated arm, watched the last glimmering of life, like a flame expiring in its socket, until, without a struggle or a groan, his soul returned to Him who gave it.

The captain and mate were both deeply affected, more especially the former, and he alluded briefly to many little incidents connected with Henry during his sojourn in his family. He had frequently known him to forsake his amusements and retire to his chamber to pray. When informed by the physician that he could never again see his home, he wept bitterly, and begged so earnestly to be permitted to accompany the captain on his present voyage, that, for humanity's sake, he could not refuse.

An hour having elapsed, preparations were made for the sequel. His hands were crossed and fastened together with spunyarn ;

"No useless coffin inclosed his breast,"

but we wrapped him in his blanket, and carried him on deck to the carpenter's bench, where the crew were requested to take a final look before he was launched into the deep. The body was then sewed up in the blankets, together with a quantity of ballast at the feet, and the whole securely lashed. The gangway was unshipped, and the body laid upon a plank in such a position that, when inclined, the feet should strike the water first. The captain and first and second officers stood just abaft the gangway, the cooper and boat-steerers near the mainmast, and the crew were assembled on the opposite side of the gangway. The third and fourth officers were stationed on either side of the body, and all was now ready for the final ceremony.

"Haul back the mainyard !" was the order.

This was silently obeyed, and gave to the ship a stately motion in the water. The captain, who was too much agitated to officiate, requested me to read a chapter in the Testament, there being no prayer-book on board. I selected such passages as I thought the most appropriate for the occasion, and read them so as to be distinctly heard by all the crew, wishing, although with but little hope, that the words and the occasion might have a beneficial effect upon the feelings of some of my shipmates. I hoped they might awaken a few sober reflections that would tend to harmonize the elements of discord that to a certain extent opposed a barrier to our social intercourse.

The service being ended, there was a moment of silence, and I do not believe there was an eye present unmoistened by a tear.

"Let go there !" said the captain.

The two officers shoved the plank a few feet beyond the gangway, quickly inclined it, and the body slid with a plunge into the water.

"Brace forward the mainyard there, Mr. Grasper !"

"Aye, aye, sir !" and as the ship once more resumed her course, I turned to catch a glimpse of a fading object that, deep in the blue element, was melting away like the faint trace of a cloud.

Four years subsequent to·this event, I sailed through the Hervey group by moonlight, and saw the beautiful isle of Raratonga rise like a dark knoll from the water. To me the circumstance was of peculiar interest, for with it I associated recollections of the little boy whose home was once here, and where perhaps at that moment an anxious mother was dreaming of an absent son. How often has she counted the breadfruit harvests, and scanned the dim horizon for the faint glimmering of a sail ! In vain has the sister woven garlands of flowers plucked from her native hills for her truant brother. But grieve not for him ; holier fingers have twined for him chaplets of amaranth, where, in brighter realms, he heeds not the storm that chants a requiem o'er the troubled ocean.

CHAPTER IV.

RUSTICATIONS AT THE CAPE DE VERDES.

A week passed by, and with favoring gales we were driven from the storms of a northern winter to the sunny South, where, a month after our departure, the barren peaks of St. Nicholas loomed in the horizon. I must pass hastily over any reference to the Cape de Verde Islands, for there are few features connected with them on which memory dwells with pleasure. Yet I envy not the disposition that would look with indifference upon the conical peak of Fogo, conspicuous above the clouds, its sides furrowed by many a deep channel, where the fiery torrent has rolled down to do battle with the element that surges against its base. Although in most instances the scenery of these islands was cheerless enough, there were picturesque valleys, where the sea-loving cocoanut rustled in the breeze, and the golden orange, half hidden by the rich foliage, sent forth a grateful perfume. Here at times streams were leaping from crags and falling in cascades, where on either side rose the dark volcanic rocks, giving a sombre effect to the scene ;

and in fancy it would seem that in this green valley alone rustled the wide-spreading banana, while all beyond was solitude and desolation.

The geographical position of these islands, lying as they do about four hundred miles west of Cape de Verde on the coast of Africa, renders them a favorite place of resort for outward-bound whalers, where, for sea-biscuit, prints, and domestic goods, they can purchase fresh supplies at reasonable rates. They are a dependency of Portugal, and, as might be supposed, far behind the age in intelligence and civilization. The forbidding appearance of the country may be adduced as a plea for its present condition ; a sterile soil, intense heat, continued droughts, and the rainy and attendant sickly season, are serious obstacles in the way of advancement. There is, however, no lack of government officials, whose corrupt politeness, bordering on servility, but ill accords with the courtesies of refinement. In plain words, most of them are a parcel of importunate beggars, and in making the assertion, I am supported by the opinions of nearly all who have held intercourse with them. I will here mention a circumstance that occurred, as an illustration of this leading characteristic.

Our captain had a fine Panama hat with a broad brim, an admirable protection from the scorching rays of the sun, and no wonder it excited the cupidity of some of the official lazzaroni. It was at a Custom-House somewhere on the island of St. Nicholas that the collector became enamored with its fair proportions, and he begged to be permitted to try it on. He then very nicely adjusted his own chip-hat upon the head of Captain Buck, and called upon the attendant officers to witness the improvement the exchange had made on the person of the latter. Their opinions perfectly coincided with his own, but our skipper meanwhile had arrived at an opposite conclusion, and the chip-hat was returned with all the politeness he was master of, much to the chagrin of the swarthy Portuguese. This, however, did not check his perseverance ; there was a circuitous method of accomplishing an object that was not to be attained by direct means.

In due season, the supplies began to come in ; stalwart negroes drove diminutive pigs before them with a string fastened to the leg, (a custom practised in every portion of the globe where pork is a staple) ; coal-black negresses bearing baskets of oranges on their heads, and little urchins skipping down the pathway, half hidden by bunches of bananas. The purchases were made, and the captain's red calico made an ostentatious display, in the turban form, on the head of some portly wench, while old and young of both sexes were crunching voraciously at the *bolash* (bread). Preparations were now made for departure, and dispatches sent out for the stragglers, some of whom were discovered drinking *aguadénte* in the guard-room with ragged soldiers, and others riding donkeys no bigger than a good-sized Newfoundland, much to the diversion of the natives. The moment being opportune, an official, wearing the royal livery with ventilated elbows, tipped his hat politely to our skipper, and begged the honor of escorting him once more to the Custom-House. He was there informed by the collector, in a most affable manner, that the systematic course adopted by the government of Portugal required that an accurate "Outward Manifest" of all exports be made, to be submitted to the Bureau of Internal Commerce for statistical purposes. This required a blank bearing the broad stamp of the Arms of Portugal, price one dollar. Duplicate blanks of "Outward Entry and Permit" were also required to be filed away among official documents, besides the observance of minor formalities, which would cause delay, and increase still further the amount he had already disbursed for the benefit of the royal treasury. Captain Buck remonstrated, but the collector was inexorable, and things were in a most interesting position, when the latter once more expressed his surprise that an American captain should be so insensible to his interests as not to acquiesce in a change that would add to his personal appearance, and which also would accord with the tastes of the gentlemen present. Our skipper took the hint, and a formal transfer of the white Panama was made for an old " chip," that was lost during the first gale. The subsequent ratification, consisting of a profusion of bows and compliments, savored strongly of " There shall be perpetual peace and amity between," &c. ; and the captain, with ill-concealed chagrin, was escorted from the premises, while the guard did him the honor to present arms.

I had not the pleasure of visiting Porta Praya, the principal city of this group, and situated on the island of St. Jago, compensating in some respects for the inferiority of the towns in the rural districts. I do not believe that the town to which I have first alluded contained a house that could boast of a glass window. I visited a dilapidated fort, erected in a commanding position, but everything bespoke ruin and decay. The coarse grass was creeping over the plastered ramparts, while perhaps a dozen guns of various calibre were pointing their rusty muzzles through the embrasures.

After procuring such supplies as we could at St. Nicholas, we bore away for St. Jago, the principal island of the group, and which we reached the next morning. Like the others, it was a commingling of rugged peaks and sterile hills, here and there relieved by sequestered valleys clothed with bright verdure, some of them dotted by neatly whitewashed houses, half concealed by the foliage.

It was at one of the rustic villages of this island that the captain proposed landing the morning of our arrival, and on this occasion also I obtained permission to go in the boat, where I was sure of an opportunity of tugging at the oar, under a broiling sun. I should have mentioned before that I was not attached to either of the boats, a circumstance for which I was probably indebted to an accident that occurred to me the morning we were leaving port ; I hope the reader will pardon me for introducing it at the present time. We were " fishing" the larboard anchor ; some eighteen or twenty of us had clapped on to the fall, and were hauling away to the tune of

"O, it's an Oldtown skipper and a Nantucket mate ;"

the huge cat-block was toggled aloft, and happening to be directly beneath it when the decimation took place, I was the victim. The larboard port was triced up, and Mr. Short was on his hands and knees looking out to superintend his share of the business. Suddenly the toggle gave way, and down came the block upon my head (not fairly), and glancing, struck Mr. Short full in the rear with such violence that he made a headlong plunge through the port, and only saved himself from falling into the water by seizing hold of the anchorfluke. I was knocked down senseless, and, in my fall, another with me. When I recovered, I was on the quarter-deck, covered with blood, and supported by a couple of shipmates, while the captain was trying his hand at surgery on two or three ugly gashes upon the back of my head. It was during the time I was confined to my bunk, recovering from the effects of the blow, that the watches and boat's crews were chosen ; and when I was able to come on deck, I learned that I had not been assigned to either of the boats, but was to be one of the reserve which remains aboard while they are in pursuit of whales.

As I before said, I obtained permission to join the crew, and off we started in the starboard boat, the waist boat keeping company. In due season we were laying on our oars just outside the surf, and looking for a convenient place to land. Several officious ebony-colored individuals ran along the beach, and with loud cries and gesticulations gave us to understand that a little farther on, there was a cove protected from the swell of the sea by jutting rocks. Our boats were soon hauled upon the beach, abreast of the town, and a guard placed around each to prevent accident from the thieving propensity of the natives. The captain was waited upon by a young man of prepossessing appearance, who politely informed him that he was chief in authority at this place, and that any assistance he could render him in the way of trafficking would be cheerfully tendered ; a civility that was accepted. and an amicable understanding at once existed between them. Almost his first inquiry was, if there was a doctor aboard.

The captain referred him to me, and to avoid compromising the Planet's dignity, I confirmed the assertion, mentally wishing drugs and medicines at the bottom of the sea ; at the same time, passing rapidly in review the long catalogue of ills that flesh is heir to, and wondering what I should do if it happened to be a case of hysterics, my " vade mecum" and hartshorn being absent.

The invalid proved to be an African female slave, suffering from debility, owing to a recent attack of fever. I left some simple directions, intending to call again the next day.

The courtesy of the young gentleman did not cease here ; he invited us to accompany him to his house a short distance up the valley, a request with which we cheerfully complied. It was a snug little tenement, neatly whitewashed within and without, with lattice blinds. There was also a large paved court, the interior of which I did not see at first. We were ushered into a plain apartment where his lady was sitting, and that interesting ceremony, an interchange of compliments, where neither can comprehend the other, was inflicted with the best grace possible. Since then I have frequently wondered whether Señora took me for a sample of American doctors. There was certainly nothing in my costume suggestive of sentiments flattering to the craft ; for on that occasion I wore a pair of coarse duck trowsers, a blue woollen shirt, and a sennet hat ; but my hostess was evidently indifferent to secondary considerations, and her winning manner established a familiarity that was foreign to embarrassment. The captain and his newly-found quartermaster soon took their departure, leaving us to entertain ourselves as best we might. The apartment was plainly furnished, and the walls, as is usual in Catholic countries, were decorated with pictures of the saints and scriptural scenes, but there was an air of refreshing coolness about it that was delightful, after so fatiguing a pull. Near by was a grove of orange trees, with the golden fruit peeping out from the luxuriant foliage.

There were several African female slaves in attendance, and at a word from my entertainer, one of them left the room, but presently returned, bearing a plate of large oranges just plucked from the tree, and, kneeling down, presented them to me. This was an act of servility uncongenial to republican feelings, but in the present instance it was of trifling moment, and as an appreciation of Señora's attention, I applied myself to the juicy fruit, she, meanwhile, looking on very complacently.

I hardly knew how we should entertain each other, but accidentally espying a guitar-case under the table, and which I found contained a veritable instrument, at my request she favored me with several national airs. Our musical soirée having terminated, at her invitation I accompanied her to the court adjoining, where I saw some dozen slaves of both sexes engaged in a variety of occupations, and I blushed to see how scantily some of the younger females were attired, and who evinced not the slightest embarrassment at our approach, but chatted as familiarly with their mistress as if the sunshine of life had never been darkened by a cloud.

In due time I received a summons—Señora expressed her regrets—the last *adios* were uttered, and we parted.

CHAPTER V.

SOME ACCOUNT OF THE "PLANET" AND HER PROPENSITIES.

ONCE more we were all aboard, pigs squealing, turkeys gobbling, and chanticleers crowing; luscious bananas were clustering around the stern, and hanging as ornamental appendages from the stays, while oranges and cocoanuts were scattered about in the greatest profusion. Good-bye to this quarter of the globe : when next we revel upon terra firma, it will be somewhere in the broad Pacific. Every stitch of muslin the old " Planet" would bear was crowded on her, for we had no time to lose if we would reach the northwest cruising-ground in good season, where, amid the fog, we were to fight " polars" and " bowheads" in the icy Arctic and stormy seas of Kamtschatka. On we bounded, the old " Planet" creaking and groaning, like a fretful child, at the additional task imposed on her : down she would plunge at an approaching sea, as if hastening to the shock, and, though slightly shuddering, the old lady always rose gayly above it, while with evident satisfaction she tossed a shower of brine upon her time-worn decks as she dashed recklessly on to meet another.

Like the fickle sex, the " Planet" had her faults ; but after all, we can hardly blame her, doomed to such perpetual servitude as she had been for more than twenty years, cruising for the sperm whale in tropical seas, and again, her cordage brittle and hoary with northern frosts. Dark rumors were abroad respecting her, concerning unearthly sounds and supernatural appearances that had been heard and seen during a storm, suggesting legends of haunted tenements, for her decks had been stained with the blood of murder, and there was no seaman on board who would have dared to whistle defiance when the storm-god was shrieking through her cordage. But the worst feature in her eventful history occurred during her previous voyage. She was " hove-to" in a gale in the Pacific that had continued for several days, and with helm lashed " a-lee," she came to, and fell off with so much precision while struggling with the huge seas, that she inspired a feeling of confidence among her officers and crew, who little dreamed of the frightful change that was so soon to come over them. The starboard watch had the deck that morning; the second officer was at the carpenter's bench, and the doctor, cooper, and carpenter were in the stern boat, amusing themselves by "scrimshoning" (designing upon) whalebone. Suddenly, a mountain-wave rose high above the bulwarks and descended like an avalanche upon her deck, carrying all before it, and sweeping seven souls into eternity, who, but a moment before, were as conscious of security as if dwelling in their far-off homes. The second officer was transfixed by a spar that was torn from its lashing. Of those in the stern boat, the doctor was never afterwards seen, but the cooper and carpenter struggled for a long time; and although their voices were unheard, they could be seen, with outstretched arms, as they rose on the crest of a wave. Bulwarks and stanchions were carried away; the comings of the main-hatch started, main and mizen masts went by the board, and every boat on the cranes, together with the spare ones overhead, were stoven: in short, the "Planet" was a wreck.

I recollect an instance of her taking us by surprise. We had been "hove-to" for three or four days off the river "Plate," (Rio de la Plata,) and the weather being cold withal, we had huddled together under the lee-side of the house, and a number of heads were crouched behind the stiff collars of monkey-jackets for protection. Suddenly she shipped a sea that, carrying away the gangway, came rolling aft like a flood. As might be supposed, there was a general scrambling; some sprang for the stern boat, while others bolted for the rigging, and I never witnessed more agility in a gymnasium than was displayed by Folger on that occasion; for at a bound he cleared the bulwarks and was in the lee mizen rigging, up which he scampered until he reached the futtock shrouds. A hogshead of water was poured down the steerage, while the lee state-rooms were afloat. After a brief interval, we saw the bald head of old John protruding itself above the scuttle, his *tout ensemble* having the appearance of being completely drenched, and, all things considered, he looked like an apparition of Neptune rebuking the storm. The illusion was in nowise dispelled by his subsequent proceedings, for as soon as he could open his mouth, he poured forth a volley of curses in choice Celtic, first upon the winds, then upon the waves, and lastly upon the ship, swearing that if "he had got to be drowned, it should never be below hatches."

A week had passed since we saw the gray peaks of St. Jago sink beneath the horizon ; and was it fancy or not, but our commander seemed to pace the quarter-deck with a firmer tread than before ; orders were more frequent, and rigidly enforced.   We hoped it was an illusion, but too soon it became a reality, for daily the gulf of distinction impassable grew deeper and broader, until the perspective of our future lot looked vague and uncertain.   Each had recourse to his own philosophy ; wisely destroying the few relics of civilization I still retained, 1 plunged at once into the mysteries of the slop-chest and attired myself in its coarse woollen garments—no guernsey frocks, for I detest them ; and my monkey-jacket and short-six proved my best companions during the voyage.

An incident occurred one Sunday morning which served to impress us forcibly that discipline would be strictly maintained.   As for me, I was mute with astonishment, for it was the first affair of the kind I had ever witnessed ; but during subsequent rovings, I have learned to look upon a denouement of this nature as a before-breakfast amusement.

"Mr. Short," said Captain Buck as he came on deck, " who were those men in your watch you found sleeping last night ?"

" Old Bill and War'ick, sir."

Here was a firebrand thrown among us.   We were as merry a group as could be around the windlass : some reading, some mending, and others raising the wind generally.   Bill himself was astonishing me with an instance of his personal prowess in the China seas, when, on board of an opium clipper, the officers and crew kept at bay two armed junks.   On this occasion he had himself vanquished seven men, and was already speaking of a tall fellow, with a long lance and hat as formidable as Mambrino's helmet, when he heard his name pronounced by Mr. Short, and suddenly breaking off, remarked, " Now, bullies, you are going to see some fun ;" and so the sequel proved, for Bill's opinion perfectly coinciding with that of Captain Buck, no one was disappointed.

" Order Bill aft !" continued the captain.

" Fleet aft, there, Bill !"

" Billy, love, you won't tell of me ?" whispered a quizzing individual, trying to look affectionate.

" I'll bet my lay against any other man's in the ship, that that soger fights rats in the run before night," said another.

William moved aft with a sort of devil-may-care air, until he reached the line of demarkation, the galley, when he was checked by the command of, " Stand where you are !"   The captain advanced.

" Then you are the d——d soger that slept on watch last night, are you ?"

" I laid down a little while towards morning, sir, but there was a good look-out stationed all the time between the night-heads, sir."

" Suppose there were a hundred look-outs between the night-heads, does that give you any right to disobey orders ?   My orders are, that no man shall sleep on watch.   I'd a mind, when I first began, to make an example of you ; but bear it in mind, that if I ever catch you at it again, I'll knock seven bells out of you !   Go 'long ; I've done with you."

" But I was tired ; besides, the law allows seamen so many hours rest."

" What !" exclaimed the captain, almost stupefied with astonishment, " dare you talk to me about law ?   Go forward, sir, this instant."

Unfortunately for Bill, his propensity for " fun" left him standing irresolute, but in a moment a huge fist laid him sprawling in the lee scuppers, and the next, the hands of Mr. Grasper as he knelt upon his breast, compressed his throat like a vice, until the extremity of William's nose changed from a rich vermilion to a beautiful plum color.

" Fetch on the bracelets here, some one," shouted Mr. Grasper ; " we've found a live sea-lawyer, and the cap'n's just got out a writ of *habeas corpus.*"

Bill was speedily ironed, and escorted below by two or three officers, while one of the boys seated upon the heel of the bowsprit was carelessly humming the rogue's march.   He was confined in the run, on low diet, for the three days following.

Our skipper had just got his hand in.

" You, War'ick !   Come here !"

" Alas ! poor Yorick !" as Chips used to exclaim with a tragic air ; he was as verdant as the meadows where he pastured his cows. I don't wonder he saw no harm, when night came, in stealing a little rest upon the hard planks.   It might be truly said that he rose with fear and trembling to comply with what sounded to him like a death-warrant ; and he moved slowly aft, sliding his hand along the bulwarks for support.

" Did you sleep on watch last night, War'ick ?" commenced his interrogator, with a most annihilating scowl.

" Yes, sir ; but I got up as soon as Mr. Short told me to "

" Didn't you know it was against orders ?"

" Yes, sir ; but some of the sailors told me it wouldn't make any odds, as long as the folks in the cabin didn't find it out."

I thought I could distinguish an expansion of the captain's left cheek, as though his tongue was there.

" Suppose, sir, I should have you heavily ironed, and kept in the run a week on a pint of water and three biscuits a day ?"

No reply, but the culprit shivered visibly.

" Well, I'll let you off this time ; one's enough for to-day, but look out for the next.   March !"

I have anticipated a hundred times the cogitations of an old Jack when he is accommodated with lodgings in the " run."   Does he console himself with thoughts of vengeance, or by rummaging around with his hands in bracelets after the raisin keg ?   Day after day he is doomed to hear the clatter of dishes overhead, while his fertile imagination conjures up visions of barbacued pigs, bean soups, and smoking duff.   Hardly a ray of light can penetrate through the trap to his submarine dungeon, and, solitary and disconsolate, he stows himself away among sundry boxes of " small stores" and harpoons in reserve.   Nevertheless, he has several very consoling reflections : although he may be somewhat annoyed by the rats, he is spared that interesting pastime of scrubbing deck ; and if a faint sound of grating and plashing may sometimes reach him, it comes only as a vision of some far-off evil, from which he is perfectly secure ; he can laugh at the recollection of that ominous summons, " draw water."

In obedience to an order, I was one day rummaging about one of the cabin lockers for something, when the steward raised the trap to give the prisoner his daily allowance. I stole a glance into the dark vault, from which arose a sickening odor of bilge-water, and it was some time before the obscurity of the place would admit of my seeing a shadowy outline perched upon a box at the further extremity, with its fettered hands clasped complacently before it, and both its feet braced resolutely against a sampson-post, to preserve an equilibrium. There he sat, patient and resigned, like every politician who has been deserted by his constituents—a martyr to privileged intolerance, owing to liberal sentiments he sought to disseminate among his less aspiring shipmates. Bill's was emphatically a case of " principle *versus* privilege."

CHAPTER VI.

GAUL AND HIBERNIA.

DURING the checkered course of existence, we occasionally meet with happy dispositions too wavering to incline them to any fixed notions of enjoyment, and with whóm the asperities of life, by grinding and polishing, or, in the present instance, by familiarizing themselves with them, may be made to harmonize with each other, and who, by easily conforming to whatever position fortune has assigned them, jog happily along in shadow and sunshine.

Our little community was blessed with a few such anomalies, whose happy temperament was ruffled by neither scowls nor duty, and it was always a pleasure to observe their smiling faces and spontaneous efforts. I do not mean to say they were more industrious than others, but that they performed their duties to the best of their ability, and praise and reprimand were received alike with indifference. They were active and willing, and, as such, merited and received to a certain extent the approbation of their officers.

Most conspicuous among these was our Vulcan, a Canadian

Frenchman from Montreal, a young man of perhaps five-and-twenty, and who, when he first came among us, spoke not a word of English, but in which, before six months had passed, he was tolerably proficient. Nearly every day, when the weather would permit, his anvil rang out as merrily as it did on the banks of the St. Lawrence, and he was ever disposed to render a service to a shipmate, for he was a favorite with all. However, he was not exempt from the more arduous duties incident to his new profession ; but in storm or calm, alow or aloft, his merry song was sung as cheerfully as ever. He, for one, escaped contention and abuse, and though glad he was with us, I could not but regret on his account the accident to which we were indebted. He had come from Canada with his brother, both designing to seek employment in the United States, but missing the route of their proposed destination, they found themselves at one of our seaport towns, where some prowling land-shark, by holding out brilliant inducements, set at naught the resolution of the unsophisticated Gauls, and in perhaps an evil hour, they were persuaded to ship. But here a sad mistake occurred, either through their ignorance of our language or the selfishness of the owners, for they were both assigned to different ships, fitted out for at least three years' cruises—the one a sperm whaler bound for the Indian Ocean, and the other a right whaler destined for the Pacific. Protestations were unavailing ; and their only satisfaction, while both vessels were anchored in the bay preparatory to sailing, was for each to recognize the other from opposite bulwarks, for all visiting was prohibited. Like others among his shipmates, he had experienced the tender passion, and a certain *jeune fille* had wept at his departure. But change of scene and occupation often accomplish wonders, and before we had reached our port of destination he spoke of his courtship with indifference. What volumes might be written on the inconstancy of man! Two years afterwards, amid the noise and bustle of Commercial Wharf in San Francisco, I was recognized and accosted by an old shipmate, who revived many a reminiscence I had consigned to oblivion. I inquired particularly after the Frenchman, whose name I have forgotten, and learned that he had cruised awhile amid Arctic fogs, and chased the sperm whale within the tropics, and finally, when the ship had touched at

New Zealand for supplies, he effected his escape, became enamored, and married one of the dark Mowree girls.

There was another, too, whose humorous face should not be forgotten, and this was Bill, the Irish steerage boy. Stationed as he was between two fires, the steerage and the forecastle, cuffed and growled at by the occupants of one to extinguish any embryo notions of ambition he might entertain, and formally driven forth as a deserter whenever he trespassed within the barrier of the other, he retained his equanimity in a remarkable degree, though occasionally varied by a spirit of opposition. I remember on one occasion Bill's being caught napping. We were somewhere in the South Atlantic; the middle watch had the deck, and a more lovely moonlight never shone upon the slumber of a weary seaman. Bill had in some respects judiciously chosen his position, certainly as regards convenience, for, seated upon the windlass, with his monkey-jacket beneath him, he leaned pleasantly back against the iron brake, with both his arms extended upon it; on the other hand, it was too exposed for him to escape detection should the officer of the watch come forward, but provided he confined his beat to the quarter-deck, the tryworks afforded a safe protection in the rear. That night, however, Mr. Short took it into his head to visit us, and his lynx-eye immediately discovered the delinquent. He went around in front to obtain a better view, but Bill's was a *bona fide* sleep, and the stern gaze of the officer was unheeded. Whatever punishment Mr. Short meditated inflicting, none of us knew. After a momentary contemplation, a thought suddenly occurred to him which relaxed his features into something like a smile, and holding up his finger for us to be silent, he walked aft on tiptoe, and presently returned with a quantity of soot from the binacle.

First of all, some spun-yarn was provided, and his extended arms secured in the position they had naturally taken, then his feet were fastened to the windlass, and, strange to say, the sleeper was unconscious of the joke that was being perpetrated upon him. And now commenced a series of delineations upon his round and ruddy face. First, a formidable pair of eyebrows that nearly met, and a streak down the nose, gave him a ferocious appearance; next, a pair of fine curling mustachios, and two curved lines extending from either cheek-bone to the chin, somewhat relaxed the severity of expression. The taste of the artist then took a different turn, and by delicate touches the whole field was covered with quadrants, semicircles, and various geometrical problems, giving him the most farcical appearance conceivable. I have since seen many a tattooed savage in the South Seas, but Bill eclipsed them all. The temptation to laugh was too strong for human nature to look upon with indifference, and the suppressed titter that was first heard when Mr. Short commenced his sketch, had gradually increased, and by the time the finishing touch was given, nothing but peals of laughter was heard from all on deck. I laugh when I think of it ; and Bill awoke, and thinking himself merely fettered, laughed too, making his position more ludicrous than ever. The moon shone brightly, and his white teeth glistened in broad contrast to his sooty face. But the worst of it was not yet over for poor Bill.

" Draw me a bucket of water, there, one of you."

The brine was forthcoming, and Mr. Short elevating the bucket, poured its contents over the head of his now gasping victim ; after this he was cut adrift, when he sought refuge in the steerage by the speediest route possible.

And so we jogged along, days and weeks passing rapidly away, while we busied ourselves with the daily routine of ship duty. Every little incident that occurred to relieve the monotony, had to us its peculiar interest; even the phenomenon of a shooting star, during the silent watches of the night, would call forth an observation. When the bright gems of Ursa Major were no longer visible above the horizon, we felt that the last link that united us to home had been severed, but amid the constellations that spangled a new firmament, we traced out that enduring symbol of faith, the Southern Cross.

4

CHAPTER VII.

SOMETHING MORE ABOUT MR. GRASPER.

The increasing coolness of the atmosphere betokened our approach to higher latitudes, and when off the Rio de la Plata, we received the usual quota of squalls and rough weather ; but we were now better prepared for the encounter, for our crew had by this time become wonderfully metamorphosed into old salts, at least as pertained to externals ; most of them during leisure moments having experimented upon the wardrobe of the slop-chest.

I should perhaps have mentioned before that our stations at masthead had not been idle, and frequently we were startled from our occupations by the clear, sonorous words, " Ah ! b-l-o-w-s !" After the usual questions and responses, boats were lowered, but all in vain, their whaleships being evidently aware of the proximity of cold iron, and after spouting defiance a few times, scampered off to windward, while our oily anticipations vanished as smoothly as the commodity itself.

An incident that occurred in these latitudes is worth noticing, not on account of any extraordinary danger connected with it, but as being of frequent occurrence to those engaged in this profession. About the middle of the forenoon, a school of whales was " raised ;" the mainyard was promptly laid aback, boats were lowered and off in pursuit. The chase somehow or other got an inkling of the matter, and led off to windward in fine style, the boats following as fast as their sturdy oarsmen could propel them, until by the aid of the glass neither whales nor boats were visible. There were but six of us remaining aboard, and if I except the cooper, who acted as shipkeeper, but who was too infirm to render any active service in case of emergency, there was but one able seaman remaining. The weather was unusually fine, and so long as it continued, no one was apprehensive of danger ; we could now range the deck fore and aft without control, and some were even bold enough to watch their opportunity and venture into the cabin, from which I afterwards saw two or

three foraging parties returning with spoils of " soft tack" and ginger-
bread.

Just after noon, we descried a dark cloud rising rapidly in the
horizon. All who have sailed in these latitudes know how surprisingly quick a squall will arise and overtake a vessel ; in this
instance, we had barely time to let fly our top-gallant and flying-jib
halliards, for we were working to windward, before it was upon us.
We had but one alternative—to up helm and let her drive until we
could reduce sail, for we could only let go and clew-up. I never
saw braces work so hard as on that occasion, for it required our
utmost efforts to give the main yard a cant. The rain fell in torrents,
and beat with such fury, that it was almost impossible to look to
windward, and we must have scudded twelve or fifteen minutes before we could bring the ship to the wind. The old cooper was almost
beside himself with anxiety, for the responsibility devolved upon him.
During the squall, I recollect seeing him stumble forward, frantic
with excitement, to execute an order he had just issued, to haul
down the flying-jib, which was now fluttering in ribbons from the
stay. By some mistake, he seized hold of the sheet instead of the
downhaul, which he could hold just as easily as he could lead a mad
bull by the horns. At every jerk, I expected to see the poor man's
head fly from his shoulders, but still he clung to it with the tenacity
of despair, though momentarily threatened with dislocation ; and
several times I heard him exclaim distractedly, " God help us ! The
old man 'll think I'm running away from him."

In about half an hour the squall had blown over, and as soon as
the atmosphere had become sufficiently clear, we discerned something like a speck upon the water to windward, which proved to be
one of the boats ; in due season the others hove in sight, and soon
after we were happy to welcome our shipmates safe on board. I
should, however, except Mr. Grasper, who, while " hooking on," was
not sufficiently on his guard ; the boat having swung under the
counter, and rising on a sea while the ship settled down, he received
a blow upon his broad shoulders that bent him to the loggerhead.
Of this accident I reaped the bitter fruit. Every day for more than
a week, I was indulged with the humane occupation of rubbing the
bruised flesh, while at the same time he nearly distracted me

with questions upon the relative merits of embrocations and liniments.

One day I had an opportunity of retaliating upon him for this persecution. Being of plethoric habit, he was frequently troubled, after over exertion, with a "rush of blood" to the head, and which was sufficiently evinced by his unnaturally suffused countenance. It was on one of these occasions that he came to me complaining of a "terrible oppression aloft," and inquired whether I could do anything for him. I examined his pulse with indefinite delay, then staring at him with all the solemnity I could assume, pronounced him in a critical situation, intimating at the same time that there were strong symptoms of pericarditis.

" The devil, though ! What would you prescribe ?"

" Phlebotomy !"

" Flea bottom me ! Why, what's that ?"

" Venesection."

" Look here, my boy : the mizzen spanker-gaff wants scraping, and I'm goin' to haul the ship up three pints nigher the wind one of these days, and give some of you a work-up job. When you talk to me, I want you to talk plain English. You don't know me yet." (Here Mr. Grasper gave a rotary motion to his herculean shoulders, while his mouth went into convulsions.) " Translate that word you said last."

" Bleeding, sir !"

" O Moses ! Why, I wouldn't be tapped for anything. I was only bled once in my life, and that was in Turkowana (Talcahuano.) The doctor fussed over me for two hours before he hove his iron. He said I had the dreadfullest arm to bleed he ever saw."

The most elaborate reasoning failed to convince him at the time, and I left him vacillating between the propriety of my prescription and the physical derangement consequent upon having his arm punctured. However, about the middle of the afternoon, he called me aft to the companionway, where the steward had just placed a basin of warm water. Mr. Grasper had planted himself firmly upon deck, with his right arm akimbo. His shirt-sleeve was rolled up from the left arm, which was extended at right angles with his body, and terminating in a ponderous fist ; with lips rigid by muscular contraction, he looked for all the world like Bacchus endeavoring to personate Hercules.

"Get your lance there, doctor; I'm goin' to be bled!" he shouted as soon as I had passed the galley.

The quarter-deck at this time presented a busy spectacle. The afternoon was fine, and Captain Buck was astride of a lance-pole, the head of which rested upon the bulwarks, where the sun's rays glistened upon the polished steel; its long taper shaft he was endeavoring to smooth with a spoke-shave. Three or four of the crew, seated upon deck, were overhauling superannuated potatoes, which they facetiously termed "scurvy pills." One of them, Old Bill, as I approached, rolled his eyes wildly, and throwing back his head, made a significant gesture by drawing his index finger across his throat from one ear to the other. Weasle was at the wheel.

Instead of bringing the lance only, I brought the case of instruments, and opening it to its full extent, laid it upon the companion-way, to the consternation of Mr. Grasper.

"Why, here! Why, what's all this?" exclaimed that officer.

"I can tell you, sir, after making an examination." Although a muscular man, Mr. Grasper's tendons and arteries were liberally incased with fat; and any practitioner will readily perceive that the opening of a vein so situated, is a more delicate operation than when it is fully exposed as in thin subjects. "On this hint, I spake." After applying the bandage, and giving him the handle of a scrub-broom to hold, with directions for him to keep his fingers continually moving, I proceeded to examine his arm carefully and deliberately, during which process I shook my head ominously two or three times.

"Why, what's the matter with you, doctor? Why don't you fire, and fall back?"

"The fact is, Mr. Grasper, I never met with such an arm as yours in my life. I don't wonder the surgeon in 'Turkowana' delayed so long before performing the operation."

"Why so?"

"Because your veins are very deep-seated—remarkably so."

"Do you think there's any danger?" he inquired somewhat anxiously, looking from me to his arm, where two or three light azure streaks were barely discernible upon a field of bronze.

"I will be frank with you, sir, and explain the nature of the case as well as I am able, after which you can judge for yourself. In the first place, sir, your arm at this point contains five veins, which, for the sake of distinction, we call the cephalic, basilic, median, median-cephalic, and median-basilic. I propose opening the median-basilic, which we usually do on account of its size ; but in your case it will be attended with danger, for by the peculiar throbbing, I judge that either the brachial or ulnar artery lies immediately beneath it." I then proceeded to apply the lancet.

"Hold on! hold on! Have I got all those things in my arm? Supposen you should cut an artery ?"

"Oh, I'm prepared for that! If such an accident should occur, I would try to check the hemorrhage by a compress ; but if that failed, I should take this instrument (removing the glittering blade of the scalpel from its casement of variegated hawk's-bill) and dissect carefully until I reached the wounded vessel, which I would endeavor to seize with this instrument, (pointing to the tenaculum,) and tie both its severed extremities. After this, I would secure it with a figure-of-eight bandage. I forgot to mention, sir, that, owing to the depth of your veins beneath the skin, unless the opening of the cuticle corresponds precisely with that of the vein, a *thrombus* will be formed, occasioned by the blood escaping into the adipose tissue."

Mr. Grasper relaxed his hold of the broom-handle, which fell upon deck, while that famous arm dropped mechanically to his side. "I guess I won't be bled to-day, Doctor ———. I see you've got a thumb-lancet ; in Holmes's Hole, we always use spring ones."

It was in vain that I attempted to expatiate upon the antiquity of the former, and to denounce the latter as a mere plaything of modern invention. He was inexorable ; and removing the bandage, and rolling down his sleeve, he intimated by his gestures that my audience was at an end. I do not know whether Mr. Grasper concluded mentally that I had been indulging a personal gratification at his expense ; but certain it is, that, during the last two months of our unavoidable relationship, he eschewed all familiarity with me, and availed himself of every opportunity for rendering my situation as disagreeable as possible.

A sense of duty, nay, respect for *bodies corporate*, (I beg his pardon,) impels me to offer a slight tribute to the memory of a great man. Yes, he was truly a great man ; for in point of dimension, he might have been mistaken for a diminutive specimen of the cetacea he was in pursuit of; yet upon occasions he was gentle as a lamb, and when in a towering passion, it was impossible to obliterate the signs of mirth that lurked about the corners of his mouth. Mr. Grasper was not without his faults—some of them glaring ones ; but over these I draw a veil, for he was a reflecting man, deeply so, and that was a redeeming quality. I have seen him puffing mechanically from his short clay pipe while he gazed at the tryworks in a fit of gloomy abstraction ; then, as if suddenly aroused from his revery by the birth of a latent germ of intellect, he would fetch a sort of blowing sound, (which I have always supposed was intended for a sigh,) while he smothered an imprecation upon the ingratitude of owners and low price of oil. Strange as it may seem, he possessed a poetic vein ; while taking altitudes, I have frequently heard him, after removing the quadrant from his eye, give utterance to the following couplet :

> " As the secant is to the half sum,
> So is the cosine to a bottle of rum."

" Still as the breeze but dreadful as the storm," I have seen him with his weather-eye lifted, hovering about our little fold like a strange sail in the offing, backing and filling, edging nearer little by little, then keeping away again until he had obtained a commanding position, when, like a hungry hawk, at one swoop he would pounce upon his victim. But I do not love to harrow the mind with the dark side of a picture, though true. Years have flown by since the occurrence of these events, and every vindictive feeling has been long since consigned to oblivion. Then come, Mr. Grasper, if your venerable hulk is still floating upon the sea of life, accept the proffered hand, and let us be friends again ere exchanging " So 'long" forever. Before we part, however, we will indulge in the recollection of one of the pastimes you were occasionally pleased to furnish us.

It is blowing a gale ; the vessel is " hove-to," and there is a heavy sea running. The captain swings below in his cot, and the mate is

officer of the deck.   Our fresh diet is stowed in a solid mass between the weather-bulwarks and the tryworks, a position, by-the-
bye, advantageously chosen, for here their swineships are protected
from the wind, and secure from any accident that might occur from
the rolling of the ship.   Between the tryworks and the main hatch,
the space is clear, and Weasle is ordered to bring some slush and
apply it to a portion of the deck to windward.   He then brings a
quantity of corn, which he hands Mr. Grasper, who scatters it
temptingly upon the greasy surface.   Humanity would suggest that
the poor victims be permitted to eke out as comfortable an existence
as possible during the brief period of their impressment, but not so
thought Mr. Grasper.   After sundry grunts, they would rouse themselves, give a shake or two to be perfectly sure that their sea-legs
were on, then proceed cautiously with their noses down toward the
corn, and in a few moments a goodly number would be assembled,
crunching away voraciously.   An ordinary lurch would not disturb
their equilibrium, for with their *toes* in the seams of the deck, they
braced resolutely ; but presently a huge sea rises, gathering strength
as it approaches, until, like an avalanche, it seems ready to burst
upon us.   Then was the critical moment.   " Hold hard there, boys,
and twig 'em !" shouts Mr. Grasper, as the wave strikes the ship,
causing her to heel to leeward, until a cataract pours over her bulwarks, while the porkers, *en masse* go sliding, biting, and squealing, into the lee scupper, looking, and with good reason, like the
most disconsolate creatures in the world.

   This species of diversion, together with shaving and decorating
them with various colors, he would never indulge in when Captain
Buck was present, for our skipper was severe in his denunciations
of it, not so much, perhaps, from sympathy for the animals as from
other considerations.   The spectacle of a lean pig hobbling about
deck with a fractured limb is anything but an inviting object, even if
one is beyond the reach of fresh dainties.

CHAPTER VIII.

"*VERY LIKE A WHALE!*"

It was a cold morning in the month of December; the cutting wind that blew fresh from the snowy mountains of Patagonia, then in sight, together with an occasional dash of brine, made us court the embrace of our monkey-jackets more ardently than ever. It could not have been later than six o'clock, when, "Ah! b-l-o-w-s!" rang out clear and distinct from the mast-head. Mr. Gurrie had the deck.

"Where away?"

"Three pints off the lee-bow."

"What is it?"

"A school of sperm whale, sir."

Mr. Gurrie paused a moment; a school of sperm whales in such high latitudes was something unusual in his experience, and he felt half inclined to doubt it.

"How do you know?"

"Low and bushy spouts, sir; they've 'milled' now, and are pinting to wind'ard."

"Well, keep your eye on 'em; here, Easy, watch her while I speak to the 'old man;' I don't think he'll lower with this wind and sea."

A moment after, and Captain Buck was on deck in *deshabille*.

"Where are they now?" he shouted, looking attentively at the crow's nest.

"About a pint off the lee-bow; say two miles off, sir."

"Trim the yards, there, Mr. Grasper; brace her up as sharp as she'll go, and call all hands to stand by the boats." Then to the helmsman, "Keep her up a couple of pints, if she'll go it—there, steady 's you go, and watch her close." He then went below to complete his attire.

All these orders were executed almost as soon as given, with the exception of the appearance of the watch below, but they soon came tumbling out of the scuttle, half clad and rubbing their eyes.

There was a " mustering in hot haste" among the boat-steerers ;
all superfluous articles they hastily bundled out of their boats upon
deck ; lances were brandished, and short warps inspected, sheaths
were removed, and the keen edges of their irons tested between
thumb and finger ; there was no idle joking among them ; it was a
moment of desperate resolve.

We had a short chopping sea on, a most disagreeable one for
boats, and through this we were now dashing close-hauled upon the
wind to forelay the chase.   Every man was on the alert, and some
had already sprung into the rigging.

" There she blows ! there she blows !" rang out simultaneously
from every mouth as the whales came up to breathe.   We were almost
aboard of them.   The captain dropped his spy-glass.

" Haul 'back the main yard, and put the line-tub in the boat.
Mr. Grasper, stand by to lower away."

" Larboard boat's crew ! do you hear there ?" bellowed that officer, frantic with excitement, as he stood bareheaded, without coat,
and his sleeves rolled up to his elbows.   " You, Brown !   You,
Fisher ! spring, I tell you, or I'll make mincemeat of you in just
seventeen and three-quarter seconds by the chronometer."

These two individuals, though partial to sausages, manifested extreme reluctance at the idea of having their bodies converted
into that article of diet, and accelerated their movements accordingly.

" You, Smith !" continued he, " hold on to that block until it turns
to a lump of silver—how dare you let go ?"   By this time leviathan
was giving us grand illustrations in hydraulics, which called forth
another exclamation from Mr. Grasper.   " In the name of Moses,
look at 'em !   Now, Abram, don't go to sea again, won't you ?   Little
darlings—hundred barrellers, every one of them."

" Are you all ready, there ?" hailed Captain Buck.

" Aye, aye, sir !"

" Well, lower away, then, and be quick about it."

" Slack away roundly—for'ard tackle—handsomely after fall !
You, Fisher ! steady, or I'll wollop you with the steering-oar."

The boat has struck the water, and her crew slide down the
" falls ; " each man knows his oar, and after a momentary delay,

away it started in pursuit, Mr Grasper shouting incoherently, and, as far as his limits would permit, capering like a madman.

In the mean time, the other officers had not been idle. Mr. Gurrie, with less noise and equal energy, had cleared away, lowered, and was off. Mr. Short had received no order respecting the bow boat, and he saw but too plainly how the battle was going : he must remain ship-keeper, and reap none of the glory. Summoning up his courage for a first and final effort, he went aft to soften the stony-hearted captain, of whom he stood in slavish awe. Every muscle in his weather-beaten face was twisted up with ludicrous effect, for the purpose of making a pathetic appeal. I know not whether it was the coldness of the morning, but his eyes wore a vitreous expression, and a bright drop glistened in either corner. Poor man ! His honor was at stake.

" I tell you, Mr. Short, you must not go. I can't spare you. I must have some one aboard that I can depend upon, for I'm going myself. Starboard boat's crew ! stand by to lower."

With a woe-begone expression, Mr. Short paced despondingly up and down opposite his boat ; and even the boat-steerer seemed to partake of his " header's" supposed humiliation.

The carpenter, who belonged to the captain's boat, exhibited some reluctance about going, for the water that morning looked wet and cold ; but Josh, who, more than a month ago, had been exalted to the post of steward, without coat, hat, or shoes, sprang immediately into his place, and away they went.

The whales had by this time become " gallied," and were scattered : some had " gone flukes," others scampered off to windward, and the first two boats seemed no nearer the chase than when they started. At last, more experienced eyes than mine saw one rise not far from the captain's boat, which was immediately pointed for it, and hardly five minutes had elapsed before they reported it was fast. I managed to get hold of the telescope, and was well repaid for my temerity. The dark back of leviathan, as he dashed on to windward, was plainly visible amid a sea of foam, tinged with the blood that was bursting in jets from his spiracles. The boat, not far behind, was flying along with equal or diminished speed, as the line was either checked or slackened around the loggerhead, not skimming, but cutting through the seas, and half hidden by sheets of foam.   An experienced officer was at the loggerhead, to tend line, and the boat-steerer, with his hatchet, stood ready to sever it, should the emergency require.   It was a grand, but, nevertheless, a cold sight.

Soon after, Mr. Gurrie returned on board, sulky at his bad luck, and gave idle spectators a job at reefing topsails; it was not long before Captain Buck made his appearance also, while Mr. Grasper, in the larboard boat, was stationed by the prize.   All were thoroughly drenched, and the captain's boat, usually so trim and neat, bore traces of the recent conflict : lances and irons were sheathless and bent ; the hatchet, thollpins, bailer, and other indispensables, were scattered promiscuously about, and here and there dark patches of blood were conspicuous.

Some half dozen shivering wretches climbed over the bulwarks, seeking refuge below and a change of garments.   Josh soon appeared in a warm woollen shirt, with his collar "all abroad," and looking ruddy as ever.

"Well, Josh," said the cooper, "what do you think of whaling by this time ?"

"Great, sir ; nothing like it ; a dash or so of fresh-water spray, but none the worse for that.   Mr. Easy struck him in the 'life' the first dart, but I did feel a little squeamish about the gills when I smelt the warm blood."*

CHAPTER IX.

WHEREIN IT WILL BE SEEN THAT WHALING IS NO JOKE.

ALL was now hurry and bustle ; the wind was gradually increasing, and we were compelled to work sharp to save our prize.   A line was got out, and made fast to the whale, which was still a long way

---

* When a whale, after being mortally wounded, spouts blood, the effect of the odor arising from it is frequently such as to produce nausea and vomiting upon those within its influence.

off, and various turns were taken about the bitts and belaying-pins ;
then commenced a long and tedious job of hauling, which continued,
I should think, about two hours, after which we ventured to look over
the side.

It proved to be a young sperm bull, say a fifty-barreller. There
he lay stretched out alongside, his brown back just exposed, and undulating gently with the motion of the water. The little instrument
that had carried death to the monster was buried nearly to the
socket in his side, and from the pole a portion of the warp was still
dangling.

With considerable difficulty a chain cable was passed around it,
and secured amidships, while a strong hawser attached to the flukes
was made fast to the windlass. A squad was sent below to get up
the cutting falls and gear, and in due time the ponderous blocks were
swinging from the mainmast. The carpenter and his assistants busied
themselves about erecting a stage over the side, under the supervi-
sion of Captain Buck, and spades, with their long slender shafts,
were taken by the boat-steerers from their resting-places, where
they had grown rusty, and resharpened ; besides, there was a mustering of cutting-pikes, and all the indispensables that had long been
forgotten.

By the time our preparations were completed it was past noon,
and all hands were knocked off for dinner, which consisted of the
usual quota of junk and bean soup. It was a matter of doubt with
some whether we would be able to save even a " blanket-piece," for
the wind had increased to a gale, and although the fastenings had
been left well slackened, the whale was surging up and down in
a manner that threatened every moment to part them ; about one
o'clock the hawser, the strongest rope in the ship, went with a snap.
All hope of wearing ship, and getting the whale to leeward, was then
abandoned, and our only alternative was to work cautiously and save
what we could.

I do not wonder that Mr. Easy exhibited considerable reluctance
at the part he was to play, and that the boat-steerers congratulated
themselves for the time on the inferiority of their stations. Captain
Buck, with a rope around his waist, had gone out upon the stage, and
with a keen spade had been churning the whale's back during the

intervals it showed itself above water, and after a while had succeeded in making a tolerable hole to " hook on to." Whaling etiquette
required that whoever steered the captain's boat, usually the fourth
officer, should go down and hook on. In ordinary weather there is
no great difficulty attending the process, for persons are stationed
upon the stage with sharp spades to drive away the numerous sharks
that are always prowling about in low latitudes ; and I have seen a
" calf" that bore the impress of their teeth. In the present instance
there was no danger of this kind to be apprehended, for the weather
was too cold ; but what was worse, there was a fearful sea running that sometimes raised the whale nearly to a level with the
deck, then sinking low in the troth, a broken wave would bury it in
a cauldron of foam. In vain the whisky bottle was freely tendered;
glass after glass disappeared, but human consciousness retained its
perceptive faculties as vividly as ever. To refuse compliance with
his duty would have lowered Mr. Easy in the estimation of his inferiors, and suggest imputations on his courage. No, it was necessary
for him, as Mrs. Chick has it, to " make an effort."

Mr. Gurrie took his position upon the scaffold, and after a momentary preparation, Mr. Easy, bareheaded and barefooted, with a
halter—not around his neck, but under his arms—passed through the
open gangway and joined him.

" Now, my boy, don't be afraid," said Mr. Gurrie in his gruff way.
" Keep cool, for I can hold you till you are black and blue. Does
the knot hurt your back ? If it's too tight, say so, and I'll alter it."

Mr. Easy sprang lightly upon the fall, slid rapidly down, and in a
moment was kneeling upon the whale's back, with the huge iron hook
in his hands, endeavoring to thrust it into the hole prepared for its
reception. Before he could accomplish this, a sea broke over and
washed him off.

" Catch the iron ! Catch the iron !" shouted a dozen voices as he
struggled in the water to regain his position. This he succeeded in
doing, and again renewed his efforts ; but when he would almost effect his object, the combing of a sea would compel him to grasp the
iron for support, and thus he would lose all he had gained. Once
more he was washed off, and again he grasped the harpoon, but this
time it failed him ; loosened and bent it drew from its hold, and soon

disappeared; he was now swimming and struggling in vain to regain a footing upon the whale; but it would be easier to scale a precipice than, unaided, to have climbed that smooth convex surface, perpetually in motion.

"Quick! be quick, Mr. Grasper! the iron's drawn; throw another!" cried the captain.

With a hop, skip, and a jump, that officer snatched one from the carpenter's bench, and with a ferocious expression of countenance hove it with all his might, and buried it to the socket in the whale's back. But his assistance came too late; before Mr. Easy could reach it, a huge sea lifted him over between the whale and the ship, and buried them both in its foam. Most of us looked aghast, thinking him crushed; and seeing him drawn up apparently lifeless by Mr. Gurrie, I felt that my worst fears were realized, or at least that he was seriously injured. A privileged crowd gathered around him, and upon this occasion I was one of the number. He was stunned by the shock, and I was at first apprehensive bleeding would be necessary. A couple of officers carried him aft, where he soon revived, though unfit for duty during the remainder of the day.

"Don't give up the whale," thought Captain Buck. "Come, John, down you go!"

This was addressed to our friend John the Scotch boat-steerer, who came next in rank, as he steered the mate's boat. But John was wide-awake to his own interests, and any appeals to his ambition or sense of duty he would offset by the argument before him; although the "mountain-dew" under other circumstances would have proved a most acceptable beverage, he was now firm enough to resist its allurements, and his excuses terminated with a flat refusal.

Tom, an American boat-steerer attached to the waist boat, and who, like old John, was an experienced hand, was next called upon, but he too muttered something about "asking impossibilities," and "sided" with his companion. I could not help thinking that the whole was a grand exhibition for our young aspirants to whaling honors.

There was but one boat-steerer remaining, and that was Jim Hussy, a Canadian. Smart and active, he was always at his post in any emergency.

" Come, Jim ! what d'ye say ?" said Mr. Grasper, slapping him on
the shoulder. " Go down there and hook on, and shame those cow-
ards. Will you go ?"

" Go ? Yes, to the devil, if you want me to. I say, steward,
stand by to give us a horn."

The bottle was passed, and Jim emptied his glass at a draught ;
then divesting himself of his shoes, he tied the rope around his
waist, and hardly touching the fall, leaped down upon the whale's
back. Seizing the hook, he fastened it at the first attempt ; then
grasping the harpoon to steady himself against an approaching sea,
he bawled out as loudly as he could, " Haul ! you santapedes, haul !"
Jim himself was immediately hauled up, but not without a thorough
immersion. I cannot attribute his success to superior skill, for Mr.
Easy, who killed the whale, was his senior in years, and more experienced ; but whether indebted to luck or otherwise, he deserved
credit, and for a time was quite a lion among the uninitiated.

As before remarked, we had all sorts of dispositions, and the sentiments pertaining to actors in greater events were displayed on this
occasion ; for how often is it in every-day life that we see a meri-
torious act, when it comes under the cognizance of envy, distorted
and perverted from its true meaning, while that amiable quality endeavors to persuade itself that either the author's motives were
selfish, or the deed the result of some fortuitous circumstance ! Although a cruel humiliation to John and Tom, they had no right to
rob Jim of his laurels ; and their sarcastic allusions to drunkenness
and insanity were unheeded by the mass.

But time is too precious to waste in idle comment ; so, leaving
Donald and Jonathan to their mutual consolations, I must hasten to
the brakes. How surprisingly hard they worked as blanket-piece
after blanket-piece ascended to the main yard ! Two or three debu-
tants attempted a song, but they all proved abortions, and failed
miserably.

I will here explain, for the benefit of those unacquainted with the
profession, a few terms that must necessarily occur. After the hook
has been fastened to the blubber, the captain, or whoever may have
that duty assigned him, commences cutting about a foot on either
side of the hook, and as he cuts, the men heave slowly at the brakes,

while the fish is gradually turning. Having hoisted the strip nearly to the main yard, one of the officers, (in the instance before us, Mr. Gurrie,) with a two-edged pike, plunges into the strip of blubber, and cuts a circular hole about a foot in diameter. Through this the bight of a rope is passed and toggled, then attached to a tackle overhead. This being done, the strip is severed immediately above the toggle, and by the aid of guys, is swung over the main hatchway. This is called a "blanket-piece," and is lowered to the between-decks, which, together with the space appertaining, constitutes the "blubber-room," and the process is repeated until every blanket-piece has been safely deposited. They are then cut up into square pieces, called "horse-pieces," of convenient size for tossing, by persons sent below for that purpose, a task usually devolving upon the laggards.

After a sufficient quantity of horse-pieces have been provided, the work of boiling commences. The carpenter is stationed near the •tryworks with a mincing-knife and block, and as he needs them, calls out "Horse-pieces." These are tossed from the hold with pikes, where, by similar implements, they are thrown into a heap near the mincing-tub. The boiler in his turn calls out "Mincing-pieces," and there are always supernumeraries ready to obey the requisition. After boiling sufficiently to extract the oil, they are removed from the kettles with a large skimmer. These are called "scraps," and are laid in a pile, to be used as fuel. The oil is then baled out into a large copper cooler, which is lashed to the tryworks, preparatory to being stowed below in casks. It may be as well to add, that the process of boiling, once commenced, continues day and night; and during seasons when the fish are plentiful, there are few occupations more laborious than whaling.

But to return. Our skipper was cast in the mould of perseverance; instead of a single blanket-piece, as predicted by some, we fairly stripped the carcass; but the head, with its rich store of spermaceti, we could not save, and with its loss vanished our anticipations of ivory teeth and "scrimshoning." Before cutting adrift from it, I had a good view of its "square" head, and long, narrow jaw, armed with its white teeth, and pendent in the water. The sea in our vicinity was literally covered with albatrosses, boobies, petrels, and other oceanic birds, giving a lively effect to the scene. Some

5

bold bird would dart at the carcass almost beneath the spade, and tearing off a portion with its sharp beak, would fly away, to be in his turn pounced upon by his fellows, while their harsh, discordant cries mingled with the shrill piping of the gale.

Having cut adrift, we wore round, and scudded away under reefed topsails. It blew too hard to think of lighting fires that night, and all our efforts were directed towards clearing up ship. Ashes were scattered upon deck for security of footing, and all superfluous lumber was stowed away in some nook or other. Before nightfall we had the satisfaction of seeing the Planet in tolerable order, and heartily wearied with our day's work, we sought refuge in our bunks, to await the events of the morrow.

CHAPTER X.

" BILIN' OUT," AND ITS INCIDENTS.

The morrow came, and with it an abatement of the gale, whereupon preparations were made accordingly. Many were the mutual congratulations among the officers at their good fortune. Mr. Grasper, with arms akimbo and an air of martyrdom, declared that, " for his part, he didn't care whether they took oil enough to fill cabin and all, for he could stow himself away in the maintop." Mr. Gurrie, too, professed himself perfectly willing to " give bedding and bunk a free passage over the fore-sheet, if necessary ;" while Messrs. Short and Easy reverently nodded their heads in approval.

Such a mustering of old garments ! Complete " tarring down" suits, and " jumpers" greasy with age, were forthcoming ; and then, indeed, for the first, and for some of us the last time, we indulged in the realities of whaling. The carpenter was at the block with his knife, and the boat-steerers mustered around the boiling apparatus. Folger and Weasle, spade in hand, were sent below to the blubber-room, and a requisite number were stationed near the hatchway to pitch horse-pieces, and others to pass them to the boiler, after they had been minced. Some three or four of us had the bitterest pill to digest, (so thought I at the time,) for, with sleeves rolled up to our elbows, with hand-brushes we scrubbed the "gurry" from the bulwarks with lye. Captain Buck bustled about with great officiousness, and I give him credit for being versed in all the mysteries of his profession. The starting of a hoop or the removal of a stave must be done with precision; like a skilful general, his glance was everywhere. There was no use in Mr. Grasper endeavoring to look fierce that day, or assuming any of his terrific scowls, for in almost every instance he broke down, and usually wound up his abortive attempts at severity with one of his dry jokes.

Before we were fairly under way, I recollect seeing Chips, who had served an apprenticeship as supernumerary in one of our theatres, and whose personifications of Iago, or the victim of Bosworth Field, would frequently distract him in the midst of his occupation, go to the "comings" of the hatch and exclaim, as he stared down with a haughty look at Folger, his inveterate enemy—

> "What! will the aspiring blood of Lancaster
> Sink in the ground! I thought it would have mounted."

Folger brandished his spade for an instant, and I thought he would have thrown it; but better counsel prevailed, for a moment after, he plunged it more fiercely than ever into the greasy mountain before him, cutting away indiscriminately to the right and left, without regard to the proportion of his horse-pieces, until poor Weasle fled aghast; and well he might, for in less than ten minutes Folger was assisted upon deck with a frightful gash in his right foot, so that he was *hors du combat* for the time. The spade, like the adze, is a dangerous implement in the hands of an inexperienced person, and should be used with the utmost caution. One circumstance alone, of almost daily occurrence, served to keep Mr. Folger's antipathy green in his memory, and that was, the partiality of the carpenter for his services to aid him in sharpening his tools; this being countenanced by Mr. Grasper, he never resumed his position at the crank of the grindstone without vowing vengeance, while the rapidity of its revolutions, an index to his sentiments, frequently called forth an encomium from his tormentor.

The work of boiling commenced. Thick volumes of smoke rolling upwards, gave the Planet's drapery a dingy hue, and sometimes the eddying wind would whirl the smoke in our faces, nearly driving us from our occupation. To turn from the snowy mountains and look at the fires, which, with their greasy fuel hissing and crackling, were burning merrily, was a pleasant but tantalizing sight. It would have been unsafe to venture in close proximity to them, for, independently of the execration such trespassing would merit, I have seen more potent arguments resorted to, and the offender driven forth amid a shower of scraps. Still, we had reason to be grateful. Our first whale had been taken, and the weather was favorable for boiling out; besides, the wind was fair, and we had every prospect of a speedy passage around the Cape, to warmer latitudes in the broad Pacific.

Night came at last, but with it no cessation from toil. The fires sent forth a lurid glow, and we pitched and minced by their light; during occasional intervals of relaxation, we managed to keep our eyes open by sleepy jokes. There was with us an old whaleman we called Sampson—not from any resemblance to that Israelite's distinguishing quality, for, on the contrary, he was simple, and not overburdened with strength. He had recently returned from a three years' cruise indebted some ten or twelve dollars to the owners, who generously forgave it—an act of charity alone that entitles them to flexible medals. He felt uncommonly good-humored that night, and entertained me with many a tale both comic and tragic relating to whaling; then, in the goodness of his heart, he promised me, on our arrival at Bedford, to take me to a "bunkum outfitter" he knew, where I could get any kind of shore toggery ("none of your slops") I wanted for almost half price; and he even went so far as to consult me on the propriety of seamen wearing "claw-hammer jackets" (dress-coats) ashore.

We gossipped until the propensity to sleep was irresistible, and, complying with a hint, I skulked with him to the booby-hatch, and watching an opportunity, we cautiously descended in pitchy darkness. Then we commenced groping towards the starboard wing, where a quantity of old rigging was stowed. Sampson stumbled over one of the cutting pendants, and fell against a stanchion, yet nothing but a suppressed " Murder" escaped him. I was more fortunate, and reached a coil of rigging without accident, and feeling about to ascertain the precise locality, my hands encountered something that I conjectured to be a pair of whiskers, and which further search confirmed, but the object might have been a corpse as regards animation. We left the sleeper to his dreams, and neither Sampson nor I ever discovered who it was. We both crawled on near the wellroom, where some old sails formed an inviting couch, but had hardly lain down before the aperture through which we had descended was darkened by the outline of a human figure ; then we heard the measured tread of some one coming down the ladder, then another and another succeeded, until I began to think the whole watch had deserted the deck.

" I believe they've tracked our wake," whispered Sampson, starting up ; then, disguising his voice, he said, as gruffly as he could, in a low tone, " Go back, you sogers, go back ! use a little judgment about it ; if you all skulk, you'll have old quiddle quaddle (Mr. G.) after you." But there came not a word out of the darkness, and we could hear them, like ghosts in a pantomime, as they took up their positions around us. A deep, heavy breathing soon disturbed the stillness, and I judged from the sound, that Sampson was snoring for a wager, with a " mezzo soprano" on my left. I slept, and none but those who labor know the sweets of reposing on the misty shores of Lethe.

After a brief slumber, I was awakened by some one pounding and pinching my leg, with exclamations of, " Oh! oh !"

" Hallo ! hallo ! there. Who's that pounding me ?"

" *Oh !* dear, doctor, is that you ? Do just take your boot-heel out of the small of my back, for I'm wedged in here, and can't stir."

It was poor Weasle. He had extended himself fore and aft, between me and the pump-well, while I was stretched out athwartships ; by the incessant lee-lurching of the ship, I had gradually slid to leeward, until my feet came in contact with the first thing that could give me steady support, and which proved to be the spine of Weasle. I lost no time in relieving him from his painful predicament, and giving him a place beside me.   It must have hurt him, for he told me " he dreamt he was a whale, and that Mr. Grasper had fastened to him."

Again we slept, but it could not have been long before every sleeper was simultaneously aroused, and on the alert, by a well-known bellowing at the scuttle.

" In the name of Moses !   Tumble up here, every ——— soger of you!   Don't let me get my boarding-pikes afoul of you ; if you do, I'll make the horse-pieces fly."

" Marlin-spikes and cat-harpins !" whispered Sampson.

Then there was a pause, for no one answered.   Every man felt himself too strongly intrenched to risk a battle in the open field ; for we could see, without being seen, and Mr. Grasper, on his part, was too skilful a general to storm a fortress single-handed, without a perfect knowledge of the enemy's strength; he knew, too, that he had made some bitter enemies.   For my part, I contemplated beating a retreat through a dangerous defile of casks and lumber out into the blubber-room, and thence to the deck, but second thought convinced me that it would be impracticable in the darkness.

A violent stamping and a volley of imprecations came next, but we answered not a gun.   He then had recourse to another system of tactics.

" You, War'ick!   You, Weasle !   You, Brown !   Answer me this instant, every one of you.   I know you're there."

" Aye, aye, sir ; I'm comin'," said Warwick, without attempting a parley.

" Shall I answer ?" whispered Weasle to me.

" Yes ; be quick !"

" Sir !"

" Oho !   So you've woke up at last !   Up you come, sir, before I get my grappling-irons on to you and taughten your weather-leach."

" I can't go," again whispered Weasle ; " I'm afraid he'll misuse me, he talks so savage.   Dear me ! why *didn't* I stop in the blubber-room !"

I told him to follow close upon the heels of Warwick, who had now commenced ascending the ladder, and who would be the first to confront Mr. Grasper ; and by watching his opportunity, he might slip away unperceived. He did so, and escaped without notice ; but the moment Warwick emerged from the scuttle, the powerful hand of Mr. Grasper was upon him, and I believe that here he expended his pent-up rage, for we could hear a shuffling of feet on deck, while his tongue, like a swivel on pivot amidships, was rolling out grape and cannister; among his invectives, the words " Jupiter !" " Moses !" and " Mince-meat !" were conspicuous.

At Sampson's suggestion, we all started *en masse*, and crowding out of the scuttle, marched down the deck in close array to the scene of our labors, where we filed away unmolested to our respective duties.

Nothing of further interest occurred during the night. It only remains to be said, that in a day or two all our horse-pieces were " tried out," and the oil, which did not exceed thirty barrels, was stowed away in well-coopered casks in the lower hold. I had almost forgotten to mention, that while boiling, a merchantman came rolling down to us before the wind to procure a supply of tobacco, which we furnished him.

CHAPTER XI.

"CAPE HORN FEVER."

OUR anticipations of fine weather off Cape Horn were soon put to flight, for we were driven by adverse winds as far as the fifty-eighth degree of south latitude. " As the days begin to lengthen, the cold begins to strengthen," thought some of our number. It was January, and for more than eighteen hours out of the twenty-four the sun was above the horizon.

In less than a week, our sick-list had increased to an alarming degree. Among the catalogue of ills were head, tooth, and a variety of aches ; besides, there were symptoms of decline, and morbid appetites accompanied by indigestion, but by far the greater portion consisted of chronic rheumatism. To treat this medley, I was vested with full discretional powers to act as the emergency might require,

and even a superficial observer would have been at no loss to assign
to most of these maladies their true cause. For the credit of the
recruits, I will state that the epidemic was not confined to them
alone; among those laid up with the most trivial disorders were
some of the oldest seamen on board. Like the Salem witchcraft, it
had progressed too far, and our officers were led seriously to reflect
upon its probable duration.

Mr. Grasper came on deck one morning, determined to have a
general hospital delivery.

" Doctor, what men are those sick below ?"

" Old Bill, Sampson, Fol——"

" There, there, that'll do ; steady 's you go. We'll begin with Old
Bill. What's the matter with him ?"

" Toothache, sir."

" Toothache, hey ! What kind of a sickness is that for an old
man-o'-war's-man like him to knock off with ? Why don't you pull
it, and not let him make a loblolly boy of you ?"

" I offered to do so ; but he says it's ulcerated, and that all of his
teeth have four curved prongs. The last dentist he applied to
frac——"

" Hold on ! hold on ! Mrs. Grasper in the bullrushes ! Order him
up there, Mr. Short !"

" Bill !" called that officer at the scuttle ; " you are wanted on
deck ! Come, bundle up here in a hurry."

And bundle up he did as soon as practicable, with his meagre face
swathed up in strips of old flannel, and over all was fastened a soiled
guernsey frock, something after the fashion of an Esquimaux hood.
He made a desperate·effort to look faint.

Mr. Grasper and the bystanders could hardly suppress a smile.
The former stepped up, and laying his hand upon his shoulder, with
an air of mock kindness, said, " William, my boy, what ails you ?"
I will here premise that it would have been difficult to determine
which was the senior in years.

" Oh, Mr. Grasper ! if you knew what a dreadful state my face is
in. I haint had a wink of sleep for the last three nights," and then
he fetched a groan.

" Sawry ; I'm sawry, William. Take that chafin gear off o' your head, and let me have a look ; perhaps I can do something for you. Why, your eyes look like a couple of grummet-holes !"

" I'm afraid I shall catch cold, and get the toothache worse for ——"

" O, no, you won't ; the doctor 'll be responsible for that, won't you ?"

I nodded in affirmation.

Piece by piece Bill removed the drapery from his head, and look at him as you would, there were no signs of protrusion or ulceration on either cheek.

" Your face don't look sore, William ; perhaps it's your tooth that aches ?"

" Yes, sir, dreadfully."

" Doctor, go and get your irons."

I requested permission to make an examination, to ascertain whether the case required the turnkey or the forceps, but he opened his mouth with so much reluctance, that I could make nothing out of his directions, so I deferred my observations until I had returned with both instruments.

A considerable elongation in his features had taken place during my absence, and when he saw the cold, shining steel, he declared that his " toothache was gone, and he'd rather not have it pulled," then resolutely pursed up his mouth.

" Come, Bill," said I, " don't be babyish ; think of those seven men you killed on board the opium clipper." But my appeals were in vain, for he maintained the firmness of a stoic.

" Open those scouse-coolers this minute, or I'll pry 'em open with a marlin-spike !" exclaimed Mr. Grasper, showing his true colors, and seizing Bill by the collar. " Down you go, there, agin the bitts— open your mouth, I say."

Making a virtue of necessity, Bill sat down upon deck, and leaned against the bitts, and with many entreaties for me not to hurt him, opened his mouth. Nothing can be more annoying to an operator than the infantile quibbles of his subject, and when they come from one grown gray with hard knocks, the dentist should be a prodigy of patience. As soon as I had the opportunity, I made a liberal incision with the usual instrument, and applying the forceps, despite his kicks and struggles, I laid the cause of his woes in his lap. A prolonged groan escaped him, and the tears actually trickled down his cheeks. With a salutary admonition, he was ordered to appear on deck when eight bells were struck.

"Let me see," continued Mr. Grasper: "there's Folger, I haint seen his face in some time. Show him up."

Mr. Folger made his appearance, and went to the weather side, then leaning upon the bulwarks, he looked out upon the water. O! for a sympathizing friend at that moment to share his meditations! But he saw nothing save the dull bank of clouds in the horizon, and the dreary waste of ocean, where each heavy wave that rolled across the monotony seemed an incubus to his melancholy. The snowy albatross, with its broad, extended wings, sailed swiftly by, as if, in its free and joyous flight, it sported amid warring elements, and mocked his misery.

For a moment Mr. Grasper's attention was occupied with issuing some necessary order, which Folger hearing, hastily whispered to me, using my name instead of the "handle."

"Tell that ogre I'm sick—dying, anything you please, so that I can keep out of his sight; but above all things, pray don't let him prescribe that villanous compound of his."

Further requests were interrupted by the return of his inquisitor, who, in this instance, assumed one of his affectionate looks, and laying one hand upon Folger's forehead, and the other upon his chin, as a veterinary surgeon would do in a similar emergency, he proceeded deliberately to open his mouth and look at his tongue. Although that organ did not protrude to exceed an inch, Mr. Grasper professed himself satisfied, and expressed a conviction that it indicated an "unhealthy tone of the diaphragm."

"Feel of his pulse, doctor; feel of his pulse, and let us know what you think of him."

I complied, but could detect nothing in the arterial throbbing that would indicate a derangement of the system. Folger hardly knew which way to look to keep his countenance.

"What do you say? Let's bleed him," said Mr. Grasper, looking fierce.

Folger raised his eyes with an expression of horror.

Not seeing the necessity of resorting to " flea-bottom-me," I counselled otherwise.

" I'll tell you, doctor, what I think 'll bring him 'round—a large handful of salts, dissolved in a quart of warm water."

" Mr. Grasper !"

" Why, that's nothing at all ; it's a great deal milder than to set down by a bucket of salt-water, and sip it with a tea-spoon until you feel better."

As nearly as I can judge, he made me put between three and four ounces of epsom salts into a tin pot, which I took to the galley and filled about two-thirds full of warm water ; and the fair Rosamond never received the poisoned goblet with more reluctance than did Folger the rusty tin pot, with its nauseous dose. I wash my hands clean of *this* affair ; should this ever meet the eye of Mr. Folger, of whose whereabouts I have been ignorant for the last five years, I beg him to remember that the deed was not perpetrated at my suggestion.

There are times when great minds, beset by difficulties, rise manfully to assert their greatness, and, like wounded stags, turn at bay to defy their persecutors. Such was the spirit manifested by Folger on this occasion ; placing the cup calmly upon the carpenter's bench, he coolly returned the withering look of Mr. Grasper.

" You have given me an over-dose, sir ; and I don't mean to make a drug-store of my bowels to accommodate any man."

" Mercy on us ! Now, don't go to sea, Abram, won't you. Why, doctor, we've got an Esculapius in disguise !" Then to Folger— " Look you here, my lark, your wings ain't fledged enough to fly far yet ; if you go to showing ' black-skin,' I shall touch you under the ' life,' and set you spouting blood in just seventeen and three-quarter seconds."

" There's reason in all things, sir. A part, if you compel me to, I drink ; but the whole—never !"

Bravo, Folger ! That was " bearding a Douglas in his hall ;" but your temerity availed you nothing. By threats, accompanied with an ominous brandishing of one of his " boarding-pikes," he compelled his unwilling patient to carry the cup to his lips, when a spasmodic twitching in the epigastric region was perceptible to all

" Drink, drink ! or I'll put a *tunnel* down your throat."

Folger took one swallow, and the same phenomenon again occurred ; but his tormentor was resolute, and he was compelled to force down about half a pint : after which Nature would be obeyed, and a violent retching was relieved at the lee bulwarks. For a short time after this he was sick in earnest; but when he recovered, the lesson was not forgotten.

Half a dozen others were summoned up, and their cases disposed of with less ceremony ; the result was that, out of nine or ten serious maladies, but three persons were really invalids.

I will close this chapter by mentioning an accident that happened at this time to our cook. For years he had been near-sighted in his right eye, and which at times he found to be very inconvenient. One morning, in coming from the forecastle, his sound eye came in collision with the windlass-brake, with such violence that for a time he was deprived of the use of it. I gave him almost the only remedy I had, a weak solution of sulphate of zinc, of which he made two or three applications during the day, and by night found himself considerably relieved. Had he rested here, all might have gone well ; but not comprehending the principle of inverse ratio, he adopted the axiom, that like causes produce like effects, adding, in unlimited proportion. Consequently, during the night he deluged his eyes with the solution, so that by morning he was an object of commiseration, for he was totally blind and a laughing-stock to the crew. He did not fully recover the use of his visual organs for several days after his ill-timed experiment.

CHAPTER XII.

JUAN FERNANDEZ, AND WHAT HAPPENED THERE.

WHAT cool and delightful evenings ! How brightly the full moon rises from behind the white clouds, and steadily pursues her course through the blue ether, while our ship, as she dashes along, joyfully welcomes the southeast wind. Some of the inmates of the deep seem influenced by Nature's harmony; for many a phosphorescent streak marks the course of porpoises and albicore in their gambols alongside and under the vessel's bow. We were sailing down the coast of Chili, and, after seeing nothing but sky and sea, together with a few barren mountains, for more than four months, our eyes were to be gladdened on the morrow by the green hills of Juan Fernandez.

For the objects of our voyage, it was not necessary that we should visit this island; but dissensions having arisen among the officers, it was determined by mutual consent that Mr. Gurrie, bag and baggage, should be left here. These difficulties had extended to the crew, each siding with his favorite officer, if favoritism could exist; so that anything approximating to Odd-fellowship among them had long since vanished. It was rumored, and confidently believed by some, that at the critical moment Mr. Gurrie would renounce his intention; but their estimate of his character was too superficial. He had said that, " if there was a rock in the ocean big enough to hold him, he'd leave the ship;" and he was not a man to be diverted by trifles.

The wished-for morning came; far ahead something like a faint cloud was seen in the horizon, and the welcome cry of " Land, O !" was heard once more. We were dashing rapidly along before the wind, and soon the " cloud," at first barely discernible, loomed more distinctly, and the delicate tracery of mountain, hill, and ravine was pencilled in mist. Gradually the sunlight burst forth, and the light vapors stealing along the mountain-side, rolled up to the summit and disappeared; Nature's handiwork in its beauty and sublimity was before us. There were deep valleys, whose furrowed sides were clothed with a sea of verdure, sweeping upwards in gentle undulations to the dark ridges. Everything wore an air of inspiriting freshness, that can only be appreciated by those who have long been sojourners upon the ocean. In a miniature bay, and standing off-and-on, was a bark, her white sails in beautiful contrast with the dark-green foliage. It proved to be the C——, of S——, Captain D——; her boats were ashore, engaged in fishing. Of the finny tribe an abundance may be found in these waters, and they are easily taken.

In due season, the main yard was hauled aback, and preparations for landing Mr. Gurrie commenced. The starboard boat was first lowered, into which jumped Captain Buck with a picked crew, who pulled off for the bark, probably to seek advice or investigate those points of law touching the part he was to play in the affair. The result of their deliberations we could never learn ; we only know that when he returned, he drew up a paper stating that " he (Mr. Gurrie) was acting of his own free will, and that he (Mr. Gurrie) relieved Captain Buck from any consequences that might ensue." This interesting document was formally signed, sealed, and delivered in the presence of ———.

Then arose a murmur of discontent among the brethren, especially the starboard watch. With all his failings, Mr. Gurrie was a good seaman, and never indulged in familiarity with his subordinates. He was a man who in storm or calm was cool and self-possessed, and in matters pertaining to seamanship, a person in whom we had every confidence. I reverted to the days of Robinson Crusoe and Selkirk, and to the adventures of the latter the case of Mr. Gurrie bore a strong resemblance. Alexander Selkirk, an officer, became dissatisfied with Captain Stradling, and declared that rather than be " straddled" over by him any longer, he preferred remaining upon an uninhabited island in the midst of the ocean. Hezekiah Gurrie, Jr., an officer, became dissatisfied with Captain Buck, and declared that rather than be " bucked" about by him any longer, he preferred remaining upon any rock or island in the middle of the ocean. When I saw his athletic proportions clothed with a pair of dark-blue trowsers and shirt of the same color, over which a pair of broad white suspenders were crossed, I thought it needed but the huge chako and musket to complete his equipment as a grenadier. His chest, bedding, and other little items of personal comfort, were brought up and lowered into the boat, together with a quantity of beef, pork, and sea-biscuit ; last of all, he shook hands with us, accompanied by the usual " so'-long," and descended himself.

Mr. Grasper, who commanded the boat, had been exceedingly officious that morning, arising perhaps from a consciousness of the responsible duty he was called upon to perform ; he even condescended to hint to me that he anticipated nothing short of open mutiny, headed by Mr. Gurrie himself, so soon as the boat should reach the shore, and had consequently provided himself with a brace of pistols and a sheath-knife. With a picked crew the boat shoved off, Mr. G. waving farewell; the old cooper, who was given to the "melting mood," dropped a tear to his memory.

We watched its receding form until it reached the shore, where it remained about fifteen minutes, and then returned, nothing having occurred to disturb Mr. Grasper's equanimity. Mr. Gurrie had again shaken hands with the boat's crew, wishing them "greasy luck" as he assisted to shove off the boat. Although, like Selkirk, he preferred solitude, I do not think he was the man to say,

> "I never heard a sound so dismal as their parting oars."

On its return, the boat paid a visit to the bark, by which we were favored with an exchange of diet; for it brought us a load of fish, a luxury after sustaining nature so long upon the contents of the "harness cask."

With nothing further to detain us, we squared the main yard, up helm, and away, the bark keeping company; and by sunset the green hummock of Juan Fernández loomed dimly in the twilight.

That night, unknown to me, a demonstration was made by a certain clique in behalf of their absent officer. A quantity of provision, boatcompass, sail, and other necessaries, were secretly stowed away in the waist boat; and it was arranged by Mr. Easy, who headed the plot, and who had now become third officer, that during the middle watch, he, the cooper, carpenter, and two of the boat-steerers, should lower away, the fall and blocks having been previously greased to prevent noise, and return to the island we had just left. At the critical moment, when everything was prepared, and each man stood by with a small bundle of clothes, the cooper's fortitude deserted him. The "old bridge" had carried him safely over; besides, he had broken bread and eaten salt aboard of her, and why then shouldn't he love her? No; at the eleventh hour he concluded to cling to her, like an affectionate son to his mother's bosom. She had never deserted him, and he would never desert her. Entreaties and expostulations were unavailing; like an epidemic, the feeling of disaffection extended to all, and the plot was abandoned through the

instability of one of its members.   I know not whether Captain
Buck ever heard of it, nor do I recollect having previously mentioned it.

CHAPTER XIII.

ON ETIQUETTE, DIGRESSING TO DOMESTIC QUADRUPEDS.

FOR nearly a week after leaving Juan Fernandez, we " gammed"
(kept company) with the bark, and as pertained to sailing qualities, she and the Planet were pretty fairly matched, although
the latter was considerably the larger of the two.   The monotony
of existence was thus relieved by frequent visits to each other, and
which, without material interference with our duties, was an agreeable and useful diversion.   It changes the current of the feelings
that are perhaps brooding over wrongs, real or fancied, and relaxes
for a moment the efforts that imply fear and obey !   Old friendships
are burnished up, and new ones cemented ; besides, new faces are
seen, and new voices heard.   Compliments, too, in their way, are
exchanged ; and the amicable feeling that characterizes an interchange of sentiment ashore is usually maintained at a " gam."   If
the captain with the starboard boat's crew visits his neighbor, the
mate of the vessel visited returns with the crew of the larboard boat,
and *vice versa.*   Upon these occasions, I have been told that the respective cabins are disguised by extra scrubbings, and fancy table-
covers and curtains are brought forth from their resting-places,
where they have become mildewed.   I can testify to the fact of sundry suspicious-looking messes having been brought forward to undergo a culinary operation, and by humoring the steward, he would
now and then indulge me with " soft tack."

It came my turn one day to go in the boat.   After leaving the
captain at the man-ropes, the warp was hove on deck, and the boat
hauled forward to the fore-chains, up which the crew climbed to the
bulwarks.   As a matter of courtesy, one of the bark's crew jumped

down into the boat, to prevent it from staving against the ship's side. We are prone to draw comparisons favorable to ourselves, and in this instance, I flattered myself that the C—— was in every respect inferior to the Planet, both as pertained to comfort and convenience, and even beauty, for everything wore a slovenly look, from the main truck to the water-ways. Our entertainers, however, were assiduous in their endeavors to please. I shall not forget the kindness of the second officer, who took me into his state-room and initiated me into the mysteries of his chest, commenting upon each article successively drawn forth. They, too, had taken a sperm whale, and the till of his chest was enriched with its trophies. He kindly presented me with two large ivory teeth, explaining minutely the process of grinding and polishing preparatory to " scrimshoning."

I must not forget to mention the young steward, who gave me a two-ounce vial of porpoise-jaw oil, used by jewellers for watches, pure and clear as crystal ; he suggested, that for greasing razors it was far superior to the ordinary process of " slushing them with auguintum," (Ung. Hyd. Mite.)

One day the first officer of the C—— paid us a visit, and among a crew of various climes and colors was one of Afric's sable sons, in his way an expert dancer, and no one appreciated this agile talent more than Mr. Grasper. I at one time thought the poor negro was condemned to martyrdom to gratify his mirthful propensity. He capered to a charm, at least so most of us thought ; but still Mr. Grasper would have it that the right heel was not thrown far enough aft at the terminus of each figure. With the perspiration streaming from him, he was compelled to continue his antics until he satisfied in this respect ; *i. e.*, in one grand finale, his arms and eyes classically raised, with a slight concavity of the spine, and the heel thrown back at an angle of fifteen degrees from the true perpendicular of the body.

For more than a week we continued to visit by day and signalize by night, and some began to hope for a change of wind that would compel us to part company. Before this consummation, an accident occurred that gave me an idea of my importance. Chips, by some unlucky accident, fell from the between-decks upon a tier of casks in the lower hold, and was removed almost senseless to his

6

work-bench abaft the tryworks.   Instead of mending, he continued
to get worse.   Weasle, like the good Samaritan, offered his assistance, but Folger passed by with a disdainful scowl.   I had recourse
to bleeding, which revived him, and other remedies that were required, I hinted it would be necessary to procure from our consort.
A boat was accordingly lowered and placed at my disposal; this
time I was not compelled to sit upon a thawt and tug at the oar, but,
seated upon the gunwale, I was entertained by the lively conversation of Mr. Easy.   A few more such accidents, and I might have
been aspiring enough to entertain notions of superiority.

Soon after, we parted company, nor did we meet again for several
weeks, when, by a singular coincidence, both of us arrived the same
day at Maui.

Since leaving port, we had been pestered by rats, and instead of
diminishing, these unwelcome intruders continued to increase until
they became an insupportable nuisance.   A large water-tank, between decks, and not closely covered, had a pump leading to it from
the galley.   About this time it became an object of strong suspicion with me, owing to the peculiar taste and odor of the water,
suggesting recollections of cats in a well.   I had subsequent reason to believe that my conjectures were well founded: upon examination, the *debris* at the bottom of the tank was found to contain
short gray hairs and detached horny substances, bearing a close resemblance to claws, together with sundry cartilaginous shreds, the
whole affording strong evidence that at no very remote period animal decomposition had taken place.

The weather being favorable, Captain Buck determined upon a war
of extermination, and that was, a thorough smoking out.   Accordingly,
all necessary garments were brought on deck, together with provision sufficient for a three days' smoke.   The first step in the process
was to calk every little aperture through which the gases might
escape ; next, a huge iron pot was suspended in the blubber-room,
beneath the main hatch, and into this was thrown tinder for igniting, also a quantity of charcoal and sulphur, so that the rats, instead
of snuffing up the balmy air of the tropics, were to be suffocated by
the combined effects of carbon and sulphuretted hydrogen.   The fire
having been lighted, the hatches were put on, calked, and carefully

battened down, as well as the companionway, steerage, and forecastle scuttles, to render them as nearly air-tight as possible. Of course there was little or no work done during the two days following; and the weather being unexceptionably fine, we enjoyed the temporary respite from our labors.

To walk the hot decks of a ship at sea over a burning fire produces sensations similar to those occasioned by traversing the bed of a crater, where mephitic vapors ascending from deep fissures and subterranean detonations, evidence the element that is raging beneath. I could not help *calculating* to a nicety our distance from the coast of Peru, the prevailing winds, and the quantity of provision and water the boats would carry, each with its respective complement of men. Fortunately, we had no occasion to resort to this alternative, and after the fires had burned two days, the hatches were removed. A sufficient time having been allowed for the escape of the foul and influx of fresh air, Mr. Short was requested to descend to make observations, with the salutary caution to scream in case he found himself suffocated. But the rats were " game," and although many of them lay stretched in death, the sleek sides of more than one of them were palpitating on the cabin floor. Again the hatches were replaced, battened down, and continued so during the remainder of the day, and that following, after which they were removed, and the rats thrown overboard by scores; though not quite exterminated, they gave us no further inconvenience during the remainder of the passage.

CHAPTER XIV.

A CALM, ITS INCIDENTS, AND CONCLUSION.

A CALM at sea has its inconveniences: the rolling of the ship, the flapping of sails, and the glassy surface of the ocean that radiates with intensity the burning rays of the sun, seem to betoken a pause in existence; the lull of voices, the almost painful silence that reigns on board and around, suggest reflections upon a universe without animation. If it occur at evening, I know of no place better adapted to quiet meditation ; the very atmosphere seems to possess a soothing power, and resigning yourself passively to its influence, a pleasing train of emotions will be awakened, harmonizing with surrounding objects.

We were becalmed one day near the line ; as evening approached the decks were neatly cleared up and swept down ; everything breathed an air of quietness and repose. The sun was hastening to the horizon, and its rays, undimmed by a cloud, were undulating upon the water, and bathing the dark hull and sails of the Planet in their golden light.

The steward and Jim Hussy, yielding to the temptation, were alternately climbing and leaping from the bulwarks to sport in the inviting element. Although such a bath would have been a luxury, I entertained too great a dread of sharks to indulge in it, and jumping into one of the boats, I endeavored instead to immerse myself in the abstrusities of that clever German, Schlegel, a volume of which I fortunately retained. The sun was just dipping, when the cry of "Shark, O !" rang out with startling effect from the mast-head. Having left the two men swimming, I anticipated nothing less than a scene of horror, but from which I was relieved by seeing them shivering upon the rail, as they stared down at some object in the water.

"There, now! What 'd I tell you ? I reckon you'll b'lieve me next time, when I say to you that I saw a man have his leg bit off by a shirk," said Mr. Grasper, with an appearance of melancholy.

It appears the men had been diving at regular intervals ; and Mr. Grasper, thinking they had continued their diversion long enough, detained them upon the rail as they were preparing for another leap, to relate to them an accident that had come within his cognizance, and during this interval the shark had made his appearance. We all hastened to the side to witness the arrival of our new visitor, which proved to be a large blue shark, (known among sailors as the " deepsea shark,") who worked his way leisurely along to the ship, with his dorsal fin above water. For a moment he remained motionless, then, turning slightly upon his side, we saw his small round eye look inquiringly up, as if wondering what could have induced the swimmers to discontinue so innocent a pastime. Whatever were his meditations, he did not indulge them long ; for Mr. Easy hove a " gig" through and through him, giving him a most unceremonious start from his reveries upon fresh joints. We all clapped on to the line and hauled together. The monster's weight was incredible, and when I looked over the side to watch his ascent, he was writhing his body and lashing his tail with fury, and his open jaws displayed two or three ghastly rows of saw-like teeth, which at intervals he would gnash together with such vehemence as to be distinctly heard above the noise and confusion attending his capture. With great difficulty he was drawn half way up the side, when the iron drew, and he fell back into the water where, after moving about leisurely for a few moments, with his entrails protruding from the wound, he disappeared and was seen no more.

If there be any object throughout the whole structure of animated creation for which I entertain an invincible abhorrence, it is a shark. Anthropóphagi are bad enough, but they may be tamed ; whereas the shark seems created expressly to lend a terror to the sea, and to prey upon human flesh. There is something indescribably loathsome in the appearance of the huge ground-sharks I have seen among the islands of the Pacific, when drawn upon deck or ashore ; the very eyes seem to speak murder, and their teeth torture ; and often, while swimming in crystal waters, over fields of coral, the thought has flashed across me that perhaps at that moment a pair of eyes were staring at me through labyrinthine branches, and that some monster was waiting either the impulse or opportunity to drag me mangled and bleeding to its submarine grot. Too many instances of their murderous propensity have come within my cognizance to diminish this antipathy, and I can fully participate in the feelings of the sailor, when he captures his arch-enemy.

We were becalmed nearly a week, and Captain Buck, thinking the opportunity favorable, all hands were turned to scraping and scouring the ship's sides, preparatory to painting. After the stagings, formed of spars and planks, were properly arranged, and the decorations of the Planet commenced, I was swung over the stern to erase and paint in large characters her name, and, although making no pretensions to artistic merit, Captain Buck complimented me on what he was pleased to term my success. We painted her black outside, with formidable ports, giving her bulwarks a dash of lead-color within. The day we were occupied with the finishing touches, it became necessary to fasten the running rigging up to the fair leaders, where it was secured, without reference to service in the event of an emergency.

It was only at sunset that appearances indicated a change in the weather. There was a heavy bank of clouds skirting the eastern horizon, that wore a threatening look, and some of the knowing ones affirmed it was a weather breeder. No notice was taken of it, however, and as evening advanced detached masses were seen gradually rising, although with us there was not a breath of air stirring. Suddenly a vivid flash seemed to rend the dark mass to its centre, and the low rumbling of thunder that immediately followed sounded ominously as it reverberated in the distance. These signs of an approaching storm were too startling to be disregarded, and, at the sacrifice of our day's work, the watch was called upon to render the running rigging accessible ; before this could be accomplished the storm was upon us, a tempest of wind and rain. We up helm and let her scud before it, and I thought our spars would go before we could reduce sail ; but fortunately, accomplished all that was required without accident. The wind being fair, we drove rapidly along, and by morning it had settled down to a steady breeze, that carried us safely to the green hills of Maui.

Having hastily sketched a few of the incidents that served to beguile the monotony of a six months' cruise, without attempting anything like a concise narrative of events, I must say *au revoir* to the reader, whom I hope soon to meet again amid scenes that shall be mutually congenial.

END OF PART FIRST.

SEQUEL TO THE FOREGOING.

T HE writer of a romance is at liberty to dispose of his characters as he pleases. I wish that in the present instance I could do the same ; but a regard for the feelings of others, more interested than myself, compels me to draw a veil over the events that characterize the sequel. Yet, without meriting censure, I think a few remarks may be safely hazarded relative to those who have figured in the foregoing pages. It will be necessary to premise that several made their escape, but more were discharged ; it is upon the causes that led to this result that silence is maintained, not on my own, but on account of others.

With Captain Buck, and Messrs. Grasper, Gurrie, Short, and Easy, I have not yet had the pleasure of a subsequent interview. I have never since heard of my old friend the cooper. The blacksmith, as was before noticed, deserted, and was married in New Zealand. O'Connor, in company with steerage Bill and Weasle, attempted his escape at Lahaina ; and while trudging leisurely along the beach, in an uninhabited district, they were beset by three natives who came to capture them. He and his companions were provided with clubs, but at the critical moment, Bill and Weasle threw down their weapons, and took up a commanding position on an eminence a short distance off. O'Connor knocked down the first native, whose temerity exceeded his discretion, which brought the others to a parley. The articles of capitulation conceded that he should ride into town on a donkey, accompanied by Bill and Weasle on either side, who were to retain the free use of their arms. This last clause coinciding with the views of these two persons, the treaty was formally ratified by their ready acquiescence, and the strange cortege that moved into town, without a precedent in the annals of constabulary deeds, threatened to revolutionize this branch of municipal regulation.

One of the foremost hands, subsequently promoted to the rank of boat-steerer, was struck by a whale on the Northwest, and instantly killed.

John, the boat-steerer, discharged at Lahaina, shipped on another vessel for a cruise in the Arctic, where he narrowly escaped with his life. Being out one day in pursuit of whales, they came upon a " cow and calf," and John up iron and let drive, when madam, resenting the indignity, elevated her flukes, and brought them down with such violence, that the boat was shattered to fragments, precipitating all into the water, whence John arose, clinging to a piece of the wreck, and growling like a polar bear.

One of our number, who shall be nameless, whom I have since seen engaged in commercial pursuits in Honolulu, related to me the events attending his escape, capture, and subsequent discharge, an outline of which I subjoin :—The day previous to the sailing of the Planet, he was ashore on liberty, and thinking the moment for escape opportune, he encumbered himself with a canteen of water, and as much sea-biscuit as he could, without impeding his progress, and started for the mountains. Arrived there, he passed two or three days and nights in misery without shelter, and being overcome by thirst, he descended to the bottom of one of those deep valleys in the rear of Lahaina, to procure a drop of the cooling liquid. The temptation to bathe was too strong to be resisted, there being no signs of inhabitants ; while indulging in his ablutions, he was startled by the sound of footsteps, and looking around, saw a native girl coming towards him. He was at first disposed to beat a retreat up the steep ridges in deshabille, but the " pleasant countenance and winning way of the girl," as he expressed it, " hove him completely aback." After all, it was but a woman, and with becoming fortitude, he prepared himself for the emergency. By signs she invited him to dress himself, and accompany her to her house farther up the valley. He, " nothing loth," complied, and followed his conductress for a considerable distance up the bank of the stream, then striking out into a side-path to the left, they soon reached a snug grass hut, into which she bade him enter. Here he feasted for the first time on fish, poi, and bananas ; after which she spread a clean mat for him to lie upon, and hung up a broad *kapa* for a curtain. Conceiving he had made an impression, and absorbed with reveries of love in a cottage, he lay down to sleep ; but how fallacious are human hopes ! At midnight he was awakened by the sound of voices in earnest converse, and cautiously pulling the curtain aside, he discovered his hostess in communication with two brawny natives, attired in nothing but the malo. .He was soon relieved from his suspense by the girl, who by signs expressed to him her wishes that he should accompany her visitors. Entreaties were unavailing, for nothing but money would soften her stony heart, and unfortunately, he was unprovided with any description of the circulating medium ; so over rock and stone, through bush and brake, he was compelled to travel that night, until he found himself safely immured within the walls of the fort at Lahaina.

* * * * * *

During the night, while lying off and on the port of ———, a fire broke out in the fore hold, the work of an incendiary, and before effectual means could be taken to check its further progress, the flames burst out of the fore hatchway. My informant was nearly suffocated by the smoke while asleep in the forecastle. Many of the crew, instead of obeying orders, flew at once to the boats, while others applied themselves to drawing water, and by the efforts of these, together with the personal daring of a boat-steerer, named Nicholas Peters, of R. I., who leaped into the fore hold, the better to grapple with it, the fire was extinguished. There was no peace for Mr. Grasper during the remainder of that night ; he girded on a long, straight, cavalry sword, something like a Toledo blade, stuck a brace of pistols in his belt, and, thus accoutred, performed the duty of a marine : while Mr. Short, for want of a better weapon, promenaded the opposite side of the quarter-deck with a boarding-pike. Mr. Easy had already effected his escape.

* * * * * *

Josh, and two or three others, for a brief interval turned their attention to agricultural pursuits.

* * * * * *

The merry laugh of some, is hushed—the warm hand of friendship, cold ! When the " chip" of life first swam on the ocean of eternity, it was said by Him who hove it—" Watch !" The sands of time ran still, while the thread of existence spun rapidly from the reel, and when death said " Up !" by the hand that gave it beginning it was " checked" forever.   But amid light and gloom ocean rolls on, unchanged by the storm of passion or calm of repose ; and to each light heart that has sported amid its billows, but now slumbers in its bosom, let us unite in saying, Farewell !—*requiescat in pace !*

PART II.

—

HAWAIIAN ISLANDS.

HAWAIIAN ISLANDS.

CHAPTER I.

ADVENTURES IN LAHAINA.

LAHAINA, the principal town of Maui, and the second of importance in the kingdom, is pleasantly situated on the leeward side of West Maui, so called from its resemblance to a distinct island, being connected with East Maui by a low isthmus nearly level with the sea.

From the roadstead, it having no harbor, there is something peculiarly attractive in its appearance owing to its favorable contrast to the sterile mountains in the background, rising from 4,000 to 5,000 feet above the sea. Like, as it were, an oasis in the desert, it extends for nearly two miles along the shore, a luxuriant garden, having an average breadth of nearly half a mile. The site of the town is perfectly level, with a slight elevation above the sea. In the rear, and on either side, there is hardly tree or shrub to relieve the barren aspect. Among its conspicuous objects is the long two-story wooden building with a verandah running around it, and designated " The Palace," but which, to do his majesty justice, he never deigns to notice during his visits to Lahaina.

The fort, occupying a central position, is a parallelogram, built of coral blocks, about twelve feet in height, and mounting a few rusty guns of various calibre on its ramparts, which are patrolled by sentinels in ventilated uniforms. The native church, a two-story building, and neatly whitewashed, is also conspicuous, with its red roof and steeple, surrounded by bread-fruit, cocoanut, and *kukui* trees, (*Aleurites triloba*.) The stores and dwellings of foreign residents, scattered along the shore, form a pleasing contrast to the grass houses of the natives, situated amid groves, and grouped near the water's edge. In the rear, at a much greater elevation, and somewhat to the right, two deep valleys give a pleasing effect to the landscape, their sides clothed with a dense growth of trees and underwood, and their bottoms watered by streams foaming over rocky beds, irrigating the inclined plane to a considerable extent, until absorbed by the thirsty soil. During the rainy season, they become torrents, and empty into the sea. On the mountain-side to the left, the white mission residences of Lahainaluna, with the steepled Seminary, afford an agreeable relief to the eye ; beyond, the mountain summits are clothed with forest, and frequently enveloped in clouds. The soil of Lahaina has a reddish tinge, and is of clayey consistency. According to the seasons, it is alternately dry and muddy ; and during the summer months, when there is a long absence of rain, the whirlwinds that come sweeping down the valleys carry the dust in clouds far out to sea.

With all its inconveniences, Lahaina is a most inviting spot to look upon after the privations of a sea-voyage. To one who has never before visited Polynesia, there is a novelty and beauty in everything—the commingling of civilization with semi-barbarism, and the association of native and foreigner. The light and airy cottage that we are accustomed to associate with oak and elm at home, looks none the worse though shaded by the spreading branches of the *kou*, or for having its garden adorned with exotics, interspersed with the breadfruit and cocoa palm. The thatch huts of the natives, sometimes inclosed by adobe walls, and surrounded by taro-patches and the products of their industry, have a pleasing appearance ; these, together with the frequently gaudy attire of their inmates, strutting leisurely along, or chanting a *mele* beneath shady banana groves, lend a picturesque effect to the scene.

On the 20th April, 1849, I was, like Jack, "all abroad," and, in reverting to the incidents of that period, I have classed them among the happiest of Polynesian reminiscences. Without being frowned upon as an intruder, with duck trowsers and hickory shirt,

I could initiate myself into all the mysteries of beer-shops and victualling-houses, (deprecating the taste,) and witness the hearty congratulations between the cruisers of New Zealand and those of the Ochotsk seas. It was during this interesting period that I made myself fully acquainted with the domestic economy of a Hawaiian household, though the taste for *poi* was subsequently acquired under circumstances of necessity. To trespass upon the subject of family routine, would involve too much prolixity; suffice it to say, the research should be cautiously ventured, and not unfrequently the result would be anything but flattering to morality. The dress of the males usually consists of the ordinary trowsers and shirt; but among the wealthier class there is nothing to distinguish their garments, both in quantity and quality, from those of more favored communities. The female attire possesses nothing attractive. Without regard to material, whether the embroidered fabrics of China, or the printed cottons from the looms of Fall River, they fashion their robes like loose gowns, with formidable *gigot* sleeves, pertinaciously rejecting any innovation on their established custom.

It has been remarked that Hawaiians are proverbial for their hospitality; without combating any encomium upon their virtues, I must observe, that friendship will sometimes degenerate to selfishness. Whether from predisposition in my favor, or acting under a momentary impulse, a native, whom I shall call John, saw fit to shoulder himself upon me, inviting confidence by his apparent sincerity. He was a good-looking fellow, speaking English with tolerable facility; and having cruised two or three seasons on the northwest, he believed it his prerogative to inveigle any of the craft, no matter by what means, into an appreciation of his attentions. On his account, I am sorry to add that from me his gleanings were small, for chest I had none, and the small bundle of necessary apparel could never incommode me by its weight. As to shoes, I wore my only pair, and between soles and uppers a struggle had been long going on regarding the propriety of separation.

The first object that seriously engaged his attention was a large fancy quilt, and which he suggested was admirably adapted for a curtain of ceremony. I had no great partiality for it, although not insensible to its convenience. During the voyage it had covered a

bust of General Cass, which had been presented by a friend—the
artist who executed it ; but whether typical or not of that states-
man's downfall, I found it fractured in several places on my arrival,
and with feelings of regret I consigned the relics to a resting-place
among the coral reefs of Lahaina.   I gave it to him at once.   Next,
a figured pongee with a dashing border attracted his attention.   This
he begged for his wife, and it was readily bestowed, for she was a
pretty and obliging woman.   As his wants increased, my stock diminished ; and with feelings of alarm, I contemplated the contingency of "pitching horse-pieces" in the Arctic.   Any hints regarding my needy condition—for, unfortunately, I had nothing in the shape
of a legal tender—he would offset with a cozy embrace, informing
me that the poi calabash was always at my service.   I could eat
the taro fresh from the oven, for then there is something agreeable
about it ; but, after seeing John, *sans culotte*, and girded with nothing
but a *malo*, pounding away at it with a stone pestle upon an old
board, with the perspiration streaming from his body, my stomach
refused to encounter it.   Nalfmu, his wife, would sometimes oblige
me with a bunch of bananas ; and through her influence, we were
now and then regaled with the inviting spectacle of a roaster.   However, I ultimately effected an arrangement with the proprietor of a
victualling-house, thus avoiding the prospect of lingering starvation.

It was several days before I ventured to trespass within the precincts of royalty.   Crossing a stagnant pool where the " mud-hens"
were quarrelling with each other, I sauntered leisurely towards the
Palace, expecting to see the royal standard of Hawaii waving from
the balcony, and grooms and pages in livery bustling about with the
officiousness of menials.   But not a sound came from its deserted
halls.   Both railings and columns of unmentionable architecture expressed a contempt of paint, having withal a venerable aspect ;
the most interesting feature was its plastered walls, whose whitewashed surface offered a tempting field for the designs of native
artists.   Whether original or otherwise, they certainly produced an
astonishing effect ; for, without adhering to any particular school
of the art, the dash of coloring (charcoal) was laid on in bold outline ; and *tableaux* of animated figures, with explanatory hieroglyphics, were grouped about the door-way.   At the first glance, the

delineation of a centaur would indicate an acquaintance with mythology ; but a broad Mexican saddle, with its uncouth stirrups, giving it a modern appearance, made one unable to reconcile the discrepancy. At times, there was an approximation to sentiments of a tenderer nature, and amorous designs gave a clue to the propensities of their authors. Appropriate mottoes were frequently subjoined, such as " *aloha maikai oe o pua loke*," (love to you, my rose,) but again there were characters so unique that it would have required a Champollion to decipher them. I had the temerity to trespass within the portal ; though destitute of ornament, the spacious rooms and solid floors have a substantial appearance. I know of no better place in Lahaina for enjoying the sea-breeze and a commanding prospect, than its balcony or roof. In one of its rooms is held the Police Court ; and the broad hall is occupied by the Circuit Court, during its annual sitting. Of late years, more attention has been paid to its appearance, with reference to wilful mutilation. The walls are sound, and it may yet be rendered an ornament to the town in which it stands.

At this time his majesty, Kamehameha III., was visiting Lahaina, and during his sojourn he usually remained at the residence of the Young family, the *élite* of Hawaiian nobility. He frequently rode out accompanied by his attendants, managing his horse with ease, and had the appearance of being an accomplished equestrian.

CHAPTER II.

O'CONNOR'S EXPERIENCES.

I was one day strolling through the bread-fruit grove at the southern extremity of the town, indulging a few consolatory reflections at the expense of that misanthrope, Zimmerman, when I was startled from my revery by a familiar voice singing:

> " I dug his grave with a silver spade ;
>   O ! bullies, O !
> And I lowered him down with a golden chain,
>   A hundred years ago !"

7

Immediately after, it changed to, " Hard a-port there, shipmate! and keep your luff, or you'll be aboard of me."

In the direction whence the sound came, I espied the gable of a hut just peeping above a clump of sugar-cane.

" Ship ahoy! Who are you?" I hailed.

" Avast there, doctor! and heave aback. You are trespassing on my cruising-ground!" returned O'Connor, whom I now recognized.

I lost no time in entering the humble portal, and there, stretched out upon a pile of mats in " inglorious ease," was the hero of the donkey; inhaling at intervals, from a short, stumpy pipe, the aroma of the fragrant weed. He was a shade darker than when we had parted on shipboard, and his costume was a *mélange* of civilization and barbarism. Instead of the striped flannel shirt, he sported a fancy regatta with a flowing collar; a Turkey red *paú*, or wrapper, was substituted for duck trowsers. He wore a fragrant necklace of the yellow drupes of the *Pandanus odoratissimus*, and his head was encircled by a formidable wreath of mountain fern. There were half a dozen dusky belles and beaux in the apartment, reclining upon the soft mats of the *lauhála*. The whole seemed an apparition of the drowsy *tableaux* in " Midsummer Night's Dream;" and I felt like exclaiming with Snout:

> " O Bottom, thou art changed!
> What do I see on thee!"

After passing congratulations and comparing notes, O'Connor proceeded to recount a few items of personal adventure that had transpired since his escape.

" In the first place," said he, " after leaving the fort, I commenced beating about for something to do. I was determined not to reship without a little rustication. So one day I packed up and started off for the other side of the island. A lucky stroke I had my 'pass,' or I should have been arrested a dozen times as a runaway. Well, I forged ahead until I reached the mountain, and here I hove-to for the night; for, you know, it's rulable to make any port in a storm. The next day I commenced climbing over hills and ridges as barren as those of St. Nicholas, and it was a good half day before I reached the desert on the opposite side. I was almost choked, for since morning I had been sweltering in the sun without a smell of anything to drink, and here I stood on a plain, miles in extent, without a sign of either tree, shrub, or water. I edged along to the seashore, and followed the smooth beach for three or four miles, until I reached a little village of dried haystacks. Here I halted for a snack. I bolted into the first house I came to, and made motions to an old woman catching fleas. She handed me a calabash of villanous liquid, that reminded me of a fermented waterbutt; and if you'll believe me, I had to pay a *real* before she'd give me a drink of the abominable stuff.

"I was lucky in finding a white man, who told me he had lived for years in Wai—— Wai—— something, I forget the name, and that he raised potatoes in the mountains, and speculated in horses and cattle for a living. He offered to hire me to drive cart from the diggings to the beach, and as the wages were fair, I signed articles on the spot. I said I was lucky, but I believe I was unlucky, for I find I was never cut out for a farmer. D'ye see, the cattle here aint like the cattle at home. In the first place, I had to have native boys to tackle 'em for me, and then, you know, I can't talk a word of Kanaker, (the only language they understand,) so that when I said 'port' and 'starboard,' I might as well have whistled to the wind. Things went on in a fair way until the fifth day. I was driving a cart-load of 'spuds' down the mountain, for the haystacks, and when about half way, the starboard beast got huffy, and began to make leeway; so, thinks I, my lad, I'll just clap a stopper on to your cutwater, and bring you to. I took out a coil of rope I always carried in the cart, and made a running bowline, which I tried to throw over his nose. Some how or other they both got wind of the game, and with tails triced up as taught as martingales, they started down hill like a pair of 'fin-backs.' They went as if the devil had 'em, and the old cart bounded over the rocks, scattering 'scurvy pills' all the way! They must have shaped their course by compass, for they kept the track, and I watched them until they looked no bigger than a pair of sucking calves. D'ye think I followed? Not I. I jumped on to a rock, swung my tarpaulin, and sung that good old song—

'O! storm along!
O! my roving blades, storm along, stormy!'

"My farming jig was up. I squared yards with the old fellow, and

bore away for this port.   I arrived four days ago : went down and
shipped aboard the O——, bound for the Arctic ; got an advance,
and I'm living it out.   I rent this house, I do, and these squaws and
Kanakas are my hired servants.   A man must live a little while, you
know.   In less than three months I shall be on the nor'west, chasing 'bowheads' in the fog, and up to my eyes in 'gurry.'   But
never mind, a man's all right if he can only keep a 'shot in the
locker.' "

O'Connor was a good sample of the reckless roisterly sailor.
Free and easy, at the same time prepared for any emergency, the
impudence that would prompt him to tweak the fur hood of an Esquimaux belle, relapsed into a sentiment of unqualified self-assurance,
while paying court to the less circumspect charmers of the Southern
Isles.   We gossipped together for an hour or more ; and on shaking
hands, wished each other " so-'long," with the same levity and indifference that characterized our first meeting on shipboard.   Sailors,
of all classes, are least disposed to brood over severed friendships,
whether transient or permanent.   Two days after, he sailed, and I
have neither seen nor heard of him since.

CHAPTER III.

A LAWYER ABROAD.

AMONG the guests of the victualling-house, I noticed a person
of perhaps five-and-twenty, whose seedy attire accorded so well
with my own unpretending habiliments of blue drilling, that, after
a little random conversation, a mutual feeling of sympathy began to
germinate, and we were drawn together by the intuitive perception
inherent in " birds of a feather."

Allaire, my newly-found acquaintance, wore a " pepper-and-salt"
frock-coat of undeniable antiquity, which hung around him like loose
drapery, with the exception of the sleeves ; these were so tight
that the elbows, by urging a continued remonstrance, had effected a

compromise. His lustreless cravat of black silk, notwithstanding the climate, was girded tightly around his neck to the chin, and the frayed extremities of a calico shirt-collar occasionally struggled for an existence above it. His pants, of threadbare doeskin, seemed a redeeming feature. A dilapidated beaver or broad-brimmed Panama was usually adjusted several inches in advance of the facial angle. He had a peculiar gait, wiry and elastic, as if treading upon springs, the right shoulder hitched up, while the other was correspondingly depressed.

He was an Englishman, and, with all his oddities, was qualified by birth and education to move in a higher sphere of social relations than that into which the chances of adventure had thrown him. He had, I think, obtained a degree at the college from which he graduated, besides receiving the diploma of jurisprudence ; and with safety it may be added, that, at the time of which I am writing, but *few* persons in the kingdom could boast of higher literary attainments than Mr. Allaire. Strange to add, he had reached the Islands about six months previous, on a Yankee whaler.

At his request, I removed, with the few relics of the " slop-chest" I still retained, to his residence. It was a medium-sized grass house, situated in the vicinity of the Palace, owned and occupied by a huge female named Kai-hu-nui, whose blood gave her a sort of precedence over the fag-end of Hawaiian nobility. She had a charming little protegé named Lá-ni (Heaven), about twelve years of age, full of roguish mirth, and whose cheerful disposition seemed to neutralize the acerbity of her surly godmother. Though Allaire had rented one-half the house, (the line of demarkation being a fancy calico curtain,) the old Hecate always looked upon me as a vagabond interloper, without ever deigning me a grunt of civility.

In future pages I shall probably have occasion to speak of shampooing, or *Lomilómi*-ing, but never again of the manner in which I have seen it practised upon her. Mrs. K—— would extend herself upon the mats, face downward ; after which, a powerful man would elevate himself upon her back, and pace up and down her spine with the measured tread of a wire-dancer. This she esteemed a luxury, and it was a favorite remedy on occasions of indigestion.

In disposition she was selfish. I could never leave a bunch of cigars, or other trophies of a foraging expedition, upon the table in our apartment, without finding them more than decimated on my return.   Whenever, during my peregrinations, I could filch a wreath of flowers, and afterwards present it to the pretty Láni, she would knit her formidable brows, and utter in a deep " primo basso," " *Nána* KELA *háole !*" equivalent to, " Mercy ! what impudence !"

The furniture of our apartment was simple enough : at one extremity was a dais for sleeping ; it was covered with mats, and, save two or three quilts and pillows, there were no other pretensions to bedding.   Allaire had a little rickety trunk in one corner, filled promiscuously with newspapers, pamphlets, (he was an assistant editor,) and clothing.   The table, of liberal dimensions, was innocent of covering.   Here were scattered manuscripts, briefs, books, plugs of tobacco, with sheath-knife for cutting, and an indefinite quantity of pens, pipes, and the minor requirements of a literary *dilettante.* Among the tomes, I noticed, in neat calf binding, the " Hawaiian Statute Laws," " Peregrine. Pickle," an odd volume of the " Edinburgh Quarterly," and a dozen others equally acceptable to a pair of loiterers.   By far the most significant object was a pile of empty Cologne bottles in one corner of the apartment ; and I could not repress the natural inquiry as to what he had done with his barber pole.

" You must know," said Allaire, " that a sign is not always an indication of occupation.   Necessity may compel a man to swallow home-brewed malt, though at the same time he would evince a decided preference for Cognac.   *Ergo,* as our statutes impose a duty of five dollars per gallon on imported liquors, containing four per cent. alcohol, our Galens wriggle over it by augmenting their stock of perfumery and cosmetics, including eau de Cologne, superior Baywater, Ambrosia, et cetera.   These we purchase *ad libitum*, and, after imbibing the essence of ideality, in the shape of peppermint and wintergreen, we soar away to Olympus amid an atmosphere of bergamot and rosemary.

Whatever might have been Allaire's propensity in this respect, there was no manifestation of it in my presence.   His " nippers," if he indulged, were taken abroad.   We often strolled out together, lounging through the groves, and initiating ourselves into the mysteries of domestic economy.   A six months' sojourn had not been unimproved by Allaire, and, in nautical phraseology, he "knew the ropes."

One evening he inquired of me whether I was familiar with botany.

"What do you mean?"

"Simply, whether you are acquainted with the appearance, properties, and legitimate uses of the plant *Dracona terminalis*, or *Awa?*"

I replied, that my knowledge of it was limited to a brief botanical description; and that I was aware its root was used by the natives of the Pacific Isles for manufacturing an intoxicating beverage.

"Well, then," said my Mentor, "just put on your hat and favor me with your company this evening. Ah! I had nearly forgotten. I think it advisable we adjust our bedding, by way of anticipation!"

Little Lani looked archly at us as we left the house, and, shaking her finger, said:

"*Ua iki au ko olúa héle ana,*" (I know where you are going.)

"*Hea' ka héwa*" (what of it)? returned Allaire, laughingly, as he closed the door.

After leaving the house, he guided me by a route I had never been, through a forest of cocoanut and kukúi trees, cane jungles, and, what was worse than all, over the unavoidable margins of "taro-patches," where a false step would have precipitated us into the "slough of despond." Lights were gleaming at intervals through the groves; and as if these were insufficient, the barking of dogs announced our proximity to thatch homesteads. We soon entered upon a well-trodden path through a banana grove, which conducted us to a habitation, where, through the chinks of the door, we saw a light burning, and, from the sound of voices, inferred that a goodly company was assembled.

Without knocking, we entered, and Allaire was recognized by all, to judge from the storm of salutations that followed. My estimate as to the quantity and quality of the assemblage had not been premature. There were present more than a dozen natives of both sexes, old and young, indulging in a lively gossip. The group that first riveted our attention was that occupying the centre of the apartment.   Here were half a dozen young girls, some of them in *deshabille*, sitting upon the mats around a huge calabash, each girl having a small bunch of *awa* roots beside her, portions of which all were chewing.   After reducing it to a pulpy consistency between their beautifully white teeth, they would toss it into the large calabash, while their mouths were relieved from superfluous secretions by a smaller vessel placed for the purpose

Though ostensibly engaged in conversation, it was evident that the sentiments of the old folks were in the large calabash, to judge from the longing glances cast upon it.   I noticed a venerable-looking individual, (his only attire a *malo*,) who leaned complacently against the centre post, and watched intently his heart's delight.   Allaire, after firing a shot here and there, proceeded to comment upon the subject before us.

" You observe," said he, " that in preparing the root as it should be, recourse is had to none but mouths of unquestionable purity. Albeit the lips are voluptuous, the rosy cavity, with its appendage of immaculate ivory, is a model of mastication ; and as to lungs, their breath is as pure as the atmosphere they inhale.   The effect of the beverage prepared from the root is peculiar.   After drinking it, you should retire to some quiet spot where you can repose undisturbed, with your head moderately elevated ; and the dreams of an opium-smoker cannot surpass the pleasing reveries that will flit through your cranium.   Its continued use affects the skin, causing it to peel off.   To notice the epidermis of some of these lank gentry who have been long indulging, reminds one of a snake during moulting season.   Of course, I speak as an ' outsider.'   You shall see for yourself presently."

Knowing that the preparation of the root was *tabooed*, or prohibited, I was surprised to see a young man present who sported a red band on his hat, one of the insignia of a constable, and I sought an explanation.

" Let me again impress upon your mind that there is no kingdom in the world where appearances are more deceptive than in this. That fellow yonder is no more a constable than I am.   His mother has probably been making a red flannel-shirt for his father, and by way of coaxing him to weed the taro-patch, she has condescendingly sewed the trimmings upon his cap. Gold bands, you have probably noticed, are the rage among all classes and colors ; but don't deceive yourself into the belief that they are criterions of rank, for the king's jockey sports a broader one than his majesty."

Our colloquy was interrupted by an exclamation from some of the girls of "*Ua páu kakóu !*" (we have done,) meaning that they had finished. A stout native then approached the calabash of masticated roots, and half filled it with water from a smaller vessel. After this, he rolled up his sleeve and commenced kneading the mass with his hand until the liquid assumed the appearance of soap-suds. Then, from the inner fibre of a cocoanut husk, he fashioned a sort of bird's-nest funnel, which was to serve the double purpose of purifier and strainer, and holding it over one of the small drinking vessels, he poured the liquid into it as it filtered slowly through, while the minute particles or *impurities* adhered to the strainer. The drinking vessels consisted of glass tumblers, earthen bowls, cocoanut shells, and small gourds. As fast as they were filled, they were handed to the company, who received them with undisguised satisfaction. Allaire appropriated one of the gourds, and gave me a glassful of the opaque liquid, insisting that I should drink it. I moistened my lips, and returned the repulsive mixture.

"Chew the root, man, and you'll find the beverage more palatable."

I did as directed, and was agreeably surprised to find that it had a pungent, aromatic flavor, leaving in the mouth a sensation similar to that produced by chewing cinnamon or cloves. I then drained the contents of the glass, (the first and only time I ever drank *awa,*) and waited patiently for the result.

Meanwhile, the old man continued to ladle out the contents of his vegetable punch-bowl, with all the officiousness of a master of ceremonies. Allaire, I think, drank two gourds of it. The grimaces of the old folks, as they sipped from their delectable goblets, were suggestive of a domestic tea and knitting-work party.

Its influence was speedily manifested upon some of the girls, who assumed a variety of attitudes, and commenced a *húra*, or chant, that will not admit of description. The young man with the red band, after a few oratorical gestures, seized a large *poi* calabash, and with a stone pestle commenced a series of spiritual rappings. As for me, I could never perceive, from that time to this, that I was in the slightest degree affected by it. But Allaire, whose libations had been copious, soon began to manifest symptoms peculiar to persons who are " three sheets in the wind ;" that is, eyelids drooped, nether jaw slightly ajar, while the head lacked stability of position, giving to his physiognomy an air of innocent stupidity, as much as to say, "Oh, don't be afraid ; it's only me !"

Presently he raised the empty gourd, and poising it gracefully upon the extremities of his fingers, and emphasizing each word, said :

. " Doc. ! permit me to say to you, in the language of the immortal Swiveller, ' May the wing of friendship never moult a feather !' (Here succeeded a fit of nodding.) I intend bringing forward several interesting cases at the next session of Cupid's court."

He continued giving birth to his incoherent wit, interesting only to the brain that conceived it, and the more ludicrous as he afterwards attempted to lick it into shape.

It was past nine when we returned the salutations of the dusky bacchanals. The night was dark and cloudy, and Allaire, who preserved his equilibrium in a wonderful degree, voluntarily took the lead to pilot me through a labyrinth of trees and taro-patches. I grew nervous as we approached the deceitful margins of the latter. He was several paces in advance, and barely discernible in the obscurity. Suddenly I heard a plunge, followed immediately by a terrible floundering. Cautiously I reached the spot, and to my dismay saw my quondam pilot immersed to his neck in a pool of muddy water, and clutching nervously at a clump of sugar-cane that grew on the brink.

"Just in time, Doc.," said Allaire. " I'm trying to decline the esculent noun *arum*, (taro,) and I want your assistance."

I pulled him out, and in doing so, received a liberal coating of the black mud with which he was completely covered. We then kept close together, and proceeding more cautiously, reached our quarters without further adventure.

*   *   *   *   *   *   *

Five years have flitted imperceptibly by, five seasons of buoyant hopes and darkening sorrows, to leave their indelible impress upon the brief span of human endurance ; and yet, barely a point in time, insignificant as the thistle-down that floats upon eddying winds, when thrown into the great cycle of eternity. Old friendships, hallowed by endearing associations, have been rudely severed, and new ones cemented. Scenes of joy and gladness, and a host of bygones, fling around us a halo of soothing memories to charm for a moment, ere, dim and lustreless, they pale before the stalking phantoms of reality.

Poor Allaire ! His is a coral tomb in tranquil depths, where myriads of tiny architects have woven a fairy grot of crystal corymbs and arborescent branches. Restless surges, forever dashing against rocky barriers, fling o'er him a snowy winding-sheet, and moan an eternal dirge.

From broken storm-clouds that whirl around summits of the everlasting mountains have issued solemn voices. Though, like "deep calling unto deep," mysterious tones have trembled through their dark labyrinths, and fearful spirits have ridden forth upon the blast, he will sleep securely upon his azure bed until a Mightier breathes upon the troubled ocean.

Another has gone.

Breezes of refreshing coolness rustle through the palm groves, and beneath shady canopies, where the dark and glossy leaves of the breadfruit intermingle with the silvery foliage of the candlenut, happy groups are twining garlands.

Starry night looks down upon the sleeping landscape ; mountain, valley and grove are blended in silent shadows, and hearts are throbbing.

A wail of human woe swells upon the midnight air, then dies away in tearful cadence, and lights flash dimly amid the gloom. Above scenes of terrestrial brightness, a spirit hovers—now it wings its way to the starry vault. From dark valleys creeps the nightwind, sighing mournfully among the ferns, and whispering through leafy branches ; until, across mountain heath, through wild ravines, o'er the moaning sea, and amid fragrant groves, we hear the mystic voices of the spirit-legion mingle with the gale—saying, " We live forever."

Four years have passed since the little Láni was laid to rest. The seasons roll round. Joyous sunlight gladdens the heart, and dew-drops sparkle upon the " opening blossoms of the *ohia ;*" but the rain-cloud weeps upon the mourning plumes of the pandanus, and night-winds sigh among the bleak hills of Kaa-na-pá-li.

CHAPTER IV.

ROYAL YACHT KAMEHAMÉHA.

HOWEVER agreeable it may be to indulge the propensity for loung-ing, something substantial is required to support it. The beauty of a cocoanut-tree is in nowise enhanced when one is compelled to re-sort to the tedious process of climbing to obtain the fruit. I stumbled across three of my shipmates, who asked my advice ; of course I recommended industry, and read them a chapter on the folly of idle-ness. Two of them shipped for another cruise, but the third turned his attention to digging potatoes somewhere in the Kúla district.

I have omitted to mention that the epidemic for emigration to the recently discovered gold placers of California had extended to Hawaii, and that there was a consequent dearth of foreign population in Lahaina and other towns ; though a month previous I would have bound myself that my aspirations should not extend beyond a resting-place on terra firma, at the end of that period notions of beauty had become vapid, and tropical fascinations were at a discount.

The beautiful yacht Kamehameha was at that time making regu-lar trips between Honolulu and Lahaina, and one day I determined to embark and have a peep at the capital. Packets plying between the two ports usually get under way about two o'clock in the afternoon, and long before that hour the shore in the vicinity of the boat canal is lined with natives ; some of them, passengers encum-bered with calabashes containing food and raiment, and others, friends come to say farewell; but by far the greater portion are idlers and hangers-on, who, having nothing else to do, prowl about precisely as loafers would around the docks of a city. Boats ply between the schooner and shore to convey passengers and luggage. If there be little or no surf, it is attended without inconvenience; but when the opposite is the case, the boat requires careful watching by an experienced crew to avoid being capsized in the breakers, to say nothing of a drenching.

When I arrived on board, I found the crew heaving at the windlass, the mainsail having already been hoisted. The boat was still in requisition; and this, together with canoes discharging their freights on deck, lent animation to the scene. It was a Babel of noise and confusion. There were pigs, poultry, and old women huddled promiscuously together; I noticed a silver-haired matron, with a full-grown dog in her arms, (a parody on the pugs of fashion,) expostulating with some one in a canoe about the ownership of a calabash. Some of the fairer portion had left the adjustment of difficulties to their lords, and spreading their mats, had taken up positions on the quarter-deck, where they were sporting parasols and bright yellow *leis*, or wreaths of the *lauhála*, (pandanus.) The foreigners on these occasions chiefly remain aft, having the monopoly of the cabin, but many prefer sleeping on deck, as the heat below is oppressive. Akoni, the well-known Hawaiian mariner, was our commander, a good-natured and competent person; but like most natives, the idea of discipline and respect never entered his head, and I have seen him devouring cuttle-fish with his cook, with the same familiarity that characterized feasting with his passengers.

In due season the order was given, and the anchor "peaked." Coming gracefully around, the "Kammey" caught the breeze on the larboard tack, and though light, we made good progress through the water, for she was a fast sailer. In our rear was the barren island of Kahuláwe, and on our right the rugged peaks of Maui; La-inái loomed on the left, while in front were the densely-wooded ravines and cloud-capped summits of Molokái. With a freshening breeze, we dashed along, until Lahaina seemed but a narrow strip of verdure fringing the base of a barren mountain; and gradually as we opened the broad channel between Maui and Molokái, we caught the full force of the trades that sometimes sweep through these inter-island passages with the fury of a tempest.   Without reducing sail, we scudded rapidly before it, and while others were chatting and laughing, I was watching the novelty and beauty of the scenery.   But familiarity begets indifference, and during subsequent passages I have found more agreeable entertainment in noticing incidents of character than indulging poetic abstractions.

Not the least interesting spectacle was to witness their preparations for supper, a duty which usually devolves on the old men. Young cocoanuts and melons, before unnoticed, now made their appearance, and the sennit lashings of huge calabashes were unfastened and their contents investigated.   Fishes, that looked as though they had been embalmed for at least a century, made to native eyes a tempting display beside the everlasting *poi*, and large lumps of the forbidden flesh resembled miniature islands in calabashes of salt and water.   There were famished-looking dogs that took up positions favorable for observation, and maintained an equilibrium despite the rolling of the vessel.   Any person who has ever seen a Hawaiian at his meals, and noticed the dexterous manner in which he twirls the glutinous mass around his fingers and conveys it to his mouth, and heard the hearty smack that follows, can never for an instant entertain a doubt of his sincerity.   No unnecessary delay is occasioned by formalities, and their meals are soon dispatched and everything snugly secured, after which they laugh, joke, and chant their *meles.*

Before sunset, we had passed Lahaina, and the low, barren portion of Molokái, stretching out towards the west, was on our right.   As the broad disk was resting upon the horizon, its farewell rays lit up a strange but touching scene.   Every head was uncovered, every whisper hushed, and the voice of prayer ascended in the still evening.   Nothing could be more appropriate than for hearts of sincerity to offer up their humble acknowledgments to their Creator under the broad canopy of heaven.   But these devotions are of late years omitted ; deteriorating influences have begotten more the fear of worldly contempt than reverence for spiritual duty.

Their preparations for sleep occasion them no inconvenience. Mats are spread and *kiheis* unfolded ; laughing and joking, they good-humoredly lie down upon the hard deck, both sexes, old and young, huddled promiscuously together. Sometimes the deck of a schooner is completely encumbered ; and occasionally during the night, when looking at the prostrate sleepers with their heads covered, I have seen a solitary form arise and commence a silent attack upon the calabashes. We had with us a chief and his wife from Hawaii, who, with their attendants, monopolized the long-boat, and whom the plebeians around looked upon with reverence. Her grace was portly, and had a haughty manner of intimating her wishes. The boat was lined with soft beds and counterpanes, besides containing other articles conducive to comfort. Two or three female attendants paid attention to umbrella, fan, and spittoon, while his lordship appeared to be a nonentity. There is, perhaps, no nation where the distinction between noble and plebeian is more strongly defined than among the Hawaiians. The former are characterized by corpulency or powerful proportions and a majestic gait ; while the latter, according to our taste, are more agile and delicate, possessing their peculiar beauty in a greater degree than their superiors. Some one hinted to her ladyship that I had a miniature which had been fortunately saved from the wreck of personal property, and as she expressed a desire to look at it, I handed it to her. After closely scrutinizing the face, coloring, and more especially the embossed case, she returned it, observing, in a primo basso tone, " *Maikái, likapú he wahíne máole,*" which a bystander was kind enough to interpret, " Good ! it resembles a native woman." Without comment on her taste, I thanked her for the compliment, wondering that I had never before detected the affinity between Saxon and Polynesian beauty.

Accepting the invitation, I shared the mat and *kihéi* of one of the natives, who are generally kind and hospitable, expecting a similar return ; and yet it is remarkable that in their language they have no word expressive of either thanks or gratitude. On one occasion, while going from Honolulu to Lahaina, we had rough weather, and the spray was continually dashing aboard, causing such as were unprovided to shiver with the cold. I gave my blankets to an old woman crouched down near the companionway, who, looking up, simply remarked, " *Lokomáikai óe,*" (you are generous.)

CHAPTER V.

HONOLULU.

As soon as it was light, the barren mountains of Oahu were in sight, looking if anything more sterile than those of West Maui ; but they were relieved by the bright verdure that seemed nestling in the valleys and sometimes creeping along their ridges.   There was little or no wind, and for a short time we were becalmed off Diamond Head.   This is an extinct crater, and its peculiar formation, with its stratified cliffs rising from the plains of Waikikí, renders it a conspicuous landmark for vessels approaching Honolulu.   It was nine o'clock before we caught a light breeze, and the water being clear as crystal, the most delicate formations of coral could be distinctly traced on the bottom as we glided along.   Waikikí, with its extensive cocoanut grove, was on our right, and the broad plain of Honolulu and the smiling valley of Nuuánu were every moment becoming more distinct.   As we approached nearer, I was agreeably disappointed in the appearance of the town, it being much larger and more regularly laid out than I had anticipated.   Few vessels were in the harbor, but these, anchored near the temporary wharves, gave an air of business to the scene, which was enhanced by the appearance of the substantial warehouses clustering near them.   The passage through the reef is somewhat intricate ; but it has been carefully buoyed, and with a commanding breeze, vessels may enter and depart without difficulty, the breakers rolling in sheets of foam on either side.   The harbor is small, and I have seen it filled with shipping, which also obstructed the passage, while a number of vessels for want of room had anchored, and were lying off and on outside the reef. The "Kammey" worked like a top, and by ten o'clock she was snugly moored in the lagoon, and boats and canoes were waiting to convey passengers to the shore.   By invitation, I took up my abode at the " Hotel de France," a clean-looking building, with a comfortable verandah and a yard well shaded by trees.

Having frequently visited Honolulu during the last few years, it may be well to notice it more particularly, to avoid repetition here-after ; although, from its intimate association with California, there are thousands to whom a recapitulation of what they have seen will be of little interest. Like San Francisco, it has made gigantic strides in improvement, and become a city. The stranger who promenades its streets, but for the distant landscape, would fancy himself at home, or what would come nearer the truth, in an English or American colony.

The town, with all its neatness, has some irregularities in the arrangement of its streets, which, instead of crossing at right angles, sometimes intersect each other diagonally, forming triangular and irregular lots. A few of them are inconveniently narrow. The principal is Main Street, a broad thoroughfare bisecting the town through its entire length, stretching away to Pearl River on the west, and to the plains of Waikiki on the east. This is crossed at right angles by Nuuánu Street ; commencing at the sea and passing through the compact portion of the town, it descends a gentle declivity, and continues up the beautiful valley of Nuuánu, adorned by villas and luxuriant vegetation, until, at a distance of seven or eight miles, it terminates at the " Páli," or an abrupt precipice, memorable in Hawaiian annals as the spot where the hosts of the King of Oahu took their fatal leap before the victorious arms of Kamehaméha the Great. The streets are generally kept neat and clean, and the light or substantial dwellings of foreigners are scattered at irregular intervals on either side ; some of them are elegant. The material of which they are built is wood, and sometimes of coral blocks taken from the reef; these being covered with cement and tastefully shaded, resemble granite or freestone, and the dwelling, with its verandah and green venetians, has an inviting appearance. The dilapidated native huts scattered here and there are mere excrescences, and are fast disappearing.

Among the public buildings of Honolulu is the Government House, a two-story edifice, substantially built of neatly dressed coral blocks. It was formerly occupied by the Legislative Council during its sessions, but is now devoted almost exclusively to offices of the Home and Foreign Departments. Over the arched gateway of the court has been placed, by way of ornament or effect, the gilded diadem of

8

regal dignity.   In the erection of the Custom-House, reference has
been had to service rather than architectural decoration.   It is a
plain three-story building, conveniently located near the water.
From the harbor, the eye seeks in vain for a more attractive object
than the Market, situated near the principal wharf.   It is neat and
appropriate, and would be an ornament to any town.   The Court-
House, bounded on the east by Fort Street, and a short distance
to the right, is a more elaborate structure than either of the others
referred to.   It is subservient to the requirements of Capitol, Halls
of Justice, and ecclesiastical convocations.   These buildings are all
of coral, and within the circuit of one-fourth of a mile of each other.

The Palace, on Main Street, is barely visible, owing to its confined
situation, being surrounded by massive walls of coral, inclosing a garden of young trees ; but it is roomy, having spacious apartments, some
of them decorated with the relics of antiquity, and others with the
designs of art.   The Fort, situated at the water's edge, is, like that
of Lahaina, used more as a prison than a national defence, and at
any hour of the day two or three sentinels may be seen lounging lazily
upon its ramparts.   At the present time there are substantial wharves,
where vessels of a large class may lie alongside and discharge their
cargoes, while the emulous competition of the native boat-boys for
your *real*, strongly reminds one of larger cities.   Within a few years
carriages have been introduced, and neat equipages roll along the
streets that were formerly disturbed only by the equestrian or small
vehicle drawn by hand.   With reference to the latter mode of conveyance, which is occasionally resorted to at the present day, I
cannot conceive that any ignominy should be attached to its proprietor for having a couple of lazy natives to drag it, thus diverting them
from idleness, or perhaps worse.   I have seen in the East Indies the
sedan employed, but have never learned that a breath of reproach was
incurred by those who adopted this means of conveyance.   As to
society, Honolulu is not a whit behind the age, and the associations
of refinement pertaining to more extensive communities may here
be enjoyed, though in a minor degree, and *fêtes*, balls, and excursions are frequently the order of the day.

The street scenes are of "all sorts"—a medley of costumes
and creeds—colors and castes.   The worshippers of Fo step ner-

vously along in their flowing robes of embroidered silk, and the straggling Lascar readjusts his turban as he leers at the native syren. Garments that would be cynosures upon the Boulevard are in juxtaposition with dress-coats that might have distracted belles half a century ago. A distinguished citizen once remarked to me that he admired Honolulu because fashions of all climes and ages were tolerated with impunity. Muslin robes and chameleon parasols are no longer apparitions, for the sunlight is reflected in the coquettish smiles of northern beauty where parties *à la mode* enjoy a picnic amid the classic scenes of Hawaiian mythology. The native belles merit a passing word. Hand in hand they lounge leisurely through the street, sometimes with wreaths upon their heads, or, again, they sport a fine Panama with a broad, black ribbon. They are usually occupied with staring at the show-windows that exhibit the most gaudy display of recently imported millinery, and some of them would dispute for an hour upon the respective merits of head-dresses. Though prodigal of their smiles, they are sensitive to ridicule, and a vocabulary of invectives is sometimes showered upon the offender who trespasses beyond the limits of propriety. It is interesting to witness the meeting of two old persons, for with all their faults, the Hawaiians are an affectionate people, and their warm hearts are ever open to the impulses of humanity. First, there is an *alóha* of recognition, then an embrace, accompanied by collision of noses; after which follows a wail of discord, to be succeeded by grimaces and mutual congratulations.

The market presents a busy scene in the morning. Neatly-attired widows, who advertise for " a few select gentlemen, &c.," trip along the clean streets accompanied by their servants, and visit it to select fresh joints. It is thronged by old and young of all classes and colors, haggling about the price of fish, poultry, and esculents of every description. There is laughing, jostling, and joking, and everywhere an air of good-humor. The old women of the stalls have an Israelitish propensity for coin, yet their cupidity is tempered with caution. If you toss them a piece upon which the nose of either her Majesty the Queen or that of the Goddess of Liberty has by some mishap received a contusion, in nine instances out of ten it will be rejected.

An animated spectacle may be witnessed in the streets every Saturday afternoon, when nags and hacks of every description are pressed into service. On these occasions, the natives are arrayed in all their finery; the men in black or white trowsers and clean Panama hats, (their rims invariably drooped,) and the females in their silks and muslins, their hats and necks decorated with wreaths. Either from convenience or habit, in sitting upon their steeds the females have adopted the custom of their lords; and girding their waists with Turkey-red, or some other gaudily-colored fabric, they make a flaunting display of their skirts fluttering in the wind. Waikiki appears to be the favorite place of rendezvous; and at any time during the afternoon, the road is thronged with Amazonian squadrons and detached horsemen dashing by at headlong speed, and scattering the dust in clouds. I have seen two parties, each composed of male and female riders, coming at full gallop from opposite directions, and without checking a rein or swerving to the right or left, come in full collision with each other, whereby several were thrown headlong to the earth, and more or less injured. As might be supposed, accidents are of frequent occurrence. I was at Maui on one occasion, when a girl, with the recklessness of exuberant spirits, was galloping along the street, and just as she had reached the road leading to the chapel, the horse became frightened—suddenly stopped, and the girl plunged headlong upon the rocks that abound in that vicinity. Her skull was fractured, and she survived the injury but a few hours.

CHAPTER VI.

THE SAME CONTINUED.

THERE is another feature of Honolulu which I noticed during my last visit, and which would be an interesting subject for the contemplation of our professors of the agile talent at home; I allude to the dance-houses. These places of diversion have multiplied throughout the city, and a congregation of some description is of almost nightly occurrence. Dancing is an agreeable pastime, and the recreation might be conducted without detriment to the natives; but an assemblage of this description is little better than a rendezvous for assignation. The appearance of the girls in foreign costume strongly reminds one of the Mexican *chulus* at their fandangos, and to do them justice, some of them display their forms to advantage, and dance and waltz gracefully. Though looked upon as a moral pest, the legislature as yet has done nothing towards their suppression. It is a delicate task for jurisprudence to draw the exceedingly nice distinction that exists between right and wrong. It would be deemed arbitrary to prevent a convivial party from assembling in a public room and dispersing at the appointed hour.

The civil and religious institutions of Honolulu are progressive, and afford a pleasanter theme. Her Christian associations of various denominations, her united charitable institutions, library society, diffusion of knowledge by the press, and the association for the development of agricultural resources, and above all, the impartial administration of justice in her courts, are not only evidences of the constituent elements of society, but they give Hawaii pre-eminence over all other kingdoms whose resources are confined to as limited territorial dominion. Already, from her own contributions, has a mission been established in Micronesia, which has been warmly welcomed by the natives of those groups, and she has thrown out, as it were, a band of pioneers to explore the field of the Marquesas. The hospitality of her citizens to those whom shipwreck and misfortune have thrown upon her shores has been frequently noticed; and though abounding in vicious temptations, the seamen who roam the streets can offer no excuse for their indulgence. There is a library appropriated exclusively for their benefit, and there are those whose duty it is to offer the consolations of spiritual advice to such as may require them.

In its appropriate place, I should have noticed the leading features of the surrounding country, which, though in the main devoid of the characteristic beauty of the South Sea Islands, still possess much that is attractive. The absence of trees at first strikes the observer as the principal defect, and although no efforts have been spared for their introduction, they never attain the luxuriant growth that ren-

ders them so attractive in other portions of the group. The soil is in
many places light and porous, and excavations to the depth of a few
feet disclose a stratum of volcanic cinders, which, together with the
slight depth of the superincumbent earth, retards the natural growth
of vegetation.   A sinuous stream that waters Nuuánu Valley, disembogues into the sea on the western side of the town, and at a short
distance from the shore a few scattered cocoanut-trees rise from its
banks.   The extinct crater of Punchbowl, bounding the plain in
the rear of the town, is a conspicuous object for the eye to rest upon,
owing to its peculiar formation and commanding appearance.   It is
crowned with a rude battery, and its sides, at almost regular intervals, are deeply furrowed, leaving prominent ridges standing forth
like the bastions of some antiquated fortress.   Here may be obtained
a grand view of the surrounding scenery ; and Waikikí plains, the
city with its shipping, and the distant mountains of Ewa, together
with the sea and its fringe of breakers, are spread out like a vast
panorama.   The mountains in the rear, rising to no great elevation,
are crowned with a luxuriant growth of vegetation, which between
the ridges creeps down into the valleys in bright strips of verdure.

By far the most pleasing feature is Nuuánu Valley ; descending the gentle slope from the level of the town, you ride leisurely
along the smooth road, and on either side are green fields, diversified with snug cottages, native huts, and miniature gardens, having
a picturesque effect.   Continuing to advance, the road gradually ascends, and on either side rise more substantial residences, their inclosures adorned by shrubbery, both native and exotic.   Neatly
painted mile-posts are placed at regular intervals, affording convenient reference, and at the distance of a few miles, the town is
shut out by the winding of the valley and the projecting mountain
spurs.   A perceptible change in the atmosphere is now experienced ;
and the streamlet, almost before unnoticed, is seen leaping from crags,
or heard rippling over its stony bed by the roadside.   The valley
has grown narrower, and its sides are covered with a sea of verdure variegated by the bright foliage of the candlenut.   Scarce a
house is to be seen, and the heavy vapor sweeping along the mountain's side and descending into the valley has a chilling aspect.
After fastening your horse behind a woody knoll, to protect it from

the violence of the wind, which sometimes, compressed by the mountains, comes sweeping like a tempest through the gorge, you ascend to the brow of the *páli*, or precipice, and a view of unsurpassed grandeur bursts upon the sight.   It is one of those scenes to attempt a description of which can never gratify the curiosity of the reader, and is only embarrassing to the writer ; to be appreciated it must be seen.   On either side, hemmed in by mountains, you stand as it were at the circumference of a vast amphitheatre, and look down upon the varied landscape beneath.   Broad forests sweeping away from the mountain's base, seem dwindled into shrubs, and hill and valley, with smiling aspect, are like the inequalities that characterize a garden of art.   Often a narrow streak in the reddish soil denotes the course of a road, which is lost by the winding of a valley or an intervening hill, when its continuation beyond is again marked until lost in the distance.   On the left the prospect is bounded by the amphitheatre of mountains, which, extending around toward the sea, terminate in blue ridges almost blending with the sky ; in front extends the broad ocean, and the whitish tinge of the water near the shore denotes the coral barrier.   A spiral path for horses has been constructed down the face of the cliff on the right, and the scene is occasionally enlivened by the natives from Kolau toiling up its steep ascent, with their beasts ladened with produce for market.

In their way, there are associations connected with the *pali* deeply interesting, embodying events whose result was the subjugation of a kingdom.   After sustaining a vigorous siege, the forces of the King of Oahu, unable longer to hold out against the superior discipline of the warriors of Kamehameha, retreated up the valley, until their course was checked by the abyss, into which they leaped, and their bones were left to bleach beneath the rugged cliffs of Koláu.

CHAPTER VII.

INCIDENTS OF SOJOURN.

"MINE host" of the "Hotel de France," though possessing the whims and oddities peculiar to a Frenchman, was an obliging land-lord, and displayed no little skill in catering for the wants of his guests, for he was *au fait* with all the mysteries of his pro-fession. It was sometimes amusing to witness his paroxysms of anger with his attendants, and his futile efforts to express himself in the native vernacular. The Hawaiian is a dialect not so copious that its words may be pronounced without regard to accent or em-phasis ; of all nations, the French, like Cockneys, are least qual-ified to give it expression, and their ludicrous efforts sometimes de-generate into absolute absurdities. In the attempt of the latter to say *haole*, (foreigner,) we have *'áole*, (no) ; and by rejecting the as-pirate in the word *hána*, (labor), we have the signification of the pres-ent participle of a verb. I can imagine that in the attempt of the latter to repeat a correspondingly arranged line of poetry in Hawaiian, we should have something as ludicrous as,

"The 'orn of the 'unter is 'eard on the 'ill."

But Monsieur was above paying attention to all these little minu-tiæ, and without regard to punctuation or syntax, he would pour forth a heterogeneous mixture of French, English, and Hawaiian to one of his boys, who, with mouth agap and projecting eyeballs, was only paying attention to the frantic gestures by which to obtain a clue to his master's wishes. Sometimes I have seen them, after withdraw-ing to a safe distance, shrug up their shoulders and give utterance to their favorite expression, *a-óle páha*, (no you don't.) But with all his foibles and eccentricities, he was a good host, and his guests will remember with pleasure his attentions.

At this time I had a roving commission, and abundant leisure to perfect myself in a course of Hawaiian, a taste the natives are always pleased to indulge. For the convenience of the reader, who may not have one at hand, I will give a hasty description of their houses, which we may possibly have to frequent during future rambles.

Having selected a suitable locality, a number of strong posts are driven into the earth in parallel rows, leaving an area for the interior, in accordance with the taste of the proprietor. The portions remaining above ground vary in height from three to seven or eight feet, with a distance of three or four feet between each other ; upon them are laid rafters, forming generally an acute, or at least a right angle at the ridge. Outside of both rafters and posts, *áhos* (wattles) are fastened with sennit, made from the fibre of the cocoanut-husk, at short distances from each other, giving the uncovered frame a sort of lattice-work appearance. It is then ready for thatching, and for this purpose the coarse grass called *pili* is used, which is so laid on as to render them water and weather proof. When more than ordinary pains are taken with them, the natives have a fashion of braiding the grass on the outside, which gives them a somewhat tasteful appearance ; however, an ordinary grass-house that has seen service, if viewed at a short distance, looks much like a weather-beaten haystack. But appearances are often deceptive, and the interior of these primitive domicils is more inviting than their exterior would lead one to suppose. They have usually a good door with hinges, and square apertures at the sides designed for windows, and these have shutters. The floor is strewed with dry grass, and covered with mats made of the *lauhála*, which are either few or numerous, coarse or fine, according to the taste or wealth of the owner. Partitions are formed by curtains, usually of some gaudy material ; and for beds, if unprovided with bedsteads, they have mats of a fine quality ; for the manufacture of these, the leewardmost island, Nihau, is famous. Their pillows are stuffed with *púlu*, a substance resembling the down of a thistle. Almost every house can boast of a few chairs or table manufactured from *koa* wood, the mahogany of the Pacific, besides chests to contain their apparel. One corner is usually devoted to calabashes and feasting 'arrangements, also agricultural implements, if the proprietor be a laborer. During the night a tin lamp is suspended from the centre pole, affording them sufficient light to sleep by, which they always require, having an invincible dread of *akúas*, (ghosts.)

After remaining in Honolulu nearly two weeks, I was fortunate in making the acquaintance of Mr. Linton L. Torbert, a planter of East Maui. At his invitation I consented to accompany him to his plantation at Ulupalakúa, (ripe breadfruit of the gods,) he having chartered the "Kammey" to call there on her way to Hawaii. On the day appointed we embarked, but if the confusion I had before witnessed at Lahaina was noticeable, it was now increased tenfold. There were several members of the Mission, with their families, whose stations were among the windward islands; they were encumbered by servants, who in turn were surrounded by friends come to take leave. It was past four o'clock, the hour for departure, yet there was no movement on the part of those natives who resided ashore towards leaving the deck. There were wailings and frequent contact of noses, and the word *alóha* predominated above every other. But this delay was finally obviated by the kindness of a gentleman, formerly of the Mission, who with a slender ratan, a rod of love, laid it gently across the shoulders of both male and female, and the *alóha* was speedily changed to *auwé!* (oh dear!) while a simultaneous rush for the canoes was the result of its application.

Without incident worth noticing, we reached Lahaina the following day, and having discharged passengers and cargo for that place, we continued on towards Hounaúla, (red earth,) the name of Mr. Torbert's landing. When off the deep gorges of Oluálu and Ukamehámé, we encountered one of those *momókus*, or whirlwinds, which sometimes sweep down from the mountains with fearful violence. In an instant our jib was fluttering from the stay in ribbons. With but little sea-way, the water was lifted and whirled over the deck fore and aft, and before we could let go halliards, the schooner was ploughing her way along, almost bulwarks under, to the consternation of our lady passengers. We soon passed the last projecting point of West Maui, and opened the broad bay of Malía, where we had a good view of the low isthmus, uniting as it were the two islands; also the lofty summit of East Maui, Haleakalá, (house of the sun,) looming darkly above the clouds to an elevation of 10,000 feet above the sea. Mr. Torbert had left us at Lahaina, and ridden over the mountain on horseback, so that we had no other pilot than a native woman, a wife of one of his foreign employees. To a person unacquainted with the localities, it would be difficult to find the precise anchorage, for there is a uniformity in the appearance of the shore that to an inexperienced eye hardly offers a landmark. Captain Akóni kept the woman constantly on the look-out, and by the lights on shore she managed to discover the spot, and letting go our anchor, we soon had the satisfaction of hearing juvenile voices laughing and shouting from the rocks.

CHAPTER VIII.

"RIPE BREADFRUIT OF THE GODS."

Mr. Torbert lost no time in coming alongside in a canoe, and with the native woman, Mrs. Sinclair, we paddled ashore. Here I found two persons who had long been engaged in his service, and to whom we shall have occasion to make future reference. They had just returned from a hunting excursion, and the result of their sporting was a few braces of wild pigeons. One of them, the husband of our pilot, whom we called " Long Jim," was a tall downeaster; the other answered to the name Steve, who was likewise an American, and savored something of the backwoodsman, for he was expert with the axe. They were both clever souls. Steve bustled about for a supper, and, with the assistance of a native, soon returned with a quantity of fish wrapped up in leaves, and smoking hot from the oven, besides a large calabash of poi. We all sat down upon the mats to enjoy a hearty repast, and a person must be a Stoic to avoid augmenting his acquaintance on such an occasion. Having supped, in company with the two, I strolled along the beach, while they entertained me with all the little items of gossip and scandal about Ulupalakúa. But this was done for talk's sake and to become more intimate; a more harmonious little community never jogged along among the green hills of Maui.

In the morning I found the premises to consist of a good-sized yard, containing a large stone storehouse, and two or three thatch arrangements of smaller dimensions. There was also a boat-shed; and chain cables, spars, old rigging, cannon-balls, &c., recalled to mind the ship-yard of " Richard Quilp, Esq." At an early hour the natives began to assemble, and the work of discharging commenced. The merchandise was conveyed in boats as near to the shore as practicable, when it was carried by islanders, who stood ready to receive it, to the beach above high-water mark. During the morning a canoe filled with girls made its appearance from behind a projecting point, who by their laughing and singing seemed to court attention. Presently the outrigger flew high in the air, and they were swimming around the canoe, which had been purposely capsized. After a brief interval it was righted, and one of the youngest assisted into it, to bail out. One by one they emerged from the sea and resumed their seats, wringing the brine from their dark tresses, and laughing merrily as ever.

About nine o'clock, bullock teams with heavy carts, which we had seen descending the mountain, arrived, driven by native boys, to convey the merchandise to the plantation. The only portion of this that was visible were a few bright cane-fields, which the inequalities of the mountain-side permitted to be seen. The road, a good one, could be traced at intervals until it ascended the last hill, a distance of three miles. The carts being ladened, we set out at a slow pace, for the road was a continued ascent, and before the oxen had finished their journey they were panting with heat and fatigue. There is hardly tree or shrub by the wayside to relieve the lonely aspect, except frequently large clusters of the *cactus* rising above the coarse grass. I have always thought the road to Ulupalakúa—and I have travelled it often—as wearisome as that of the Hill of Science; if the hospitable proprietor would only establish a sort of half-way house for the benefit of visitors, he would be looked upon as a public benefactor.

Having ascended about half way, one of the teams, in a fit of desperation, broke away from the road, dragging the cart alarmingly near the edge of a dry water-course, and I anticipated nothing less than a general stampede. Fortunately, the boys succeeded in quieting them, and I had now a lesson to learn regarding the propensities of cattle that had once roamed wild among their native hills.

By some accident the chain that connects the cart with the yoke had become wound around the tongue, and the boys were making a great ado among themselves as to who should clear it. Impatient at the delay, I stepped up to the nearest bullock, with a loud " stand-over" that was meant to intimidate, and laid my hand upon the chain. At the present day I have a confused recollection of describing sundry gyrations in the air, until brought to a sense of consciousness by familiar contact with the earth. This was the first and last time that I interfered with cattle in the Pacific. As hill after hill rose with its steep ascent before us, my sympathy for the panting beasts gradually relapsed into considerations of personal comfort. To have mounted one of the carts which they seemed hardly able to drag after them, would have been worse than walking, and our only resource was to halt frequently. By noon we had still the interminable succession of hills ; the last was the climax of perpendicularity, and after reaching its summit we all sat down to rest, for the village of Ulupalakúa was before us.

A conspicuous object was the tall white chimney of the boiling-house, rolling out volumes of black smoke ; and around this were grouped the mills, rind and drying-houses. The road leading to the open space in the centre was lined on either side with the grass-houses of native laborers. Other domicils were also scattered about in different parts of the plantation, their cultivations lending a pleasing effect to the landscape. On either side were bright fields of cane in various stages of growth ; and in their appropriate places, large groves of bananas and extensive fields of taro were waving in the breeze. Roads intersected each other, and along some of them carts were conveying their juicy loads to the mills. Around these were assembled old and young, chiefly females, who were feeding them, while others carried the crushed rind to dry. The mills consisted simply of upright iron rollers with the requisite machinery, which was worked by oxen, and the expressed juice was conveyed by subterranean channels to vats in the boiling-house. All seemed animated and happy. The boys sang as they drove their teams ; the females gossipped and joked while performing their duties. Independent of these there were carpenter, blacksmith, tinsmith, cooper, &c., pursuing their vocations. The proprietor and director of this industrious community, sorrounded by the smiling evidences of prosperity, possessed a more solid basis for enjoyment than they who hoard wealth amid the dens of a city. The house of Mr. Torbert, though thatch, was a large and substantial building, having porches in front and rear. The principal ornament of the interior was a well-selected library ; the most comfortable appendages were the broad table, suggestive of things that might happen, and the spacious beds. The door of one of the small rooms in the rear was open, and from the rafters were suspended countless bunches of bananas in every stage of perfection. The cook-house adjoining, was almost surrounded by banana-trees.

It is unknown to what circumstance this district is indebted for its name—" Ripe-breadfruit-of-the-Gods"—for tradition makes no mention of its abounding with the name-giving tree. At the present day the surface of the soil is hardly diversified by tree or shrub, unless a short distance farther up, where it is clothed with a heavy and almost impenetrable growth of forest. At an elevation of more than three thousand feet above the sea it possesses a climate cool and invigorating ; and nothing save actual convalescence can be more agreeable to invalids who have been languishing in the heated atmosphere of the lowlands, than to ascend to this temperate zone and enjoy the breeze, cool and fresh from the mountains. During the night heavy dews fall, and the air is sometimes so chilly that an additional blanket is required. Its commanding prospect is not the least of its attractions ; the broad ocean, the barren island of Kahuláwe, with the rocky islet of Molokíni in mid-channel, the rugged mountain of Lanái and a portion of Molokái, are all beheld at a glance. In clear weather the shipping in the roadstead of Lahaina, a distance of thirty miles, is discernible ; and there is also a view of Malía Bay and the barren mountains of West Maui. Looking seaward, the mountain-side is diversified by hill, plain, and valley, where sheep and cattle are grazing ; and on the left there is a broad tract as black as Erebus, where, in ages beyond tradition, the lava has made its way to the sea. With a telescope you may here and there detect a solitary hut ; and occasionally a faint cloud of smoke shows where the native is preparing the land for cultivation. Small hamlets are scattered along the shore, and near the landing, a prominent feature of the landscape is an extinct crater known as Miller's Hill, its rugged cliffs washed by the waves.

The soil of this district is exceedingly prolific ; though the period for the ripening of sugar-cane is necessarily of greater duration than would be required in the lowlands, this deficiency, if such it can be called, is amply compensated for by the superiority of its quality. I have surveyed every field, yet do not recollect their aggregate area ; but there are several hundred acres under cultivation, and in planting, such reference is had to convenience that there is always a portion fit for cutting at any season of the year. In a paper recently read by Mr. Torbert, before the Hawaiian Agricultural Association at Honolulu, it is stated that sugar-cane was first noticed among these islands at Ulupalakúa ; whether this circumstance is to be attributed to accident or to its partiality for the soil, it is certain that the sugar here manufactured is of superior quality. This, however, is in some degree owing to the attention bestowed upon its preparation ; for, unlike the system pursued by many plantations on these islands, the whole process is conducted upon principles strictly scientific. I believe, however, it has a formidable rival on the leeward Island of Kauái, where are also extensive cultivations of coffee ; but I am certain of having seen the prize medal in the possession of Mr. Torbert.

The system pursued in conducting the plantation is worthy of remark. The attention paid to morality and sobriety has, in a great degree, been conducive to its prosperity. With reference to occupation, there are no harrowing distinctions drawn between the foreigners engaged in his service. The visitor at Ulupalakúa, be he high or low, rich or poor, sits at the same table with the most humble artisan. There are some who have formed matrimonial alliances with the native females ; and to these a sufficient quantity of land has been allotted, also the necessary time for its cultivation. Attention has been paid to the construction of suitable houses for the natives ; during a severe *kóna* (southwest tempest) that swept with violence over the land, I have seen Mr. Torbert inspecting their condition, and from such as were dilapidated removing their inmates to others more commodious, and providing those who needed them with warm and comfortable garments from his own house. The condition of the natives in his employ is in many respects superior to that of those who draw a precarious subsistence, by occasionally cultivating and fishing on their own account. Their pay is sufficient to provide for their necessary wants, and the food served out is good and abundant. They are well clothed, and contented and happy.

At an early hour the horn sounds, and the laborers assemble, each knowing his respective duty. In due time it again recalls them to their morning meal, after which they return to their occupations, and at night they come flocking in with their implements to the storehouse, where those permanently engaged receive their rations, and the day-laborers their pay, usually a paper certificate redeemable in merchandise on demand. During the " cutting season," large numbers, both male and female, assemble from Kaupó and the districts adjoining. The scene then is one of increased industry and animation.

Such was its condition during my early visits to Ulupalakúa; but whether subsequent events have rendered it necessary for the proprietor, like those of other plantations, to resort to the labor of Chinese coolies, who as an experiment were imported in 1851, I cannot say; but in any event, shall hope that the energy and perseverance which have characterized his efforts may have success for their ultimate reward.

CHAPTER IX.

PLANTATION LIFE.

To have seen us jogging along together in unison, one would suppose us to be a model community of Socialists who had crept up into our eyrie, where we could observe without being observed. Our elucidations of humanity were drawn from various sources; though composed of divers elements, the result of habit and association, our enjoyments were in common, and a mind aspiring to superiority in its intercourse with those around it, would have been an object of commiseration in our home among the mountains. From the proprietor down, we had all seen service in whalers ; and the hand that swung the sledge or shoved the plane, could with equal facility handle an oar or trim a sail. After the toils of the day were over, we would assemble beneath the porch in the cool evening, and comparing notes, revive old reminiscences.

There was one of our number, the old gray-headed cooper of Nantucket, (Heaven rest his soul ! for he has gone to render a long account of deeds done in the body,) whose domestic troubles afforded unsympathizing hearts a continued source of diversion. He had united his destinies for weal or woe with those of a Kaupó girl young enough to be his grand-daughter, and who, as the novelty of matrimony wore away, was uncharitable enough to cast reflections upon his venerable locks, and otherwise animadvert upon his rheumatic infirmities. But all this was meekly borne by the object of her acrimony ; and it was only when she would actually desert him, to seek obscurity among her native hills, that his grief found utterance in tears and lamentations. To have solicited either work or favor from him at these periods of desertion would be requiring an impossibility ; for, wringing his hands and forgetting his infirmities, he walked frantically up and down, recounting his woes to all he met, at the same time an object of mirth and pity. There was a person residing on the plantation who had seen as many years as the cooper, and between these two old men existed the bitterest animosity. This was the only instance of mutual ill-will observable among us, but it was so perfectly harmless in its results that it gave to the monotony of daily routine the spice of variety. On the occasions alluded to, the cooper's arch-enemy would wag his head with a satisfied look, and with a shade of sarcasm remark, "*Kupanáha !* (astonishing!) the cooper's got his tantrims ag'in, fal de dol diddle dol dido !" and whenever they met, the wrinkled features of the one, as far as was possible, expressed exultation, while the eyes of the other shot cannon-balls.

An express would be forthwith dispatched to the beach, and in due season a couple of *káikos* (constables) would make their appearance with their insignia of office—caps with red bands and formidable clubs. Of course a resort to their services drew largely upon the

9

cooper's exchequer, and if empty, as was usually the case, he had
recourse to a loan, as an affectionate husband is in duty bound to do,
after which the minions of the law would take their departure over
the mountains to bring back the recluse.   To do this required
a day or two, and I have known three days to elapse before
she was returned to the desolate homestead.   With a mixture of
sulkiness and shame, she would enter the house, while the cooper
followed with humility, and closed the door.   The bonds of matrimony are sacred, and it would have been a bold eye to peep through
an aperture of the thatch and witness the arguments resorted to
on that occasion.   With pardonable curiosity, we could listen at a
respectful distance, and no one was more delighted with the scene
that was to follow than our old friend, who would interpret the native portion of the colloquy ; but the cooper's English was generally
too expressive to require comment or explanation.   Sometimes the
interview commenced with an ominous silence that would continue for several minutes ; then a few incoherent words in the native
tongue, in a tone of reproach, succeeded, without eliciting a reply.   Next, expostulations in mingled native and English would be
heard in a louder voice; the more amusing to us, for, save a word or
two, neither of them understood the language of the other.   After
this had been indulged in a reasonable length of time without a word
on her part, I was at first thrown into consternation by repeated
smacking sounds, very like the contact of a hand with an inviting portion of flesh, (usually resorted to in instances of refractory children ;)
when the silence was at once broken by a loud *auwé !* (oh dear!) and
then were heard the unfeminine expressions of *elemakúle !* (old
man !) *puáa !* (pig!) *nihoóle !* (toothless !) and a copious vocabulary of
Hawaiian reproaches.   Poor cooper !   He literally " had as much
trouble as a married man," and they could only compromise their
difficulties by his promising to purchase a new dress, or sundry articles of finery gratifying to her savage fancy.

One day, the very picture of despair, he requested me to step down
to his house with him and look at his wife, and if she pleased me, he
would procure a divorce and sell her to me for a reasonable compensation.   The district of Kaupó is famous for its beauty, and madam
was a fair sample, for she was delicately formed, without that sen-

sual expression peculiar to many of the Hawaiians. From the cordiality of my reception, I have not the slightest doubt but that she fully concurred in her husband's wishes, and to avoid incurring any suspicions of insincerity, I declined his offer, by saying that I was so erratic in my movements that I could not make up my mind to assume the responsibilities of matrimony ; also, that the necessary outfit would be too expensive.

" Don't mention it," said the cooper ; " here's my house and all its furniture, (consisting of a chair, table, bedding, three calabashes, and a poi board,) and a large field of taro, (two-thirds of an acre,) that I'll throw in gratis to give you a start."

I begged him not to think there was any want of appreciation of his kindness on my part, and finally convinced him that, situated as I then was, a mere visitor, such an alliance would be wholly impracticable. Their union having never been prolific, he questioned me as to the propriety of adopting a child, " to see if it wouldn't kinder get her wonted." On this subject I told him he was the more competent to judge, and wishing that he might never have a recurrence of his afflictions, I left him.

About ten days after my arrival, it was rumored through our little village that there was to be a wedding—a double wedding the same day—and all the old gossips were on the *qui vive*, for the bridegrooms were foreigners. They were both widowers, and on inquiry I learned that one was our friend Steve, and the other Jack Burns. Both resided at opposite extremes of the plantations, and Jack declared he had lived in Kalíhi (garden) long enough "without a blossom." It has been said that " the course of true love never runs smooth," and such was the case in this instance, for up hill and down dale they were compelled to go to reach Wailúku, the nearest missionary residence, and distant nearly twenty miles. I did not see the wedding party, which started away at an early hour, but about four o'clock in the afternoon the sound of juvenile voices announced its return, and all eyes were directed to the road winding down the hill from the Kúla district. Here was seen the whole party trooping along, some on horseback, and a large retinue on foot, and all making an ostentatious display ; some with white Panamas decorated with ribbons, and flashy silks, others with wreaths, Turkey-red, and white muslin robes. The old superannuated dog Tiger and his younger companion immediately ran up the road as far as the rind-house, where they stationed themselves, and whether congratulatory or not, commenced a series of barkings, which continued without in-termission until the arrival of our guests.

There was no more work during the remainder of that day, and natives and foreigners assembled to offer their congratulations. Un-doubtedly there were many present who would have been glad had a wedding happened every day, for preparations for a feast had been going forward. In passing an opinion upon the relative merits of the young brides, I would do so without disparaging the taste of either Jack or Steve, for marriages here, as is frequently the case at home, are more matters of convenience than otherwise. Steve had married the sister of his deceased wife, who had always resided in his family ; but despite her finery, the nasal organ was decidedly too broad to favor any pretensions to beauty. I believe, however, she has proved a serviceable helpmate, and am certain that their union is in a fair way of being blessed with a numerous progeny. Mrs. Burns had a lighter complexion, and was in every respect more attractive than her companion, but her happiness was brief. Like many an old acquaintance, she has bidden farewell forever to the bright scenes of Ulupalakúa.

Torbert went out, gun in hand, and shot a large hog ; two of the boys ran up, and seizing it by the ears, called out, after a momentary examination, *Ua máke !* (he's dead !) upon which Keáne Líli, our quartermaster, approached with a large blood-letting instrument. The hog was speedily dressed and roasting under ground. A short time after sunset he presented a ghastly appearance, when his proportions, undisturbed, were carried into the rear porch on a wooden trencher. There were numerous hillocks of roasted taro and sweet potatoes, besides poi enough to feast all the natives of East Maui. The females preferred sitting upon the mats and supping *à la Turque;* but the foreigners, and there was a goodly number of us, monopolized the table, which was groaning beneath its feast of fat things. In ad-dition to the substantial fare with which we were always provided, there were sundry approximations to pastry, (we had no thorough-bred cook,) and oysters that had vegetated in the beds of the Atlantic, together with a surfeit of fruit, and what was better than all, we were entertained with the dry jokes of our host, burnished up for the occasion.

It has been the policy of Mr. Torbert to "marry off" those engaged in his service, whether native or foreigner, as fast as possible, and in some instances the plan is a good one. To a foreigner, it is often attended with inconvenience ; for, in marrying one of its members, the bridegroom usually has the entire family "shouldered on to him," and frequently relatives of questionable affinity. Recently, Mr. Torbert has been empowered by the authorities to marry upon his plantation, and with natives the affair is conducted with little ceremony. A man and woman conceive they were made for each other, make application, and if no obstacle exists they are forthwith united in the store, which is filled with spectators.

Mr. Torbert's was a versatile talent. Though possessing a taste for music and the fine arts, he was modest of his accomplishments as an amateur. A year or two prior to my arrival, he had stumbled upon a German musical-instrument maker in Honolulu ; a bargain was struck, and the artist carried off to Ulupalakúa, where, after breathing the pure atmosphere of the mountains for a few days, he was installed in the workshop, and provided with materials for making a seraphine. The instrument was completed, and in the still evening the natives would gather around to listen to the strange harmony that stole softly over the hills and awoke the woodland solitudes. But an El Dorado was discovered on the adjoining coast, and all eyes were turned towards Maui for a garden. The seraphine was ignominiously consigned to obscurity, where, in a dilapidated grass-house, encumbered by rickety furniture and lumber, it was speedily covered with cobwebs. The fingers that glided over the ivory keys now drafted a vessel, and sharp axes in the hands of Yankee pioneers decimated the forest trunks that for ages had flourished undisturbed. A schooner was built, launched, and freighted on the owner's account, with the produce of his plantation. She was called the "Chance," and consigned to the chances of waves and fortune. It was during the period of her absence that I arrived.

I found a guitar in Honolulu, that had made its way there from the Spanish Main, where it had probably charmed brunettes and timed their movements in the equivocal steps of the *samucuéca.* This I carried with me to the plantation ; and also prevailed upon Torbert to rescue the old seraphine from oblivion. But the responses of the finger-board were often in startling discord, and it was only from a limited number of chords that harmony could be produced.

One evening the main apartment presented an interesting scene. Around the broad *kóa* table were seated several of the foreign employees, reading. Though isolated among the mountains, some of them were deeply absorbed in continental politics, while others culled statistics from American documents, and a visitor was poring over an illustrated edition of Robinson Crusoe. Upon the table before them were a bunch of ripe bananas and a plate of finely powdered sugar. The doors were open, and in the back porch were three or four little girls, attendants, whose duty it was " to brush away insects ;" and, as is often the case with little folks when they have nothing to do, making a great deal of noise.

A couple of elderly females were indulging in an interminable gossip. Torbert and I were alternately talking and thrumming upon the instruments, when suddenly a prolonged shriek of human agony chimed in with horrid symphony to our harmony. The effect was electric : books and instruments were dropped, and when Torbert, without hat or coat, started off in the direction whence the sound came, the women, with distorted features, screamed, " *Akúa !*" (ghosts.)

We listened, but the cry was not repeated. The old resident informed us that it was probably the effect of fear upon some native who fancied himself the victim of a supernatural visitation. His conclusions were correct. Upon his return, Mr. Torbert informed his anxious audience that, far down amid the cane-fields, he had found one of the strongest natives in his service panting and helpless, and covered with a profuse perspiration. In the dark, he had been encountered by the spirit of a deceased relative that had seized him by the throat and endeavored to strangle him. These spirits, like their deities, are always bugbears to terrify. Between the former and the living there is no bond of spiritual communion, while the latter are regarded as synonyms of pestilence and scourge. It is somewhat remarkable that at the moment the man screamed, the cooper's wife, more than half a mile distant, responded and went into convulsions. The "ghost-seer" was her relative. Almost palsied with fright, the old cooper tottered up to the house for assistance, and we in turn were startled by the apparition of his livid countenance.

Two weeks passed rapidly away, when surveying duties called Mr. Torbert abroad ; at his request I accompanied him, thus bidding adieu to Ulupalakúa for several months. Subsequent adventures here will be reserved for future pages

---

CHAPTER X.

HAWAIIAN ROADS

AT an early hour our horses and knapsacks were prepared, and in company with a gentleman from Honolulu, we commenced ascending the Kúla road. It wound through cane and taro fields, and from an eminence we had a fine view of the plantation, with its cultivated portions regularly laid out, interspersed with houses and banana groves. The road winds to the left, and, with occasional ascent and descent, continues through the district of Kúla, at an elevation of more than 4,000 feet above the sea, until it gradually descends towards Makawáo. It was a mere bridle-path across open fields and through strips of forest that covered the face of the mountain above us, where it was encircled by a belt of clouds. The trees of the lower edge were low and scraggy, but often affording an agreeable shade ; around their trunks and from their branches were parasitic vines enwreathed and hanging in festoons. But few houses were passed ; near some of them natives were clearing the land for agricultural purposes.

We reached the residence of Mr. William McLean (since deceased) at noon. Nearly five years have elapsed since I visited

Makawáo, and although my recollections of it are not very distinct, I thought it at the time one of the most charming spots I ever beheld. A vast inclined plane was diversified by forest and small copsès of woodland, together with deep valleys and broad cultivations of sugar-cane. There were good roads ; and the number of houses, both native and foreign, evidenced a larger population than those of the district through which we had just passed. The residence of Mr. McLean was situated in a garden perfumed by the mingled odors of rose and geranium, and was also shaded by the wide-spreading branches of the majestic *kóa*. Among the fruit-trees I noticed the peach ; but a lower temperature is requisite for it to attain perfection.

A week of delightful recreation had been passed at Makawáo, when we mounted our horses at an early hour and set out for Lahaina by the road running parallel with the sea-shore. From Kalepolépo, on the south side of the isthmus, around by the way of Waikapú and Wailúku to Makawáo, will be found the best road in the whole group, for the level nature of the land favors its construction. Along the shore on the north, a better could hardly be expected, and with a few slight improvements, it would be admirably adapted for a carriage-road. The few houses seen by the way were principally fishermen's huts, but at Kahulúwe there was quite a hamlet, with several storehouses, and though possessing no available harbor for shipping other than small coasters, it is the port to which the produce of Makawáo and the lands adjacent is conveyed for exportation.

We traversed the sandy plains and hills of Wailúku, ever memorable in Hawaiian annals as being the spot where Kamehaméha landed with his fleet of canoes from Hawaii and fought his first battle on Maui, whose ultimate result was the complete subjugation of the leeward islands. The name of the stream that issues from the deep gorge of Wailúku signifies "carnage choked," and from present indications, it would appear to have been appropriately applied, for the trade-winds that sweep over this desolate tract, whirling the sand into ridges and miniature cones, daily disclose fresh evidences of the slaughter. We saw numerous skulls and bones, some of them quite perfect, but others crumbling, and all bleached to a dazzling whiteness in the sun.

Wailúku, distant fifteen miles from the residence of Mr. McLean, is a neat and pretty village, with roads and paths winding among numerous taro-patches and cultivations. The houses generally were more commodious than those we had seen on East Maui. The mission residence, school, and church, were its chief attractions ; a short distance in the rear rose the barren mountains of West Maui.

Though a hasty meal had been provided for us previous to setting out, an invitation to breakfast from Kualáni, a chief who resides here, could not be declined without manifest indifference to his hospitality ; giving our horses to the boys in attendance, we accompanied him to his house. Though of thatch, I considered it preferable to many frame-houses of greater pretensions. It was spacious and airy, and the simplicity of its furniture rendered it still more attractive. His wife, a portly female, and of higher rank than himself, was sitting upon a pile of fine mats, and gave us a cordial *alóha* as we entered, but she did not change her recumbent position while we remained. There were a number of female attendants or visitors, some with long *kahílis* to brush away insects, and others merely looking on, laughing familiarly and making comments. A snowy table-cloth was spread, and adorned with dishes of white porcelain, together with polished blades and silver forks, and our fare, consisting of fresh fish, roast duck and pork, fowl, taro, potatoes, breadfruit, and coffee, was served up to correspond. Kualáni himself presided as master of ceremonies. We were both amused and complimented by one evidence of his taste. This was a large curtain of silk handkerchiefs, each emblazoned with the likeness of " General William H. Harrison," a relic of the campaign of 1840.

We loitered here for an hour, then remounted, and passed through the smaller village of Waikapu, (consecrated water,) and without drawing rein, continued on until we diverged from the cart-road to the bridle-path that winds over the mountain. Here we dismounted and tightened our saddle girths, and I had yet to see a Hawaiian road in all its deformity, that which crosses the mountains of West Maui. I would observe, that with all her improvements, Hawaii is sadly deficient in roads ; except where natural facilities are offered for their construction, they consist usually of miserable paths winding through bush and brake, frequently making long detours to avoid a narrow ravine that might be spanned by a bridge, and running along the brink of a precipice, where a false step would precipitate horse and rider to destruction. With reference to the road in question, its present route cannot well be avoided, unless one were constructed by the sea-side. But this would be a work of immense labor, and would require more time and money than skilful engineering. From its summit, this portion of the mountain descends in rocky ridges to the sea, terminating in abrupt cliffs, into which the ceaseless dashing of the waves has worn caverns.

After a short halt, we commenced the steep ascent by the zigzag path, leaning forward in our saddles, and sweltering beneath the rays of a burning sun. A tedious ride brought us to a cooler region, where the coarse *pili* was waving, and here the comparative smoothness of the path for a short distance afforded an opportunity for cantering our horses.

Torbert kept the lead, our Honolulu friend the middle, and I the rear, for this reason—our leader had the best horse, and was almost daily in the saddle, while I was fresh from the region of tar and greasy substances; besides, I had become so lacerated by the Mexican saddle, that trotting was insupportable. Sometimes, in looking ahead, I would see horse and rider suddenly disappear, and after a while emerge from the opposite side of a ravine as I reached its brink to contemplate with dismay the route to be pursued. On these occasions, Torbert would look back and call out jocosely, " Keep up, keep up, or you'll lose your way." I mentally wished I could see his horse rolling down from one of the steep ridges, so that I could have a temporary respite, while expressing concern for the accident. In one place the rocky wall rises perpendicularly, where the path is insufficient for two horsemen to ride abreast, and on the other side is an alarmingly steep declivity, interspersed with rocks and other uninviting objects. To avoid any unpleasant meditations in passing this spot, I started my horse at full speed, but with over-caution, drew the right rein too strongly, and the result was that my knee was dashed against a projecting rock with such violence, that for a long time my foot hung powerless from the stirrup. My humble advice to all novices on Hawaiian roads is, to ride with shins and thighs incased in greaves.

The descent of the mountain on the opposite side was infinitely worse than the ascent, for in some places it was literally leaping from rock to rock, and our animals seemed to pick their way by instinct. A most welcome sound was the faint roaring of the surf, which could now be seen fringing the bright landscape beneath us, and after a brief interval our panting steeds were galloping along the smooth sandy beach towards a couple of shady trees, where we halted to refresh ourselves.

A pleasanter road was near the shore, and as if accustomed to it, our horses immediately broke into a canter. Here we passed the small hamlet of Oluálu, with its cool stream issuing from the dark mountain gorge in the rear. But few trees or cultivations were to be seen, and the average breadth of the bottom-land, between the mountain and the shore, was perhaps half a mile, though in some instances it was more than double that distance. The mountains of Molokái gradually came in sight, and at four o'clock we passed the stony district of Launiupóko, and were soon after gratified by the sight of the cocoanut grove of Polanúi, the suburbs of Lahaina.

CHAPTER XI.

RAMBLES ON MOLOKÁI

AFTER passing two days in Lahaina, surveying duties required the presence of Mr. Torbert on the island of Molokái, ten miles distant, and for this purpose a whale-boat was provided to convey us across the channel. He had availed himself of the services of a young graduate of the Seminary of Lahainalúna, named Richardson, who, accompanied by his friends and others, swelled our number to fifteen persons.

We started at an early hour, and pulled along outside the reef, until the western point of the island had been reached, when our sail was set to the stormy wind sweeping through the channel. Our greatest source of inconvenience was our younger passengers, who, accustomed to their canoes with outriggers, seemed to think their safety depended upon keeping the boat on even keel, when the reverse was the case ; for it is obvious that if a boat have the wind abeam, it will be less liable to accident by having a list to leeward, thereby elevating the weather-side, which serves· as a bulwark against the waves, and by rising with them, frequently prevents their breaking aboard. Incessant baling was required, and between watching squalls and seas, our excursion was anything but agreeable. Without mishap we shaped our course through a boat passage in the reef, and landed upon the sandy beach of Molokái.

A group of natives, male and female, came down to welcome our arrival, and seemed to vie with each other in their officiousness about carrying our baggage to the thatch-house that was to serve as headquarters. · This place appeared to be a rendezvous for young ladies, and no wonder a stranger becomes rapidly proficient in Hawaiian. Their attentions were gratuitously forced upon us, and had we given them permission, they would have carried chain, taken compass ranges, and to the best of their ability, calculated the areas of trapezia and parallelograms. We noticed one conspicuous among her companions by her graceful proportions and exuberant spirits, who rejoiced in the euphonious but sacrilegious appellation of Ka-i-o-a-lá-ni, (the food of heaven.)

Our first care was to purchase a good-sized pig, which was killed, dressed, and left to roast in the oven. The surveying this day consisted chiefly of ranging along the beach for a base-line, and setting up convenient stations for the operations of the morrow. We returned tired and hungry to our domicil, and after referring to notes and delineating sundry geometrical problems, Mr. Torbert ordered the cook to bring in the pig, that had by this time undergone a duplicate roasting.

This description of cooking, with but slight variation, is common throughout Polynesia : a hole is dug in the ground, in which a fire is built; over this are piled stones, which become thoroughly heated ; with these the pig is stuffed and surrounded, after which it is covered with leaves, usually banana, and earth or other substances heaped over them to retain the heat. Sufficient time having elapsed, the food is removed, cooked to a nicety. Our pig was served up on a wooden trencher in fragments, emitting a delicious odor for hungry stomachs, and to set-off, we had a huge calabash of poi. As the reader may not recollect the mode of its preparation, I will briefly allude to it. The taro (*Arum esculentum*) is roasted in the manner described, and the outer portion having been removed, a small quantity at a time is laid upon a board, slightly hollowed out for that purpose, when it is beaten into a pasty mass with a stone pestle. The task is laborious, and devolves on the men, who strip to it, and have a calabash of water near by, into which they frequently dip their hands, to aid them in removing the glutinous mass from the board to which it adheres by pounding. When properly prepared, it should be without lumps ; after this, it is removed from the board to large calabashes, into which is poured a sufficient quantity of water, so that by kneading, it may be reduced to the consistency required ; that is, sufficiently tenacious to adhere to the fingers, while, by a dexterous twirl, it is conveyed to the mouth. It is then set aside to ferment, a process requiring two or three days. In this state it bears some resemblance to yeast, and is of a light gray color. The accomplishment of feeding one's self can only be acquired by long practice, and though my efforts at first were a source of diversion to the natives, they subsequently complimented me on my proficiency in the art. I was now for the first time compelled to make a trial of its merits, which was done by cautiously venturing one finger, and in endeavoring to convey it quickly to my mouth, its immediate vicinity received the greater portion. However, having made a beginning, the taste was soon acquired, and instead of one, I used three fingers. When our repast was finished, Torbert affirmed that I had lowered the contents of the calabash by three inches. After us came our-attendants, and although they fell-to voraciously, there still remained a sufficiency for the morrow.

We breakfasted early, and prepared for our tramp up the mountain. Blankets were bundled up, and natives hired to carry them, besides one to act as quartermaster, also a few supernumeraries to make themselves generally useful. As we set out, old and young assembled to witness our departure, and some of the children accompanied us for a considerable distance up the path we were following. Richardson had found an old man, one of the ancient *régime*, to guide us to the bounds of the land, the name of which I do not recollect. The stations erected at appropriate points were piles of stones, and sometimes stakes were thrust in at the top, to render them more conspicuous. By noon we had ascended as far as Mr. Torbert thought necessary, though still a long distance from the northern boundary of the land. Upon Richardson's inquiring where it was, the old man leaned upon his staff, and pointing in the direction of the clouds, exclaimed, " *Ma-o-á-á-á !*" meaning that it was still at an indefinite distance.

After partaking of a hasty lunch and erecting a cairn, we commenced descending from the ridge in a line parallel with the shore. This was no easy task, for the side was steep, from which large trees were projecting, and clothed with a heavy growth of underwood, through which we sometimes slid and crept. The only sounds were our voices and the faint murmuring of the stream rippling over its stony bed at the bottom of the valley, for not a warbler enlivened these solitudes with its notes. The descent accomplished, we made a momentary halt to perform necessary ablutions, and an opportunity was afforded of seeing how the natives drink without a suitable vessel. This is simply done by bending over the stream and throwing the water into the mouth with one hand.

The ascent of the opposite side was now to be encountered, and this was attended with danger to those who lagged behind, for our train was stretched out at wide intervals. It was steep, and those who pioneered the way would, in climbing, frequently detach stones and rocks from the loose soil, which went bounding and crashing through the bushes, until checked by a tree or the bed of the valley. These projectiles could be heard, but not seen, and the moment a person accidentally started one, he would call out " *Málama okóu !*" (look out for yourselves,) and skilful dodging was sometimes required to avoid them.

On reaching the summit of the adjoining ridge, we halted for our stragglers to come up. When a native arrived, he would bawl out, in true Hawaiian style, to accelerate the movements of those behind ; who in turn would reply with something equivalent to " O, mind your business," while we could hear them floundering among the bushes below. Our quartermaster came last, a boy about twenty years old, and whose voice we frequently heard as his calabashes became entangled among the branches. He was completely begrimed with mud; although the atmosphere was cool, the perspiration was pouring from him in streams, and I believe at that moment he heartily wished that such an appendage as an empty stomach had never existed. Again, after crossing a narrow tract of level land, we had another descent to make; but this was attended with less difficulty. From the summit of the opposite side, we looked up the adjoining valley on our left, and a white streak amid the dark-green foliage was the foam of a waterfall. The opposite bounds of the land were now being traced, and our old gray-headed guide, with his long staff, took the lead; but almost every vestige of a path had been long since obliterated. For years he had not traversed these scenes, and sometimes he gazed about bewildered. We finally struck into what had once been quite a thoroughfare, and he walked on, chanting to himself in a low tone. I requested Richardson to go carefully behind without disturbing him, and listen to what he was singing. When he returned, he said he was "singing about the time when the roads were plain, and the land was covered with houses and strong men." Poor old man! He had outlived his generation; and had witnessed the last gathering of warriors among his native hills, and heard the last war-song chanted. He now lived to see a relic of his race fast disappearing before the innovations of the foreigner. Portions of his body were fancifully tattooed; and I noticed three figures upon his neck, which were said to be a mark of distinction.

Evening overtook us when the descent had been but half accomplished, and in looking over the ridge we were fortunate enough to discover a native house at the bottom of the valley, half hidden by a banana grove. It was past sunset before we reached it. The old man and his wife were hospitable enough to offer us the best their house afforded, which at that time consisted of bananas and poi. Of these and the fragments of our pig we made a tolerable meal. For several reasons, I spread my blankets upon clean mats under a shed, where the night was passed comfortably.

While continuing our occupation the day following, my attention was attracted by a green embankment commencing far up the valley, the bottoms of all of which incline towards the sea, and preserving a level as it continued its course along the side of a dividing ridge, winding in and out among projecting spurs, until intersected by the inclined plane of the elevation along whose side it ran. I at first took it to be an old line of fortification, but on inquiry, learned it was an aqueduct, constructed with immense labor in the days of Kamehaméha the Great, to convey a portion of the water from the valley to the uplands requiring irrigation.

Three days were spent in this vicinity, after which we took our departure for Keluaáha, the residence of Mr. H——, the missionary stationed on this island. We were accompanied by a young native, one of Richardson's friends, who took great pride in exhibiting his *palapála* (diploma) authorizing him to plead at the bar. Mr. Torbert reached the village about three P. M., and without pausing to rest, with characteristic energy, immediately commenced operations. He had preceded me by half an hour, and I found him on my arrival surrounded by the entire juvenile population, wondering what he saw so interesting about Keluaáha as to require such careful inspection through two parallel strips of *keleáwe*, (brass.) It would be unnecessary to recapitulate the incidents that transpired during a four days' sojourn at the residence of Mr. H——. Again we had mountains to ascend and valleys to cross ; but by far the most agreeable feature to revert to is the hospitality we enjoyed, and the cordial manner with which it was tendered. The snug cottage with garden and fences, the school-house and church, and the harmony of domestic economy, were strongly associated with recollections of home. Mrs. H—— informed me that she had been a resident there for eighteen years.

Much has been said regarding the charitable disposition of the natives of this district; without questioning the plan or principles adopted for their instruction, it may be observed that there is a possibility of inculcating too ultra notions of propriety, and I will cite an instance that occurred during the season when southwest gales were prevalent. On one occasion, a schooner, I think it was the " Emma," owned by James Y. Kanehóa, Esq., Governor of Maui, visited the small bay of Kanakakái, and while lying there, was overtaken by a storm, and dragging at her anchors, she drifted towards the reef, by surging against which she carried away her rudder. A vessel without a rudder is as useless as an " ox in a pit," whether Sabbath or not, and as soon as the weather would permit, the defect was remedied, to be prepared for any emergency. The day happened to be Sunday. Previous to the storm, a number of natives had engaged their passages for Honolulu ; but having seen the captain labor on the Sabbath, for his own preservation, they came on board and gave him to understand that they could not conscientiously comply with their agreement, and when the weather permitted, he was forced to depart as he came.

Bidding adieu to our kind friends, we returned by the road we had come, and in company with Richardson, called upon the chief judge of the island, his father-in-law, where we were hospitably entertained until the arrival of the boat. The house, a large adobe one, is neatly plastered and whitewashed, and being situated on an eminence, commands a fine view of the surrounding country. Here I indulged so freely in poi and milk that I could never endure the sight of the mixture since.

The next day our boat arrived, and being hauled as near to the shore as the reef would allow, we were carried to it upon the shoulders of natives, and with no breeze, shoved out into the open sea.. There were no trades that day, and we had a long pull beneath a burning sun. The strong wind of the day previous having left a heavy swell, our boat rolled about in an unpleasant manner, and Richardson was so affected by it that he leaned upon the gunwale, excessively sick. For a change, I sat down to an oar, and while rowing, it accidentally slipped from the row-lock, when I fell backwards at full length. To say nothing of sundry contusions, I seriously fractured a large calabash and its cover, the owner of which muttered invectives until we reached Lahaina. Here, for a brief interval, I bade adieu to the Sandwich Islands.

10

CHAPTER XII.

KA-LE-PO-LÉ-PO, AND THE "OLD PLANTATION."

Six months have been passed among the deep cañons and pine-clad mountains of the Siérra Neváda, and we are once more galloping along the smooth sandy beach, with foaming breakers on one hand, and the dark gorge of Oluálu on the other. Everything wears a smiling aspect: the native huts, the fishing canoes outside the reef, and the dark rocks, offer a familiar welcome. Even the barren mountain, whose obstacles are again to be encountered, appears less formidable.

Having accomplished its passage, I "kept away" to the right, skirting the common by the sea-shore, and after a ride of five or six miles, reached the small village of Kalepolépo. Its name has been appropriately bestowed, and may be rendered into English as " superlatively unclean." It consists of a few grass and frame houses situated upon the land of Waiakóa. During the year 1850, the increased commerce of this group tended greatly to its improvement, and at almost any time one or more vessels might be seen anchored in the bay, chiefly Californian traders. The place is built upon sand, and during the strong gales prevalent from November to March, the low embankment is frequently overflowed by the heavy swell from the southwest. Its locality, in a commercial point of view, is perhaps the best that could have been selected with reference, at that time, to the chief article of export, the Irish potato. Situated on Malía Bay, and about one-third the distance from East to West Maui, it has good roads leading to it from various cultivated tracts in the potato district, or Kula, from 4,000 to 5,000 feet above the sea; also from Makawáo, Waikapú, and Wailúku, besides being on the direct road from plantations on the leeward side of East Maui to Lahaina. The anchorage is good for vessels of every class at the distance of half or three-fourths of a mile west of the town, while vessels of lighter draught can anchor nearer in. There is a reef skirting the shore, partially bare at low water, and which in some degree breaks the force of the waves during the southwest gales.

The fish-pond immediately in the rear, and running nearly parallel with the town, is now almost filled up, but it was formerly extensive, being a royal prerogative. The site of the old town was located farther back, the pond extending between it and the sea-shore ; but for the last twenty years vegetation has ceased in many places, thereby exposing the sandy soil to the full force of the trade-winds that sometimes sweep violently across the common, raising the sand in clouds. Thus, during successive years, deposits have been made in its waters, forming a tolerable foundation for the present town ; and all that remains of the pond is fast disappearing beneath the sand-clouds that are daily driving across it. *Momókus* (whirl-winds) occasionally occur, and though of brief duration, their effect is sometimes embarrassing to vessels that drag at their anchors, while the water is whirled over them in masses. They are always unpleasant to those residing on shore, who usually retreat to their houses to avoid the blinding sand. Although the bay is often exceedingly rough, the natives boldly venture out in boats, or their canoes, where at times they may be seen fearlessly standing or sitting upon their outriggers.

The general appearance of Kalepolépo is desolate in the extreme, but a relief is afforded by the majestic background, with its hills, valleys, and broad belt of forest, the dark summit of Haleakalá towering above the clouds, at an elevation of nearly 10,000 feet above the sea. No fresh water can be procured here within a distance of several miles, unless during the rainy season, when it is sought for among the deep ravines, where it is found in pools. On the common, near the sea-shore, and between Kalepolépo and West Maui, are extensive salt-ponds. Into these the sea is admitted by small channels, and by its evaporation, the salt is found in snowy crystals thickly incrusting the bed of the pond, when it is piled in small conical heaps by the natives, and covered with grass or leaves to protect it from the sand and dirt. Not far from the town, upon the arid plain, are numerous relics of mortality, and, as at Wailúku, this Golgotha is alternately covered and exposed by the drifting sand. In crossing this plain the galloping hoof scatters crumbling bones to the eddying winds, and hastens their commingling with kindred dust. Among the sand-hills of Palauéa, five miles distant, I have seen

children erecting pyramids of skulls, and inclosing them with an-
cestral bones.

After leaving Kalepolépo, my road, for three or four miles, was
over the hard sand beach, and passed through a hamlet with a grove of
cocoanut-trees, which, though small, is very inviting, and forms an
agreeable contrast to the desert by which it is nearly surrounded.
Leaving the shore on the right, the road winds through a succession
of low sand-hills, some of them curiously formed into miniature cones
and embankments, and scantily covered with vegetation, chiefly the
creeping convólvulus.   It was solitary and cheerless, and continued
so for two miles, before a soil was reached sufficiently arable for the
cultivation of sweet potatoes or melons.   Though stony, it now became firmer, while the hills were clothed with the coarse *pili*, here
and there relieved by the yellow-flowered *ilíma* bushes.   The appearance of the country improved with the ascent; the grass grew
firmer, while the soil was darker; the low *ilíma* was exchanged for
the bright foliage of the shady candlenut, and here and there, small
clusters of *arkókoa* afforded an agreeable diversity.   A solitary hut
now and then betokened that the confines of civilization were once
more being approached, and soon after, the district of Ulupalakúa
in its beauty and fertility was before me.

It was pleasant to revisit the "Old Plantation;" and after galloping along the road through the cane-fields, I halted for a moment
upon the knoll that overlooks the little village.   It was evening, and
from the tall chimney volumes of black smoke were ascending, and
occasionally a fork of flame shot upward through the gloom.   As I
rode leisurely down to the old homestead, the dogs sprang out to
give me a boisterous welcome, and after dismounting, it was counter-
signed by the cordial grasp of Mr. Torbert.

I noticed several new faces present, an indication of increasing
prosperity.   Accompanying my friend to the boiling-house, where
he was superintending the natives who watched the bubbling cal-
drons, we seated ourselves on a pile of dry rind, used for fuel, and
I gleaned from him all that had transpired during my absence,
domestic and political, including the redoubtable attack of the French
on Honolulu, and the theft of the yacht "Kamehaméha."

After remaining at Ulupalakúa for several days, with Mr. Torbert

I revisited Lahaina and Honolulu, and on our return, accompanied him on a surveying excursion to Kúla, the incidents of which will be reserved for the following chapter.

CHAPTER XIII.

S U R V E Y I N G   I N   K Ú L A .

AT an early hour the boy especially appointed for that purpose was sent out to bring in the horses, of which we have quite a "stable" at Ulupalakúa; and having prepared our baggage, which each man carried behind his saddle, and secured our surveying instruments, we started off for Kúla by the Makawáo road. Our party consisted of Mr. Torbert, Mr. A——— (a son of one of the missionaries, who was familiar with the native tongue), and myself. After a three hours' ride, we reached the house of Mr. S———, on the land of Koonólu, which was to serve as headquarters during our operations. In this instance, the necessity of looking out for an old native who knew the bounds was obviated by the presence of the *konohíki*, or overseer of the chief who formerly owned the land, and who received, with very bad grace, a letter from his superior requesting him to render us all requisite assistance, and quietly yield up his authority.

Our task was commenced by sending a native up through the forest with white flags, to affix them at its upper edge, on either bound of the land. A considerable time elapsed before the white beacons were visible, for the forest was pathless and the distance long, the elevation sought being far above the clouds. Both altitudes and angles were taken by theodolite, an instrument almost indispensable for surveying in this country. Our distance was obtained by chaining across the breadth of the land for a base-line.

Directions were then given about cutting a wide path entirely through the forest from its lower to its upper extremity, and also about continuing the survey from where we then were, by compass, to the sea-shore, a distance of more than twelve miles; after this, Mr. Torbert took his departure, leaving us to finish the remainder of the job. My first care was to secure the services of four strong natives for the bush-work, and after breakfast we set out for the scene of our labor.

Having provided ourselves with all that was requisite, we started away about eight o'clock in the morning, crossing the ravine that divides Koonólu from Kohéo, to cut a pathway through the forest along the southern boundary of the last-mentioned land. Our path for a considerable distance was through the potato cultivations, where the natives were commencing their labors for the day. Boys were scampering among the trees and driving together the cattle, while some of the men lounged lazily around the carts, to yoke them; girls, with their hair braided behind, or hanging about their faces, were trudging leisurely along with calabashes in hand, and chanting their songs, though their garments were dripping with the heavy dew they had brushed from the bushes; the birds were singing their matins, and though warblers are scarce, there is no spot throughout the group more musical than the groves that skirt the forests of Kúla.

We soon passed the limits of cultivation, and stood on the edge of the forest. Everything was dripping with moisture; for though the scorching rays of the sun were lighting up the broad isthmus between the two promontories, they had yet to creep over the lofty summit of Haleakalá before reaching us, where, at an elevation of 5,000 feet, we were almost shivering in the coolness of the morning. Unlike the forests of the continents, lofty and comparatively open, those of Polynesia are low, dense, and obstructed by a heavy underwood; and although wanting in height, their frequently twisted trunks and crooked branches remind one of some of the scraggy forests of South Australia. Our natives commenced their labors by a general smoke, striking fire with flint and steel, and each inhaling half a dozen whiffs from a short wooden pipe. Then, with tough poles about six feet long, they commenced beating a path, relieving each other at short intervals, and chopping down with a hatchet such small trees or bushes as obstructed their progress. We made but little advance that day; they told us that on the morrow we would reach the spot where the trees grew larger, and *kahi-kulóa*, (in bygone days,) their ancestors, built their war-canoes.

We retrograded by the path we had made, and reached the house of Mr. S—— at sundown, where, after partaking of a substantial supper, we retired to rest at an early hour, and enjoyed a comfortable repose between sheets of the native *kappa*. On the morrow we resumed our duties, and by noon had reached the locality mentioned by our guides. It had little or no distinction from the surrounding forest, except that at this elevation the timber was heavier, though more scattered, and that the surface of the land in this vicinity afforded a comparatively level resting-place.

A century ago and these solitudes had echoed the busy sounds of the artisan, who, with fire and rude implements of stone, modelled the fleets of his kingdom that were to battle upon the " eight seas of Hawaii." Here were huts with their families, and up and down the mountain we had traversed, bearers of burdens were ascending and descending, while their lordly taskmasters presided over all. One of our guides seemed to be fully sensible of the broad distinction that existed between Hawaii as it then *was* and as it now *is*, for, striking the *koalípi* (axe) deep into the trunk of a tree, he exclaimed, " *Naaupó lákou ia manéwa—ákamai mákou kéia manéwa*," (they were ignorant then, but we are expert now.)

We were now among the clouds, and at times completely enveloped by them, and once a smart shower compelled us to seek refuge under the remarkably curved trunk of a koa-tree that for years had lain prostrate, and the vines and underwood that had grown up around its sides seemed to protect, while it afforded shelter for us all. It was not until the afternoon of the third day that the decreasing size and peculiar appearance of the trees indicated our approach to the upper edge of the forest, and open strips of land were passed, without resorting to either pole or hatchet. After crossing a narrow marshy space, we emerged completely from the bush to the coarse grass and stunted shrubs, where, from this lofty eminence, over forest and cloud, we looked down upon the landscape beneath. Our natives collected some dry fuel, and we were soon sitting around the crackling flames, which sent forth an acceptable heat in this cold atmosphere. By an optical illusion, the extended horizon seemed to rise to a level with the eye, and the rugged summits of West Maui, Molokái, and Lanái loomed up before us, but Kahuláwe was hidden by intervening ridges. We were at too great a distance to discover minute objects, but the localities of Wailúku and Waikúpa were recognized by the bold outline of mountain and shore. Here were strawberry vines in abundance ; during the summer season the fruit is plentiful, as is the case on the uplands of most of the islands. When I visited this district a year later, the path we had made was almost obliterated by the underwood and fern that had sprung up; the latter everywhere clothes the mountain-side like a garment.

On the following day the services of our native laborers were dispensed with, and having secured the assistance of a Yankee, whom I shall call Arnold, and hired a boy to follow with the horses, we commenced our observations by compass, chaining from station to station, and following the bounds towards the sea-shore that had already been pointed out by the *konohiki*. Unavoidable delays prevented an early start, and the difference between this and our previous labors was perceptible in the intense heat and absence of water, for the land below this forest belt is open, or scantily covered with shrubbery, while the soil becomes more arid and stony, and the sinuous course of rocky ravines may be traced, until, like dark threads, their windings are lost upon the broad isthmus or common. The sterility of the soil increases with the descent, until near the base of this portion of the mountain, a distance of seven or eight miles from the cultivated tracts, the reddish earth is covered only with coarse grass and the low *ilíma* bushes, and dark ferruginous rocks are scattered thickly around. Our road lay for more than twelve miles through this description of country, unenlivened by either house or tree that could afford a shelter.

Half way down the mountain we found a pool of pure rain-water in a rocky basin, and which proved most acceptable to us, for we were parched with thirst, more especially Arnold, who contemplated a bath, but that would have been taking liberties with this provision of nature. Our guide discovered a cave in the ravine sufficiently commodious to contain us all ; and as there was no prospect of our reaching Kalepolépo that night, we concluded to camp out where we were. While erecting a cairn of stones upon a slight eminence for a conspicuous bound, we discovered strange proceedings among our quadrupeds ; the native held fast to the tether ropes, and they were galloping around him at full speed, prancing and performing evolutions generally. We were too distant to render him assistance, and A———, our linguist, shouted "*Péla!*" (as you are ;) but the native probably concluded that it was easier to direct than to perform, for a moment after my horse shot off at a tangent, while the broad Mexican stirrups were beating time upon his back. Together with Arnold's mule, which had been quietly browsing a short distance off, we were spectators of the scene, and not three minutes had elapsed from the time my animal first conceived the notion of liberty, before he had disappeared among the hummocks that skirt the common. Arnold, full of commiseration, mounted his mule and galloped off in pursuit, soon disappearing among the low hills, while we who remained set about making ourselves comfortable for the night. Our natives needed no instruction, for they collected an abundance of dry grass to line the cave, and filled the vessels with water ; but as to fire, our resources were small, owing to the want of fuel, which consisted merely of dry grass and bits of wood that had been washed down the ravines. A small tree grew near the mouth of the cave, and I requested one of the men to break it down, and lay it upon the fire ; but he replied, "*Laáu ála—kápu!*" (sandal-wood—prohibited !) It proved to be a bastard species of the precious shrub growing solitarily amid this scene of desolation, and although the Hawaiian Government have "tabooed" the sandal-wood, I must beg its indulgence for what may be construed a violation of the law, by pleading the emergency. Its branches, which, with further preparation, might have exhaled a grateful odor in the Temple of Joss, when thrown upon the fire, sent forth a cloud of smoke that nearly drove us from our quarters. At dusk, Arnold returned without any tidings of the horse, and wanted to know what "we'd got to eat :" he was welcomed to our frugal meal, consisting of sea-biscuit, cold boiled taro, and water. We bundled ourselves up for the night, and slept miserably.

Early the next morning, I trudged off on foot for Kalepolépo to find the deserter, but could glean no tidings concerning him ; I then had recourse to offering five dollars reward for horse, sad-

dle, and bridle, which sent three or four native equestrians scouring over the plain in pursuit.   On my return to camp, when
about half way, I found him standing by the roadside, and well
secured, for the rope, in trailing behind, had caught under a projecting root ; all was safe, except the heavy stamped leather that
covers the saddle, which was missing.   It was found upon the common, nearly a month after, and returned to Ulupalakúa.   During the
forenoon, while chaining along, we came to the brink of a deep ravine, winding and cavernous, and in calling to each other, our voices
echoed and re-echoed along its rocky passages.   I asked one of the
natives what it meant ; he said it was *akúa*, (a ghost.)   We reached
Kalepolépo at noon, and were indebted to the courtesy of a merchant
of that place for our dinner.   On our return, I saw the *konohíki*
peeling the bark from an *ilíma* bush, and chewing it.   Upon inquiry, he informed us that he was troubled with the *náhu*, (" gripes ;")
and if his manner of chewing was an indication of his sensibilities,
his pain must have been intense.   I was never before aware that
this bark possessed carminative properties.

Mr. Torbert was at Koonólu, and the next day we had the
claims of the quondam konohíki to adjust   He had two or three
patches, of from one to half an acre, under cultivation, situated remotely from each other, upon the land of Kohéo, of which we had
just taken the dimensions.   As it would spoil the appearance of an
estate to have three or four independent inclosures scattered in its
midst, Mr. Torbert proposed giving him a piece of land of such dimensions as to equal the aggregate areas of those he claimed.   "No,
he would not do that ; he'd appeal to the Land Commission."   It
will be necessary to state, that at a sitting of the Privy Council, a
law had been passed, granting to every native in fee-simple such
pieces or parcels of land as he lived upon or cultivated ; this
also extended to deeds of purchase, in which was inserted " native
rights respected," and hence arose the *kuliána* or " rights" system,
in the construction of which, broad license was granted, at least so
it would appear to a foreigner unacquainted with the tenure of native
fiefs.   An instance in question came to my notice during a sojourn
in Lahaina.   A citizen of that town had purchased a strip of land
situate in the suburbs, called Polanúi, conspicuous for its grove of

cocoanut-trees. A regular sale was made by the chief, the acknowledged owner, to the purchaser, who, on attempting to take possession, found an obstacle in his way. This proved to be an old woman without a shadow of pretension to real ownership, who consented to the sale, provided there should be no transfer of the cocoanut grove. As the remainder of the land extending to the mountain was barren, this grove constituted the principal object of attraction. An investigation took place, and it was proven that her grandfather had built a wall around the sprouting trees to protect them from the ravages of swine, and that the plaintiff, when not abroad, had resided there from childhood ; consequently, the purchaser was nonsuited. It was sometimes carried to a ridiculous extent in Lahaina. A boy could hardly take your horse to browse by the roadside without being accosted by a venerable individual with *málo* and staff, who intimated that a suspension of proceedings would be desirable, as he had a *kuliána* on that particular spot, whether public or not. I do not allude to these instances with a sentiment of disrespect towards the Board of Land Commissioners, who would never condescend to absurdities ; their duties have been both complex and difficult. The law framed for the purpose of securing to common natives homesteads which they can call their own was humane, for it relieves them forever from a state of vassalage and the feudal tenure by which they formerly held their estates, and concedes to them the rights and privileges of freemen. To obviate difficulty, it would be advisable for those purchasing lands to ascertain definitively of what these " native rights" consist. I have never ascertained the result of the *konohíki's* litigation.

CHAPTER XIV.

"THE SICK WIND."—A WRECKING PARTY.

THE month of January wore on. The azure skies became gradually overcast, and watery clouds, creeping up from the southwest, floated like a gloomy pall overhead. Everything betokened a *kóna*, or southwest gale, called by the natives *"makáni mái,"* (sick wind,) owing to the cold, wet weather attending it. By the careless exposure of their persons during these seasons, many of them engender future disease.

Such were the appearances noticed one afternoon at our landing; and not wishing to encounter the bleak hills with a tempest in perspective, I accepted the invitation of Bob, our storekeeper, to remain with him, instead of plodding up the dreary road to Ulupalakúa.

At midnight we were awakened by sounds of the gale; the storm-spirits were abroad, and a tempest of wind and rain threatened to tear the well-secured thatch from the rafters, as it howled with fury around the low stone walls of our shelter. The beach, a few yards distant, was bounded by a solid wall, or massive boulders of ancient lava; and the incessant roaring of the breakers against these giant ramparts was, like the pealing of thunder, in wild harmony with the storm.

The morning broke gloomily. Though the rain had ceased, tempestuous clouds were hurrying rapidly before the wind, enshrouding the mountain summit and the green cane-fields in their humid folds. The once smiling canopy seemed strangely contracted to a gloomy, concave vault, frowning upon the landscape, and chilling every warm feeling associated with it. In the southwestern horizon, an incubus of leaden clouds was lowering upon an ocean flecked with foam, where snowy crests danced upon its broad surface, until wave after wave, rolling heavily in, hurled themselves against the rocky barrier, to burst upward in sheets of foam and spray, and fall in showers by the distant roadside.

Not a native was stirring. As if in anticipation of the storm, canoes had been hauled upon the rocks and secured, but the wind was making sad havoc among the loose thatch of some of their tenements. We mustered around and collected such dry fuel as we could find in the shed, and built a fire in the house. The tea-kettle was filled, and some sweet potatoes thrown into the fire to roast; and with these, together with a scanty ration of yesterday's soup, we made a tolerable breakfast.

As soon as the weather would permit, I started for the plantation. The road was slippery and often obstructed by deep gullies, where rain-torrents had foamed the night preceding. Damp winds were whistling across the bleak hills and among ghostly clusters of the cactus; and as I toiled up the monotonous ascent, the brow of each successive hill seemed to bear the mocking impress, *Excelsior!*

The cooper was the first person I encountered on my arrival. He communicated the alarming intelligence that the whole village had been destroyed, and would fain have me believe that what I saw was merely the apparition of what had been. The old grass-house occupied by him as a workshop had been completely demolished, occasioning a serious disarray of his casks and lumber generally. Two or three other dilapidated tenements had been blown away, and the sides of a few which had started were propped up by poles. Though in some instances the cane bore evidence of the furious blast, no serious damage was done.

This gale, with abated violence, continued for several days, and its effects were observable throughout the leeward portions of the group. In Lahaina, a Californian trader dragged at her anchors, capsized off Lanái, and every white person on board perished, while the natives saved themselves by swimming. Numerous houses and trees were prostrated. In one instance, a cocoanut-tree was torn from its roots and whirled over a house in the rear of which it grew. A blast swept through the eastern valley, and that specimen of architecture, the palace, being directly within the range of these *momókus*, portions of the roof and railing of the verandah were torn away. As this has been of frequent occurrence, though as often repaired, the government have at present concluded to let Æolus do his worst, for when I visited it three years afterwards the building remained in *statu quo*. It was during this gale that the yacht "Wanderer," commanded by Captain Boyd, whose tragic fate at the Solomon Islands has excited so much interest in the minds of all, saved the lives of half a dozen natives who had been drifted to sea in a whale-boat schooner. A bark, which the evening previous had sailed from Honolulu for Lahaina, was fifteen days in reaching its port of destination.

A month subsequent to these events, when the weather was fair, but by no means settled, our villagers were thrown into no small excitement by the appearance of a native constable, or *káiko*, dashing at full speed along the Lahaina road, with Spanish leggings and a gaudy poncho fluttering in the wind. He reined in his steed at one of the mills and dismounted. A crowd of idlers gathered around to learn the news, for Mr. Torbert had been absent nearly two weeks, and the state of the weather would not admit of the usual labor. He brought the intelligence that a Californian schooner had been capsized off Lahaina, and every soul lost; that she had a large quantity of specie on board, and that the Governor had offered a reward for any information respecting her, or where she might be found. As a clue to aid the search, he further stated that a few evenings previous a native who was out in his canoe had discovered a dark object like the hull of a vessel floating past him, which he was afraid to board, conjecturing it to be an *akúa*. Upon a cross-examination, he said it was drifting down the channel towards Kahuláwe, a barren island, opposite the southwest point of East Maui.

Here was an antidote for ennui; for want of better occupation, I had just been making an accurate survey of the cooper's taro-patch in the rear of his house, which I drafted on a large scale, indicating by appropriate hieroglyphics where might be found the largest growth of the esculent vegetable; also, such portions as had become deteriorated by trespassing pigs, and for all of which he professed eternal obligation, while he hung it up as an ornament in his apartment. The foreign employees had busied themselves in various ways, but chiefly with their homesteads and domestic arrangements.

Dispatches were at once sent out for " Steve," who resided at one extreme of the plantation, and for " Long Jim," who occupied Kalîhi at the other. These soon arrived, and providing ourselves

with two or three telescopes, we ascended an eminence to reconnoitre the shores of Kahuláwe. Every black rock alternately appearing and disappearing amid the dashing of the surf, that bore a
supposed similitude to a schooner's hull, was commented upon *pro*
and *con*, until it was finally decided that we should procure a boat
and go in search of it.

The cooper talked largely about salvage and general averages, and
insisted upon going ; though his weight would have been but a trifling encumbrance, his rheumatism could not be other than a serious
counterpoise to his services, so we promised him a share of the spoil,
if he would remain quietly at home.

Five of us started down the mountain, about the middle of the
afternoon, each with his blankets, while we carried a small quantity
of sea-biscuit in a knapsack. We made for the landing direct, and
taking Bob by storm, told him we would listen to no opposition, and
that he must accompany us as soon as he could get ready ; an invitation to which he manifested ready compliance, much to the consternation of his wife, *Páli*, (precipice !) At his request she folded
a couple of blankets, and with considerable reluctance filled a small
calabash with nicely prepared poi, which, together with a bundle of
pái kálo and the sea-biscuit, was to furnish us with supper and breakfast, for we intended passing one night only on the island. Dan engaged the services of a stout young native named Makaóe, (sharp-
eyes,) whose former residence on Kahuláwe qualified him to act as
pilot and guide, and having hired a dilapidated whale-boat, our party
of seven took its departure from Honuaúla.

As the boat shoved off, Mrs. Páli ran out of the house, shouting,
" *Aóle páu ko káua aló—ha !*" (our love has not ceased yet.)

Aóle, pualóke, (no, my rose,) replied Bob, laughing, and amid the
cheers of the natives who had assembled to witness our departure, we
set the sail to the light breeze and slid smoothly over the quiet water.
It was evening, and there was not a cloud in the sky ; the stars shone
brightly, and had it not been for the leaky condition of the boat,
which required incessant baling, the excursion would have been delightful. We skirted the southern edge of the rocky islet Molokini,
which rose an apparently inaccessible cliff in mid-channel, and soon
after the bold outline of Kahuláwe loomed distinctly before us. By

Makaóe's direction the boat was headed for a small cove that formed an excellent boat harbor, and which is frequently resorted to by fishing canoes; as the surf was but trifling, we shot in through the narrow channel into still water, and a moment after hauled the boat up high and dry upon the smooth sand beach. On either side our position was bounded by projecting spurs extending to the sea, and terminating in abrupt cliffs, while the level bottom intervening was but limited. Our first care was to provide a suitable place to pass the night; some of us had already begun to cast inquiring glances towards the lee-side of a large cactus which grew near the shore, when Makaóe, the all-provident, directed us to a cave close by, formed by shelving rocks, and crowned by the ruined walls of an old *heiáu*, (heathen temple,) frowning gloomily in the dusk of evening. To this we conveyed our baggage and provision; after which all set to work collecting dry grass for our beds and drift-wood for a fire, of which there was an abundance, while Makaóe disappeared with a calabash up one of the ravines for water. The bright flames emitted a cheerful warmth, and lighted up the dark rocks, which re-echoed the mirth of a convivial party indulging their appetites with the vegetable diet Mrs. Páli had provided.

None of us feeling inclined to sleep, it was arranged that our guide should remain near the cave, to guard against contingencies that might occur, while the rest of us ascended one of the ridges and awaited the rising of the moon, to light our ramblings along the shore. After climbing the steep ascent, we sat down in the coarse grass until the full moon, which was already lighting up the sky behind the dark mountains of East Maui, should make its appearance. Mount Haleakalá stood forth in bold relief, rising darkly from the ocean, with its summit enveloped in clouds. These gradually assumed a more transparent hue, until the bright orb shone calmly forth, spanning the broad channel with its silver rays, and shedding a mellow light over the dark ridges and ravines we sought to traverse. These inequalities of the surface, like those of the other islands, radiate from the centre to the sea; and being of frequent occurrence, and often precipitous, they are serious inconveniences to travelling. We rambled near the cliffs, where we could look down upon the rocks below, to discover if there were any signs of a wreck. By some accident, Bob and I were separated from the party, and thinking we had continued our jaunt far enough for that evening, we again reclined upon the sweet-scented grass, while he entertained me with some of his adventures in the South Seas, for he had been a great rover. Presently we saw a human figure creeping up the side of the ravine towards us. Neither of us could conjecture it to be other than the troubled ghost of some departed hero, for we believed the island to be uninhabited. Bob sprang to his feet, and hailed " *Owái la ?*" (who's there.)

" *Oau no !*" (nobody but me !) It was Makaóe, who, afraid to remain among the *akúas*, had joined us to avoid the unpleasant reflections of solitude.

CHAPTER XV.

THE BIVOUAC, AND RETURN.

INSTEAD of returning by the route we had come, it was arranged that we should pick our way along the rocky shore beneath the cliffs ; and as a hint for our companions to do the same, we set fire to the coarse grass, which would prevent their retrograding by the old path, and compel them either to ascend higher up the mountain, or, like ourselves, follow the shore. Our party discovered the main boom of a schooner reposing quietly upon the rocks, where it had been thrown by the waves ; also a small " hatch," and two canoe paddles, which had drifted upon these barren shores. The boom, a long, solid spar, remained where we found it, but the others were carried to our camp as trophies of success. Jack Burns and his squad soon returned, bearing between them the top-gallant yard of a ship, with its sail, both in a dilapidated state, occasioned by their surging against the rocks. There was a little wrangling about who should occupy the centre of the cave, but this was settled by Bob, who took up a squatter's claim, and thrust his head under a shelving rock, forming an aperture that extended indefinitely towards the interior. Soon after, when we were all snugly wrapped in our blankets, he withdrew, alleging there was " a strong graveyard smell," and finally took up his quarters in the open air.

The morning dawned brightly; and although it was evident we should discover no trace of the schooner, it was mutually determined that we should make ourselves more intimately acquainted with Kahuláwe. For this purpose, we divided ourselves into two parties: Steve, Long Jim, and Jack Burns, to constitute the first, and to take the northern route; while it was arranged that Bob Waldron and I, together with Makaóe, should bear away towards the south, both parties to advance until they met, when all should return across the island to the point of starting. The theory in itself was plausible, but would not bear reducing to practice. We ate the poi at once, preliminary to making an equal distribution of the remaining fragments of boiled taro and sea-biscuit, a task that was performed by Bob, who had reference to party interests. Then strapping the knapsack on Makaóe's shoulders, we started away in opposite directions.

The air was charming; a light sea-breeze was fanning across the hills, where the shrill cries of the plover, as they winged their way to the more elevated regions, and the bleating of the wild goats, alone awoke the solitude. We strolled leisurely along the brow of the cliffs, occasionally looking over to reconnoitre, or, by our united efforts, starting a huge crag from its insecure resting-place, to watch it as it dashed into the foaming caldron beneath. Sometimes we would launch a massive boulder down the steep side of a ravine, which, like an avalanche, went leaping and bounding, carrying all before it, until dashed into fragments by collision with the rocks below. Waldron was afflicted with a mania for chasing goats, and during this pastoral occupation, he described several summersets, to the great diversion of Makaóe. His efforts were ultimately rewarded by the capture of two beautiful kids, whose tiny limbs were too weak to follow the bold leaps of the dam from rock to rock, who, deserted by the flock, was looking down from a craggy eminence and bleating piteously for her young. Dan suggested taking them both to his wife, who had frequently manifested a fondness for pets, but we fortunately argued him out of it, for they could not have survived the disastrous return. We gave them their liberty, and had soon the pleasure of seeing the mother skip down the rocks to join them. Makaóe very sagely remarked to Waldron, that if he would only catch the mother, we could all have some milk.

The difficulties of the excursion had been greatly underrated ; the ravines were so steep, and of such frequent recurrence, that our progress had been greatly retarded. It was noon before we had fairly reached the southern portion of the island, or little more than half the distance we proposed accomplishing by that time. The general aspect of the land was desolate in the extreme ; the reddish, sterile soil being unrelieved by either tree or shrub, and everything seemed parched up by the burning rays of the sun. There was neither stream nor spring upon the island ; our thirst was quenched at the pools of rain-water, where rocky basins had furnished natural reservoirs. We here halted for a consultation, whether to cross the mountain and reach our bivouac, or to continue on until dark, when, at the rate we had travelled, we would be exactly opposite the point of starting. The former was decided upon, though mentally upbraiding ourselves with neglect of duty towards our companions. We did not attain the greatest elevation of the island, which presented the leading features of the portion we had traversed ; that is, " stale and unprofitable." At one place was passed what had once been a grove of *akókoa* trees, but nothing now remained save an area covered with withered trunks and branches, bleached as white as skeletons in the sun, the bark having been stripped from them by the goats. We saw *akókoa* and a few shrubs growing farther up the mountain, and these, together with a few stunted *wiliwili* trees, were the only living representatives of the vegetable kingdom worth noticing.

In passing through a small clump of *akókoa* shrubbery which lay in our route, Waldron called my attention to the condition of a pair of black " doeskins" I wore on that occasion. They were completely ruined by the white milky substance that had exuded from the tender branches we had broken in forcing our way through ; though white as milk, it was of a glutinous nature, and from it the natives manufacture bird-lime.

Tired and hungry, we reached our quarters about the middle of the afternoon, and found everything as we had left it. The limited stock of provision had been completely exhausted; and our only resource for procuring a new supply was to wade out upon the coral reef and gather *biche de mer*, or trepang, and such shell-fish as the *echinus*, or sea-egg, and limpets. The latter roasted were palatable, but the trepang I could make nothing of; though soaked and broiled upon the embers, it still continued as tough as sole-leather, and I was compelled to discard an article of diet that would have caused a Celestial's eyes to sparkle with delight. Waldron was afflicted with a most immoderate appetite, and the whole catalogue of mollusca disappeared from his hands with marvellous rapidity; the "lily pups," as he termed the limpets, were swallowed raw as he took them from the rocks. Makaóe, who shunned the *biche de mer* as an Israelite would pork, contemplated with astonishment the facility with which the slimy strips, contorted by heat, underwent the masticating process, preparatory to digestion. At sundown, the appetite of this "genius of famine" was in some degree appeased, and we all went out to collect a pile of drift-wood for the evening; after gossiping until sleepy, we retired for the night.

The morning returned, but not the missing party, and numerous were the conjectures as to what had befallen them. Makaóe thought they might have fallen over a precipice during the night, but Waldron and I concluded they were too wise to grope about pitfalls in the dark. After waiting until eight o'clock, with no tidings from them, I proposed that we should ascend the mountain, with Makaóe for our guide, to see whether they had strayed in that direction; accordingly, we all started off, following up a ravine, until a dividing ridge formed a better path. About a mile and a half from the camp, Waldron gave out and returned, and soon after Makaóe said something about *éha kúu wawái*, (sore feet,) so we dismissed him, while Bob and I plodded on together. Our path soon led through a broad valley of considerable extent, and down a cliff that formed its lower bound, water was trickling as it oozed from the ground above, which had been thoroughly saturated by the recent rains. We continued up the valley, the soil of which was tolerably fertile; it bore traces of having once been extensively cultivated with sweet potatoes, and here we beheld fresh traces of wild hogs ; it was by far the pleasantest portion of the island we had seen. My shoes had by this time been torn from my feet, so that I was compelled to lash the soles on (like sandals) with strong vines, which grew here in abundance. Bob, too, became dissatisfied, and wished to return, but I begged him to hold out a little longer, until we could see the ocean on the other side ; though we had both given up the object of our search, he finally consented, and half an hour afterwards, we saw the continuation of the broad Pacific, having travelled about four miles from our camp. We did not reach the highest point, but even here were seen remains of an extinct crater, perhaps half a mile in diameter, circular in form, and of shallow depth ; it seemed like a basin formed by the sinking of the earth, without disturbing the growth of vegetation that covered it. On our return, we set fire to the dry grass, which, easily igniting, was consumed with great rapidity, for the wind by this time was blowing freshly ; it continued to burn for nearly a week, and served as a beacon for vessels coming from Honolulu.

On our arrival in camp, we found the lost ones awaiting our return, laughing at us for our pains, while Waldron was comforting himself with dried fish and sweet potatoes. It appears that about noon they discovered two fishing huts, tenanted, as they said, by *old folks;* but whether such was the case or not, they found sufficient entertainment to detain them there for the remainder of the day and the following night. They brought with them a small quantity of dried fish, also a few roasted sweet potatoes, the only vegetable cultivated on this island. It was now about eleven o'clock in the forenoon, and it was put to vote whether we should venture to sea, or remain where we were until the wind should somewhat abate, for the channel was very rough.

It was carried in the affirmative by a majority of one ; and collecting our equipage, we deposited it in the boat, which cracked ominously as we launched it over the spar into the water.

It was only after we had shot out beyond the headland of the cove that we experienced the force of the wind, which swept violently through the passage. These inter-island channels during a storm are more dangerous to boats than the open sea, for instead of the long,

heavy swell of the ocean, there is a short sea that is almost continually " combing," threatening to swamp any open boat. It was precisely
such a sea as this that we had to encounter ; and five minutes after
leaving the shore, I would have forfeited any visions of prospective
enjoyment to have been snugly moored again in the cove. But we
had drifted far to leeward of it, and beyond, there was nothing but a
rock-bound coast, against which the waves were beating furiously.
The sea was so heavy that we could not head the boat for Maui, but
were obliged to keep away before the wind towards Lanái in an
opposite direction, and the prospect began to look alarming. The
wind also blew so strongly that we set the sail without the sprit ;
I tended " sheet," which I gave a turn round the after " thawt," and
held the end ready to slacken away in case of emergency. Jack
Burns was at the steering oar, and a better fellow for that all-important post could not have been selected ; Long Jim and Waldron sat
on either side of the mast ; Bob and Makaóe baled incessantly,
while Steve was lying prostrate against the stern sheets, deathly sea-
sick. Had I felt the least inclination to nausea, the sight of those
wild waves roaring around us would have dispelled the sensation.
The boat would shoot upon the crest of a wave, then suddenly plunge
into the trough below, but the careful eye of Burns watched every
sea, as with mathematical precision it struck us at right angles
with the stern. Once a wave broke amidships, completely covering Waldron, besides adding greatly to the water that had already
found its way through the seams of the boat. Presently a sea
raised us high on its summit, then suddenly receding, the bow fell
with such violence upon the water that the two boat-carpenters, Bob
and Waldron, expressed their belief that the " coffin" would be
" stoven" by a similar occurrence. Once more it fell, but with less violence, until the third time, it descended with an appalling crash, and
the flood that rolled aft explained too well the nature of the accident.
All crowded into the stern of the boat, and at that moment I believed
we were going down at once. The two carpenters quickly went
forward to ascertain the extent of the accident, while I gave the
sheet to the winds. Calabashes were broken, and every person who
could, commenced baling. The five minutes that followed were the
most painful I ever experienced before or since. It was playing the

game of life and death, and our excitement was intense as we watched the result of our efforts, seeing whether we could master the enemy that was gaining upon us with rapid stride. The native had stripped as soon as the accident occurred, to buffet the waves: and although a most expert swimmer and diver, I doubt whether he could have survived long amid those seas. The wind blew in squalls, and so violently that we could not hear each other's voices from opposite extremities of the boat. Presently Bob returned, and reported that the " garboard streak," or lower plank that attaches to the kelson, was split from the bow to " amidships," and that at each plunge it opened an inch forward ; that the bow beams had started, and he had left Waldron to hold them together. At his suggestion, and being the lightest, I stood upon the gunwale, and reaching as high as I could, with a sheath-knife, cut the stay of the mast ; and taking this and a blanket, I went into the bow of the boat, endeavoring to pass the blanket under and secure it by the rope. This required many efforts, for I could only work as the boat rose on a sea ; at each downward plunge I was compelled to hold fast, for the impetus was sufficient to throw me headlong ; as it was, my head and arms were frequently under water. After considerable labor, I accomplished the task, and returned to baling, leaving Waldron lying at full length and holding the beams together with his hands, in which position, half immersed, he remained for nearly an hour.

To make a long story short, after two hours' suspense, we were once more in comparatively still water, between Molokíni and Maui ; and getting out our oars, we laughed at the danger we had undergone, as we swept slowly in towards the rocky shore, where a number of natives were assembled to witness our arrival. When within a few yards of the beach, the steering strap parted, (a miracle that it had not happened before !) and as we had unshipped our oars, the boat was unmanageable ; accordingly, we jumped into the water, waist-deep, and held it, to avoid collision with the rocks. What the *akókoa* bushes had ruined in appearance, my exertions in the boat had rendered useless for service, and I preferred remaining in the water to running the gauntlet through a bevy of females, until one of them, observing my discomfiture, kindly loaned me a shawl to reconcile any deficiencies that might exist between garments and their duty.

They had watched us with glasses from the plantation, and when the sail disappeared they gave us up for lost. Our troubles were forgotten while indulging in a warm supper provided by Mrs. Páli, who looked commiseratingly upon her husband as she said, "*Mai máke oe,*" (you were most dead.) The experiences of that day furnished a salutary lesson to us all, never to go wrecking without a conveyance suited to the emergency, lest the wreckers become the wrecked.

CHAPTER XVI.

CAVERNS—MOUNTAIN AND SUBMARINE.

There is a natural curiosity two miles south of Ulupalakúa, which, though limited in extent, is worth the attention of tourists. It is a cavern about half a mile in length and of limited breadth, probably formed by the cooling of the outer edges and upper surface of the lava, while that beneath rolled out in a fluid state, and this at a period beyond tradition, when the angry goddess Péle, from her ancient throne, had poured forth the vials of her wrath to desolate the fields of the superstitious Hawaiians.

I forget the occasion, but it was a holiday, and as the cave was said to be a famous pigeon-roost, some half dozen of us, with our fowling-pieces, made up a party for a hunting excursion. Mrs. Páli and Mrs. Burns accompanied their husbands, to visit acquaintances residing in the immediate vicinity of the cavern. The weather was unexceptionably fine. After leaving the cane-fields, we came upon the homesteads of the natives—grass-houses, with their groves of banana-trees and small cultivations of mountain taro. This portion of the estate is bounded by the premises of Steve, consisting of a substantial grass-house and its appertaining outbuildings; near by was a walled inclosure of small irregular blocks of lava, which abound in this vicinity, containing a number of porkers; and the whole was almost surrounded by a grove of banana-trees. It required no strenuous arguments to prevail upon its proprietor to shoulder his gun and accompany us. The two girls added their entreaties, and Mrs. Chapman slipped on one of her best *holokús* (dresses) and joined her companions. We led the van, and the matrons and half a dozen boys brought up the rear.

The appearance of the country as we advanced was more rugged, and the travelling exceedingly difficult; the ancient lava being somewhat decomposed, its surface was covered with a light but rich soil, hidden in its turn by thick bushes and creeping vines, so that out of the narrow trail that had been worn, it would be a fatiguing task to pick one's way over the sharp stones that covered the surface; as it was, our path was tedious, and we were compelled to advance in single file. With the exception of here and there a shady *kukúi*, there were no trees, though the ground was thickly covered with bushes. We lost sight of the plantation by intervening hills, and for miles the eye wandered over a solitary tract to the sea-shore, seldom relieved by the lonely hut of the native. There were no streams, no groves, not even a warbler to enliven the scene; a broad black belt of scoria lay like the pall of desolation upon the southwestern shore. These hills and valleys had once been cultivated, and numerous habitations dotted the landscape, but the events of half a century have left only the relics of a once numerous people; frequently we stumbled against low walls rising in terraces upon the hillside, but now overgrown with creeping plants.

After an hour's walk, a shout from some of our party in advance announced that the cave had been reached. We stood on the brink of a circular pit, as nearly as I can recollect about fifty feet in depth, and the same extent in diameter; its walls were precipitous and rocky, often perforated with deep holes; the bottom was covered with vegetation, and here were growing several large *kukúi* trees. The entrance to the cavern was by a fissure in the rock on the *markái*, or sea-side.

Our guns being ready as we approached, the solitudes re-echoed the bang, bang, that was heard as the pigeons rose in the air, and half a dozen fell at the first discharge. Steve, who professed to be thoroughly acquainted with their habits, said we would have abundance of leisure to explore the cave and the surrounding country, if so disposed, for the pigeons would not return again until afternoon. Accordingly, we all descended by a narrow path down the face of the rock, and at the entrance found torches, composed of dry bushes and stout weeds, that had been prepared by natives who resort to this cavern for water. These we unceremoniously appropriated. Those of our party acquainted with the locality took precedence, and we commenced the descent through the aperture on our hands and knees, and soon emerged into a chamber of pitchy darkness. The glare of our torches flashed over a broad chamber, perhaps fifteen feet in height; its sides were visible, but the lower extremity was buried in gloom. The outer edge of the lava having cooled first, the liquid mass, in its passage through, had sometimes adhered to the compact portions, and congealed in grotesque shapes: from the arched roof that rose over us like a dome, dark masses were pendent, tapering gradually from their bases like the stalactites of limestone caverns. The presence of the glittering spar existing in those concretions was wanting, to throw out coruscations by torch-light, which here only brought forth in bold relief the more prominent masses, while others were lost amid the deep solitude. The floor was covered with fragments of lava, and in one place was a small pool of pure water that had percolated by drops through the rocks above; this afforded a display of native economy, for the element being a rarity in this region, the cavern is a natural reservoir for those residing in its immediate vicinity. Light wicker frames had been constructed and placed beneath the dropping water; over these were laid banana leaves, having a convenient slope, and which served as conduits for the liquid that was received in large calabashes, placed at the lower extremity, and which we found filled with pure cold water.

This ancient repository for the dead had perhaps never re-echoed the mirthful voices of so merry a party as now explored its gloomy arches and dark recesses; the children, laughing and shouting, led the way with the torches, often pausing to light the path for others whenever they reached a dangerous pitfall. Once the vault seemed contracted to a narrow tunnel; emerging from which, we entered a spacious chamber, whose dome was too lofty to be illumined by the dim light of our torches. Here I noticed several small heaps of broken lava that had been piled up by the natives, but I know not for what purpose. Bob suggested extinguishing all the torches, to which we consented, and taking them from the hands of their bearers, he trampled upon the ignited portions, to the consternation of the women and children, who, with true Hawaiian superstition, were afraid of the *akuas* (ghosts) of deceased progenitors that haunted the apartment. The darkness was painfully profound, and none of us ventured from our position; having a moment to reflect, we found ourselves covered with a cold perspiration, consequent upon exertion in the confined and chilling atmosphere. After listening to the protestations of the females against such proceedings, Bob drew a box of matches from his pocket, and relighted the torches.

Nearly an hour had been passed in this dismal vault, when we crept through the aperture, and emerged once more into daylight. Four of our party concealed themselves beneath trees to await the return of the pigeons in the afternoon, while two or three of us, for whom a tramp among the hills possessed greater attractions than tender joints, shouldered our guns and marched off. The females proceeded to pay their morning visits to acquaintances, of which there were about a dozen families in the neighborhood. During our ramble, we approached a house, half hidden by a clump of *kukúi* trees; and not far off, heard a continued clicking sound, which Bob informed me was some one beating *kápa*, or native cloth, and soon after, seated beneath a low natural arch, admirably adapted for the purpose, we saw a septuagenarian engaged at this almost obsolete occupation. She relaxed her wrinkled features into something like a smile as she welcomed us with a half-stifled *alóha;* but soon after, replacing the pulpy mass upon the dry log, she took up her square wooden beater, and the monotonous sound of click, click, click, in rapid succession, awoke the solitude.

Farther up the mountain, we discovered the ruins of an old *heiáu,* or temple, almost overgrown with young trees and creeping vines. All that now remained of it were two low compactly-built walls running at right angles with each other. A commanding site had been chosen by the priests for its erection, where they could celebrate

their orgies amid the sublimities of nature.   In front was the broad
extent of landscape, diversified by hill, valley, and scattered groves,
bounded by the sea-shore ; on the right, half concealed by projecting ridges, loomed the barren island of Kahuláwe, and on the left,
the snow-clad summits of Máuna Lóa and Máuna Kéa rose in
grandeur above the clouds.   In the rear was an almost impenetrable
forest.

During the afternoon we returned to our companions at the cave,
and learned that their patience had been but poorly rewarded, and
assembling the stragglers, we made our way towards home.   The
pigeons spoken of are not indigenous to Hawaii.   They were originally carried there, and reared as are doves at home, of which they
are the same species.   Many of them have become wild, and brood
their young in caves or perforated cliffs.   The food found in their
crops is usually the seed of the broom-corn, which grows wild upon
the mountains.   Along the lowlands and upon the broad common that
unites East with West Maui, plover are abundant, but exceedingly
shy.   They are called by the natives *koréa*, from the peculiar sound
they emit when flying.   The higher class of game consists of wild-
ducks that congregate around pools in uninhabited districts, and
among swampy tracts or taro-patches.   Turkeys have also strayed
abroad, and become as shy as their species in our western forests,
and a long range is required to reach them.   They are usually hunted
on horseback.   In the forests wild hogs are found, some of them
formidable fellows ; but the inequalities of the land and the dense
growth of underwood prevent the pursuit of them by sportsmen.

I was much interested by a visit made one day in company with
Mr. Torbert to some ancient wells situated in the midst of the mountain forest.   His object was to ascertain the exact distance from the
water to his house, with a view of laying at some future period conduits for its transmission ; and for this purpose we carried compass
and chain.   The distance, I think, was a mile and a half in a
straight line.   We found a circuitous path leading to them ; and
having ascended about two miles, emerged to an opening in the
forest, where the mountain at this point seemed to have formed a
shallow basin, unobstructed by trees, and perhaps half a mile in circumference.   The bottom was covered with coarse grasses, and the

ferns that everywhere grew in rank luxuriance were frequently clinging in parasitic clusters around moss-covered trunks, and nourished
by the humid atmosphere. In one or two instances, these completely
obliterated all traces of excavation, and in descending to examine
the wells, we were compelled to proceed carefully, feeling our way
with poles, to avoid being ensnared. These reservoirs, perhaps
twenty in number, were scattered about the basin, and nearly all of
them contained pure water. There is no authentic account of their
having been made, or resorted to, subsequent to the discovery of the
islands by Captain Cook, and this, together with other circumstances,
would indicate that the population was on the wane prior to his arrival.
As the various lands extending from the sea-shore converge towards
the mountain's summit, it is probable that each district had its own
wells, and that they were visited by their respective proprietors.
Mr. Torbert proposed making an extensive excavation, thus uniting
all the wells into one reservoir; as they are never known to be dry,
the plan is a good one, and might be adopted with comparatively
trifling expense. It unfortunately happens that the leeward portion
of these islands is sadly destitute of water, but nature has in some
respects compensated for this deficiency by the heavy dews;
among the streams and valleys of the lowlands more thrifty and
well-conditioned cattle cannot be seen than those whose only moisture
is obtained from the grass upon the mountains. The natives place
broad calabashes under the drooping leaves of the pandanus-trees,
which abound in this vicinity, to receive it as it drops, so that their
beverage is literally the sparkling dew-drops. The wells alluded to
are nearly five thousand feet above the level of the sea.

Near the landing at Honuaúla, there is a remarkable submarine
grot, which might furnish as poetic a theme as that spoken of
by Marriner at the Tonga Islands, and adopted by Byron in his
"Island." Descending from the road among the dark rocks that
bound the sea, to a huge boulder conspicuous amid those around it,
a loud, hissing noise is heard, like steam escaping from a safety-
valve. This is occasioned by the motion of the sea. When it
recedes, the air is forced down through the aperture by atmospheric
pressure with a peculiar sucking sound, and as the wave returns, it
is forced outward again with the hissing noise before mentioned, so

that the phenomenon is momentarily repeated. This breathing-hole is twenty yards from the shore, which is bold and rocky. The cavern is reached by diving from the rock to the depth of twenty-five feet, when the entrance is discovered, a broad, dark passage, into which the diver turns and swims boldly for about fifteen feet, then ascending gradually, he emerges to the white sandy beach of the interior.

None other than expert divers and native " mermaids" have ventured into this Syren chamber, and their accounts of it are marvellous. Besides describing a wonderful marine plant, to which they attribute medicinal properties, they say that their bodies look white—" as white as the snows of Máuna Lóa." The cavern, being on the western side of the island, is only visited when the sun is past meridian and unobscured. Even then, the rays of light refracted at those azure depths, and faintly transmitted through the gloomy passage, can only illumine the vault with a sepulchral glow.

In bidding adieu to Ulapalakúa, I do so with regret, for with it are linked the earliest impressions that have combined to foster a taste for Polynesian adventure, and to instil an appreciation of Hawaiian hospitality, both native and foreign. Though it lack the waving groves and gushing fountains of poetic imagery, its rocks and broad fields possess a fascinating power that lends a charm to every incident associated with them. Not the least pleasing reminiscence is to review again the happy and contented faces that have lent animation to scenes where nature has poured out her harvests of plenty ; and I cannot forbear expressing a conviction that the efforts of the enterprising proprietor will be successfully rewarded ; also the hope that he may long continue, as he has ever been, an example of perseverance to those around him.

CHAPTER XVII.

KAWAIHÁE—TRAGEDY—COURTSHIP.

If the recital of incidents possessing little interest has not already grown wearisome, let the indulgent reader skip over an interval of two years, and join me on a pleasure excursion to Hawaii, the largest island of the group, and which perhaps neither of us has yet visited. Though our conveyance is one of the small coasters that cruise among the islands, she holds her way with a will against the southwest wind, and in earnest of her efforts, is scattering the brine fore and aft in fine style.

Our first port of destination was Kawaiháe, a town situate on the northwest side of the island ; and as the schooner had just come into the possession of owners unacquainted with the ports of Hawaii, it was deemed prudent to hug the wind as closely as possible until near enough to the shore to discover the locality sought. The morning was fine, and the unclouded rays of the sun shone with dazzling effect upon the lofty snow-covered summits, trending with gentle declivity to the clouds. The bold outline of hill and valley became every moment more distinctly defined, and the broad landscape swept upward in varied undulations to the dark summit of Hualalái. There were strips of white sand-beach, flecked with black rocks of lava, the whole sometimes relieved by clusters of cocoanut-trees, giving shelter to a few grass-huts. Beyond, the soil looked dry and parched, and huge boulders were scattered thickly over the surface, which was now and then varied by black serpentine streams of congealed lava. Farther up, the scenery improved, being diversified by green hummocks and tempting groves, but there was not even the shadow of a rill to lend an air of life and freshness. The black jagged rock connecting two green hills like a wall would be a perfect gem, could we but trace the silver thread of a mountain stream leaping from crag to crag in its giddy course. Beneath the white clouds, a belt of evergreen forest encircles the mountain ; above, there is naught but desolate grandeur.

By noon we were anchored off the port of Kawaihâe. This was one of the most lonely places dignified with the name of port I had ever visited ; it consists merely of half a dozen framed houses, scattered at wide intervals along the rocky shore, and perhaps a couple of dozen native huts, suspiciously separated from each other ; a few cocoanut-trees charitably extend their broad plumes over the miserable abodes that craved their protection.   With all its. faults, Kawaihâe must not be too hastily condemned, for it is but the humble gate to a paradise among the mountains ; I mean Waiméa, distant from the shore eight miles, and enjoying the temperature of perpetual spring, at an elevation of 7,000 feet above the sea.   It may be that " distance lends enchantment to the view," but from what I could observe of it by the aid of a powerful glass, I should judge the scenery around to be lovely.   At this place may be seen the ruins of one of the largest *heiáus* to be found throughout the group, but as our stay was limited, I did not visit it.

With Kawaihâe is connected an historical incident of considerable interest, for here Keóua, (the eldest son and successor of King Kalaiopú, whose name is so intimately associated with that of Captain Cook,) who was the last rival of Kamehaméha I., was barbarously assassinated.   A melancholy interest attaches itself to this last of a race of kings.   Not content with his acknowledged supremacy over a portion of the island, he aspired to the sovereignty of the whole, to which he considered himself the legitimate heir.   The battle of Keéi was fought, in which his brother was slain and his followers routed, Keóua himself taking refuge among his adherents in Hilo, on the eastern side of the island.   Among them he resided for several years, but in 1789 he marshalled his forces for a final attack upon those of Kamehaméha upon the western shores.   He took the road across the island by the way of the volcano, and encamped in its vicinity.   During the night an eruption occurred, by which eighty warriors were destroyed.   He continued his march, and engaged with the forces of Kamehaméha, under his chief Kaiána, at a place called Kailikíi, or the southernmost portion of the island. Here he was defeated and compelled to retreat, but was overtaken by the victorious army, when another battle was fought, and his forces completely destroyed, Keóua saving himself by flying to the mountains, attended by a few faithful followers. After roaming amid the forests for some time, he determined to abdicate forever in favor of his fortunate rival, and for this purpose he requested permission of Kaiána to pass through his forces unmolested. This was granted, and he embarked in a canoe near the scene of his discomfiture, and sailed along the western shores to surrender himself to Kamehaméha, then residing at Kawaiháe.

On his way thither he stopped at several places where the inhabitants, who were devotedly attached to him, testified their pleasure at seeing him by various acceptable presents, and some of them prophesied with lamentations that he would never return. Kamehaméha, with characteristic magnanimity, renewed the assurances of his kind intention ; but there was with him a ferocious chief, named Kéeaumóku, who had determined on his death. Kamehaméha was standing upon the beach, surrounded by his chiefs, when the canoe bearing the fallen king approached, and fearful lest the royal clemency should be manifested in his behalf, Kéeaumóku waded into the water, and seizing hold of the canoe with one hand, despite the threats and remonstrances of the chiefs on shore, he stabbed Keoúa to the heart with a dagger, besides several of his friends who came in the same canoe. This is but one of the many dark scenes in Hawaiian history.

I was somewhat surprised at meeting a transient acquaintance at this place, whom I had not seen for more than two years, and who, for a week previous to our arrival, had been on a visit to Waiméa. It was Dr. L——, of San Francisco, and for want of better occupation at the time, I proposed a stroll along the beach, to which he readily consented, and I afterwards discovered he had an object in view.

It appears that about a year previous, on a visit to this place, he had found a modest and unassuming little girl, (I quote his own words,) whose simplicity of manner had completely won his esteem. He had indubitable proof that her deportment was moral, and had consequently bestowed upon her various testimonials of his regard, such as wreaths, dresses, pin money, and a piece of gold, all of which she was pleased to accept, and in earnest of reciprocal sentiments, she smiled bewitchingly, banqueted him on fish and *poi*, bestowed an oc-

12

casional kiss, and whispered *alóha*. The doctor had made no decided progress in his suit, owing to his ignorance of the language; he could smile, and " look unutterable things," and even brush away the flies with the *kahíli*, as she reclined upon the mats, but the main thing, a mutual interchange of sentiment, was out of the question. I saw at once his object ; he wished to avail himself of my services as interpreter.   I promised that my best efforts should be exerted to promote his proxical courtship, provided his intentions were honest.

He led me a long way from the town, over a sandy beach, to a small grove of cocoanut-trees that were leaning affectionately seaward, their branches rustling in the breeze.   Here were three or four houses, and one of them conspicuous amid those around it, by its elevated position and rude wall of lava, was said to contain the object in question.   A dilapidated canoe-house in one corner of the inclosure, containing two canoes, denoted some pretension to property ; besides, there were sundry other articles, such as nets, poi boards, a stone-pounder, fractured calabashes, and two or three samples of hardware ; in short, the ordinary appurtenances of a Hawaiian household.   The doctor's claims gave him the right of precedence, and much to my surprise, we found the Hawaiian belle reclining upon light mats of the pandanus, supported by pillows, while two or three old women were assiduously engaged fanning her, and a third attendant was dressing her hair, giving the scene an effect semi-oriental, semi-barbaric.

" Isn't she pretty ?" was the first question.

I confess that I was disappointed ; from the doctor's description, I expected nothing less than a paragon of beauty and excellence ; though certainly interesting, pretensions to superior charms would have been ill-founded.   She possessed in an ordinary degree the characteristics of Hawaiian beauty—hair black and glossy, and brows prettily arched, but, what is unusual, the orb beneath shone with a dim lustre ; with reference to the nasal organ, there was a tendency to fullness of nostril, though whenever she smiled two rows of unexceptionable teeth were displayed.   Her air of unsophisticated innocence contrasted so strongly with the vivacity peculiar to native girls at her age, that I suspected she had received her tuition from the officious mammas, who flattered themselves that their *protegée* was every way worthy of aspiring to the hand and purse of an M.D. She wore a loose white muslin robe, and her small ankles and feet were concealed by white stockings and morocco slippers. A pair of broad gold earrings, and several showy appendages of the same material upon her fingers, were evidences of the doctor's prodigality. Around her neck, suspended by a black ribbon, she wore th identical piece of gold, which spoke volumes in her favor.

She received us with an affectation of languor, without changing her recumbent position. I was introduced as a confidential friend, which was interpreted without any embellishment. It is unnecessary to recapitulate the conversation that ensued, in which the old women took a conspicuous part. " Had she ever resided in Honolulu or Lahaina?" " No. Her peregrinations extended only to Waiméa and the districts adjoining. In their opinion, girls who frequented such large towns, and were fond of travelling, were no better than they should be. For their part, they didn't approve of rearing children in ignorance. The child could read, write, sew, and sing, and was in fact superior to the ' ordinary run ' of girls." One of them inquired of me, I thought rather seriously, whether the doctor was in earnest ; also as to his general character, and ability to maintain a wife and *her family* with becoming dignity.

By this time I had concluded that he was perpetrating only a serious joke, and that his " earnest regard" was stronger than his love. I replied that I had always thought him a nice young man, possessing all the qualifications for making a young lady happy ; that he was sometimes eccentric, and required careful watching ; and that it consequently behooved them to " keep an eye to windward," for so good a daughter required the most amiable of husbands.

The hair-dresser fidgeted about, and ventured to hint that a certain piece of land in the district of Kohála was then in the market, and was remarkable for its large growth of taro and sweet potatoes. Meanwhile, the young lady (I have forgotten her name) had dispossessed the doctor of his chain, and twined it about her neck with true female vanity, while his diamond ring was sparkling upon her *thumb*. To a question of his, whether she would accompany him to Honolulu, she replied, " Yes, if you'll marry me before I go !"

We remained here about half an hour, and then returned to the party at the landing, which had been augmented during our absence by a few straggling foreigners and a number of inquisitive natives of both sexes.   Captain B—— having transacted his business in this place, we had nothing further to delay our departure.   How the doctor's suit subsequently progressed I could never learn, for that evening he sailed for Honolulu, and I for Kailúa, nor have we ever seen each other since.

CHAPTER XVIII.

K A I L Ú A .

THE land-breeze, ladened with sweet perfume, came tardily that night, but cool and fresh from the mountain.   The full moon smiled upon the melting undulations of hill and valley, chasing the giant palm-shadows from the tranquil lagoon ; and the steady rustling of the gale, as it rippled the moonlit water, mingled with the monotonous roar of the breakers, to lull the sleeping landscape.   The extended sails smiled a welcome, and hurried us once more along the dark shores of Kóna.

The following morning found us a long way from Kawaiháe.   The district of Kóna wore the same general appearance that we had noticed at Kohála, except an apparent increase of sterility along the shore, for it now presented an almost unbroken barrier of black lava, against which the waves were surging with a noise like distant thunder.   In some places were spacious tunnels beneath the surface of the rock, open to the sea, and communicating with the air by large irregular fissures.   Compressed within the narrow limits of these subterranean passages, the waves are hurried along with immense power, until they escape from their dark caverns, bursting upward in lofty jets and clouds of foam and spray, with an effect indescribably grand.   Few huts were seen, and these, grouped together in solitary hamlets, only gave a more marked aspect to the general desolation.

I said we were going to Kailúa, which means either *Ocean Cave* or *Two Seas*, but neither of us knew where it was, and we had only a few desultory directions for our guidance. Summed up, they amounted to a good-sized town, in which the church and governor's house were conspicuous ; then, after " rounding the black pint," we would see a battery of guns. Add to this a few scattered cocoanut groves, and our sailing directions were complete. At noon we observed a double canoe under sail, containing three persons, and standing along the shore just outside the breakers. We hauled upon the wind sufficiently to form an angle of meeting, determined, if possible, to press one of them on board as a pilot. In due time the canoe was alongside. Its occupants were an elderly couple and a lad about fifteen years of age. It was from Hilo, ladened with fruit, and bound for Kailúa. The old man placed the boy at our disposal, who came up to me with a knowing look, and inquired in good English whether I knew him.

" No ; who are you ?"

" Máuna Lóa," (great mountain.)

I recognized him at once, and in order to be sure, pulled his slouched hat off his bullet head, and found his bristly hair cropped short as ever. He had grown incredibly ; two years before, while leading a rambling life on East Maui, I had taken the young vagrant into my service ; if surveying or other duties called me abroad, Máuna Lóa, much to his annoyance, had a knapsack strapped on to his shoulders, and occasionally endured forced marches on an empty stomach. In sporting, he was serviceable in various ways, for he sometimes carried the gun, and always the game, and it was his duty to climb the cliffs and scare the pigeons from their rocky nests. In cooking, fishing, and running errands, he was generally useful : the art of polishing boots he had acquired in Honolulu. However, he ultimately became so mischievous and saucy, that I gave him indefinite leave of absence ; since then, he had led an erratic life, with various occupations, from setting up ten-pins in Honolulu, to weeding taro-patches in Lahaina, and he now very coolly proffered a renewal of his former services. He was given to understand that a seat upon the windlass bitts, and keeping a sharp look-out, would be the most becoming position he could then occupy, a hint he was careful to take, and he remained at his post until we dropped anchor in the roadstead of Kailúa at half past one o'clock.

In point of scenery, this was the most interesting spot visited since leaving Lahaina ; like most native villages, the houses were distributed with greater reference to convenience than regularity. Exclusive of the few substantial dwellings of foreigners, they consisted chiefly of the ordinary grass-houses, which, from a superficial observation, were scattered over the area of a mile. Situated in the rear of the village, upon an eminence, was the house of Governor Adams, built, I think, of stone, and neatly whitewashed, having extensive inclosures. The church was of liberal dimensions, and occupied a central position ; it singularly happened that the steeple, which had been standing for years, fell with a crash about fifteen minutes after we had landed. There were several varieties of trees, but the cocoanut was most conspicuous. The anchorage is protected on the north by a low point of lava, extending into the sea, forming a tolerable protection against northerly winds. Here were a number of rusty guns of various calibre, either mounted on indifferent carriages, or lying upon the ground. This point, which is composed entirely of lava, was formed by an eruption from one of the craters of Hualalái, about fifty years ago, but whose fires have long been quiescent. In its course the molten flood destroyed several hamlets and plantations, filling up a bay twenty miles in extent.

The soil of Kailúa and its immediate vicinity is thickly covered with volanic evidences, but towards the mountain, where the soil is deeper and richer, are the cultivations of the natives. Here the banana, sugar-cane, melons, mountain taro, and sweet potatoes are thriving. At a greater elevation the soil improves, consisting of a rich vegetable mould and decomposed lava, where the bread-fruit, orange, and *ohia* grow luxuriantly. The latter is the apple of Hawaii, a red and juicy fruit, and so strongly resembling that of the temperate zone, that when an apple finds its way to this group, it is called by the natives " *ohia háuri,*" or foreign apple. The average height of the tree is twenty feet, having oblong pointed leaves, which are not perennial ; like those of the deciduous plant it resembles, they wither and fall during the winter months.

Southeast of the town are several lava caverns similar to the one described in East Maui ; that was reached by descending, while these are tunnelled into the side of the mountain ; one of them, called Lanikéa, is of considerable extent, and contains a large pool of brackish water. As is the case throughout the entire sea-board of Western Hawaii, Kailúa is sadly deficient in fresh water.

It was the design of Mr. L——, the owner, who accompanied us, to purchase a cargo of oranges, sweet potatoes, and poultry for the San Francisco market, but several traders having recently been here, these staples could not be procured ; our informant, Mr. Rice, an old resident, intimated that at either Kealakekúa or Keauhó, the desired produce might be obtained, without much difficulty. The sun was at this time about three hours high ; we rowed back to the schooner, took in two additional oarsmen, making seven of us in all, and started for Keauhó. Again our directions were either indifferently given or carelessly observed, resulting in a long and tedious pull, without discovering our place of destination. A few days previous there had been a gale from the southwest, which had left a heavy swell setting on shore from that direction, and to avoid the rollers that were breaking heavily along the whole extent of coast, we stood well out, and a landing at any point seemed impracticable. The shore was a uniform line of black rocks ; add to this the unchanging background of the mountains, the interminable array of cocoanut-trees, and the similarity in appearance of the hamlets successively passed, and an excuse may be offered for our want of success.

It was near sunset when we reversed our course, and before we had accomplished half the distance, night overtook us. It was quite dark, for the moon had not yet risen, but we could hear the breakers boiling under our lee like a caldron; in this way we rowed for three hours, guided by them and the lights that glimmered at intervals on shore. We reached the schooner at eight, with garments drenched and strong appetites.

CHAPTER XIX.

" THE PATHWAY OF THE GODS."

AT four in the morning the anchor was weighed for Ke-a-la-ke-kú-a. We continued fanning along until daylight, when the breeze left us becalmed, in company with two small native schooners, one ahead and the other astern.   Calms are the chief annoyance incident to voyaging in Hawaiian waters, and passages are usually made to lee-ward of the islands, where they are of frequent occurrence.   This inconvenience is in some degree obviated by the land breeze that blows gently from the mountains before midnight, and extends a short distance seaward, so that experienced coasters usually hug the shore. This has reference to the larger islands ; in most of the channels the northeast trades blow uniformly.

We did not reach Kealakekúa until the middle of the afternoon; this extensive bay will ever be memorable in Hawaiian annals, as being the spot where the celebrated voyager, Cook, met his untimely fate.   The narrative of this event is too familiar to require further attention.

Its name is derived from a remarkable landslide down the face of a precipitous cliff that rises abruptly from the water near the head of the bay ; it signifies, " The Pathway of the Gods."   The tradition connected with the spot is, that on one occasion a mythic divinity, in his anxiety to cross over to the south side of the harbor, chose the most expeditious route instead of making a long detour, and, in an unbecoming attitude for an immortal, slid down the steep descent, making so decided an impress that his path is visible at the present day.   Posterity has never been enlightened as to the nature of this urgent mission.

In the cliff are several caverns, which were formerly used as re-positories for the dead.   On the north side of the bay, where the fatal battle occurred, was the once populous town of Ka-wa-ló-a, now a small hamlet, and inferior to the villages on the east and south-ern sides of the bay.   We found here a Californian trader, that had just completed its cargo, and from the captain, Mr. L———, learned that his only alternative would be to proceed at once to Keauhó.

A landing was with difficulty effected, owing to the heavy surf. The passage was intricate, and bounded by jagged rocks. With a native pilot, we watched an opportunity and shot in on a roller, and about midway, turning suddenly to the left, reached the beach without accident, although it was only by skilful management that the boat was prevented from being stove. A crowd of natives were lounging upon the shore, some of whom assisted us to haul up our boat, after which we passed through the village of grass-houses, on our way to the residence of Mr. Cumming, Collector of the Port, and an American. This and the adjoining outbuildings were pleasantly located. They were built of stone, plastered, and neatly white-washed. The dwelling had a verandah in front, where we enjoyed the sea-breeze, and watched the movements of the natives of both sexes, who were gossiping good-humoredly and hanging lazily around. Mr. Cumming advised us to take horses and proceed directly to Keauhó, and by ascertaining the condition of the supplies at that place, we would avoid the trouble of visiting it in the schooner, if a cargo was not to be procured.

Before leaving, a well-dressed young native came up from the crowd, and shaking hands with me, inquired whether I recognized him. A second look discovered it to be the lawyer who accompanied the surveying party to Molokai, and who was so fond of exhibiting his *palapála*, (diploma.) With him, as with Mark Meddle, " costs, actions, and damages must have arisen like sky-rockets in his aspiring mind ;". for he had steadily worked his way up to the dignity of either police magistrate or district judge, and had become a person of considerable importance in his own estimation. He insisted on my accompanying him to his residence, a short distance to the left of where we then were. It proved to be a substantial grass-house, comfortably furnished. Its occupants at the time were his wife and her sister, both young and pretty, and neatly attired, the latter having her head encircled with a wreath of flowers. He introduced me to them as his friend, and I was much pleased with their modest deportment and courteous behavior. They invited me to be seated, and his wife provided a large plate of delicious oranges, also a bunch of choice bananas.   After leave-taking, I found L—— sitting in the verandah, waiting patiently for a native to saddle a couple of horses he had just hired.

We mounted, and rode through the village ; then turning short to the left, ascended the heights above the town by a good path, and galloped along the road to the north.

Our route lay across the most rugged tract of lava I had yet seen, but over it a good road had been constructed by filling the inequalities with fragments, and covering the whole with grass and earth.   There were deep chasms, and huge black masses had been thrown up in every conceivable shape, the very picture of chaos.   It seemed as if a vast flood, while in a semi-fluid state, had, by some mighty agency, been rent asunder, and whirled and tossed by a tempest of elements, until congealed in its present form.   We had no time to make any minute examination, but continued on, gradually descending, and passing through small hamlets along the sea-shore, which was an uninterrupted wall of lava, against which the sea was violently surging.

We rode by a classic spot in Hawaiian history, Kuamú, for here, in 1819, was fought the decisive battle which forever banished idolatry from this group.   The heathen party was commanded by Kekuaokaláni, (the God of Heaven,) and Kalaimokú, who commanded the forces of King Liholiho, was cousin to the former.   The morning of the battle, a messenger was dispatched to the heathen party, to effect, if possible, a reconciliation ; but the young chief, urged on by the priests, was inexorable, and so bitter was the hatred of his party, that the messenger with difficulty escaped with his life. The forces of Kalaimokú occupied the sea-shore, while those of Kekuaokaláni were intrenched behind a wall farther up.   The battle commenced ; and after some sharp fighting, the latter were forced from their position, and fell back a short distance.   Here the young chief rallied his warriors for a final effort, but being himself faint from loss of blood and unable to stand, he sat upon a fragment of lava, loaded, and fired his musket twice upon the advancing party, but soon after, receiving a ball in his breast, he fell and expired. His courageous wife, Manóa, had fought by his side during the day with a heroism worthy of a better cause.   After his death, seeing

Kalaimokú advancing with his sister, she craved their protection, but ere it could be extended, a bullet pierced her brain, and she expired by the side of her husband. The spot is still shown where this brave and affectionate pair received the last rites of sepulture. This incident is beautifully described by Mr. Ellis.

We reached Keauhó at sunset, and proceeding at once to the only framed house in the village, I was agreeably surprised to find it occupied by an old acquaintance, Captain O———, who had renounced his allegiance to Neptune to render homage to that peaceful divinity, Pomona. This was evident from the fact of his having on the mountain-side an extensive cultivation of squashes suffering from drought, and upon which he was constantly invoking a liquid blessing from every passing cloud. The village consisted of perhaps twenty-five houses, but save a few pandanus and cocoanut trees, and here and there a creeping convolvulus, I do not recollect seeing any other signs of vegetation. There is a small cove here, of sufficient depth of water and capacity to afford a safe harbor for two or three schooners, though somewhat obstructed by large blocks of coral.

This spot is interesting from its being the birth-place of Kamehaméha the Great, and the relics of one of his war-canoes is still shown to visitors. It is now subservient to more humble purposes, for at the time I saw it, it sheltered a fine brood of young turkeys.

L——— was in luck; he could obtain here everything desired, and it was arranged that Captain O——— should return with us to Kealakekúa and pilot the schooner into the harbor. After partaking of a hasty supper, we started off with two horses between three persons. This inconvenience, if such it could be called, (for I preferred walking,) was obviated by alternately changing situations. The distance between the two places is about four miles, but ere it had been half accomplished, it had become so dark that we were compelled to pick our way carefully over the uneven surface of the lava. Captain O——— suggested reaching the schooner by way of Kawalóa, situate on the north side of the bay. Accordingly, we struck off from the road, intending to " shape a course" by the sea-shore, which was still a good distance off. The present instance furnished a happy illustration of " the blind leading the blind." After patiently guiding the horses, and feeling the way with our hands, with no prospect of ultimately bettering our condition, we questioned O—— more closely as to his knowledge of localities. The result was, that he " didn't know, but *guessed* he could find the way." Our only hope was in discovering a native from whom we could obtain information. After a long delay we were successful, and learned to our dismay, that, owing to steep precipices, it would be impossible to reach Kawalóa by the shore, and that we must retrograde as we had come. A few invectives were muttered, while mentally wishing our guide had remained at Keauhó ; but after gaining the highway once more, unfriendly sentiments vanished. We reached the hill whence we had started, and turning to the right, commenced the descent towards Kawalóa. The path was steep and winding, being covered with loose fragments of lava. L—— considered it dangerous, and dismounted, but I retained my seat in the saddle, though the quadruped that bore it would sometimes brace himself resolutely and slide on " all-fours."

Captain O—— pointed out to us on the left a dark tumulus, built of lava blocks, where the body of Captain Cook had been burned. On the eminence to the left was the spot where his observatory had been erected. Soon after, we reached Kawalóa, but its inhabitants had retired to rest, and our march through the town was only disturbed by dogs, which kept up an incessant barking. The houses looked dilapidated and gloomy, and the dark shadows of the cocoapalms seemed to heighten the effect.

On arriving at the shore, we hailed the schooner, which we knew was anchored somewhere in the darkness, but obtained no reply. O—— suggested appropriating a canoe, but this would have been unfair, without the owner's consent. We therefore concluded to separate, and beat about the village until we could find some one who would ferry us aboard. L—— remained upon the shore, while O—— climbed over a wall into a yard, where he was instantly beset by dogs. I returned by the path we came, to a hut where I had noticed the twinkling of a light. Proceeding cautiously towards it, and looking through a small aperture in the thatch, I saw an interesting spectacle. An elderly couple, wrinkled with age, whose appetites had got the better of their slumbers, were seated in the middle of the apartment, loosely attired with soiled *kapas,* and having a calabash of poi and a few dried fish between them. They were having a feast of fat things. That innocent appendage to a Hawaiian household, a lank cur, was seated upon his haunches, staring gloomily at them. He must have either seen or heard me, for I was aroused from my eaves-dropping by a sudden yelp, upon which I knocked hastily at the door. The old man called out:

" *Owái óe ?*" (who are you ?)

" *He hóa, no páha,*" (a friend, perhaps.)

" *Ai páha ; heá ka méa mákemáke oe ?*" (perhaps so ; what do you want ?)

" *Mákemáke au e héle malúna o kou wáa, ma ka móku kialúa ; mai Lahaina mai, úa ku mai kéia la,*" (I want to go in your canoe to the schooner from Lahaina ; it arrived to-day.)

" *O! maikái, e héle mai oe malóko nei,*" (ah! right ; come inside.)

These preliminaries are seldom resorted to, but as I had disturbed him at a most unseasonable hour, he was perhaps justified in propounding a few inquiries. Having entered, they invited me to join them, but I declined, alleging that I had friends waiting for me ; he received the hint with indifference, and continued his repast. This concluded, he lighted a lantern and accompanied me ; at my request, he pointed out the cocoanut-tree that had been sawed off, and upon which was nailed a sheet of copper, with an inscription almost illegible, to the effect that, " Near this spot fell the renowned circumnavigator, Captain James Cook," &c. It is a pity that some suitable testimonial has not been erected to the memory of this unfortunate voyager, whose life was devoted to the advancement of science. We also went down to the rock where he received the fatal stab while ordering the marines to cease firing. This has been sadly chipped away by devotees who have made a pilgrimage to Kealake-kúa. The name of Lóno (Cook) is reverenced by Hawaiians, and they modestly attribute to themselves the causes that led to the fatal result. If there be no monument here to record his fame, his memory will ever be cherished in the hearts of his countrymen, and he will be remembered by all, as one whose achievements, though peaceful, were unqualifiedly great ; and who, for accuracy of observation and extent of discovery in this ocean, stands unrivalled among cotemporaneous or subsequent voyagers.

CHAPTER XX.

LOITERINGS IN A HAWAIIAN VILLAGE.

EARLY in the mörning the anchor was weighed, but the breeze being light, we did not reach Keauhó before ten o'clock. As we entered the harbor, the sight was anything but tranquillizing to weak nerves. We were steering for an iron-bound shore, where the surf was beating with a noise like thunder, and bursting upwards in sheets of foam. Had the wind failed us, it would have been unpleasant to anticipate consequences. Though the entrance was narrow, we had a commanding breeze that carried us safely in, where we anchored and moored the schooner by ropes made fast to cocoanut-trees.

From the sensation produced among the natives, I should judge that arrivals were unfrequent at Keauhó, for the adjoining rocks were covered with curious idlers, and re-echoed their boisterous welcome. The water, which does not exceed two fathoms in depth, is beautifully transparent; and over the white sandy bottom are scattered clusters of coral and shells. Floating upon it were canoes filled with girls, who paddled around us, laughing and singing in high glee. Frequently, when the outriggers came in collision with each other, the occupant of one canoe, by a dexterous movement, would capsize those of the other into the water, a joke that was taken in good part, and some of these amphibious damsels seemed to manifest a preference for the briny element.

Sometimes half a dozen heads were dotting the surface on one side of the schooner; then, by a simultaneous movement, all would disappear and presently be seen shooting upwards on the opposite side. They swam about, plashing the brine in each other's faces, and when fatigued rested themselves by clinging to the outriggers. One of these girls, perhaps fourteen years of age, possessed an ornament that might excite the envy of our belles at home, and which so enhances female beauty. This was the most exquisite (indulge the word) head of hair I ever beheld in Polynesia. While swimming, it was either trailing behind her or hiding her face; but was only seen to advantage when its possessor was basking on shore, where she allowed it to float loosely upon her shoulders. Black, wavy, and glossy, and unrivalled in fineness, its peculiar beauty was noticed by all on board, from the owner to the sailor. The juvenile portion of the community seemed greatly to preponderate, and our deck was soon encumbered with them.

We remained here three or four days, and during that time took on board twenty thousand oranges and a large quantity of sweet potatoes, besides pigs and poultry. The oranges grow upon the mountain-side, about three miles distant from the beach, and are brought down by the natives in large baskets made of the pandanus leaves, one of which is suspended from each extremity of a pole and carried upon the shoulder to the shore. One morning, in company with L——, I ascended the mountain to where the fruit grew. The ascent was gradual, and our path at first lay over a field of broken lava ; but as we advanced this was covered with a red or brownish soil ; and here we found extensive cultivations of the sweet potato and melons, all looking thrifty. Farther up were groves of bananas, with their yellow fruit pendent ; and the soil continued to improve as we neared the edge of the forest. Here, the land was beautifully diversified by hill and valley, whose gentle declivities were sometimes shaded by groves of bread-fruit, and the dark foliage of the orange thickly studded with its golden fruit. That unique plant, the papaya, was also growing here, its luscious treasure clustering around the upper portion of its slender stem ; and I also noticed a species of fan-palm. There were several small inclosures of thrifty-looking coffee-trees, ornamented with their red berries. A feeling of regret naturally intrudes itself that such valuable land should remain uncultivated. Its prolific soil would yield an abundant harvest of either coffee or sugar-cane ; but it now nourishes a tangled forest, luxuriant in its wildness.

We saw but few native houses, and into one of these we entered. Its only inmate was a superannuated woman, who was endeavoring with her almost palsied fingers to braid a mat. She wished us *alóha,* and bade us be seated. Being fatigued by our morning walk, we cheerfully complied with her request.

There is often a melancholy pleasure in conversing with these old

people of the ancient *régime* ; their day has gone by ; they have indulged for the last time in their pastimes.   The ordeal of civil warfare that has so often desolated their homes, and the foreign pestilence of later years, have left them unscathed ; they now live to see
but a relic of the stirring thousands that once trod these hills ; their
homes, and all they once held sacred, are passing into the hands of
strangers.   I was much interested in the conversation of this old
woman, who became animated as she reverted once more to the
scenes of her childhood, interspersed with tales of " flood and field."
At L——'s request, I inquired whether she recollected the death of
Captain Cook.   Her reminiscences of the events of those days were
faint ; still, she recollected the circumstances attending it, and spoke
reverently of King Kalaiopú.

" *Naáupó na kanáká ia manéwa,*" (men were ignorant then,) she
remarked with great earnestness, alluding to the age of darkness
and superstition.

Having refreshed ourselves, we wished   our kind entertainer
" *alóha nui oe,*" (much love to you,) and returned to the beach, which
we reached about one o'clock P. M.   The word *naáupó*, used by the
woman, means literally *dark-bowelled*, the Hawaiians conceiving that
their intellectual faculties are interwoven with the viscera ; but they
are not singular in this respect, for sacred writers make allusion to
" bowels (σπλάγχνα) of compassion."   I was one day amused in Lahaina, by the remark of an old man to another, with whom he had
had a quarrel some time previous.   The latter was endeavoring to
conciliate him by every reasonable argument that suggested itself,
when the other, after listening patiently to all he had to advance,
simply remarked, " My bowels are not right towards you," and
walked away.

On Sunday morning I visited a singing-school, held in the native
church, which could not be more primitive ; it was simply a large
oblong grass-house, open at both extremities, and on one of its sides
A rude pulpit had been constructed, but the only seats were flat
stones placed upon the finely broken lava that constituted the floor.
Besides the young of both sexes of Keauhó, natives had also assembled from the villages adjoining, and a goodly number of happy faces
were congregated beneath the humble roof.   The men occupied the

seats in the rear, while the young ladies sat in front, and some of them, more fastidious than their companions, had brought small mats for their convenience. A few of the girls were neatly attired, and wore silk shawls or scarfs over their muslin dresses, and white stockings and slippers. The chorister was a stout, athletic native, an intelligent-looking fellow, and sported a slight moustache; he wore a fancy regatta shirt, carelessly adjusted over a pair of ———, I hardly know what to call them, for they were certainly not pants; they appeared to be a medium between the sailor and Chinese trowsers; however, there was no mistaking their quality; I distinctly read in faded blue characters, semicircularly arranged, "Superior Brown Dril———," the remainder was lost by a fold in the garment.

Their songs were sacred, and set to music, each person having a book, and it was surprising to witness their proficiency, for nearly all were more or less acquainted with the notes; but the greatest difficulty the chorister had to encounter was the democratic propensities of his juvenile pupils, whose discords rang out with startling effect; precisely the same giggling, whispering, and looking for places occurred, observable in a singing-school at home. The voices of the Hawaiians have not the flexibility and compass peculiar to the Tahitians, which harmonize so sweetly, and in whom music appears to be innate, for they are unacquainted with its theory; but such as they are, it is pleasing to hear them chanting airs familiar, and reviving associations of one's native land.

After these exercises had continued for an hour, a horn was blown to summon the people to church, and a large number of both sexes soon collected. The principal man of the place, whose name I do not recollect, was well dressed, and sat in a chair that was provided for him; he courteously offered to have one brought for me, but I declined the favor, preferring to sit on a mat near his wife, who had invited me to attend, and who, during the service, always found the hymn given out and handed me the book. The minister was a venerable-looking man, and dressed in a suit of black; the text given was from the Proverbs of Solomon, but I cannot now recollect the chapter or verse. I regretted that my knowledge of the native tongue was too limited to enable me to comprehend connectedly the discourse, though some portions were distinctly understood; what-

13

ever might have been the nature of his remarks, the most profound attention was observed by his hearers. It was pleasing to witness the devotion of this congregation, for there were many present who had once been Sabbath-breakers and idolaters, and I was led to reflect that the services of those who had reclaimed them from their heathenish customs, and many of their vicious habits, were often too lightly estimated ; it has been urged by cavilers, that efforts have been made to instruct these natives in " things" utterly beyond their comprehension. Admitting that their minds are too simple to grapple with the subtleties of theology or metaphysics, they are sufficiently clear to comprehend the difference that exists between right and wrong, at least in their extremes, or to understand the simple command, " Thou shalt have no other gods before me." The reverence of the Christian for his God, or the heathen or devotee for his idol, may be equally sincere; yet, though in grove or cloister the latter convoke to his aid symbols for a faith he vaguely feels, but yearns to possess—a spiritual longing inherent in the minds of both —we cannot compare them with a hope of obtaining results equally beneficial, for the moral effect of the one is inversely to that of the other. Examine this principle in whatever phase it may exist, whether among enlightened or heathen nations, and it will be found that, while the one concedes knowledge and life, the other involves ignorance, and, not unfrequently—death.

CHAPTER XXI.

SPIRITUALITY AND PASTIME.

AFTER service, in company with several natives, I walked over to the village adjoining, which proved to be more extensive than Keauhó. Its grove of cocoanut-trees was delightful. Like the entire sea-board of Kóna, the ground was covered with fragments of lava, and near the shore were the ruins of several *heiáus*. They seemed appropriately located for the celebration of infernal orgies, beneath the dark shade of the cocoanut, where the ocean was forever surging against the rocky rampart on which they were built.

Two days before leaving the village, a small coaster arrived from the leeward islands, and seeing some half dozen native passengers enter a house, I went in soon after to ascertain if there was anything new stirring. A young man was bending over some object at the extremity of the apartment, and apparently absorbed in deep grief. On inquiry, I learned the object of his lamentation was a coffin, containing the remains of a deceased brother. This coffin was placed on a sort of dais, covered with a cloth, and, suspended from the rafters, was a fine musquito-net, that enveloped it in its folds. These relics of mortality had thus been preserved for nearly two years, to awaken at intervals the grief of relatives, whose abode was beneath the same roof. This is not a solitary instance. Similar occurrences are frequent with Hawaiians, who esteem it a privilege to mourn over the remains of departed friends and relatives.

The transmigration of souls was once a popular tenet of theirs. A ludicrous illustration of this occurred at Oahu many years ago. An old man had lost a relative which he conceived to have become metamorphosed into a wild cow, that seriously retarded the growth of his taro and sweet potatoes. Being out one day in the field, he discovered the object of his solicitude quietly feeding beyond his inclosure, and climbing over the fence, he proceeded reverently towards it, saying, " Much love to you !" The cow raised her head, and returned a wild look for the salutation ; but the other continued, and calling his deceased relative by name, said :

" I've come to see you this morning. If you want anything, I'll give it to you ; but my bowels don't feel right towards you when you come into my *páa* (yard) and destroy my vegetables, because what you don't eat you trample down."

But the longer he discoursed, the more belligerent was the attitude assumed by the supposed relative, who refused to be pacified, and with a sudden bellowing, made a headlong plunge, whereupon the old man threw down his *óo*, (a kind of spade,) and beat a precipitate retreat for the wall, which he hardly cleared as the cow reached it. Then, without cherishing a vindictive feeling, he turned calmly around and said, " That was wrong, for I intended no harm, and you know how I love you."

A parallel incident occurred during my stay at Honuaúla. A female, in a state of monomania, swam from the shore one night to a small rock which was barely disclosed at low water. This place is famous for sharks; although she could not be seen, her voice was heard amid the darkness, as she clung to the rock, calling for her deceased relatives, whom she now believed to be sharks, to assemble around her. She was relieved from her perilous situation by a canoe.

On the northern side of the harbor at Keauhó, the black point of lava extends for a considerable distance into the sea, and in connection with a slight indentation in the shore, it forms a cove, where the surf rolls heavily. At any hour of the day, children might be seen running out on this point with their surf-boards. Watching their opportunity, they would plunge into the sea between two rollers, with exceedingly nice judgment, reaching the wave at its culminating point, and just as it was " combing," shoot in upon its crest, amid foam and spray, with the velocity of a race-horse, and shouting in wild delight.

What the sled is to the child at home, the *pápa*, or surf-board, is to the juveniles of Hawaii. I determined one morning to join them in their sport; and having signified my intention, about twenty girls, of various ages, and a dozen boys, promised to give me instruction. I preferred confiding myself to the management of the two oldest girls, who were more experienced. A board, four feet in length, and rounded at both ends, was provided for me. This, when used, is placed beneath the breast and held firmly between the extended arms, at an angle of about fifteen degrees with the level of the sea. The boys wore *málos*, the girls, loose gowns; and not wishing to be encumbered with superfluous " gear," I adopted the fashion of the former. The shore receded quickly, so that at a distance of ten yards we were beyond our depth. The surf rolled in heavily, and with my two instructresses on either side, I swam seaward. The spent rollers we suffered to pass beneath us, but as our distance from the shore increased, they were not to be disregarded; and when we saw a wall of water rise up before us, and come rolling in like an avalanche, we dove beneath it, while it broke and foamed above us. I should have said that *I* dove, for, like fishes, the girls could sink at will, and without any apparent effort. This peculiarity I have also noticed among the pearl-divers of the Southern Ocean, who, by giving a slight spring upward, sink easily, and turn beneath the surface. I have frequently attempted it, but without success, though by trial have remained under water as long as expert divers.

The breakers were frightful. Though a good swimmer, and familiar with winds and waves, I would never think of buffeting voluntarily such a formidable array of cataracts without a host of guardians. The roar was incessant, and almost deafening; still, we kept on. It is a strange sight to see the horizon of vision contracting before you and rising rapidly towards the zenith, until you look upon an impending wall of liquid blue, imperceptibly melting to a delicate pea-green with a snowy crest. There is a commingling of beauty and sublimity, of stern majesty and power. It is the mighty bolt that shatters the groaning timbers of the ship, and scatters the fragments upon the froth of its rage. But my fair guardians mocked its impotence. With a laugh and a shout, saying, "*Lu kakóu,*" (let us dive,) each clasped a hand, and in tranquil depths we hid from the billow that thundered above us.

Having obtained a suitable distance, we waited for a roller, and started upon its crest; but the art of surf-riding is not so simple as it would seem. With my companions on either side, I flew rapidly along for a few seconds; but somehow or other the wave always receded and left me in the lurch, while they shot ahead in a sea of foam. I sported in this way for fifteen minutes, until a roller caught me as it broke, and wrenching the board from my hands, whirled me along in every conceivable attitude; and on recovering from the shock, I was compelled to abandon my aquatic sports for the remainder of the day. After bathing in the sea, the girls always pour fresh water over each other, carefully washing their dark tresses, for they say salt water impairs their beauty.

While receiving cargo, we were pleased with an instance of native economy. A large proportion of the sweet potatoes purchased came from the districts adjoining, and were transported to Keauhó in canoes. One of these diminutive transports, heavily laden, came alongside, and by some mismanagement, the upper tier of baskets fell into the water, and the contents of some were scattered upon the sandy bottom, or among the coral branches, where, at a depth of twelve feet, they could be distinctly seen.   The owner, an old man, had no idea of permitting the sacrifice ; so, divesting himself of his garments, and with a basket in one hand, he dove down and commenced filling it.   After remaining below as long as he could, he would ascend to the surface and empty it, repeating the process until he had collected all.   The baskets that had not burst were more easily disposed of, for taking down a rope, he attached it to them, and they were drawn up.

At two o'clock in the morning, the land-breeze blowing freshly, we cast adrift our moorings, weighed anchor, and stood out of the harbor.   With a pleasant breeze, we reached Lahaina the same day.

Again I would beg the reader's indulgence for the interval that must necessarily occur while rambling upon Asiatic shores and islands in the Eastern Archipelago ; promising that our next visit to this group shall be brief and final.

CHAPTER XXII.

THE GREEN HILLS OF HILO.

ONCE more, O Hawaii ! we view thy snowy peaks, rising like "twin giants" above the blue wave, thy broad belt of forest enshrouded by white rolling clouds.   The barren cliff, the woody hill, the winding valley, and the grassy plain, all harmoniously blended in the distance, fading and glowing in shadow and sunshine : but, above—above all !—those hoary summits ! rising solemn and grand in the clear cold sky, where cheerless sunbeams glitter upon their everlasting snows.

It was a pleasant morning as we bounded rapidly along before the N. E. trades, towards Hilo, the paradise of Hawaii ; having received our pilot on board, at noon we were safely anchored in its

ample bay. All who have visited Hilo concur in admiring its scenery. The bold outline of Mauna Loa and Mauna Kea, in the background ; the broad lands, sweeping gradually up to the clouds, diversified by valleys, gentle declivities, and scattered groves, watered by sparkling streams that wind among them and empty into the bay, render it, for beauty and sublimity combined, unrivalled by any other view in the Pacific. The town itself would hardly be noticed, so dense is the grove that conceals it. Here, the dark foliage of the bread-fruit is relieved by sprinklings of the bright candlenut ; and the tender leaves of the plantain, fringed by the wanton breeze that rustles through them, are in pleasing contrast with clusters of the sombre pandanus. As if to add an exquisite finish to the landscape, slender annulated trunks of the cocoa-palm have been scattered through the groves and upon the sandy margin of the bay, nodding to the gale that sports with their waving plumes.

When the shades of evening were reposing on land and sea, I have frequently watched the glimmering of lights far up the mountain-side, sometimes flashing up and as suddenly disappearing, then burning steadily, betokening habitations unnoticed in the broad glare of day. Near the shore the beacons were more frequent, and around the vast semicircle of the bay bright fires flashed at intervals amid the dark groves. These, together with the cheerful sound of voices in harmony with the faint roar of the surf, combined to form a pleasing picture of Polynesian tranquillity.

The harbor, or bay, derives its name from the town, and is situate on the N. E. side of the island, forming a safe anchorage for vessels against all winds, except from the northeast. Near the southeast shore there is a rocky islet covered with cocoanut-trees ; and from this towards the N. E. extends a shoal for a long distance ; so that the entrance is on the western side, where the land is bold and the water deep. During a strong northeast wind, the sea rolls in heavily, and the shore is lined with breakers. On these occasions boats from vessels, instead of effecting a difficult landing on the western side, which is most thickly settled, usually resort to the southern shore, where a small stream affords them a secure retreat. This is called Waiakéa, and waters the district of that name, constituting the southern boundary of Hilo. The soil of this district and its vicinity is exceedingly prolific. Sugar-cane and coffee have been cultivated to a considerable extent ; and these, together with *púlu*, a soft silky substance that grows in the mountains, and used for upholstering purposes, are its staple exports. A defect, if such it can be called, is its climate, which is too moist. Showers are of almost daily occurrence, but they serve to array nature in her brightest colors.

The day after our arrival, Captain C—— and I landed to pay our respects to B. Pittman, Esq., an American, and collector of this port. Following the road from the beach, we soon came in sight of his premises. The residence, a thatched-roof cottage, is situated in a garden, ornamented by shade-trees, flowering shrubs, and choice exotics, tastefully laid out in walks and parterres, and the whole kept in beautiful order by Amoy coolies. The effect was also heightened by the appearance of the roads leading to and in front of them, for they were clean and free from weeds, all other obstructions being removed. Several neat dwellings have also been erected in yards adjoining, for the accommodation of guests or friends who resort to Hilo to enjoy its scenery and the hospitality of their entertainer. By this laudable display of taste and industry, Mr. Pittman has thrown around him the comforts and associations of an American home, and has constituted himself the enviable possessor of the most beautiful homestead in the group. Its merits are not confined to externals alone, as those can testify who have been the recipients of his hospitality.

Hilo is one continuous grove, bisected by a road a short distance from and running parallel with the shore. On either side are scattered native habitations, or the more substantial residences of foreigners.

The premises of Mr. Coan, the resident missionary, adjoin those of Mr. P——. They are charmingly located upon a commanding eminence ; but whatever attractions the interior of the residence may possess, viewed externally, the whole is a style of architecture strangely at variance with a tropical landscape. The sharp gables and the shingled roof, clipped primly off to the clap-boards, remind one of a snug little New-England homestead nestling beneath the shade of birch and maple. Though wanting in artistic effect, there is a moral connected with it that impresses an observer favorably ; for we may reasonably suppose that its possessor still retains the primitive tastes of his native land, and for confirmation it is unnecessary to look beyond the cordial hospitality extended to the visitor, whose habits and pursuits accord with the requirements of social intercourse.

Beyond the neat inclosure, and towards the sea, there is a broad open space, surrounded by groves, and watered by a sparkling rill that ripples through it. It is a kind of public pleasure-ground, where happy groups may romp to their hearts' content over the bright green-sward.

Three streams disembogue into the bay; one of them, Wailúku, rises among the hills of Maúna Kéa, and after pursuing its serpentine course for several miles towards the sea, pours over a ledge of basaltic rocks into a deep round basin ; when the volume of water is heavy, owing to rains, and the sunlight unobscured, the " maid of the mist" rises brightly from its clear waters, and this constitutes the Rainbow Fall of Hilo. The stream then winds through a valley, foaming among rocks, until it reaches the shore. The other two, of less extent, Wailáma and Waiakéa, bubble up in springs not far inland, forming several large fish-ponds or preserves in their course, (a royal prerogative,) and empty on the south side of the bay. Waiakéa is tolerably deep, and I have paddled a canoe upon its clear waters for nearly half a mile, until it became obstructed by the inclosure for the ponds. The fish that inhabit them are a species of mullet, and are much esteemed by the chiefs for their delicacy of flavor.

After dinner, at Mr. Pittman's request, I mounted his horse, and with a native boy for a guide, visited the Rainbow Fall. The ascent was by a narrow path, through cultivations of coffee, sugarcane, taro, plantains, melons, &c., and after a short ride we reached the scattered hamlet, situated in the immediate vicinity of the fall. The occupants levy contributions upon amateurs and others visiting this spot, by tendering their services in a variety of ways, such as holding the bridle while the horse feeds, watching your garments, which have been deposited upon a rock, while you enjoy the luxury of a bath, or telling you what you already know. The best view is obtained from the lower side, where may be seen at a glance the fall, with its dark cavern behind, the deep basin, and the amphitheatre of terraced rock, covered with a luxuriant growth of fern, nourished by the spray and humid atmosphere. The bed of the stream above the fall is broad and rocky, but in the absence of much rain, is confined to narrow limits. This torrent has worn deep and smooth reservoirs in the rock ; at the time I visited them, the stream being comparatively low, they had no connection with it, and in one of these smooth basins I enjoyed a refreshing bath.

Not far from its mouth, and where it is intersected by the road passing through the town, the course of the stream is among rocks, frequently broken by miniature cascades and foaming rapids ; in one spot there is a broad, deep pool, bounded on the left by a precipitous cliff. During the latter part of the afternoon, its banks are lined with boys and girls, who resort here to bathe. We have often amused ourselves by tossing *reals* or *medios* into the water, and seeing the children leap from an elevation of twenty or thirty feet, and catch them before they reach the bottom.

Hilo is the rendezvous for all who purpose visiting the celebrated crater of Kilauéa, which is distant thirty miles, or a day's travel, though a day and a half are usually required for the journey. This celebrated volcano is in the district of Púna, in a southwest direction from the town, and its locality is indicated by the snow-covered summit of Maúna Lóa that rises above it.

Until within a recent period, Hilo has been spared the inundations of lava that have devastated the southern and western shores of this island ; but in the spring of 1852, an eruption of lava occurred in the forest, several miles in the rear of the town, communicating with the great crater by a subterranean passage. The molten mass ran slowly seaward, destroying forests and vegetation, filling valleys and levelling mounds, attended by the ordinary volcanic phenomena, and as its sluggish course was watched, it was at one time feared that Hilo would be swept away. But after vomiting forth lava for several days, and scattering over the town cinders and the light capillary glass, called "The Hair of Péle," the fires of this new crater suddenly ceased, leaving a wide field of ruin and desolation. Although they have remained quiescent since that period, I noticed one morning a low white cloud hanging over the spot, the more remarkable as in no other portion of the atmosphere was a vapor to be seen, and by the aid of a telescope, I saw columns of steam shooting up from black chasms, or slowly ascending from the fissures that rent the dark mass in every direction.

One night while on board the ship, I was awakened by Captain B——, to look at the reflection of the fires of Kilauéa upon the sky. The whole southwestern firmament was in a tremulous glow, like that occasioned by a vast conflagration ; there was not a cloud to be seen, and the stars, though clear overhead, were obscured in that direction by the intense brightness.

Hilo, for a few years past, has been a port of entry, and is becoming a favorite place of resort for whalers ; I have counted eighteen in the harbor at once ; in this respect it ranks next to Lahaina. Its commerce is principally coastwise, few vessels lading here for foreign ports, and its produce, and that of the districts adjoining, is usually conveyed to Honolulu and Lahaina for reshipment. The potatoes with which whalers are supplied are brought around from the district of Waiméa, for they do not appear to thrive in the humid atmosphere of Hilo. Before leaving the place, I visited Kilauéa, and the incidents of the journey will be reserved for the following chapter.

CHAPTER XXIII.

A TRIP TO KILAUÉA.

THE day selected for our journey was unusually fine, and as there was neither ship nor visitors at Hilo besides our own and ourselves, I prevailed on Captain B—— to become a *compagnon de voyage.* Our rendezvous was at Mr. Pittman's store ; and it being generally nown that a visit to Kilauéa was contemplated that morning, we found quite a congregation of natives, some with horses to hire, and others to hire themselves. It was amusing to witness the competition among them, each vociferating the merits of his beast, while those of his neighbors were either " spavined, knock-kneed, or wind-broken."

We could not please all, but engaged a couple of horses at the ordinary price, ten dollars each ; also a native boy, about sixteen years of age, and a man to carry our blankets and sleeping clothes. These were disposed of in large calabashes suspended to a pole, which our attendant carried across his shoulder.

We started away at nine o'clock, intending to pass the night at the half-way house. After crossing Waiakéa, we travelled through the district of Púna, on the western boundary of which the crater is situated. I had supposed that on leaving Hilo we would commence the ascent of the mountain immediately, but instead, the road is across a beautiful tract of country, wild, or but partially cultivated, having hardly a habitation to relieve its solitude. We rode slowly, and the natives had no difficulty in keeping up with us. At noon we stopped at a small hamlet by the roadside, where, after dismounting and giving our horses free range, we went to a house and ordered some refreshment. Here we remained long enough for our entertainers to roast a fowl and boil some taro, after which we mounted and continued our journey. Though a long distance from the sea-shore, our ascent had been so gradual as to be imperceptible, and it was only as we advanced that the increasing coolness of the atmosphere indicated our elevation. We had passed through but one small copse of woodland, and at the place where we halted, the country was open, and the land uneven and rocky, being thickly covered with coarse grass and fern. An extensive and gently undulating plain was crossed, covered with a beautiful mantle of waving ferns, stretching away as far as the eye could reach. It was perfectly straight, and the soil being a rich vegetable mould, we were somewhat inconvenienced by the mud. While admiring the wildness of the scenery, we could not but regret that so much valuable land was suffered to remain uncultivated. The sites are eligible for plantations ; and there being no impassable ravines or obstacles to hinder the construction of broad roads, easy access could be had to Hilo, and a prolific soil would yield an ample harvest.

About the middle of the afternoon we diverged from the main road

to one on our right, and this looked more like ascending than anything we had yet seen, for a hill rose up some distance ahead of us.
Before reaching it, the road became almost impassably muddy, the
horses sinking nearly to their knees at every step; but having attained the eminence, the path became firmer, and the continued
ascent more perceptible. Here was first encountered the *pahoihói*,
(satin rock,) or exposed lava of peculiar conformation, smooth and
uneven, and over this our progress was slow. Small hamlets were
occasionally passed, and at one of these a woman came out to
inquire where we were going. On being informed, she replied:
"*Núi lóa ka áhi ma ka 'Lúa o Péle' kéia manéwa!*" (the fire now at
the cave of Péle is exceedingly great.) Péle was the goddess in
Hawaiian mythology who came with her family from lands beyond
the heaven, (horizon,) and took up her abode in the crater; hence
the native name, the "Cave of Péle."

We jogged on until the half-way house was reached, from which
it is only half a day's ride to the volcano. In this district, houses
were scattered along at no great distance from each other, but the
whole picture was lonely in the extreme. The uncultivated soil,
partially covering rugged rocks, the distant forest in gloom, and the
chilling aspect of the mountains, with the now inconveniently cool
atmosphere, were in striking contrast to the scenes we had left that
morning.

The shades of evening were now setting in; and being in a perspiration from the exertion of walking, for a few miles back I had
mounted the native boy in my place, I felt thoroughly chilled by the
sudden halt, and leaving B—— to look after the baggage, made
direct for the cook-house, to find warmth among its embers. This
was small, and a miserable fire was smouldering near the centre,
enough to stifle one with its smoke, for there was no aperture to
permit its escape. I found some half dozen of both sexes rubbing
their eyes; and going into their midst, divested myself of boots,
and reclined at full length upon the mats. Some more brands were
thrown on to the fire, and for a trifling compensation, I obtained the
luxury of a *lomilómi*. This simple word conveys to those acquainted
with its meaning, ideas of a pound, pinch, and squeeze, and, when
properly performed, the process is a universal remedy among Ha-

waiians for all diseases, imaginary or real. I have seen portly females extended upon the mats, face downwards, while juveniles, barefooted, were dancing upon their backs, and this they considered a luxury. But, jesting aside, the effect upon wearied limbs by the manipulations of experienced hands is soothing. We were soon laughing and joking, for any one, if so disposed, can make himself perfectly at home in a Hawaiian household, nor is it looked upon as an intrusion or undue familiarity. Our conversation was interrupted by the appearance of the host, who, for the benefit of future visitors, I will state was a sinner and a hypocrite ; harsh terms, but nevertheless true. He may be easily recognized by his stunted form and ambling gait, while his eyes either stare at you obliquely, or are bent upon the ground.

His abrupt inquiry was, " What do you want to eat ?"

I told him the best he had, and as much of it as he could conveniently spare.

He stood for a few seconds without replying, then, looking steadily upon the ground, said, " Pigs are high."

" How high ?"

" Four dollars for one so long," indicating the length by extending his right arm, and grasping it with his left hand at the elbow-joint.

I told him I didn't believe it, and that I would look elsewhere. He then gave me to understand that he monopolized the neighborhood. After considerable haggling, he promised to bring me one for three dollars ; and this preliminary being settled, he told me he didn't know where he was going to get it. Our party was ravenously hungry, and this suspense was torturing. After he had patiently listened to a few imprecations in English, he suggested, by way of consolation, that he could go and look for one, but, if the search proved unsuccessful, he was to have a dollar for his pains. I told him I would go myself ; but to this he replied good-naturedly, that I would lose my way and fall down on the *pahoihói,* (satin rock.)

By this time quite a group had collected to listen to the dispute ; and the native we had brought with us from Hilo, seeing how matters stood, and that his prospect of a supper was in vague perspective, remarked to the old man that he was *naáu po,* (dark-bowelled,) and otherwise gave free utterance to his sentiments. The old extortioner had mistaken his character. I had lived too long among Hawaiians to b'e fleeced by them, if such happened to be the propensity; and I required no interpreter, for I could pay him back in his own tongue. I was willing to pay liberally, but was determined to have what was paid for; and it may be inferred that we did not stint ourselves, when the expenses of two of us for three days, in this wilderness, amounted to thirty-three dollars.

After a while the pig was forthcoming; but, to our inexpressible annoyance, he insisted on immediate payment, as if we were not to be trusted over night. The pig was slaughtered, dressed, and a portion roasted. From this, together with taro and potatoes, also purchased, we made a hearty supper, and after us our natives. The remaining relics were devoured by the old man, who then assembled his family and offered up a fervent prayer.

Our dormitory was a large grass-house, having a raised platform about three feet high, extending through its entire length, covered with mats, and separated from the *sitting-room* by calico curtains. The night being cold, we retired early, and wrapping ourselves in blankets, enjoyed a comfortable repose.

By morning I had become acclimated, and found the mountain air cool and invigorating. Everything was covered with a heavy dew; but the melody of warblers was lacking, to give animation to the scene. At an early hour I dispatched the boy to bring up the horses, which had been tethered a short distance off, while others bustled about to prepare the breakfast. This important item passed off without ceremony, and at eight o'clock we were again under way. An important acquisition to our party was secured in the person of an old native guide we were fortunate enough to procure at this place. I have forgotten his name. For years he has resided in this vicinity, and has accompanied visitors to the volcano. He was intelligent and obliging, a happy contrast to our host of the night preceding. He carried the pig and vegetables in calabashes suspended from a pole.

The road, after leaving this place, was formed by laying poles across the rugged lava, and covering them with earth, when it could be conveniently procured. From several houses women came

out, offering bananas for sale.   We purchased several bunches, and
on one occasion, as we could not make the change, a bunch was
promised us on our return.   Beyond this settlement we lost all trace
of habitations, and indications of the volcano were anxiously looked
for.   The land was rolling and rocky ; or, rather, it seemed one mass
of ancient lava scantily covered with soil.   Here we saw the *púlu*
growing ; and in some portions of the forest, the mountain-fern grew
so high that we could not reach the top of it while sitting upon our
horses.   We were too impatient to wait for our attendants, whom
we had long since left behind, and had galloped on ; but in the midst
of a dense forest our road forked, and both paths appearing to be
equally trodden, we halted to deliberate.   It was agreed that B——
should take the left and I the right, shouting occasionally to each
other, to "keep our bearings."   We parted, and I recollect hailing
once, but not hearing it returned, rode on as fast as projecting
branches would permit, and in fifteen minutes reached an open
space, where I halted for my companion.   After a considerable
interval he emerged from the forest by the same path I had taken,
and reported that, having ridden on a considerable distance, all trace
of a road vanished, and he was compelled to retrograde.

His lynx-eye soon detected a light cloud in the distance, and in the
direction we were travelling ; this arose from the crater, which we
were now more anxious than ever to reach.

As we advanced, the road improved, with gradual descent, the soil
being composed of cinders and ashes, quite compact, and covered
with coarse grass, and sometimes bushes ; among the latter was the
ohélo, a species of whortleberry, and loaded with fruit.   We galloped at full speed, and at noon, after passing a low hill on our
left, the grandest sight we ever beheld was before us.

It was an extensive plain, nearly twenty miles in circumference,
extending to what appeared to be the true base of Maúna Lóa,
seemingly as distant as ever, and rising like a misty hummock to
bound it on the west.   Within the limits of this plain, and five or six
miles in circumference, yawned the immense pit, a thousand feet in
depth, the southern portion obscured by fiery clouds ; its perpendicular or overhanging walls of basalt rose darkly from its bed, at once
a scene of grandeur and desolation, flanked by bastions or rugged

promontories, extending into the congealed flood that in fiery waves sometimes surged against these giant ramparts.

As our guides had not yet arrived, we rode on to the small thatch hut that has been erected on the margin of the crater by Mr. Pittman, for the gratuitous convenience of visitors ; standing, as it did, alone in this wilderness, it looked the very picture of solitude. Along our path we occasionally saw deep fissures, from which arose light clouds of vapor ; a few shrubs and a heavy growth of fern bounded the wide space we were travelling, over which were thinly scattered *ohélo* bushes. Having reached the house, we halted, without dismounting, to enjoy another view of the sublime scene before us, and the magnificent prospect on our right, where Maúna Lóa and Maúna Kéa bounded, a broad plateau, diversified by hill and valley. The base of the former was dotted by what in the distance appeared to be scattered groves, but which were probably dense forests.

It was now one o'clock, and Captain B—— proposed " circumnavigating" the crater ; as we had abundance of time, I readily consented. Soon after leaving the house, we passed an extensive bed of volcanic sulphur, which we subsequently visited ; the fissures in the ground over which we were travelling became more frequent, and it was sometimes necessary to ride through a cloud of sulphurous vapor, while the dry earth, as we galloped on, sent back a hollow sound beneath the hoofs of our horses. Having reached the most elevated portion of the western side, we halted again to look at the chaotic mass below. Black as the Stygian lake, a broad *river*, congealed to rock, ran around the entire extent of the crater, carefully following the inequalities of its banks, forming coves and deep bays, while the interior was thrown up in the wildest confusion, sometimes bounding the river by rugged walls ; again huge masses were scattered about like islands, and in several places miniature cones were vomiting forth smoke and bright sulphureous flame.

B——'s horse being somewhat jaded, I took the lead, but had not galloped far before I heard him shouting to me. On returning, I found he had lost my monkey-jacket, which, for want of better " chafing gear," he had placed beneath him. As the nights at this elevation are cold, and not wishing to be without sufficient clothing,

14

I was determined to find it, if compelled to forego the pleasure of riding around the crater. We had no difficulty in retracing our steps, for the land in this vicinity was free from tree or shrub, though we were sometimes compelled to make long detours to avoid yawning chasms, among which it would be unsafe to venture in the night. I began to think we would never find it, but having nearly reached the house, it was discovered lying upon the verge of a bottomless pit, one portion of it hanging over, and saturated with the condensed steam; it had been blown from the road by the strong gusts that occasionally swept across the plain. As too much time had been consumed to think of accomplishing our project, we returned to the house, where we found the natives lying upon the ground and eating *ohélos.* Our baggage was deposited in the house, where were a few mats to sleep on, a table, and a small cupboard, but the house itself was sadly dilapidated, being doorless, and propped up on both sides by stout poles. The boy unsaddled the horses and tethered them out to feed, while the guide, with the assistance of our Hilo man, set about preparing a late dinner.

The pig and vegetables were nicely wrapped up in stout leaves and fern, and deposited to be cooked in one of the fissures, from which arose a cloud of steam. Our water was procured from a natural distillery, a short distance from the house; from a deep chasm rose a dense cloud of vapor, which was condensed by the cold air, and blown in clear drops to a small reservoir on the leeward side, around the margin of which was a luxuriant growth of rushes and fern.

B—— and I visited the sulphur bank in the vicinity of the house, which is not the least of the many curiosities at Kilauéa. It is reached by a slight descent, and crossing a short level thickly incrusted with the mineral. The bank is of considerable extent, and in many places is rent by narrow fissures, the sides of which are of a light yellow color, and from which noxious gases are continually ascending. We broke several specimens from the bank, crystallized in beautiful prisms, but of their shape I had no means of judging. Some of them were incrusted with a white substance, probably sulphate of ammonia, which enhanced their beauty. In walking, we noticed a peculiar crunching sound, similar to that produced by walking over frozen snow.

In the rear of the house are various chasms, some of them emitting steam, and others almost hidden by the rank growth of fern and bushes. Into one of these we descended for a short distance, using dry bushes for torches. It appeared to be a large winding passage, continually descending, the walls of which were dark trap rocks, and into one of its vaults I threw a torch, which burnt but a moment, and then disappeared. There is but little to be gained by venturing into these caverns, for the steam is liable at any moment to burst forth, which would cause instant death. On ascending, we saw a light cloud escaping from a fissure near the entrance, unnoticed during our descent. These are evidences of the phenomena peculiar to volcanic countries, and were probably occasioned by earthquakes, which at intervals convulse Hawaii. The vapors arising from them would imply that they have subterranean communication with the great crater.

CHAPTER XXIV.

THE THRONE OF AN ANCIENT GODDESS.

By evening, our pig and vegetables were done to a turn—a most acceptable repast, for we had eaten nothing since morning, except *okélo* berries. The night was clear, cold, and dark ; and as I sat at the entrance of our shelter, and looked out upon the bright fires burning beneath, over which hung a canopy of glowing clouds, the superstitions of the ancient Hawaiians connected with this spot naturally recurred to me. This was the throne of that fabled divinity, Péle. Here, with her fiery train, she swept over the flaming surges, the sound of whose roaring was the music of their voices ; and here, in her wild domain, she held state, visiting with a deluge of fire all who incurred her resentment. It is painful to conceive of a mythology so fearful as that which fettered the minds of the former

·inhabitants of this group. The plebeians were physically bound down to the lowest grade of serfdom at the caprice of their lords, and mentally fettered by a polytheism as cruel as it was extravagant. They were continually startled by the recurrence of phenomena, conjuring up frightful legends, which in the obscurity of ages had become interwoven with the history of their origin ; while over all hung the gloom of superstition like an incubus.

In addition to what I already knew of this strange mythology, the old guide amused us by narrating tales of the divinities of Hawaii ; also incidents that had occurred to those visiting the volcano. The tale of Kamapúa is familiar to most foreign residents of this group ; but for those who have not heard of it, I will briefly insert it, as an illustration of the supernatural powers of the fabled goddess.

This Kamapúa was a huge monster, the centaur of Hawaii ; for he was half hog and half man. His original residence appears to have been Oahu, but becoming dissatisfied with its narrow limits, he roamed abroad generally ; being something of a gallant in disposition, he found it convenient to visit Kilauéa, where he made proposals to Péle, the elder branch of the fire-loving family. She had the good sense to reject his advances with scorn ; and adding insult to injury, called him " a hog, and the son of a hog," and arose from her flaming bed with her sisters to drive him away. But this was no easy task, for Kamapúa reached the ocean by a few strides, some twenty miles distant, and sucking in seas at a draught, he returned and vomited them into the crater, to the consternation of its divinities, who sent forth volleys of burning stones and clouds of smoke and ashes, in the shade of which Kamapúa would retreat to the sea. This fierce combat continued for some time, until Péle, summoning new powers to her aid, hurled forth her molten torrents, and drove him into the ocean, amid flaming volleys, and thunder and lightning.

Our boy, who took care of the horses, had by this time torn his clothes to shreds among the bushes and rocks. As he complained of the cold, I gave him a pair of silk *pejamas* I had brought to sleep in ; and the guide having made a short prayer, we retired for the night.

The following morning was cold and clear. After partaking of an early breakfast, preparations were made for our descent to the bed of the crater. It was arranged that the boy, who had no shoes, should remain at the house to look after the horses and baggage, and to have dinner ready on our return. B——, following the example of the guide, had provided himself with a pole the day previous, to " sound" as he went along ; for old salts, who are forever fussing over spun-yarn and rigging, acquire habits of observation, while I, being naturally improvident, had overlooked this important item, and which it was now too late to remedy. Accordingly, the guide and B—— took the lead. I followed, the Hilo man bringing up the rear with a canteen of water and the fragments of our breakfast.

About forty feet below the margin of the crater, at the point of descent, is a level space covered with vegetation ; and here, within what was no doubt its original bound, we saw a small grass-house built by Mr. Coan, and occupied by him during his visits to the volcano. Our descent was continued among irregular fissures or chasms and trees, until we reached another division or broad level spot, affording a convenient resting-place. By the path, we saw a large rock, on which was faintly traced, " Kamehaméha ;" also, chiselled into it, the words, " Boyd, yacht Wanderer." We found the descent very fatiguing down the steep ridges, our path being obstructed by broken ledges and fragments of lava ; but at eight o'clock we stood on the bed of the crater, hemmed in by its rocky amphitheatre.

The atmosphere was unpleasantly hot, and over some portions of the lava there was a tremulous glow, such as may be seen arising from a furnace. Our course at first lay over the black flood we had noticed from above, the surface of which resembled a river filled with blocks of ice and suddenly congealed. It was cool, solid, and easily passed. But our guide soon called our attention to a shining, vitreous mass, that looked like molten iron, poured out and cooled. This was a recent eruption of lava, the reflection of whose light we had seen a few evenings previous, and we were compelled to make a long detour to avoid it, as it was unapproachable on account of its heat. In some places, a thin crust over the surface we were travelling crumbled at every step like frozen snow. On our right was an immense black wall, thrown up in fearful confusion, and which seemed to rise like an island from the congealed sea around it. In some places the surface was comparatively smooth, reposing in gentle undulations like the waves of the sea ; and again, having been rent by a mighty convulsion, a portion would project like a ledge above that beneath it. We were often startled by fearful detonations, that seemed to jar the igneous masses over which we were cautiously picking our way ; and at intervals, a hollow, rumbling sound, and columns of white, sulphurous vapor, bursting upward, betokened the appalling gulf we were approaching. As the chasms became more frequent, we were compelled to leap them, with the fire glowing but a foot beneath us, and in one place I stooped down and lighted a cheroot. A short distance on our left, the semi-fluid lava that had overflowed its confines a few days previous, wound its way among dark Plutonic rocks that frowned above it.

After traversing the bed of the crater nearly three miles, we ascended a slight eminence and stood upon the brink of the burning lake. It was a pit, one-fourth of a mile in circumference, and about fifty feet in depth ; but as narrow as were its limits, it contained a sight of fearful grandeur. In the centre, a dark molten mass was rolling its sluggish waves towards the east, while across it, in every direction, serpentine streaks of bright red lava wove a fiery network. The east and western portions were in a state of terrific ebullition, tossed and whirling in waves of fire, like surf against a rocky rampart ; and the sound that arose from this burning pit was like the roar of a mighty furnace. At times, a bluish or sulphurous flame would sweep o'er its surface, then quickly disappear, and the fearful blasts of the fiery whirlwind seemed lulled to repose, or dying away in ominous rumblings like the reverberations of distant thunder. But it was the awful calm that heralds the impending storm ; for suddenly, from the Cyclopean furnace, bellowing throats vomited upward blood-red jets, and as if lashed into fury, a tempest of spectral waves danced upon its surface, or whirled amid fiery maelstroms ; while, at intervals, fearful detonations seemed to rend the bowels of the earth, and spherical masses of fusing lava, flaming and hissing, were flung heavenward, to fall back into the abyss.

We gazed upon this fearful scene in silence, transfixed, as if we

stood in the presence of a basilisk, each absorbed in his own reflections, and every thought, save inspirations of the all-impressive scene,
buried in oblivion.   Like its great prototype, the mind loves to contemplate ; no theme is too vast, no object too minute to convey an
impression ; it is this delicate susceptibility to externals that affects
our spiritual being, awakening, in accordance with the sublimity of
conception, ideas of which language is no exponent, and revealing
a well-spring of future thought.   We gaze upon the tranquil beauty
of a landscape with delight, while its ever-varying features lend the
brightest conceptions of poetic imagery, and analyzing our emotions,
they yield gratitude and love ; the roar of a cataract or mountain torrent inspires us with its grandeur; but when standing in the bowels of the
earth, hemmed in by walls of adamant, with a flaming vortex on one
hand, and the chaotic wreck of nature on the other, the mind is
overwhelmed with conflicting emotions, and humiliated by the stern
comment on its insignificance.   I had gazed upon that watery
avalanche, Niagara, hurrying to its deep abyss, but with emotions
vastly different from those awakened while standing in the crater of
Kilauéa ; with the former, the face of nature was unchanged ; the
same rainbow enwreathed its clouds, its waters spake with unvarying
tone, while the stern majesty of its beauty was in harmony with surrounding objects.   But in Kilauéa, we are shut out from every vestige of life, in the presence of a more fearful element, and startled
by recurring phenomena ; with a vast plain of convulsed masses before us, the ideal of solitude and desolation, an emblem of chaos
when " the earth was without form and void."   We stand upon the
valve of a mighty reservoir of liquid fire, whose depths will forever
remain unfathomed, and of whose vastness we can form but a faint conception by the evidences around us.   From its culminating points,
Maúna Lóa and Maúna Kéa, 14,000 feet high, to the ocean that laves
their bases, Hawaii is a confused mass of lava or volcanic matter,
exposed or partially covered with vegetation, which for ages has
been accumulating ; and it is easy to conceive of the profundity of
the submarine caldron that has hove up from the bed of ocean
this mountain dome, for the escape of its fiery blast.   Fancy wanders, reason pauses to reflect ; impressions conveyed by its funereal
gloom endure forever, and we gaze upon this burning pyre of nature

with the most exalted emotions of sublimity, and with feelings of humble reverence for its Creator.

The southern portion of the crater was inaccessible from its bed, owing to the sulphurous gases arising from burning pits, and it was hidden by a dense cloud. Contrary to the advice of our guide, I ventured a short distance to leeward, but the vapors were stifling to respiration. Before leaving the lake of fire, an immense mass of rock detached itself from the western wall and fell into the caldron, with a terrific crash, causing the molten lava to surge with redoubled fury and burst upward in jets of liquid fire, in a manner inconceivably grand. On our return, and about half a mile from the lake, we visited a cone which had been thrown up by the expansive force of latent heat, and from its apex were issuing dense clouds of vapor. We returned by another route over the *island* before mentioned, and gathered some beautiful specimens of vitreous and cellular lava, exceedingly brittle, and its fractures variegated with chameleon hues. Immense chasms were passed, apparently bottomless, and throwing down stones, we could hear them bound from side to side, until the echo was gradually lost. I have sometimes thought that the natives retain a shade of their former superstition, and in this instance, but for our questions, the two who accompanied us might have been taken for mutes; our Hilo man, who at home was somewhat rakish in his habits, looked upon it as sacrilege to see us hurl rocks into the burning lake. Formerly these islanders, in passing the crater, would never eat an *ohélo* berry, without first plucking some and throwing them over the margin, exclaiming, " Here, Péle, I throw you some of your *ohélos*; some I eat myself." After gathering a quantity of a light-brown vitreous substance, or capillary glass, called " *Lauóho o Péle*," (the hair of Péle,) we commenced ascending the precipitous side of the crater, a fatiguing task, and reached the house at three o'clock in the afternoon.

Permitting ourselves but a hasty dinner, and depositing a quantity of taro and potatoes in the cupboard of the house, we mounted our horses and bid adieu to Kilauéa, having enjoyed but a superficial glance at its wonders.

This extensive crater is situate about fifteen miles from the sea-shore, on the southern boundary of Púna. Its elevation above the sea is about four thousand feet. The dimensions assigned to it by Wilkes, who surveyed it, are—length, three and a half miles, and breadth, two and a half miles ; while its depth below the surrounding plain is one thousand feet. In other words, its depth and extent are so great that, were the city of New-York removed to its bed, the loftiest spires would hardly be noticed. At this elevation, on the north there are broad tracts of level land adapted to grazing ; and, though in some places diversified with sterile hills and rocky ravines, they are relieved by dark masses of forest stretching away towards the mountains. The cattle first introduced by Vancouver propagated rapidly and roamed wild over this district, where they were pursued to the brink of the volcano and captured by the rancheros brought from the Spanish Main for that purpose. These mountain heaths are inhabited by a species of grouse that never visit the warm regions of the sea-shore, but confine their flight to the vast plains extending from Maúna Lóa on the south to Maúna Kéa and Hualalái on the north. They are prized for food, and their pursuit would afford agreeable recreation for sportsmen. I saw several flocks flying at a distance, and they bore a strong resemblance to wild geese.

The summits of Maúna Lóa and Maúna Kéa have the misty appearance lent by distance. Though the former resembles a smooth conical mound, it would be found on visiting it that its sides towards the apex were barren, and furrowed by deep ravines, while rocky cliffs and rugged masses of slag or scoria are almost insurmountable obstacles in the way of accomplishing its ascent. Its apex is a vast crater, whose fires have long been quiescent; and around its margin is thrown a mantle of perpetual snow. The same may be said of Maúna Kéa, except that it is less uniform in its contour. While the sea-shore is clothed with luxuriant vegetation, nourished by the genial warmth of the tropics, these summits rear themselves into frozen regions where no living thing is found, and where, unseen and unheard, tempests of snow and hail sweep over this wilderness of solitude and desolation.

Mount Hualalái, constituting the western foot of this tripod of the clouds, is but ten thousand feet high. Fifty years ago it was a burning volcano, and poured forth its fiery torrents to the sea, filling bays and extending the shores of Kóna by its molten flood ; and which, in future ages, by decomposition and alluvial deposits, will furnish sites for cultivation, resting upon a rocky foundation.   North of Maúna Lóa and Maúna Kéa, the fertile district of Waiméa flourishes, undisturbed by the volcanic phenomena that have devastated the southern portion of the island.   At an elevation of seven thousand feet above the sea, it enjoys a climate of perpetual spring, where plants of the temperate zone have been successfully introduced, and it yields an abundant harvest of tropical products.   The northern half of the island, including the districts of Kohála, Hamakúa, and Hilo, is unsurpassed in fertility ; while on the south and west the shores of Púna Káu and Kóna are mostly barren and worthless. This, however, does not always extend to the inland regions, where, beneath a belt of clouds, the trunks of the forest wave their broad branches in a cooler zone.

Our Hilo men, who had preceded us by an hour, travelled like horses with their ladened calabashes, and, though we rode as fast as the inequalities of the road would permit, they were not overtaken until half way to our former hotel.   Here we all halted for the old guide to come up, who presently emerged from a clump of low trees, and skipping as nimbly as a child over the *páhoihói*.   We soon reached the scattered huts of the settlement, in passing one of which a girl came out with a luscious bunch of bananas, reminding us that it was an equivalent for change due on a former purchase.

At the house we found two French Catholic priests journeying from Hilo across the island, whom we invited to share our supper. The elder, though possessing an austere countenance, proved an agreeable and intelligent companion.   During the evening we amused ourselves with reviewing portions of the book carried by our guide, containing the autographs, and, in some instances, the sentiments of those who had visited the volcano.   It is well worth the attention of visitors as an index to disposition ; and, adopting the sentiments therein expressed as a basis, material would be furnished for a tolerable treatise on ethnology.   The opinions of some were timidly set forth ; others boldly advanced.   One admired, while another ridiculed ; and several observations on the temperature of the atmosphere and its visible phenomena would be interesting to meteorologists ; for we find it recorded that on one occasion, " during the night, *poi* froze in our calabash." In another place we notice, " I have just returned out of the crater, and seen the lake of fire, which kicks up quite a rumpus ; and, take it altogether, I think it one of the most extensive manufactories of pottery in his majesty's dominions.———, U.S. Navy." Some have manifested an unconquerable propensity for sketching ; and a few of these illuminated manuscripts were, I imagine, designed as caricatures on the goddess Péle.

Without incident worthy of note, we reached Hilo on Thursday afternoon at two o'clock ; here we found some half dozen whalers that had arrived during our absence ; also, a tremendous surf on the western shore, which compelled us to follow the beach round to Waiakéa, and take our departure for the ship by the river, the entrance to which was but slightly affected by the breakers. This is the only wind, a northeaster, that occasions inconvenience in the harbor ; and at this time the heavy swell that set in through the channel and over the shoal was so great as to compel two vessels laying alongside of each other to tranship cargo, to cast adrift their fastenings, and anchor at a distance.

During the week following our visit to Kilauéa, it rained almost incessantly, and unfortunately there was no regular communication between this and the leeward ports, so that I was compelled to wait for a passage to Honolulu, until the favor was conferred by Captain Sands, of the American ship " B——— T———."

Without having recorded a moiety of the incidents that have enlivened an aggregate sojourn of twenty months in the Hawaiian Archipelago, or having dwelt upon those topics that enhance the interest of a cursory narrative, I merely offer a concluding remark. If I have omitted any allusion to the resources of these islands as a country, or to their inhabitants as a nation, I have forfeited no promise ; the history of their natural productions, or the tale of legends and national characteristics, would be themes too prolix for off-hand sketches ; for a detailed account of these, I would refer the reader who is desirous of becoming more intimately acquainted with this interesting group, to the histories of J. J. Jarvis, Esq., and the Rev. H. Bingham ; also to that interesting book, Ellis's "Tour around Hawaii." In these it will be seen that a barbarous race in the nineteenth century has thrown off its heathen usages

and become a Christian and enlightened people, an independent
nation, and recognized as such by the great powers of earth; enjoying a government modelled to its peculiar wants, and exhibiting
in an eminent degree the liberal legislation of our great Republic,
with whose history it is interwoven, and in whose shadow it has
matured.

PART III.

—

GEORGIAN AND SOCIETY ISLANDS.

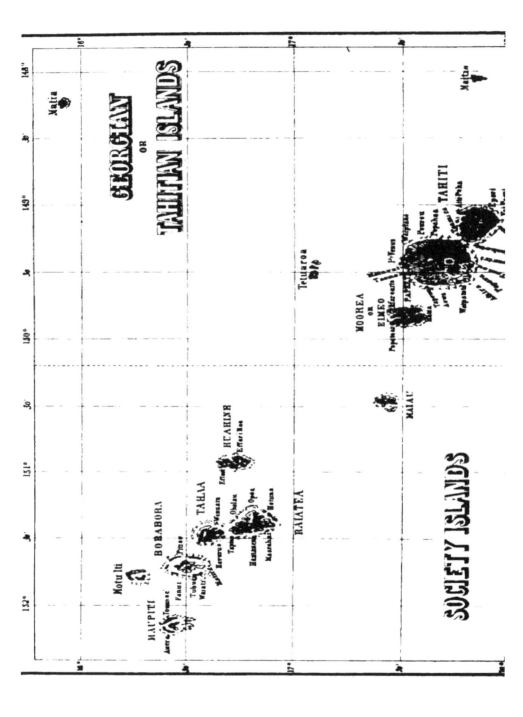

GEORGIAN

AND

SOCIETY ISLANDS.

CHAPTER I.

RAIATÉA.

ANYTHING but baffling winds! Until yesterday we had a rattling breeze, and with it should have reached the beautiful harbor of Papeéte in forty-eight hours ; but now, everything is braced sharp up, and in gaining one mile, we lose two to leeward. A parcel of weather-bound passengers censure the innocent " Eliza Mary" from truck to kelson.

We had on board twenty-two natives of the Hervey group, who were returning home, also several passengers *en route* for Australia *viá* Tahiti ; and the prospect of reaching their respective destinations was anything but encouraging.

" I say, Captain Ben," said Merton, a jovial Englishman, who loved adventure as well as an occasional glass, " have done with this ! Come, up helm, and let's away to Raiatéa ! What say you ?"

Merton had anticipated our sentiments, and Captain Ben required but little urging, for he had recently adopted that island for his home, and the Raiatéan bunting floated from the main truck of his vessel. Accordingly, the yards were rounded in, and we kept away in the direction of Huahíne, an island adjoining, and of which we were to windward.

The morning was foggy, and a good look-out was kept, lest we should have the island, or at least a reef, aboard of us before we were aware of it. About eleven o'clock, one of the Mangaía men shouted, " *Téia te fenúa !*" (here is the land,) and looking in the direction he was pointing, we could barely discern an object looming darkly amid the gloom. It was certainly land, and Merton was in ecstasies. Sleepless nights, occasioned by low islands and imaginary reefs, were now at an end, for he always shuddered at the bare idea of shipwreck, having endured its miseries twice.

It proved to be Huahíne ; and soon after, the atmosphere becoming clearer, we had a fine view of its rugged peaks and deep ravines, softened by the smiles of perpetual spring ; the bright verdure mantling around sharp pinnacles, or sweeping upward in gentle undulations, to blend with the shadows of cloud-capped summits. We passed by its eastern and southern sides, with the trade-winds blowing strongly from the southeast, and soon after saw a light hummock looming in the horizon ; this was Raiatéa, " *the distant sky.*"

Captain Ben promised us " a roast pig," together with " the best the market afforded ;" hinting broadly upon the merits of orange rum. Fore and aft there was a general exuberance of spirits. We were bearing direct for the Opóa passage ; and having attained a close proximity to the reef, we skirted along its outer edge, and this portion of the island passed in review like a beautiful panorama. Unlike any other island of this group, Raiatéa has a coral barrier extending completely around it, comprising in its folds the adjacent island of Tahóa, leaving a broad and deep channel like a vast river or lake, with numerous entrances. By a singular freak of nature, nearly every passage is bounded on either side by islets covered with a luxuriant growth of cocoanut-trees. Near Opóa, in one of the broad valleys, Mr. Platt, the owner of the vessel, pointed out a bright strip of verdure conspicuous amid the darker foliage, which he said was an extensive bamboo grove. The shore was indented with deep bays, bounded in the rear by spacious valleys, while the mountains swept down to the water's edge, hardly leaving a resting-place, and covered with a heavy growth of trees. We continued sailing in this way outside, until we reached the Ohélau passage, leading to the settlement, and bounded on either side by a beautiful islet. Between them, the water was deep and clear, but their outer sides were flanked by foaming breakers. The channel was about forty yards wide. and after passing through, we glided with equal rapidity over what appeared to be a broad, still lake ; and along the shore we could occasionally distinguish thatched huts peeping from beneath the foliage. Howard, an American, had a French flag and several private signals. These Captain Ben borrowed for the occasion, and the " Eliza Mary" made a flaunting display of bunting as she approached the settlement. A canoe filled with natives came off to meet us, and shouts of recognition were exchanged between them and some of our *attachés*. The leeward islanders having a strong aversion to anything French, one of the natives in the canoe called out in his own language, " Haul down that blackguard rag, for it's a disgrace to a Raiatéan vessel !" After rounding the last intervening point, the scattered houses of the settlement were in view ; and ranging up near the shore, we let go our anchor.

Our first impressions were unfavorable ; the mountain ridges immediately in the rear approached the water so closely as to leave but a narrow strip of level land to build upon. The mountains themselves possessed neither beauty nor grandeur, when viewed from this point ; above the lower belt of vegetation they were covered with guava bushes. Along the shore the effect was more pleasing, though at the present time too solitary to fascinate ; it was covered to the water's edge with dark groves of bread-fruit, orange, and lime trees, above which rose the slender trunks of the cocoanut. The houses seemed to be entirely deserted ; a few canoes were hauled upon the beach, and, save a dozen natives who came down and shouted to us from the shore, we saw no other indications of life. The problem was presently solved by a canoe that came off, paddled by two natives and a white man in the employ of Mr. Platt. After exchanging *iauránas*, (salutations,) George stated that old King Tamatoa was giving a grand feast up at Opóa, and nearly all the inhabitants of the settlement had gone up to participate in the festivities ; after which, an entertainment was to be given in town, by Tamáre, the opposing chief.

Our fresh provisions having run low, Merton, who professed to be in a state of starvation, ventured to inquire whether there was anything to eat ashore. George held up both hands, and exclaimed, " Plenty, plenty—the bread-fruit's just in season."

15

" Hang the bread-fruit ! we aren't Grahamites ; we want something substantial, in the shape of beef-steaks, pork chops, and hot rolls and butter ; we are starving, man."

George rolled up his eyes at the enumeration of these dainties ; as to beef, he said, the natives who wandered up the mountains for *feis* occasionally saw a wild cow ; and, further, that parties had been foraging about for every quadruped that wore bristles, stealing what they couldn't buy, as a contribution for the grand feast.   Hot rolls and butter he had eaten about ten years previous in Sydney.   This was a humiliating statement for gourmands, and very naturally led to the inquiry what they did eat.

" O," said George, " as to that matter, if we can't get a man to go, we go ourselves up the mountains, and back down a load of *feis*, and when we can't get pork or fish. we live on these and roast bread-fruit."

" And what are *feis*, pray ?" asked Merton.

" *Feis !* why, they are the best things to fatten a man you ever ate ; some call 'em wild bananas, because they grow on just such a tree, only the banana bunch hangs down and these grow straight up.   We roast 'em nicely in the ashes, and when the outside skin is pulled off they are soft and yellow, and taste something like a roasted apple."

One of the passengers had the effrontery to insinuate that he didn't believe the man knew how a roasted apple tasted, having lived so long among savages.

George imparted -numerous little items of intelligence, domestic and political ; he said that he could hardly hire a man to work, as King Tamatóa and the Chief Tamáre were making preparations to renew the war.   It was now about six P. M., and Captain Ben jumped into the canoe, (for our only boat had been stove in attempting to hoist it out to save a man's life during the recent voyage,) promising to institute a general forage among pigs and poultry, while we patiently lighted our cigars and leaned over the bulwarks to philosophize.   We were certainly in an awkward " fix :" first, it would be long before the Mangaia men would have an opportunity of returning to the Hervey Group from Raiatéa ; and our passengers for Australia were equally unfortunate, for at Tahiti vessels from San

Francisco, *en route* for Melbourne, frequently touched at that port, between which and the leeward islands communication is very irregular. As to myself, I looked upon the circumstance with indifference. It was mutually agreed by four of us, the after guard, that provided such a thing could be done, we would rent a house, and have a sort of club arrangement, until an opportunity should present itself for leaving the island, and that Merton, who aspired to the mysteries of the *cuisine*, should be caterer. The fortunes of one of our number had been somewhat remarkable : he was a native of New-York, and when a young man, had crossed over to Windmill Point in Canada, with the forces of Von Sholtz, who, with all his commissioned officers, was executed at Toronto ; having survived the three days' fight, he was among those who surrendered and were transported to Van Diemen's Land, subject to her Majesty's clemency. Here he remained until pardoned, but having been absent so many years, his regards for home had become alienated ; he spoke in the highest terms of the indulgent treatment of the Colonial Government to himself and comrades, and from my own observations in Australia, I have not the slightest doubt of the correctness of his statement. He was pleased with the country, had married, and adopted it for his home.

Captain Ben returned after dark, bringing a gloomy report on the larders of all the houses he had visited. We smothered our disappointment, determined to perish like martyrs, on chickens and bread-fruit.

CHAPTER II.

A NEW LOCALITY DESCRIBED.

In the morning we landed in canoes in front of the house of Mr. Platt, a son of one of the early missionaries ; and, as this is a sample of the first-class houses throughout the leeward, or Society Islands, I give a brief description.

An ordinary one-story frame was erected, of *tománu* wood, and

the sides interwoven with wattles.   These were plastered within
and without—the lime being prepared by burning the coral from the
reef which is a carbonate of that mineral—and neatly whitewashed.
This house had glass windows, though generally they have Vene-
tian blinds instead.   The interior is partitioned off, to suit the
convenience of the proprietor, with boards simply dressed, having no
decoration whatever.   In front, they have usually a narrow verandah.   The cook-house is situated a short distance in the rear.   Most
of these houses are raised a few feet above the ground, with only
necessary supporters, and leaving the space beneath open.   The roof
is thatched with the pandanus leaf, and viewed from the interior
of the house, with its white *puráu* rafters, its regularity and simplicity have a pleasing effect; it is far superior to the *pili* of the
Sandwich Islanders.   A few of the more aspiring natives have
adopted these houses, in preference to their own inferior ones.
The mission residences are larger, and some of them neatly furnished.   The ordinary dimensions of a house of this description
are thirty feet in length by fifteen in breadth, and about ten feet
from floor to eaves.   Their floors are usually substantial, being
heavy planks of the *tománu.*   The partitions extend only to a level
with the eaves, and the space above being left open, they merely
serve as screens, for a conversation in one apartment is heard distinctly in another.

Such of these houses as have yards are usually inclosed with rude
fences of *puráu;* but little reference is had to neatness, and the
mouldering relics in the vicinity of many of them are an index to the
diet of their occupants.   Some of these inclosures are naturally or
accidentally ornamented with beautiful orange, lime, and bread-fruit
trees, and occasionally the snowy petals of the Cape jessamine ex-
hale a sweet perfume beside the verandah.

The habitations of the common natives are primitive enough,
being of all sizes from fifteen to fifty feet in length, and some of
them twenty feet from the ridge-pole to the ground.   Their construction is very simple : the parasitic sprouts of the *puráu,* which
are well adapted to this purpose, being straight and light, are divested of their bark, tied into bundles, and placed in salt water,
where they are thoroughly immersed by the weight of large stones.

Having remained in this situation for several days, they are taken out to season ; after which they are driven into the ground, leaving the height required, usually six feet, with a space of at least two inches between each stick, which is about the size of a man's wrist. These are arranged in an oval form, and covered with the beautiful thatch of the pandanus, secured to the rafters by sennit manufactured from the cocoanut husk, and thus the entire fabric is completed without the sound of a hammer. They have but one door ; and the light admitted through this and the interstices of the sides is sufficient for their purposes. A person may stand in the house, and, by looking through any portion of it, observe all that is going on without. The interior offers a sad comment on their habits of cleanliness and industry. Unlike the Hawaiians, their houses are simply strewed with dried grass, without being covered with mats, except a few that are laid down to sleep on. During stormy weather, mats which are rolled up outside and secured beneath the eaves of the thatch, are drooped, and afford a tolerable screen. These houses have a fanciful appearance, and at a short distance might be mistaken for receptacles of poultry. However, constructions of this description which I have seen at Tahiti, where the light yellow bamboo was used instead of the *puráu*, have a beautiful appearance, and are in harmony with the landscape. But very few of them have small cultivations of taro and sweet potatoes adjoining.

At the house of Mr. Platt, I found the Rev. George Charter, a resident missionary ; also Tamáre, the rebel chieftain, together with several natives of both sexes, sitting or standing in the verandah. I enjoyed a half hour's conversation with Mr. Charter, and listened with interest to his communications respecting this group. I was at once struck with the difference between the Sandwich and Society Islanders. The latter were a handsomer race, and most of them finely proportioned : the females were prettier, and courteous and modest in their deportment, without the rudeness of the other. The dress of the males was usually a fancy regatta shirt and the *paréu*, or a couple of yards of fancy prints simply girded about their loins, and extending midway from the knee to the ankle ; that of the females resembled the loose *holokú* of the Hawaiians, but, though simple, was much more becoming. Instead of the broad yoke and

formidable gigot sleeves, they were confined at the neck by simple
bands or collars, and hung around them in loose folds, while the
sleeves were flowing or oriental.   Fine English prints, having a
delicate pink figure, were all the rage during my visit.   The complexion of these islanders is an olive brown.

My companions had preceded me through the settlement, and I
commenced my peregrinations alone, sauntering along the Broom
road, which runs parallel with the sea, and on either side of which
were scattered the houses of the natives, some of them occupied
and others deserted.   Finding the settlement to be more extensive
than I had imagined, I turned back a short distance to procure, if
possible, a horse.   Having no interpreter, I found it difficult to make
the natives comprehend my wants, for I spoke in Hawaiian.   One
of them ran off and soon returned with a native of that group, who
gave me the Tahitian designation for the quadruped, which was *púa
hóro fenúa*, or "the pig that runs on the ground."   After a short
search, a young colt was brought, without saddle, and having simply
a vegetable bridle.   This I was requested to mount, and their
charges would be in proportion to the services required.   It is almost needless to add that walking was deemed preferable ; and at
John's (the name of the Hawaiian) invitation, I accompanied him to
his house, where he promised to cook me a breakfast.   This consisted of roast fowl, bread-fruit, *feís*, and for a beverage, one of nature's choicest goblets, a young cocoanut.   The seasoning consisted
of the expressed juice of the ripe cocoanut mixed with sea-water,
having the appearance of milk.   It is called *miti*, and to one accustomed to it, is considered quite palatable.

From John I learned that Merton and his companions had found
their way to the house of another Hawaiian, an old resident on this
island, and named Maiopú, (sick stomach.)   As the distance was
nearly a mile, he carried me in a canoe, and landing, we hauled it
up on a projecting point.   The appearance of the settlement in this
direction was pleasanter, for the space between the sea-shore and
the mountains was broader, and there was more open ground.   It
seemed as if we had but just reached the thickly-settled portion, for
we were surrounded by natives of both sexes, and, among them, little
children, innocent of apparel of any description, were scampering

about in all directions, and bent on having a holiday generally. The abode of Maiopú was a snug little plastered tenement, having a verandah in front, and this was literally crowded with Raiatéan belles, some of whom were strikingly handsome, with intelligent countenances. Nearly all of them wore the white flowers of the jessamine in the lobes of their ears, or interwoven with the glossy black tresses, falling loosely upon their shoulders, or gathered into a knot behind. Some wore garlands of fern or leaves, while around the wrists of a few were bracelets of the small mottled cowrie. To judge from their animated conversation, our advent afforded a pleasing theme for comment; but as we approached, they modestly permitted us a free passage to the door-way, where we found the stragglers just sitting down to a capital feast that Maiopú had provided.

We all returned by the road, and saw many a thatched roof peeping out from the dark foliage by which it was embowered. The land near the shore is in many places very low, at times swampy, and during heavy gales portions of it are overflowed. The soil of the settlement has frequently a light sandy appearance, still it is very prolific for its indigenous products. The road was in some places completely thrown up by that troublesome species of crustacea which infests certain portions of the torrid zone, the land-crab, (*cancer ruricola.*) Their holes were numerous, for they burrowed in every direction; in some climates, they even venture into the houses and crawl about upon the rafters; they are cautious, and seldom venture far without having a hiding-place accessible.

We passed the native church, a large building, oval in form, being weather-boarded, and having green venetians; it was sufficiently commodious to seat two hundred persons. Near by was the white school-house, also the court-house, a spacious affair, consisting of a substantial frame-work, with *puráu* sides; the interior is simply strewed with dried grass, without having anything approximating to either seat or rostrum. The residence of Mr. Charter, a neat, white cottage, occupied a commanding position upon the hill, and was surrounded by a grove of fruit-trees. There is a melancholy interest connected with this settlement, for here commenced the labors of that pioneer of missionary enterprise, the Rev. John Williams, who, by his persevering efforts, built a small vessel, and carried the Gospel to the

Hervey Group, a portion of which he discovered, also to the Austral and Samóan Islands, finally receiving the crown of martyrdom from the savages of the New Hebrides, at Eromanga.

Mr. Platt was kind enough to lease us a small house for a nominal sum, and further, promised us the loan of tea-kettle, frying-pan, and sundry utensils indispensable to housekeeping.

CHAPTER III.

WE COMMENCE HOUSEKEEPING.

HAVING received the key, we proceeded at once to our new quarters. The house was small, but as well finished as any in the settlement, with a narrow hall and four apartments, green venetians, and a pleasant verandah, which was reached by half a dozen steps, and shaded by bread-fruit and orange trees that grew in the yard. The premises were well fenced, and had a good gate ; in the rear we found a nice cook-house, but neither stove nor utensil. The spreading branches of two or three cocoanut trees were waving overhead, and beneath were a few banana and papaya trees ; also the mandioca plant, and numerous creeping vines. The house had remained long untenanted, and interloping vines had forced their way between the interstices of the *puráu*, and were creeping among the blackened stones and cinders of the fireplace. In the rear a projecting spur of the mountain rose abruptly, covered with an almost impenetrable growth of guava and lime trees, the bright-yellow fruit intermingled with the foliage. Our water was to be procured from a spring in the yard adjoining.

Our first care was to make ourselves comfortable for the night, and to this effect we sent off for our bedding to the Eliza Mary. It was mutually arranged that, as one of the rear apartments was filled with pandanus leaves for thatching, the opposite one should be reserved for a store-house and dining-room, while the two front ones were to be occupied as dormitories. A supper of roast fowl and bread-fruit had been provided for us by " Sandwich Island Johnny," and this was served up promiscuously on a large platter, and partaken of in primitive style in the verandah.

In the evening we sat down upon the steps to observe the movements of our visitors, who were sitting and reclining upon the grass, wishing to offer a welcome which they knew not how to express. Having heard much of the natural talent of these natives for singing, we intimated that an exhibition of their vocal powers would prove a most acceptable diversion. Accordingly, a dozen girls seated themselves in a circle, and, after the customary simpering, one commenced chanting a strain in a minor key. Immediately after, it was taken up by her companions, whose voices chimed in with exquisite harmony. This talent is natural, for they understand not a note of music. The voices of the Hawaiians that have been cultivated are discordant in comparison. Without any pretensions as an amateur, but trusting to my operatic reminiscences, I heard the complete and harmonious intonations of the female voice, ranging from the rich, deep contralto to the clear and almost ethereal soprano. To us, in that far-off nook, this vocal melody beneath the orange-trees lent a more pleasing effect than the thrilling strain of " *Tutto é gio ja*" breathed with affected passion beneath a gorgeous canopy.

Our musical soiree having terminated, we expressed a desire to see the boys produce fire by rubbing two dry sticks together. A dozen of them started to their feet and commenced a simultaneous attack upon the fence to obtain pieces of the *puráu*, which is soft, and preferred by them for this purpose. A large piece is laid upon the ground, upon which they either sit or kneel. Along this a stick about a foot in length, held firmly between the thumbs and hands, which are lapped over each other, is propelled obliquely at an angle of about forty-five degrees. This moves slowly and steadily at first, wearing a groove in the lower piece, at the extremity of which a light dust collects as it is worn deeper by the continued friction. A faint breath of vapor seems to curl above it, and then the motion is increased until the groove turns black as the stick flies rapidly along, while the smoke rolls above it in a cloud. This is the critical moment ; should the operator suspend his labor, all would be lost. The stick flies until the groove is charred, and the powder at the ex

tremity changes from a white to a dark brown.   He then suddenly
pauses, holding the stick firmly in the extremity of the groove.   It
the dust continues to smoke, his efforts have been successful ; if not,
in vain.   After removing the stick, the little pile continues to smoke
until the fire is visible, which is almost immediately ; after which, it
is blown softly, when it communicates readily to the dry wood, now
reduced to tinder by friction.   The process is simple, and yet I have
seen it frequently attempted by persons unacquainted with the art,
who expended double the labor required without success.

A stranger might have supposed we were about commencing a
torchlight procession, from the number of burning brands ; and this
naturally suggested the absence of an important item in domestic
economy—a lamp.   One of the men volunteered to bring one, and
presently returned with something of this description ; it was a
cocoanut sawed in two, and in the centre of one of the portions
was fastened a small wick of twisted cotton rag ; it was then filled to
a convenient height with cocoanut oil.   The light, notwithstanding its
glaring effect upon the white kernel by which it was surrounded,
was dim and unpleasant, though it answered our temporary convenience.

In due season our visitors dispersed, and spreading our mats and
blankets upon the floor, we enjoyed a tolerable repose.   In the morning we breakfasted at the house of Maiopú, after which, we commenced removing our trunks and other conveniences from the brig,
assisted by the natives.   As usual, there was a crowd of them to
proffer their services ; for our arrival having been notified to the visitors at Opoa, many had hastily embarked in their canoes, and came
down to the settlement.   Trunks and boxes were lowered across
large canoes, being of lighter draught than boats, and consequently
able to approach nearer shore.

When we commenced unpacking, the yard was filled with visitors,
among whom I noticed Tamáre, his wife and daughter, whose authority among his adherents was barely nominal.   As to articles of
present comfort, I was better provided than my companions ; for I
had a capital bed, with musquito-net, besides other articles of furniture, which we shared in common.   Our trunks served us for seats,
and from our packing-boxes, Jasper and Howard, who possessed a

mechanical turn, manufactured tables—the one for the dining-room served a double purpose, being converted into a cupboard by removing the top. Our arrangement for the parlor was larger, and a fancy woollen cover that hung in folds around it, completely concealed the deformity ; this was ornamented by a beautiful solar lamp, and subsequently by marine curiosities, including some exquisite specimens of coral. The window was decorated with a pair of finely embroidered Zurich curtains, and a small piece of carpeting was admirably adapted to the dimensions of the apartment ; besides, we had a library of about fifty volumes, so that in providing for physical comfort, mental recreation had not been forgotten.

In a short time Merton made his report on the culinary department ; this was, half a dozen dinner plates, two dishes *à la mode*, a set of cups and saucers, a set each of tea and table spoons, six knives and eight forks, one large china bowl, (originally designed for ablutions, but found on inspection to answer the purpose of a soup tureen,) four decanters and a dozen goblets, a pound of table salt, one case of chocolate, and a small paper of loaf-sugar. This comprised our entire stock, except a recently baked loaf and a small quantity of pepper which Jasper had pilfered from the cabin that morning. A servant to perform the drudgery was indispensable, and·for this purpose we hired Bob, a native of Aitutáke, (an island of the Hervey Group,) and a passenger with us from Honolulu. He had been from home seven years, having served that period on board of American whalers, and in addition to his own language, he spoke English, Hawaiian, and Tahitian, so that as an interpreter he proved a valuable acquisition to us. Bob was immediately sent out for the kettle and frying-pan, promised by our landlord, while a Raiatéan boy brought us a bamboo of cocoanut oil, in quantity a gallon, which we purchased for a couple of *reals*.

Merton traversed the settlement from one end to the other, but could procure neither bread nor flour, so that his ambition to present us with hot rolls for our breakfast completely evaporated.

We appointed Bob quartermaster ; he stood upon the verandah and gave out that he was ready to listen to proposals for furnishing supplies. Some of the crowd dispersed, and soon after our ears were assailed by the squealing of pigs and cackling of fowls, while several natives came staggering into the yard with loads of bread-fruit and heavy bunches of *feis ;* two or three of them held savage-looking eels in their hands. Pork was certainly in demand, to judge by the value placed upon it, for we paid at the rate of ten cents per pound ; for inferior chickens, twenty-five cents apiece ; *feis,* ditto per bunch ; and for large bunches of bread-fruit, fifty cents each. Our store-room was soon lumbered up, and we found it convenient to transfer a portion of our stock to the cook-house, where it was occasionally subject to the depredations of juveniles, whom we found it impossible to banish from the premises.

We were sadly in need of a broom, but such a thing was not to be procured in the settlement ; the Chief Tamáre, seeing our dilemma, sent out a boy, who presently returned with a long piece of bamboo and a quantity of cocoanut husk. Tamáre sat down upon the steps, and removing the inner portion of the husk, bound it firmly around one end of the bamboo, and fashioned an excellent broom, which served us as long as we occupied the house. Several clusters of cocoanuts hung temptingly from the trees, and at our request a boy fastened a strip of bark around his ankles, leaving the space of a foot between, then by clasping the trunk with his hands, and bracing firmly with the strap, raising each alternately, he ascended rapidly, and threw down the nuts, which bounded upon the green-sward beneath.

It required two or three days before our domestic arrangements were reduced to a system, and even then we had one annoyance. Bob, who had become an important man, had hired a cook to perform the duties incumbent on himself, and who in turn found it impossible to manage without a couple of mischievous boys to wait upon him. On one occasion he suffered the fire to go out in the cook-house without lighting the lamp, and as there were no matches in the house, the situation of those who remained at home was interesting. The night was rainy, and every native snugly housed. I had been absent at the extremity of the settlement, and returning during the evening, was surprised to find the house in darkness ; ascending the steps, I was astonished at hearing strange rubbing sounds and a very audible panting, as of some one in great fatigue. A most ludicrous spectacle presented itself as I entered : in the hall was Merton, seated upon the floor, making gesticulations with two puráu sticks ;

in one of the apartments Jasper was seated upon a long pole of the same material, watching intently the efforts of Howard, who kneeled upon it, while his elbows were flying with the rapidity of engine cranks, and with the perspiration streaming from him. He was blowing like steam-puffs, and muttering incoherent curses on his luck and natives generally.

As soon as I entered both threw away their sticks and sprung to their feet, insisting on my making the attempt, which was done as soon as I could recover from the mirth their efforts excited. Having frequently practised it, I was successful, but we were careful in future to be provided with either matches or fire.

CHAPTER IV.

RAIATÉAN POLITICS.

FOR several months previous to our arrival, Raiatéa had been the theatre of strange events. To make them more perfectly understood, it may not be inappropriate to record a few items, which, though having no direct bearing upon our narrative, will exhibit the political situation of the group at that time.

While effecting the conquest of the Georgian Islands, Tahiti, and Eímeo, the French occasionally made demonstrations on the Society Islands, where at Huahíne, Raiatéa, and Borabóra, their intrigue and bribery failed, and their engagements were attended by signal defeat from the brave islanders, until British interference limited them to their present possessions. Thus, during successive years, the leeward islands were harassed by a desultory warfare, affording their inhabitants ample opportunity for displaying their warlike propensity, and familiarizing them with the use of fire-arms. The experience thus obtained has been in frequent requisition since the close of the war, for both Huahíne and Raiatéa have at intervals been disturbed by internal dissensions, having two respective parties arrayed against each other. These islands are all independent. Huahine and Maupiti have their queens, aud Raiatéa and Borabóra their kings ; but it is with Raiatéa that we at present have to do.

The name of the king of this island is Tamatóa, descendant of a king of that name, who was grandfather to Queen Pomare of Tahiti, and father to the queen-regent of Huahíne. I should judge him to be near sixty years of age ; he has a very light complexion, but something unpleasant in the expression of his countenance. To strangers, he is hospitable, but in government, a would-be despot, while his word is faithless. The present difficulties grew out of a simple instance of this arbitrary disposition. Tamatóa, the king, being absent at Tahiti, appointed a regent in his stead who partook fully of the characteristics of his master, enforcing the laws at his discretion. According to the ancient *Raiatéa háu*, or primitive form of government, the first fruits were given to the king. This custom also extended to the sea, and the first fish taken in a new net or canoe were forfeited by the possessor. On one occasion, Tamáre, chief of a western district, and next in rank to the king, had launched a new canoe, and in conformity with this law, deposited the first fruits of his success at the feet of the king's regent, who was his inferior in rank. Not content with this, the insatiate deputy called for the second result of his labors. This Tamáre refused, and gave him to understand that such an act, having reference to a person of his rank, would be without a precedent in the annals of Raiatéa. But the regent refused to be convinced, declared the property of Tamáre to be confiscate, and virtually deprived him of his authority. Tamáre felt himself an injured man, and assembled around him a few malcontents who participated in his humiliation. He explained to them the true policy of their king, which was to re-establish the ancient form of government, whereby he or his minions would be at liberty to enter their cultivation and deprive them of what they pleased, and in case of remonstrance, the old custom would be resorted to, placing the offender in a canoe and sending him adrift, without food or paddle, from the leeward side of the island.

With about fifty adherents, the chief retired to his district, and raised the standard of rebellion. The regent saw too late that he had involved himself in a serious difficulty, and a dispatch was immediately sent for King Tamatóa ; on his return, the king deemed it politic to compromise the affair with the liberal party, promising to reinstate his opponent in his privileges and immunities. This was consented to conditionally ; namely, that the private property of his adherents should be respected and no longer considered a royal prerogative ; and, further, that the king should abide implicitly by the laws enacted in the settlement, and which he had sworn to support. But this was deemed presumptuous. Tamatóa thought he had only to extend his royal clemency to receive unqualified submission, and this opposition savored of rank rebellion : his motto was, " *Aut Cæsar, aut nihil ;*" and in 1851 war was declared on both sides, and with occasional intermission, it has continued to the present day. ·

The campaign was first opened by the king, who threw out parties of skirmishers that effected nothing, and were invariably repulsed. The foreigners at the settlement never take part in these wars, and at this time they were continually startled by reports that Tamáre was coming in force to massacre and destroy all before him, for he had continued to advance until he had reached Hamanéne, or Cook's Harbor, and intrenched himself just below Captain Hunter's plantation. King Tamatóa determined to strike a decisive blow, and accordingly marshalled his forces, some three hundred fighting men, which he commanded in person. A portion of these warriors proceeded by sea to the scene of action, about six miles distant, having swivels lashed upon the sterns of some of their canoes, while Tamatóa with the remainder made his way by land. The rebel chief's line of fortification was simple, extending from the shore to one of the mountain spurs, consisting of a narrow ditch and an embankment formed of earth and cocoanut logs, cannon-ball proof, and mounting several guns of various calibre. To defend this he had but seventy-five men—like the force of the king, armed with muskets and spears. The attack was commenced in the morning, and although the Royalists were defeated, there was no lack of bravery on the part of the old king, whose infirmities prevented him from shouldering a musket. Rallying his discomfited warriors, cane in hand, he hobbled on in advance, cheering as he led them towards the intrenchments that were momentarily vomiting forth flame, until a musket-ball in the groin brought him to the ground, from whence he was borne to the rear by his attendants. The fight by sea was equally desperate ; the armed canoes delivered their fire boldly until beaten off by the cannonade from the shore. On one occasion a man while baling was shot through the neck, which checked his operations for a moment, but recovering himself, he wound his *malo* around the wound, and continued his occupation. The Liberals having gained an advantage, sallied from their intrenchments, and then commenced a bush fight among the guavas, in which these natives delight, each endeavoring to secure an advantage by strategy. In one instance two were opposed to each other, and the survivor related with gusto the stratagem by which he conquered his adversary. Both had taken positions a short distance from each other behind trees, each with a loaded musket, and watching an opportunity to shoot the other. Finally, one of them removed his hat to the muzzle of his gun, cautiously displaying it from the side of the tree, as if in the act of reconnoitering ; a moment after the report of a musket rang through the forest, and the hat was pierced by a bullet. Advancing bareheaded, he met his helpless adversary coming towards him, and levelling his piece, shot him dead.

The retreat became a rout, and those who remained in the settlement were soon aware how the battle was going by the fugitives and the wounded, conveyed to the residences of the foreigners, who maintained a strict neutrality. It was a scene of confusion ; the Royalists were certain of returning crowned with laurels to an anticipated banquet, and " sound of revelry by night ;" but instead, the road was now lined with fugitives retreating towards Opóa. What property they could not carry with them was left in the possession of foreigners, while fighting men, the youthful and the decrepit, retreated *en masse.* The wounded king was conveyed in a canoe to one of the *mótus* or islets at the entrance of the harbor, where a number of his warriors rallied around him, determined to make a final stand. The victors passed through the town, advancing until opposite this rendezvous, and would have crossed over and carried the island by assault, but for a French armed schooner that stationed itself between the island and the main. This checked their effervescing spirits ; they returned and took quiet possession of the town, which they have since retained, while Tamatóa was subsequently removed to Opóa, where he has established his head-quarters.

After this, Tamáre assumed the title of Governor, and his authority was acknowledged by the appertaining island of Taháa ; the course pursued by him has been liberal and conciliatory to all parties, whereas the king consoles himself with threats of vengeance, which he has never yet ventured to put into execution. At the Governor's (Tamáre) request, many of the royal party returned to their former habitations, but the majority continue their residence with the king at Opóa. In person, Tamáre is about forty-five years of age, tall and athletic, having an open, intelligent countenance ; his ordinary dress is like that of the other natives, with the exception of a sort of military cap and faded gilt band. In council his orations are brief and to the point. I could never detect a shade of vanity in his character ; for though holding frequent intercourse with him, he has never once alluded to his victories.

His father, who bore the same name, was a successful warrior before him. When King Tapóa of Borabóra came up to conquer Raiatéa in 1832, the former king of this island, after an unsuccessful combat, surrendered his authority to the victors ; but like the old Roman who ransomed his country with iron and not gold, Tamáre assembled his warriors from his district, and told the king it was his prerogative to rule, but not to barter away the liberties of his subjects. Accordingly, a battle was fought off Taháa, in which the invaders were repulsed with slaughter, and the independence of the *Raiatéa hau* secured.

Although the majority, both natives and foreigners, approve the policy of the governor, and would be glad to see the kingdom consolidated in his name, yet his authority is not recognized by any foreign power having intercourse with the island, for every ratified treaty exhibits the signature of Tamatóa. When the recently appointed consul for the Society Islands, B. Toup Nicholas, Esq., arrived at Raiatéa, he found the Liberal party the strongest ; nevertheless, it was necessary he should receive his *exequatur* from the king, and for this purpose he was sent for from Opóa. After the usual formalities had been complied with, it was endeavored to effect a reconciliation between the two factions. Tamáre professed his

16

willingness to resign his authority, provided the king would come and reside among them.   This his majesty partially promised to do, if his portion of the revenue already received should be granted him. The request was complied with ; but after obtaining the money, he embarked with his attendants in their canoes, proceeded to the eastern portion of the settlement, where he purchased a large amount of ammunition, and retired immediately to Opóa, bidding defiance to the Liberals.

Such was the condition of affairs at the period of our arrival. Anticipating the possibility of a war, the natives were idle, and neglected to cultivate their lands, preferring to subsist upon the spontaneous products of the soil ; the result was, that the vicious propensities that had long lain dormant were again awakened, and theft of property was of frequent occurrence.   Nor were the missionaries exempt from these depredations.   I was informed by one of them that he found it cheaper to purchase supplies from the natives than to rear them himself, owing to this pilfering propensity.

CHAPTER V.

"SAIL, O!"—NEW ACQUAINTANCES.

ONE morning Bob came running in and reported a sail off the eastern point of Taháa, to us a welcome piece of intelligence, for we hoped an opportunity would be afforded for leaving the island. Howard, who was an old sea-dog, took his telescope and went out upon the verandah to reconnoitre, and presently reported the sail to be an American whaler standing in for the harbor.   This was a damper, but we hoped at least to obtain a change of diet, if we even had to go back to the days of " good old horse," for we were destitute of salt, nor was there any to be procured in the settlement. Whoever the stranger might be, we were determined to welcome him to our humble abode.

It should have been mentioned that a division had taken place in our family a few days previous. Merton and Jasper rented a house a short distance from us, from which they came near being ejected by the propensity of the former for fresh delicacies. In a spring near the house, the wife of the proprietor kept a pet eel, which she fed every day, snapping upon the water with her fingers, when his eelship would creep out from a rocky crevice and wriggle his way to the surface to receive his accustomed portion. Of this fact Merton was ignorant. and going out one morning to the spring with his pail, he was agreeably surprised to see an inviting object nicely coiled up on the bottom, and he naturally fancied he saw the white flesh quivering in the frying-pan. Returning hastily to the house, he tied a fork to a stick, answering the purpose of a spear, and after again reaching the spring, he thrust it deliberately through the back of the unsuspecting pet. A violent commotion immedidiately succeeded, and amid the mud and confusion, the eel made his escape; the affair subsequently leaked out, and Merton was compelled to make an humble apology, but he was regarded by the woman as a monster of cruelty ever afterwards.

In a short time our new arrival anchored abreast of the settlement, and it proved to be an acquaintance, Captain A——, of the ship N——, whom both Howard and I had last seen in Honolulu. At our request, he took up his abode with us during his sojourn at Raiatéa, and from him we procured important additions to our stock of provision ; he had come for the purpose of obtaining a supply of wood and recruits.

It is hoped that the introduction of two or three new acquaintances will not be looked upon as irrelevant, inasmuch as their presence at the time was a source of convenience and gratification. Let me first present my friend Doctor Doan, who is modestly blushing at the honor thus conferred, a quality peculiar to goodness of heart; his honorary distinction, for he occupies the post of Chief Justice of Raiatéa, has in nowise chilled his social sentiments, nor biased his benevolent feelings. He is still a young man, having highly respectable connections in the United States ; at an early age the propensity for roving became irresistible ; in Europe he marvelled over the antiquities of art, and afterwards sported the poncho and sombrero to the distraction of South American belles. He " pitched and minced

horse-pieces" to his heart's content on American whalers in this
ocean, and having deserted at the Marquesas, was considered a
prodigy by the ladies, who decorated him with cocoanut oil and yellow *tumeric,* appending to his wrists and ankles ornaments of por-
poise teeth and old men's beards ; his multifarious rovings finally
terminated at the South Sea Paradise, Tahiti. In this group he had
resided nearly twelve years, three or four of which have been passed
at Raiatéa. At his house, a snug little tenement in the lower part
of the settlement, I found that he connected the pursuits of commerce
with jurisprudence and pharmacy, for numerous flashy prints were
temptingly displayed upon his shelves, which also glistened with
shining cutlery. In one corner of the apartment was a small but
well-selected library, besides a medicine-chest, partially empty. He
had married a native wife, and three or four male pledges of mutual
affection were the most boisterous illustrations of their kind I ever
witnessed ; for, regardless of parental threats, I have seen them
extended at full length upon the floor, beating a " tattoo" with their
feet, while roaring defiance.

He performed the office of good Samaritan for the settlement, and
was a strong Liberal, expounding the laws and interpreting for the
governor. He has frequently entertained us with illustrations of native eloquence and incidents of character.

In the yard adjoining lived Captain Irvine, a subject of her majesty, and a strong loyalist, a straightforward and industrious man,
attending simply to his own business ; and yet he had managed to
incur the resentment of his neighbors. We always found him hospitable and obliging, and what was better, perfectly independent of
public opinion. He had long resided upon the island, and had been
appointed pilot by King Tamatóa ; previous to this, he had been engaged in the pearl fishery, and by visiting this island, to procure
supplies of *ti-o-ó,* or preserved bread-fruit, for the Paumótuan divers,
he received that name from the natives, but it has subsequently been
corrupted by foreigners into Tio.

Monsieur Guillaume Augusté, a French trader, and his *capitaine,*
M. Flores, must not be omitted, for they were hospitable entertainers ;
and at the house of the former, I have banqueted on a variety of
delicacies, which he assured me were " *tout de Paris.*"

At the extreme eastern portion of the settlement was the residence and trading house of Messrs. Jordan & Lassiter, to whose civilities we were greatly indebted. Jordan was a Boston Yankee, and Lassiter an Englishman, yet they both jogged along together like clockwork.

These acquaintances, with a few others, constituted our social circle. They have been introduced, less from considerations of superior merit, than from a passing tribute to their attentions and hospitality. We may have occasion to refer to them hereafter.

One evening we were sitting together in the verandah, enjoying the breeze fresh from the sea, and listening to the sweet harmony of voices in the yard adjoining, when gradually I felt a strange sensation creeping over me, of which I found it impossible to divest myself. I had sat down, as I supposed, in perfect health, and this change was unaccountable ; it certainly was a symptom of illness the more unpleasant as its occurrence could be attributed to no act of my own. I arose to retire, and staggered giddily to the bed. In the morning I awoke with a burning fever. This was a new source of annoyance, for two or three pleasure excursions had just been planned out, and by this unforeseen event I was rendered a mere cipher.

A servant was immediataly dispatched for Dr. Doan, who soon after arrived, with a countenance full of commiseration, bringing with him two or three vials containing suspicious-looking mixtures. Perfectly helpless, I yielded implicitly to his advice, and swallowed his black draughts and boluses without comment. Tamáre, the chief, visited me frequently with his wife and daughter. The latter was a strange little creature, with a pretty face, and heart of adamant. Drawing the curtains aside, she would say with mock sympathy, "*Iaurána óe Támate táne,*" (Salutations to you, Thomas.) After placing her hand gently upon my feverish face, she would suddenly withdraw it, exclaiming with feigned astonishment, "*A ! méa láhi te weawéa téia mahána !*" (Why ! how warm you are to-day !) then bursting into a laugh, she would drop the curtains, and hasten to romp with her companions in the yard or upon the verandah. They brought whatever they thought would be conducive to my comfort, and I was at the time much affected by the kindness of a native woman, who sent me now and then delicacies of her own preparation, and for which I could not prevail on her to accept a farthing on my recovery.

Our model system of domestic economy was fast becoming dilapidated.   Howard was absent the greater part of the time in company with Captain A——, and Bob, whom I supposed to be a faithful fellow, proved recreant to his duty, and acted as if he were lord of the manor.   One night I called him to my room and gave him his dismissal, together with every other domestic (?) about the establishment, save the cook, for they proved worse than useless.   I frequently detected them through the blinds passing fish and breadfruit through the fence to their friends outside.   After this, I enjoyed a temporary respite.

Merton came into my room one morning, and told me that he was going to circumnavigate the island with Captain Flores in his beautiful boat, and that they had deferred their proposed trip two days, hoping for my convalescence.   I told him to be gone, and not tantalize a sick man with intelligence of that description.   He retreated laughing, promising to bring me all the news when he returned.   Soon after, Captain A—— and Howard came in to tell me that they had just returned from Opóa, where they had been delightfully entertained by his majesty, and that for the morrow a party had been made up to visit the western side of Taháa and gather oysters, both expressing regrets that I could not accompany them.   I rolled over, without uttering a word.   Thus I endured ten days of unspeakable misery and confinement.   During this time, Captain A—— lost eleven men (Hawaiians) by desertion, and took his departure, carrying with him three or four deserters from the British brig " Maid of Julpha," that had just arrived.   When this period had elapsed, I was able to make short walks to a grove of lime-trees near by, which afforded a shady resting-place, and in a few days I communicated the pleasant intelligence to the doctor that his professional services were no longer required.

Merton had a wonderful account to tell of his pilgrimage, as he called it, around the island, including musquito fights and oyster pickings—a sample of which latter he brought me.   They were rock oysters, but, though small, of excellent flavor.

CHAPTER VI.

REEFS AND CORALINES.

About this time, the month of January, it commenced raining, and continued to do so with occasional intermission for several days. Nothing could seem more dreary than our situation, for Howard and I were the sole occupants of the house at the time. Looking out upon the water, we could no longer see the misty hummock of Huahine that bounded the horizon, for tempests of wind and rain were sweeping over the ocean, and the tempestuous clouds that hung like a pall beneath the sky descended at times upon the rugged mountains of Taháa, enshrouding them in their folds. Even the shady groves by which we were surrounded, once so inviting, now wore a cold, unfriendly aspect, for they were reeking with humidity. Not a ghost of a native was stirring, and our hours seemed prolonged to days, as we listened to the beating of the rain upon the roof and the roaring of the tempest-tossed branches. We selected from our library the most gloomy subjects for perusal, as fitting accompaniments to the mental depression that floated in the atmosphere; at best the time wore slowly away, nor did we recover our accustomed spirits until the tempest had passed and the watery clouds had melted beneath the enlivening rays of the sun, as welcome to us as the truant dove with its peaceful emblem.

One pleasant day I prevailed on Howard to accompany me in a small canoe to one of the islets that bound the entrance to the harbor, promising that I would do the paddling, which was nearly two miles from where we resided. We borrowed a little egg-shell of this description of Peter, the old African, cook of the Eliza Mary, and shoved off. This was another instance of working passage, for having once taken our positions, it was impossible to change them; while I paddled, Howard baled without intermission. We soon encountered the trade-winds sweeping across the deep lagoon, and Howard suggested making a "four pint" course of it, thereby edging over towards the reef, where the water was sufficiently shoal for him to use a pole. From the shore to the outer or barrier reef the distance is about a mile, but before reaching it the water shoals gradually, and the bottom is covered with most exquisite specimens of branching, arborescent, and brain coral. At almost every thrust of the pole, some delicate formation was crushed that had cost the invisible architects centuries of labor ; the beauty of these submarine gardens was heightened by the transparency of the water, which enabled us to distinguish minute objects upon the bottom, including the sea-egg, or *echinus*, the *biche de mer*, or trepang, and various specimens of mollusca scattered over the coral or upon the sandy bed. Among these labyrinthic branches the finny tribe were gliding or sporting midway in the clear element, then, frightened at our approach, they would dart away and disappear among the snowy corymbs.

The tints or colors of these corals are white, or mingled with light gray and brown. Nothing can exceed the beauty of this marine animalculine vegetation when beheld reposing upon its bed of yellow sand, through an element as pure as liquid crystal.

Various theories have been advanced respecting the growth of corals. Sir David Brewster has attributed the existence of these beautiful marine productions, including the great barrier reefs of the Southern Ocean, such as are found on the northeast coast of New Holland, or on the western side of New Caledonia, to the incalculable labors of saxigenous, or rock-making polypi ; and has computed that the solid material formed by these invisible animalculæ, including " coraline limestone and other formations, whether calcareous or silicious, that are the work of insect labor," would furnish solid material sufficient for the construction of a satellite. Along the margin of some of these coral structures no soundings have been obtained at a depth of more than one thousand fathoms. Now, it is known that these rock-making polypi cannot exist beyond a few score fathoms below the surface ; and Mr. Darwin, who would also appear to advocate this theory, has furnished the supposition that these structures, when first commenced, were built upon foundations sufficiently elevated to accord with the habits of these invisible architects ; that these foundations during the lapse of ages have been in a gradual course of subsidence, while the structure has continued to augment by new layers of animalculine secretion upon the upper portion. This certainly is ingenious, and may appear plausible, but a more reasonable theory than this has been advanced. It has been found, by passing a current of electric fluid through water holding certain mineral particles in solution, that concrete substances resembling stones are formed. As it is known that sea-water, especially within the tropics, contains vast quantities of carbonate of lime in solution, it has been reasonably supposed that the electric fluid of the atmosphere, or that engendered by the volcanic phenomena that once existed to a great but now limited extent in these regions, may have produced these wonderful results.

There is a great difference observable between the structure of the *reef* coral and that of the exquisite corymbs that vegetate in the quiet lagoons. The former presents the appearance of a dark grayish rock, with the exposed surface more or less porous or perforated, where myriads of worms, sea-slugs, or snails, find a resting-place in these stony cells at low water, and which swarm again when the flood washes over it. On being broken, it is found to be of compact texture, and a microscopic investigation has discovered fossils.

On the other hand, the beautiful zoöphytic branches that blossom in quiet waters, are built *upon* the barrier or foundation reefs, and are the work of a distinct species of polypi, if indeed the other be the production of this genus. The animal structure of these is plainly evinced by their cellular formation, as much so as that of the honeycomb of the bee. They flourish more vigorously in shoal than in deep water, as light has a powerful influence on their growth. These lithophytic plants are by some incomprehensible process cemented to the rock, but are easily detached. I have seen exquisite specimens growing at a depth of less than a fathom beneath the surface. Corals do not necessarily attach themselves to the solid reef, but frequently adhere to rocks or other substances. There is a beautiful specimen at Tahiti, in the possession of Mr. Branda, consisting, if I recollect aright, of a single branch of madrepore, adhering to a large pearl oyster-shell, from the side of which it protrudes like an excrescence. It was found at a remarkable depth in the Paumotu Archipelago, by native divers.

But whether these reefs or coralines are the " agglutinated skeletons" of myriads of animalculæ, or, frowning and smiling, they were ushered into existence by a *coup-de-main* of thunder and lightning, we leave to the investigation of the scientific. Once more resuming our paddle, and taking it leisurely, we reach the *mótu*, after floating for an hour upon the still lagoon.

The inquiry naturally suggests itself, how came these islets to exist like scattered links of one universal chain of verdure that for more than sixty miles might have encircled the two islands ? The inference from observation would be, that the portions of the barrier reef adorned with these miniature gardens must have been more elevated than those portions of it at present exposed, which are over-flowed at high water. This structure is augmented by minute parti-cles, shells and fragments of coral, which are washed up and cement-ed to the growing mass, gradually increasing until it is raised above the surface, when these coral fragments are decomposed by exposure and the rays of the sun. Drift-wood, marine productions or plants, and other substances floating upon the sea, are deposited, and by de-composition the formation of a soil commences. At this stage, it is thronged by myriads of *crustacea*, whose skeletons are the ultimate price of their abode. These, together with the deposits of sea-birds, form an earthy stratum of sufficient richness to reproduce the germs of the pandanus or cocoanut that are cast upon it, and in time, other species of the vegetable kingdom that flourish in a light, sandy soil. Some of these appear to be thus in process of formation, and which in time may rank with their sister islets.

We found the *mótu* to be low and sandy ; its entire area could not 'exceed two acres. It was completely covered with a jungle of *pandanus, puráu,* cocoanut, and a few other varieties of vegetation, through which we often found it difficult to penetrate. The ground was in many places perforated by those industrious burrowers, the land-crabs, and the white sandy shore was strewed with fragments of coral, in every stage of decomposition. On the opposite side of the narrow channel was the larger island on which King Tamatóa found an asylum from his pursuers ; it is said to contain a spring of fresh water.

After hauling our canoe upon the sand, we retired to the interior of the island, and lighting our cheroots, sat down for a brief repose beneath the gloomy shade of the *fála* trees. So dense was the forest that the roar of the breakers upon the reef sounded like the murmuring of distant thunder, mingled with the steady breeze that was now bending and tossing the boughs above us. It was proposed that we should make our way across the island, and, if practicable, wade out to the outer reef. But a difficulty arose at the outset as to the course; Howard insisted on going to the right, and I to the left, and as neither would be convinced by the other, we set off in opposite directions. After floundering for some time through this vegetable network, I reached the shore, but, to my mortification, it was at a point directly opposite the channel, and I found that it would be necessary to wade for nearly one-fourth the circumference of the island to reach a convenient starting point for the reef. I shouted to Howard, but receiving no answer, concluded that we had both been wise in our own conceits: had the canoe been there, I would have paddled around, for to walk on the shore was impossible, as the trees in this place grew close to the water's edge, and their branches were drooping over it. The water being only waist-deep, and the bottom hard and sandy, I waded the distance, and found Howard comfortably seated on an old cocoanut trunk, and laughing at me for my pains.

We were now in close proximity to the great barrier reef, against which the waves were incessantly beating; the distance could not have been more than thirty yards, but the water was in some places very deep. With poles to steady ourselves, we picked our way by stepping upon the immense coral blocks that arose from the bottom, sometimes making long detours to avoid deep gulfs. The water deepened as we approached the reef, and Howard, who preferred dry garments to sight-seeing, retreated to the island. I continued stepping from block to block, until the water reached my shoulders, when there was nothing but a deep blue channel between me and the reef; across this I swam, and climbed up the rocky wall.

Plain, yet massive, it was one of the greatest natural curiosities I ever beheld; where I stood, its level breadth was about fourteen feet; from this, its outer portion sloped gradually away at an angle of fifteen degrees, and against it the surf was rolling heavily, sometimes washing across it into the still lagoon. This giant rampart was of both dark and light gray colors, covered in many places with marine plants, and perforated by small basins, filled with clear water; in these tiny fish were sporting. Occasionally sea-slugs are seen reposing in the crevices, and various specimens of shell-fish are scattered over it. This immense barrier has a circumference of more than sixty-five miles, inclosing two beautiful islands, whose aggregate circumference is fifty-six miles, besides having more than six channels through it, navigable for vessels of any class. It is adorned by twenty-seven islets, varying in size of from one to ten acres in extent, and nearly all of them covered with luxuriant verdure and extensive groves of cocoanut-trees. The inner portion in some places recedes gradually, and here, during the night, the natives, spear in hand, fish by torchlight; at low water, when the sea is comparatively calm, its surface is exposed, and a person may travel for miles upon this solid rock, from islet to islet, which stretch around it in evergreen links. The view from it is beautiful and impressive; on one hand you have the vast expanse of ocean, with its snowy crests, and on the other, a placid lake of varied tints, bounded by a lofty island, moulded into fantastic shapes, over which is spread a mantle of living green fringed by waving palms that lend an exquisite finish to the landscape. The average breadth of this reef, from its outer edge to the shore, is about a mile and a half; between the northern and southernmost points of Raiatéa and Taháa, the distance is two miles, and from reef to reef, five miles; these two points, receding at acute angles, leave a broad area of water like a lake, deep enough in most places for vessels of the largest class, and an admirable place for regattas.

After strolling about upon the slippery rock, and filling my pockets with conchological specimens, I swam to the island, where Howard proposed gathering shell-fish for supper; accordingly, we waded back towards the canoe, making observations by the way. At one place near the shore my comrade halted, having seen small bubbles issuing from the sand; thrusting his pole down close to the spot, and suddenly prying up, he dislodged a large crab, and hove it from the end of the stick upon the beach, which it no sooner reached than it immediately commenced a retrograde movement for the water; but hastening on shore, we caught him when he had nearly effected his escape. He proved an acceptable addition to our supper that evening. After collecting a few specimens of coral, and exploring the opposite side of the island, we again embarked, this time with the wind in our favor, and reached the landing-place in front of our house before sunset.

We found Doctor Doan awaiting our arrival, and having related to him all the wonders we had seen, he laughed at us, promising that if we would accompany him some day, he would show us marine curiosities of which we had never dreamed.

CHAPTER VII.

A SABBATH.

THE day following was the Sabbath. All was tranquil; not a wreath of smoke curled above the foliage, and not a canoe glided upon the still waters; the universal quiet and repose were emblematical of the design for which it was consecrated.

At an early hour, children, arrayed in their best attire, passed by with their books to attend the Sabbath-school, and at a later hour, adults assembled to attend divine service in their church. Whatever might have been their conduct during the week, Sunday was observed with the strictest decorum, and in a most exemplary manner. They wore their ordinary costume, though perhaps of finer quality, and with greater reference to decoration. The females, instead of going bareheaded, wore bonnets platted from the stalk of the arrow-root, which, after the necessary preparation, is of a light straw color, delicate and exceeding beautiful; but this description of head-dress fashioned from it is ill shaped, improperly adjusted, and one of the most unbecoming appendages they could possibly adopt. To judge from appearances, one would infer that the fashion introduced by the ladies of the mission about the beginning of the present century had been preserved to the present day without the slightest innovation.

Most of them carried a London edition of the Tahitian Bible in a finely braided basket or bag, to preserve it.

In company with Merton, I attended morning service. The interior of the church was plainly furnished, having simply a formidable pulpit, small altar, and comfortable seats. Through the open blinds, the sea-breeze rendered the apartment refreshingly cool. Nearly two hundred persons were assembled, and among these our Mangaía men were conspicuous by their orange-colored *tipútas,* (a garment resembling the Spanish poncho,) and all observed the most profound attention to the services, which were conducted by the Rev. Mr. Platt. We were particularly pleased with the singing, for the voices of the congregation were in perfect unison, these islanders having no other guide than a delicate perception and inherent love of harmony. I should mention, however, that occasional interruptions occurred, by wrinkled deacons administering reproof to disorderly juveniles who had brought *guavas* and *mapés* with them for a lunch during service.

A simple faith had temporarily united in one common bond of fellowship opposing warriors who had spilt each other's blood, and who were again to be drawn up in hostile array. On these occasions, personal animosities are forgotten, and the hands that to-day clasp the sacred symbol, may on the morrow brandish weapons for mutual destruction.

In the education of their converts, the missionaries of this group have had greater reference to scriptural knowledge, than instruction in the ordinary and higher branches. In consideration of the idle and warlike propensity of the natives, this course may perhaps be judicious, but I should consider it questionable ; had they exhibited the energy and *perseverance* that have characterized teachers in Hawaii, thereby discovering to the natives their own intellectual capacities, and the exhaustless physical resources at their command, a different result would have been witnessed. As it is, the majority of them are profoundly ignorant of those acquirements which would naturally instil into their minds ideas of a higher order, and have a tendency to elevate them from the degrading influences they are prone to indulge. But, too much praise cannot be awarded these laborers for the good they have already accomplished. They have fought the good fight, and rescued a nation from idolatry in its most hideous form, substituting a spiritual faith instead ; though the pathway of duty has been strewed with thorns, their hearts have been cheered by a consciousness of sincerity and the assurance of future reward.

When the missionaries were first settled in this group in 1797, they unfortunately erred in their nautical calculations, having omitted to *lose* a day in crossing the meridian opposite that of Greenwich, so that the Sabbath observed here is the true Saturday.   Since the conquest of the Georgian Islands, the French have very properly corrected this mistake, contrary to the wishes of the resident missionaries.   While at Tahiti and Mooréa the natives are worshipping, at the leeward islands the ordinary vocations are pursued.   The same is the case with the Spaniards at the Philippine Islands.

From careful observation, I should say that a greater reverence is manifested for the Sabbath in this group, Tahiti excepted, than at the Sandwich Islands, not only publicly, but also in private ; while the outward deportment of the natives would lead one to suppose that greater respect was entertained for morality.   Most families faithfully observe their devotions, and I have frequently paused to listen to their sacred melodies swelling through the groves in the still evening.

After the mission was first established in these islands, years of patient toil were consumed before beneficial results were apparent, so strongly were the natives addicted to their idolatrous customs ; when, in 1812, King Pomáre of Tahiti embraced the faith, and was baptized, he did so against the wishes of his subjects, only a few hundred of whom were hopefully converted.   So late as 1815, the missionaries estimated the number of converts throughout the group not to exceed five hundred.   Since then the work has steadily progressed, and if the condition of these islanders since their evangelization is in many respects unenviable, it cannot be attributed to the renunciation of heathenism, as some have foolishly asserted, but to an obstacle more formidable to missionary labors than the idolatry they endeavor to subvert.   It is the baneful influence of foreign innovation that in this ocean has followed close upon the track of spiritual conquest, which can hardly attain its object, ere compelled to concentrate its resources for a war of self-defence.

A comparative glance at the former condition of these islanders will exhibit the nature and magnitude of the victory that has been achieved. In many respects this resembled that of the unevangelized Hawaiians : the government was of the most arbitrary description, the life and property of the subject being at the mercy of a despotic ruler. In their domestic relations they were equally unhappy, for the tyranny of a king to his vassal was exhibited in a minor degree by the husband towards his wife, who was prohibited from his privileges and enjoyments, and degraded to menial occupations. Polygamy was common, and there were those whose profession was infanticide. Their wars were extremely desolating, and were conducted with sanguinary ferocity, the victorious party visiting its vengeance alike upon the aged and infirm, innocence and infancy. Such as were spared were devoted to slavery or heathen sacrifice.

Their notions of a future state were vague and indefinite. Though they believed in " a sweet-scented paradise" and " a foul-scented abode," both were tenanted by divinities whose attributes were fear and servile obedience to the commands of their self-constituted vicegerents. The worst feature of their fanatic idolatry was the necessity for human sacrifices ; and as the king was recognized as the supreme head of the Church, having power over subordinate rulers, the spiritual mandates were enforced by the secular arm, and the *nuncios* seldom returned without bringing their victims bleeding to the altar, over which the professedly inspired priests would chant a *Te Deum.*

CHAPTER VIII.

A TRIP TO OPÓA.

IT has before been remarked that Teó, *alias* Captain Irvine, was a staunch Royalist, and it remains to be further stated that he was the possessor of property at Opóa, the residence of the king ; this place he was in the habit of visiting frequently for trading purposes, also to procure supplies of *puráu* and coral blocks for the construction of his fences and contemplated jetty and aqueduct. These periodical trips were performed in a snug sail-boat, tight as a bucket, and which, he said, possessed the wonderful faculty of steering itself.

At his invitation, I accompanied him one morning, leaving Howard to keep house alone ; for provision by the way, we took several boxes of sardines, a few sea-crackers, and a couple of bottles of claret. Opóa is about eight miles distant from the settlement, and situate in a southeast direction ; fortunately, the day was fine, and the trades not blowing as usual, the light breeze stirring was fair. No pleasure-boating could surpass this, for we lounged easily upon the stern sheets, and the sails were so trimmed to the wind that neither of us was required at the tiller. Nanáu, our little curly-headed boy, sang, Teó smoked, and I gazed abroad at the ever-changing scenery.

The landscape, though charming, seemed the abode of solitude ; apparently undisturbed, the forest swept down to the water's edge, crowning ridges and clothing ravines ; yet along these blooming shores, for wide intervals, no hut sought shelter beneath the spreading boughs, and no voice re-echoed through the silent groves. We passed several deep bays, and at the head of one, Teó informed me, was a battery, mounting heavy guns, erected years ago by the natives, in anticipation of an attack from the French. A little hamlet, situate in one of these valleys, was called Wairáhi, on account of its large stream of water.

At eleven o'clock we reached Havíla, where the captain had come into possession of an extensive tract of real estate by his wife. This was a lovely spot, having a clear stream winding through a broad extent of level land, covered with an open grove of trees, in which the cocoanut and bread-fruit were conspicuous. At the disemboguement of the stream, the banks were walled up, and had once been spanned by a substantial bridge, but this had been suffered to decay, and all that remained for a substitute was a solitary cocoa-nut log.

After anchoring the boat near the bridge, I followed Teó into a house, or rather shed, while Nanáu was dispatched for young cocoa-nuts. In the house we found half a dozen girls, and about the same

17

complement of young men; all recognized Teó; in fact, he was known to every native throughout the group. They had been indulging in an *uté*, consisting of singing and gesticulations, a species of diversion prohibited by law. At Teó's request, two noble specimens of bread-fruit were thrown upon the fire to roast, while we strolled up the valley.

Our path was along the bank of the stream, occasionally obstructed by projecting bushes; but soon emerging to an open space, we saw several houses apparently well tenanted, where men were employed in preparing *ti-o-ó*. This consists simply in roasting the bread-fruit, and after divesting it of the rind with a cowrie-shell prepared for that purpose, burying it under ground, where it is suffered to remain for months to undergo decomposition. When disinterred, the odor emitted by the dark mass is very offensive, and yet, as an article of diet, the *ti-o-ó* is relished by the natives, and esteemed a luxury by the pearl-divers of the Paumótus.

The stream looked so inviting that I divested myself of garments, to enjoy a cool bath, while a group of children sat watching me from the banks. The water was perfectly clear, and waist-deep; the bottom was covered with sharp shells, against which Teó cautioned me, but with all my care, I wounded myself in the right foot, occasioning me afterwards great inconvenience.

Returning to the house, we found our food cooked to a nicety. Whether owing to hunger or otherwise, I fancied that bread-fruit never tasted half so delicious, and Teó was of the same opinion. This, together with our sardines and young cocoanuts, afforded us a substantial meal. The beverage furnished by the latter is something superior. To be enjoyed in its perfection, it should be tasted soon after the nut is plucked. It is then cool and refreshing, having the taste of a slightly acidulated drink. No idea of its quality can be formed by tasting the rancid liquor from the old imported nuts, for among the natives they are seldom used unless for fattening swine or manufacturing oil. I have attempted to carry these vegetable goblets to sea, but they soon become stale and insipid, more especially those that have been fractured by falling to the ground. On some of the islands of the low archipelago, the natives have no other water than that afforded by these nuts; and so expert do they be-

come, that from the ground they can look up and discover their age
and quality—an important attainment where the laborious process of
climbing is necessary to procure them. These trees are very prolific, and some are said to produce more than three hundred nuts
each during the year. I have counted upwards of sixty cocoanuts
upon one tree, in various stages of growth, where they hung in
clusters.

Our bread-fruit was the oval, a choice description. When broken
open, it was of a light straw color, mealy, and possessing a delicious
flavor.

After receiving on board the cocoanuts gathered by Nanáu,
also a few oranges, with difficulty obtained, for they were out
of season, we weighed anchor, and glided along this beautiful
shore, shaded by an interminable grove. At two o'clock P. M. we
reached the outskirts of Opóa, on the northwestern entrance of the
bay, and on the opposite side of which was the residence of the
king. At this place were some dozen houses, scattered beneath a
forest of cocoanut-trees, the occupants of which came down to the
beach to welcome our arrival. Owing to the shoalness of the water,
we could not approach within twenty yards of the shore, but a couple
of stout natives waded in and carried us off on their shoulders.
All seemed rejoiced to see Teó ; and after *iauránas* were exchanged,
the men begged to look at the new *tipis* (hatchets) he had promised,
while the girls clustered around, inquiring whether he had any new
styles of prints to introduce. All these requisitions were complied with
as soon as possible, for some stout men had been dispatched to the
boat to remove a large chest of merchandise. Several hatchets were
immediately purchased, and the enviable possessors commenced test-
ing their merits upon cocoanut and bread-fruit logs, while fathom after
fathom of flashy calico was measured off for such of the girls as
were able to purchase new *hauamús*, or dresses. These they girded
around their waists, and strutted about the premises with evident satisfaction, until one of the old women remarked, in a fit of envy, that
she " didn't like to see young folks put on quite so many airs in displaying finery purchased with borrowed funds."

Intending to call again at this place on our return, the merchandise was re-embarked, and we continued our journey. Soon passing

the last point, we opened the beautiful bay of Opóa, a sheet of crystal water, having a sandy bottom, and when visible, bestudded with exquisitely formed coralines. Its extremity was bounded by a broad valley, having lofty, irregular ridges on either side, and around this semicircle of verdure were scattered habitations, barely peeping through the luxuriant foliage. The settlement of the king is on the southeastern side of the bay, and at the time we approached it, I thought I had never witnessed a more pleasing ideal of Polynesian tranquillity and beauty. There was not a vestige of foreign innovation to mar the effect: the wicker-like huts seemed reposing beneath the boughs of this ancient grove, and towering high above all, was the gigantic trunk of an *óha*, or banian, the loftiest and most beautiful tree I ever beheld in the Pacific.

In front of his house, Teó had built a sort of jetty or butments, of coral blocks, upon which rested cocoanut logs to facilitate access to the boat, or *vice versa*. The domicil was of the most ordinary description of rustic architecture, less than the dimensions of an ordinary poultry-yard, having, like the majority of native houses, neither door, nor mats upon the floor, which was strewed with dried grass. Pretensions to a partition were displayed by a row of stakes, dividing the interior into two unequal portions ; in the smaller apartment was a long and narrow frame-work, resembling a hearse, but designed for a bedstead, which, through courtesy, he insisted that I should occupy. This, however, affords no criterion for judging of his domestic arrangements in the settlement, where his house is commodious, and perhaps better furnished than any other on the island. Our blankets, &c., were disembarked, and carried by officious natives to the house, where we endeavored to arrange them previous to paying court to royalty, and while thus engaged, we received a message from his majesty to join him at supper.

The house occupied by the royal family at that time was of the ordinary native description, with one of its sides open, and its floor covered with a profusion of mats ; the interior was encumbered by chests containing personal property, disposed of without particular reference to order. This was merely a temporary place of sojourn, while a more appropriate residence was being erected. Teó presented me first to the king and then to his consort, both of whom were graciously pleased to extend a cordial welcome, inviting me to sit upon the mats with them and partake of their repast. There was no lack of attendants, one of whom brought me a cup of tea. Her majesty sent me from her own plate the head of a boiled albicore, a favorite fish, and this portion is esteemed by them a delicacy. We had the usual complement of bread-fruit, feís, taro, and cocoanuts ; during the banquet, his majesty condescendingly offered me a portion of the *ti-ò-ò* he was eating, but though wishing to oblige him, my stomach urged a strong remonstrance.

The evening was sultry, and we were sorely pestered by musquitoes. I laid down by a miserable cocoanut lamp, endeavoring to read a piece of an old romance I had accidentally discovered, but with the dazzling glare and the natives and musquitoes that infested the house, I was compelled to abandon the attempt. About half past seven a drum was beat, and the former of our intruders dispersed. How Teó slept, I never inquired, but my experience was dismal, for I was condemned to alternate buzzings and suffocation, by covering my head with the quilt and removing it for respiration.

CHAPTER IX.

THE SACRED GROVE.

THE wonders of Opóa were yet to be seen. In former days, when idolatrous worship was the universal creed, this locality was deemed sacred above all others, not only to the inhabitants of this group, but also to those of adjacent islands speaking a foreign tongue, and all resorted here to offer human sacrifices to the god Oro. The site of the *maraes*, or temples, is on a level strip of land extending into the lagoon, a short distance beyond the settlement, an appropriate spot for heathen orgies. They are now in ruins, and remain only as monuments of human depravity.

Having signified to Teó my wish to visit them, he provided a couple of boys to accompany me, though no one could mistake finding

them by simply following the shore-road.   Passing through an extensive grove of bread-fruit trees, we emerged to an open space,
where upon the beach rose the trunks of several large *aito*, or iron-
wood trees, in shape resembling the poplar, but more shadowy and
gloomy.   We presently came to a rude fence constructed of coral
blocks and cocoanut logs, extending from the shore to the mountain;
after climbing over this, we were within the sacred precincts.
The path for a considerable distance was along an avenue of venerable trees, whose branches and thick foliage wove a dark canopy overhead, through which the sunbeams never penetrate.   Two girls who
had followed us now passed by, with their arms encircling each
other's waists, and strolling leisurely in the shade, caused the woodland solitudes to re-echo their merry songs.   Once, their lives would
have paid the forfeit of their temerity.   We turned aside to the left
towards the shore, and found considerable difficulty in picking our
way through the tangled underwood.   Presently we came upon a
solitary, upright monumental stone, about seven feet high and four
feet broad, concerning which my youthful guides could give me no
information.   We now reached one of the principal relics; it was
an inclosure, perhaps twenty-five feet in length by six in breadth,
formed of two parallel rows of massive stones, set up like slabs, and
the portions above ground varying in height from two to six feet.
The area within was covered with loose stones, across which, in
some places, huge trunks had fallen, and were mouldering; also two
skulls and a few other human relics were exposed.

I sat down upon a fallen trunk to make a sketch of the spot, but
was immediately so besieged by musquitoes that I was obliged to call
the two boys to my assistance, who commenced beating the air with
a couple of leafy branches.   After finishing the outline, we crossed
the path, and plunging deeper into the forest, reached the principal
of these relics.   This was a huge mound, one hundred feet in length
by twenty in breadth and ten in height.   It was walled up by immense slabs, some of them basaltic, others coral.   The dimensions
above ground of one which I measured were, height and breadth
respectively ten and eight feet, and thickness twenty-one inches.
We ascended this human hecatomb by a narrow space between two
of its massive supporters, and found the summit covered with loose

rocks and stones, over which a rank vegetation was creeping. Through thin crevices in every direction grew a broad-leafed plant, called by the natives *lauóha*. I also noticed several small trees growing upon it, having the formidable name of *to-pe-ta-pu-a-ta-téa*.

A more fitting retreat for consummating inhuman rites could not have been selected. Around the slender stems of the pandanus, dark leaves droop like mourning plumes from their spiral crowns, and on every side rise the ancient trunks of the *tománu*, *mapé*, and *puráu*— their commingled branches weaving a leafy canopy over these mysterious haunts, the abode of solitude and funereal gloom.

The divinity of these temples was Oro, the God of War, and numerous were the victims immolated upon his bloody altars to propitiate his favor. The divinities of these islands were numerous, but the chief was Oro, and to him, after various ceremonies, mothers dedicated their male offspring, that they might become great warriors. His was an insatiate disposition, and the most trivial occurrences would call for renewed sacrifices ; one of these was the sacrifice of restoration, which required no less than seven victims. This arose from the desecration the *marué* had sustained from an invading force, that drove its possessors to the mountains, breaking down the branches of the sacred grove with which to cook their food.

The manner of procuring victims was peculiar : when one was required, the king would send messengers to the chief of a district, who inquired of him (metaphorically) whether he had " a *broken calabash* at hand ;" a person was designated, and one of these ambassadors of death dealt him a blow upon the head, which stunned him ; immediately the others rushed up to complete the work. The body was then placed in a basket of cocoanut boughs and carried to the *maraé* in savage triumph, to be deposited upon the altar. With these sacrifices was connected a painful feature. When one of the members of a family had fallen, the others were reserved for a similar fate ; a retreat to the mountains or a neighboring island could not save them, for they were soon discovered, and hunted down for the horrid purpose. An affecting account of the last sacrifice that occurred at Tahiti is given by Mr. Williams, and which I subjoin :—

" Pomare was about to fight a battle, which would confirm him in

or deprive him of his dominions. To propitiate the gods, therefore, by the most valuable offerings he could command, was with him
an object of the highest concern.   For this purpose, rolls of native
cloth, pigs, fish, and immense quantities of other food were presented at the *maraés;* but still a *tabu* or sacrifice was demanded.
Pomare therefore sent two of his messengers to the house of his
victim, whom he had marked for the occasion.   On reaching the
place, they inquired of the wife where her husband was.   She replied that he was in such a place planting bananas.   'Well,' they
continued, 'we are thirsty ; give us some cocoanut water.'   She told
them that she had no nuts in the house, but that they were at liberty
to climb the trees and take as many as they desired.   They then
requested her to lend them the *o*, which is a piece of iron-wood
about four feet long and an inch and a half in diameter, with which
the natives open the cocoanut.   She cheerfully complied with their
wishes, little imagining that she was giving them the instrument
which in a few moments was to inflict a fatal blow upon the head of
her husband.   Upon receiving the *o*, the men left the house, and
went in search of their victim ; and the woman having become rather
suspicious, followed them shortly after, and reached the place just in
time to see her husband fall.   She rushed forward to give vent to
her agonized feelings, and take a last embrace.   But she was immediately seized and bound hand and foot, while the body of her
murdered husband was borne from her sight.   It appears that they
were always exceedingly careful to prevent the wife or daughter, or
any female relative, from touching the corpse ; for so polluting were
females considered, that a victim would have been desecrated by a
woman's touch or breath to such a degree as to have rendered it
unfit for an offering to the gods.   While the men were carrying their
victim to the *marae*, he recovered from the stunning effect of the
blow, and bound as he was in the cocoanut-leaf basket, he said to his
murderers, 'Friends, I know what you intend to do with me : you
are about to kill me and offer me as a *tapu* to your savage gods ; and
I also know that it is useless for me to beg for mercy, for you will
not spare my life.   You may kill my body, but you cannot hurt my
soul ; for I have begun to pray to Jesus, the knowledge of whom the
missionaries have brought to this island.   You may kill my body, but

you cannot hurt my soul.' Instead of being moved to compassion by his affecting address, they laid him down upon the ground, placed a stone under his head, and with another beat it to pieces. In this state they carried him to their 'savage gods.' I forbear to make any comment upon these facts, and leave them to find their own way to the hearts of my readers, and to show them how much the heathen need the Gospel. One of the assassins, whose business it was to procure human sacrifices, sailed with me in my last voyage, and not only confirmed the foregoing statement, but detailed many other transactions equally tragical, in which he had been engaged.* But painful as the incident is, it is a relief to know that this was the very last sacrifice ever offered to the gods of Tahiti; for soon after it occurred, Christianity was embraced, and the altars of the 'savage gods' ceased to be stained with human blood."

There were numerous other relics of heathenism within these precincts, but I did not visit them, as my time was limited. I left this Golgotha impressed with the conviction that a nobler conquest had never been achieved than that which wrested the human intellect from the fetters of a demon superstition.

CHAPTER X.

A STROLL UP THE VALLEY.

AFTER remaining a short time at the house, I followed the shore of the bay in an opposite direction, accompanied by the two boys, to visit the celebrated *Oha* tree. On the way, I noticed sweet potato cultivations on the mountain-side of the road, adjoining the houses of the natives. In fact, agricultural evidences were more numerous here than at the chief settlement. We soon reached the object of our visit, a magnificent specimen of the vegetable kingdom, lofty and graceful, massive, yet unique. It was a species of the *Banian Indicus*, to which it bore a resemblance, though in many respects widely different. Instead of the low, broad-spreading branches of other

species that I had seen, forming a grove with a new progeny of supporters growing downwards to take root in the earth, this arose on a
broad pedestal of what appeared to be a mass of disinterred roots,
fantastically interlaced with each other, and having a circumference
of more than ninety paces, and a height of about twenty feet.
Upon this grew the solid trunk and branches of the beautiful tree,
from which drooped parasitical shoots, pendulous in the breeze.   It
was a type of majesty and beauty.

Divesting myself of boots and watch, (coat I wore none,) and
giving them in charge of one of the boys, I proceeded to climb this
natural ladder—a task easily accomplished—and with three or four
natives descended into the interior.   Here was an apartment with
a nice floor of earth, having an area of perhaps twenty square feet,
though somewhat obstructed by the labyrinth of supporters.   The
light admitted was through the interstices of these grotesque roots
or trunks, that opposed an effectual barrier to external observation.
After remaining a short time in this vegetable grot of refreshing
coolness, we made our exit as we had come.   The natives have romantic tales connected with the old Oha, where in former days
high-born lovers obtained stolen interviews.

At ten o'clock Teó's boat was freighted, and ready to start for the
opposite side of the bay.   Before embarking, however, he took me
a short distance up the hillside, and showed me some half dozen
Irish potato plants, protected by a small inclosure.   These domestic
exotics looked thrifty, and I have not the slightest doubt that, were
proper attention bestowed upon their cultivation among the more
elevated regions, they would afford a prolific yield, and not degenerate into sweet potatoes, as some have asserted.   Just as we were
leaving, there was a general pig chase through the grove, by old and
young ; but bristles was evidently a " thorough-bred," for he led off
in fine style, sometimes skirting the sandy shore, then, striking off
obliquely, he would almost defy pursuit among the guava bushes on
the steep hillsides, avoiding with wonderful dexterity huge stones
and missiles aimed at him from every direction.   It was a chase in
which all participated ; and the children who were too young to be
of service followed in the rear shouting, while lean, worthless dogs
stood in the door-ways and barked valiantly.   Of its result I am ig-

norant, for, having exchanged salutations with their majesties, we left before the " chase" had been run down.

Our former landing-place was reached at noon, where we partook of a dinner of bread-fruit, sardines, and roast pig ; our remaining bottle of claret had moistened the palate of some prowling vintage-lover at Opóa. Teó showed me two exquisite specimens of madrepore coral of uniform size, fan-like in form, and bleached to a snowy whiteness. If beheld, they would be objects of envy to those whose ambition is to convert their mantels into marine museums. The waters here abound with these zoöphytic branches. I waded out a long distance upon the white sandy bottom. It was clear and sufficiently shoal to procure specimens which rest loosely upon the sand, without diving, for they are easily detached. Nothing can exceed the transparency of the water, and in wading slowly along, the optical illusion occasioned by the transmission or refraction of rays through a denser medium seems to raise this submarine grove to the surface with all its labyrinthine windings. Having loaded a boy who accompanied me, we returned to the shore. The corals were then washed in fresh water, to remove extraneous impurities and the unpleasant odor arising from them when taken from their native element ; after which, they were placed in an exposed situation upon the roof of a house to bleach.

Leaving Teó reclined upon the mats, surrounded by his inquisitive friends, I strolled out barefooted, for my boots, by being frequently saturated with salt water and dried in the sun, had become worse than stocks, and with no definite object in view, sauntered leisurely through a cocoanut grove on the western side of the bay. A short walk brought me to several snug native houses, having good inclosures, and upon the hillside in the rear fires were burning, where their occupants were making extensive clearings for cultivation. With all Tamáre's liberal policy, I must admit that the territory within his majesty's jurisdiction bore greater evidences of industry, as it was also characterized by greater natural beauty. Salutations were uttered as I passed, and I was invited to partake of their roast fish and bread-fruit.

Approaching the head of the bay, the thick forest again commences ; the path winds beneath the shade of the *mapé* and *puráu*, and just as the sandy curve commences, a clear stream disembogues into the sea. This was spanned by a single slender cocoanut log, and a series of gymnastic evolutions were required to cross it in safety, owing to its elasticity. The view up the stream, which was unintercepted for about seventy-five yards, was extremely picturesque : massive trunks were growing upon the verge of its banks, and in some instances their branches, projecting from opposite sides, entwined with each other, forming a shady bower over its clear waters. I returned to one of the houses and hired a young man to convey me in his canoe as far as it was navigable, and after reaching the log bridge, which was nearly level with the sea, we hauled the canoe over ' and embarked. A deathlike solitude reigned through the forest, for not even the chirping of a warbler was heard among the branches. The clear stream flowed silently over its sandy bed, eddying around moss-covered roots of the *mapé*, whose fantastic trunks rose like sentinels from the dark banks ; and the monotonous plash of the paddle was the only sound that awoke the solitude as our light canoe skimmed its way beneath an embowering canopy. It was a fitting retreat for the misanthrope to indulge his ghostly reveries ; submitting passively to its tranquil current, he might fancy himself floating upon the dreamy flood whose name is oblivion.

Having traced its sinuosities for more than a fourth of a mile, the low branches wove an impenetrable network across its surface, through which it was impossible to force the canoe with its outrigger, and we accordingly disembarked near a large *mapé* tree, into which was driven an iron staple having a small rusty chain attached. This, the young man informed me, was formerly used for securing the boats of those who visited the sugar plantation that once existed in this valley, but which had long since been abandoned. I followed him for nearly half a mile, when we emerged to an open space where were fields of taro of immense growth, and soon after, we heard the distant roaring of the stream, which now foamed in rapids over a rocky bed. A pleasant relief to this solitude was afforded by two or three native houses, situated upon its banks, and the animated voices of their inmates. Without pausing, we continued on to the ruins of the old sugar-mill, and here, surrounded by guava bushes, was the huge water-wheel, still reposing upon its rickety frame. Near by was all that remained of the boiling apparatus, with its crumbling chimney attached, and looming gloomily above the sea of verdure. The whole seemed a melancholy comment on the struggle between sloth and industry.

Many years before, a plantation had been commenced on this spot by the Messrs. Platt of Raiatéa, and a better locality could not have been selected. Entering the forest with their natives, they cleared a broad space, ploughed up the soil, and planted it with sugar-cane. A dam was afterwards built, the fall of the water affording excellent mill sites. A long sluice was dug, and the mill itself constructed. For a while, all went well ; the prolific soil yielded an ample harvest, and the sugar manufactured was of good quality, and found a ready market. But soon after, the French war broke out in Tahiti, and the infant commerce of the leeward islands was paralyzed. Internal dissensions arose among the natives, and the enterprise was ultimately abandoned for want of laborers. So complete has been the change that, save the relics enumerated, together with the trench and fallen dam, no trace of its former prosperity remains. Indeed, I did not notice a stalk of wild cane growing ; everything was covered with a wilderness of guava, above which rose the slender trunks of a few cocoanut-trees.

We followed the bed of the sluice to the dam ; thence, the bank of the stream, for a long distance ; and so dense was the foliage overhead that in no place could the sunbeams penetrate. Here, the rushing torrent seemed to have tunnelled a path beneath its leafy canopy ; and the humid atmosphere nourished in rank luxuriance creeping evergreens that twined around moss-covered trunks, and bending from their boughs trailed in the dark water, the sound of whose roaring alone disturbed the solitude and funereal gloom. The soil was a black vegetable mold, and no better evidence of its richness could be required than the luxuriant vegetation with which it was covered, including nearly every description of timber peculiar to the island, and which was easy of access. I had no other means of estimating the extent of this valley than that afforded by a superficial observation in crossing the bay, but should judge that it contained between three and four square miles of level or rolling land. The bay itself is about a mile in length, by half that distance in breadth. During our walk, we crossed a pavement of flat stones, between some of which large trees had forced their way. I counted my paces as I passed over it, and they were a hundred. My knowledge of the language was too limited to comprehend the explanation given of them by the guide ; but I distinctly understood that no *maraes* had ever been erected upon them.

Having reached our canoe, we paddled down the stream, and afterwards down the bay, to the house of the owner, whom I remunerated for his services. I then retraced the road to the house, where Teó was just sitting down to a roast pig, and wondering at my long absence. We passed a social evening, for we had numerous visitors. When we retired to rest, it was to be tortured by musquitoes. I made a promise that night that, on future excursions among these islands, my musquito-net should never be forgotten, and it has always been faithfully observed.

In the morning, Nanáu ascended a tree for young cocoanuts, and, after throwing down a sufficient supply, we once more embarked, and reached Havila about the middle of the forenoon. At the house we first visited, a group of young men were giving a pantomimic exhibition to a crowd of admiring belles, while two persons playing upon bamboo instruments regulated their movements. This description of amusement is prohibited, although I saw nothing in it that could have an immoral tendency, unless by encouraging habits of idleness.

We had towed down a large raft of *puráu* timber, aided by the erection of a mast upon it, having strips of bark peeled from the logs for stays, and our blankets tied together for sails. Before reaching Havila, Teó placed little Nanáu upon it, while we bore up for the village. There were no means of steering it ; but fortunately the mast was "stepped" well forward, and from the shore we could see the little fellow sitting upon the coral blocks on the raft, to avoid the water that covered it, as it swept steadily on over the deep lagoon. Two girls who resided at the settlement begged a passage of Teó, which he granted. Soon after reaching the raft, the wind veered around to the northwest, attended by squalls and rain. This rendered our situation extremely unpleasant, for the raft was a perfect drag, and prevented the boat from beating to windward. Our passengers then regretted that they had not followed the road along the beach, but, covering them with our coats, blankets and mats, they reclined upon the stern-sheets, and were soon in a sound sleep. Teó, on my account, proposed anchoring the raft, and proceeding to the settlement by the speediest route possible ; but this I negatived. Fortunately for the girls, a canoe from Opóa overtook us, on board of which they embarked, while we remained to tug at the oar from two o'clock in the afternoon until eight in the evening, and which I noted was a second instance of working passage, after a pleasure excursion in this ocean.

CHAPTER XI.

A POLITICO-LITERARY FESTIVAL.

A CONVIVIAL party was assembled one evening at Eelspring, (the name by which Merton's residence was designated after his adventure,) and some of the old residents of Raiatéa fancied their " stern alarums changed to merry meetings," as they quaffed the ruddy juice provided for the occasion. For want of a more suitable appendage, the table was covered with a clean white sheet, and over this were promiscuously scattered delicious fruits, some of them the first of their season, flanked on both sides by goblets and decanters containing Cognac and sherry, also pure water from the spring for the abstinent. From the rafters was suspended a rustic chandelier, fashioned by affixing cocoanut lamps to the branches of a small treetop which had been deprived of its leafy covering.

Among the guests was Dr. Doan, who, owing to a slight attack of ophthalmia, wore a pair of green goggles, but otherwise he was unimpaired, and his scintillations of wit were an acceptable contribution to the mirth-loving. As the evening wore on, there was an evident tendency to effervescence among some of the spirits assembled, and this was manifested by songs and hornpipes, and one of the party seized a herculean native by the waist, and to his consternation attempted a polka. An American seaman present ascended the rostrum, (a kind of dais for sleeping,) and commenced an oration on liberty, disparaging to the British Lion and " crumbling monarchies" generally ; this gradually digressed to the " doings of our glorious republic," his extemporaneous eloquence being frequently interlarded with " stars and stripes" and " American eagle," until hissed down by the majority, who considered the subject inappropriate to the occasion.

Merton immediately jumped up and said that the remarks of the gentleman who had just preceded him suggested to his mind a political subject : he would propose a tax on *feis* to induce industry among the natives, for as long as they could procure food that grew spontaneously in the mountains, they would never trouble themselves about tilling the soil. He considered affairs to be in a deplorable state, for whether under the administration of the legitimate or provisional governments, the consumers far outnumbered the producers, which could only be attributed to unsound legislation ; in fact, the entire department of State required reorganizing, for the offices as at present held by foreigners were mere sinecures. He said that his first proposition would require modification to bring it in shape, but he merely hinted it for the benefit of the prime minister, (meaning the doctor,) whom he saw present.

The doctor made a violent demonstration with his pocket handkerchief, and rose at once to reply. He said that " the remarks of the proprietor of Eelspring were, to speak metaphorically, like a column without a pedestal, and which he was willing to attribute to his ignorance ; for, had he taken the trouble to inform himself, he would have learned that the lands producing the said *feis* were, and had been from time immemorial, held by the chiefs and wealthier classes as allodial property, or by their dependents as limited fees ; that no portion of them had ever been considered a government monopoly since its organization. With reference to deplorable affairs, he flattered himself that a twelve years' residence in the group had enabled him to draw tolerably correct conclusions as to affecting causes, and he unhesitatingly pronounced that the chief maladies observable, both moral and physical, had been entailed upon the aborigines by resident foreigners or interloping visitors, who were in the habit of giving bacchanalian festivals and decrying immorality, while aiding and abetting it by pernicious example. He further stated, that he had never yet seen a stranger on the island who, with all his theories on political regeneration, would venture to ' put the bell on the cat's neck.' "

Some sharp shooting then took place between the two, for Merton had " caught a Tartar ;" until Jasper, wishing to change the subject, stated that he and Merton had been scribbling nonsense, and begged the doctor to criticise their productions ; but Merton, who had become somewhat nettled by the debate that was going against him, said he was not ambitious of displaying his sentiments, especially as he was to defer to the opinion of a veterinary surgeon. But the audience insisted ; and when the doctor, delighted at the idea, promised that his judgment should be impartial, Merton acceded to the request of the company. Before leaving the island, I obtained copies of their productions, which are subjoined as they were handed me.

In order to install the doctor properly in his new vocation, a dark-blue *paréu* was borrowed from a native, thrown over his shoulders, and gathered in graceful folds on the left side, something like a toga. After this, a chair was placed for him on the dais which he occupied. Apéro, a sort of sergeant-at-arms, with a bamboo in his hand, was directed to bring in an empty barrel and place it before him , over this was thrown a small damask cover, and upon it three or four books were placed in formal array.

With a dignified air, the judge arose and said he was " prepared to listen to the poem of Mr. Jasper."

A profound silence was maintained, when the individual thus addressed advanced beneath the chandelier, and (the judge meanwhile taking notes) in an off-hand manner read the following

SONG.

" Our bark is tried, our bark is true,
It loveth to bound o'er the ocean blue,
With snowy sail, still up or down,
To the zephyr smile or the tempest frown.
Away, away it onward flies,
O'er coral groves,—'neath summer skies,

18

Where pearl and shell, profusely shed,
Glitter like gems on ocean's bed ;
O'er caves where crystal treasures cling,
Where tritons woo and syrens sing ;
In azure depths, while the purple light
Flows calmer than mist of a summer night.

      " As on we bound from day to day,
Cleaving the wave 'mid foam and spray,
The song that beguiles the sunny hour
Shall cheer us again, though tempests low'r.
When the sky grows dark, and storm-winds sigh
Plaintive and shrill as the sea-bird's cry,
We'll gather our sail to the trusty mast
That creaketh ' Come on !' to the howling blast,
And over the billow we'll lightly spring,
Where revels the petrel on ' stormy wing.'
Should darkness and the tempest cloud
Fling o'er the deep a sable shroud,
The anxious vigils of the night
Shall vanish with the rosy light,
And then with joy we'll hail the day
That cheers us o'er our pathless way."

When he had finished, some of the audience applauded, while Howard said, " Spongy." The newly-constituted judge looked on with imperturbable gravity, and after the various demonstrations had subsided, arose, and said in a measured tone, " We will listen to the poem of Mr. Merton."

This gentleman having taken his position beneath the chandelier, remarked, that he " had a word to offer in apology for his subject; that it possessed not a shadow of foundation, but was merely an impromptu on what might occur." He then commenced :—

" Though years have flown by, yet in fancy I dwell
Once more on the spot where I bade thee farewell ;
Though years have flown by, still in fancy I see
Again the dark eye that beamed kindly on me.
Though Time shall roll on, and its withering trace,
The form, and each feature of youth, may deface ;
Yet the sweet recollection of happiness fled,
'Round the pathway of age a bright halo shall shed ;
And, though scenes, alas ! varied with pleasure and pain,
Through the vista of years shall steal o'er me again,

They'll beguile the brief moments that fall to my lot,
And the hours with M——n——e can ne'er be forgot.
In fancy I'll fly to her ocean-girt home,
And with hand joined in hand together we'll roam
Among the green mountains, along the deep vale,
Where sweet orange blossoms are kissed by the gale,
And where the bright flowrets perennial bloom,
To waft to the sense their delicious perfume,
And 'mid every loved scene that can lend a joy
In Nature's pure garden, untouched by alloy.

     " When the breath of Ro'hútu creeps down from the hill,
Perfumed by the incense of grove and of rill,   .
'Neath Eoline's harp, then, at eve we'll repose—
The sea-loving palm, while its melody flows,
Where murmuring branches that rustle above,
Like spirits in converse, seem whispering love.
We'll silently watch 'til a mellowing light
Serenely encircles the sceptre of night ;
And beaming soft radiance, a smile shall be shed
On wavelets that dance o'er a coraline bed.

     " When spirit-like moaning steals over the surge,
Sad anthem of ocean—funereal dirge ;
Like symbol of doom shall a magical pow'r
Fling o'er us the spell of oblivion's hour ;
O'er earth and o'er sea shall its mantle unroll,
And shed from its pinions repose to the soul.
*   *   *   *   *   *   *

     " When Time, with its sorrows, shall blight with its breath
Each pleasure of life, like the whisper of Death,
Two sweet consolations to mourners are given :——
To reflect on the past—to hope for a Heaven."

" *Tityre tu patulæ recubans, et cetera*," said the doctor, again having recourse to his handkerchief, and wiping his goggles. " *Apero !* Hand that man a banana ! I should recommend him to purchase half a dozen goats, and cross over to Maupíti and write pastorals."

Howard, who sat near by, inquired of the doctor, in an audible whisper, whether he had brought his bottle of " Preston" with him, for he certainly felt symptoms of " going off."

Jasper jumped up and remarked, with mock indignation, that their productions had not been read for the purpose of eliciting any unnecessary display of pedantry.

Meanwhile, Merton, who saw how the battle was going, retired to
a corner of the apartment, and commenced writing on the fly-leaf of
a book.

The judge " hoped that his admiration for their talents would not
tempt him to any extravagances. He was aware the poems possessed
a sort of mechanical jingle, or finger-tallying prosody, but neither of
them contained an original idea. For his part, he couldn't conceive
what there was in a simple concretion of carbonate of lime, whether
stalactite or coral, that could awaken in ' aspiring legislators or linen-
drapers' such poetic frenzy. Alluding to the first effusion, he remarked
an unlawful license, when it was stated that a pearl shell could ' glitter
like a gem ;' and he was consequently led to suppose that the writer
was ignorant of the natural history of this species of testacea. The
mother-of-pearl was a large, coarse shell externally, a pair of them
weighing from three to six pounds ; frequented deep water, where
they were found in beds ; while the ' gem,' or true oriental pearl,
was an excrescence concealed within. He was not aware that rays
of light refracted at any depth in the ocean, underwent a ' purple'
decomposing process ; that, in reducing sail on account of a storm,
it was not customary to ' gather it to the mast,' unless the vessel
should have ' standing gaffs,' as in case of ' spanker' and ' spencer'
of a ship's lower masts, when brails were rove for that purpose.
In ordinary phraseology, by reducing sail was meant to stow it upon
the yard, where it could be properly secured by a 'bunt gasket.' With
reference to the subsequent piece of mellifluence, he considered it
too puerile to require a critical notice. ' The breath of Ro'hútu'
was a very indefinite expression, for in this instance standing alone,
the word was meaningless, it being always used in connection with
one or the other of two adjectives ; as, '*Roohútu noanóa*,' (sweet-scented
Paradise,) or, ' *Roohútu námunamúa*,' (foul-scented Purgatory.) So
much for the acquirements of transient visitors. He regretted to
hear allusion made again to corals. If ' penny-a-liners' would forsake the ideal for the tangible, and convert the subject of their meditations into its legitimate uses, their efforts would be better appreciated by society. For his part, he would recommend a three days'
sojourn in a lime-kiln as an antidote for this species of mania. He
had been called upon to deliver an opinion, and had done so. With

a delicate regard for the sensibilities of the two competitors, he should decline drawing invidious comparisons, and would finally beg to be permitted to resign his functions as judge."

Having delivered his sentiments, the doctor cast off his toga, and descended from the dais to moisten his lips with a glass of sherry. By this time some of the audience had begun to yawn, and one of them, whose head had reclined upon the table during the discourse, raised it with innocent stupidity, and suggested " taking a drink all round," and adjourning " *siney diey*." At this juncture, Merton came forward and said he had a few unfinished lines which he hoped his friends would permit him to read. His request was complied with, and he hastily ran off the following

IMPROMPTU.

" When sapient critic fills the chair,
  With rubicund proboscis,
Spanned by a pair of goggles green,
  (A case of amaurosis :)
Pretending merit humbly bows
  Before his box of knowledge,
Yet, wondering how the quack obtained
  An M.D. from a college.

" To instance once his depth of search :
  A curious native sought him,
Inquiring how the cocoa-milk
  Its goblet shell was caught in.
This sage of lore, with serious nod,
  Before him took his station ;
And, finger apex on his palm,
  Replied,—'*Accumulation*.'

" A flower that blooms beside the path
  Is called a useful fixture ;
'Tis culled, and thrust into his bag
  To make a tonic mixture.
With ancient dames, profoundly skilled,
  A *savant* in cosmetics ;
With all his art, he never need
  Aspire beyond obstetrics.

    " We love him—nay, we do revere
       The talent for his calling ;
    Because he's proved himself to be
    A vampire most appalling.
    In politics, he knows his cue ;
       When vigilance relaxes,
    He pockets by his knavish skill
       Both harbor dues and taxes.

    " However, let us meekly bear
       This critical abortion ;
    When cats resort to monkey judge,
       They lose both sense and portion.
    We hope in future ———."

Merton said that was as " far as he'd got, and if they'd hold on,
he'd finish it ;" but the doctor professed himself satisfied, and willing to pass the hat as it was.

Soon after, most of the company dispersed, and Doctor Doan and
his satellites bade us good-night, and retired to West End. A few
of us, whose houses were almost contiguous; indulged in a moonlight stroll along the Broom Road that borders the beach, after which
we filed away to our respective abodes.

Jasper told me the next day, that on returning to the house, they
found Captain N——, an American, whose faculties had become
somewhat muddy, stretched out at full length on the veranda, making abortive attempts to whistle " Hail Columbia," and roaring at
intervals a line of the immortal Dibdin :—

     " Here, a sheer-hulk, lies poor Tom Bowline."

In spite of his remonstrances, he and Merton locked arms with him to
assist him home ; but on reaching the road, they found it was either
" hard starboard," or " hard aport," as their charge " was too much by
the head," and otherwise " out of ballast trim." While endeavoring to
make a short cut through the guava and lime trees, they suddenly
found themselves knee-deep in the slough that adjoins the premises
of Teó. Here the captain floundered terribly, completely bespat-
tering them with mud ; but after extricating him, he was conveyed
to his quarters which closed the adventures of the night.

CHAPTER XII.

YACHTING AMONG THE ISLES.

HAVING endured an indulgent captivity of several weeks at Raiatéa, an opportunity was afforded for bringing it to a close. One afternoon it was reported that three sail were bearing down from Huahine for the harbor, and we were all on the *qui vive*, anticipating the arrival of the strangers. They proved to be schooners, one a Californian *fruitier*, and the other two traders from Tahiti for the leeward and chain islands.

I did not visit either of them that evening, but in the morning accompanied Teó, the pilot, in his boat to the Falcon as she was getting under way, the sails being set and the crew heaving at the anchor. I was introduced to the owner, Mr. Adams, a partner of the house of K. G. & Co., at Papéete, who informed me that for novelty's sake he had fitted up the Falcon for a two months' cruise among the Paumotu and Austral Islands, and that being in need of company, the humble accommodations of his vessel were at my service ; he further insisted that I should proceed at once to the shore and return immediately with such apparel or conveniences as I might require for accompanying him on his contemplated voyage. The time was brief ; but in less than fifteen minutes my preparations were completed, and leaving Howard as proxy for *adios* to friends, I reached the schooner as she tripped her anchor and was paying-off before the breeze.

The Falcon was on her way to Borabóra, an island adjoining Raiatéa ; I found her to be a pretty craft of about ninety tons burden and a fast sailer, having " flush" decks and good accommodations below. Our pilot preferred taking us out through the Hamenéne passage, though the route was more circuitous than that of Taháa ; lest, as he said, we should get becalmed under the lee of that island. The morning was fine and the breeze steady as we swept before it over the variegated waters of the broad lagoon, bounded on one side by the ocean, and on the other by the green mountains of Raiatéa.

Adams; a Bostonian, declared that, " in its way, he had seen
nothing more beautiful," as we leaned over the rail watching the
varied appearance of the submarine garden, over which we were
gliding.   We continued in this manner within the reef for eight
miles, when we reached the Hamenéne or Hunter's Passage, opposite a deep bay, known as " Cook's Bay," for it was here that celebrated navigator first anchored on his visit to this island.

We made our exit, and Teó shook hands with us, directing the
captain to make the harbor from the south side of Borabóra, bearing
about northwest of us, and distant twelve miles ; but for reasons
unknown, we sailed around the northern side, thereby increasing our
journey five miles. · We saw our consort, the " Dos Amigos," who
had taken the Taháa passage, almost becalmed under the lee of the
island, while we had a rattling breeze, and when off the northern
point, we had nearly overtaken her.

This is one of the third class islands of this group, its greatest
length and breadth being respectively five, and two and three-fourths
miles, having an area of about eight square miles.   It is surrounded
by a reef twenty-three miles in circumference, and stretched around
its outer edge is a chain of more than twelve low islets, varying in
size from one-fourth of a mile to three miles in length.   Its harbor
is unfortunately situated on the western or leeward side of the island,
so that it is seldom entered with a leading wind.   It is capacious,
being three miles in length, and its greatest breadth from Waiáti Bay
to the islet of Tubuái (constituting one of its western bounds) is a
mile and a half; its chief inconvenience is its great depth of water
opposite the settlement.

The island lies north and south, its extremities curving towards
the west, and the curvatures of the mountain ridge of which it consists bear a strong resemblance to a figure three (3.)   From its
centre rises Mount Pahía, a perpendicular column of basalt, to a
height of fifteen hundred feet, and frequently enveloped in clouds.
Viewed from the west or northwest, this peak has a fantastic appearance, rising, as it does, like a huge gray castle, with its turrets and
bastions, above the sea of verdure that sweeps in gentle undulations
around its base.   I have visited numerous islands in this ocean, and
with reference to extent, must concede to Borabóra the unrivalled

attractions of romantic scenery with quiet beauty. Without a barren spot to pain the eye, its ridges are robed from summit to base with a mantle of luxuriant verdure, where the snowy petals of the Cape jessamine nestle amid the dark foliage of the forest, and with its clear rills gushing from a rocky fountain, (Mount Pahía,) and winding through the groves of its quiet dells, it might rival the Hesperian Gardens or the happy valley of Rasselas. As if to protect it from the boisterous ocean, a coral barrier has been stretched around it, its white surface besprinkled with the links of an emerald cordon, covered with a host of waving palms, whose broad plumes glitter in the spray of foaming breakers.

This little spot of eight square miles has been the nursery of the most daring and successful warriors the group ever produced. More than forty years ago, Tapóa, its king, by successful wars, united the Society Islands into one confederacy ; and he had proceeded to Tahiti to crown his victories by the conquest of that island, when death arrested him in his career. He was cotemporaneous with Kamehaméha I., and in some respects there is a parallel in the history of these two Polynesian champions, though, unlike his rival, he failed to consolidate a kingdom : when he perished, his deeds perished with him. From the largest island of the group as a starting-point, Kamehaméha commenced the subjugation of the smaller islands to leeward, while with Tapóa one of the smallest of the leeward islands served as the basis of his operations, and his victories were achieved among the larger islands to windward. Such a notoriety did this conqueror obtain, that to the present day among the Hawaiians a native of this group is not designated a Tahitian, but a Borabórian. Its age of heroism has passed. In 1832 the last battle of conquest was fought at Taháa, in which Tapóa, a grandson of the renowned chieftain, sustained a signal defeat. Since then its inhabitants have remained at peace, and undisturbed by the political differences of the other islands. All that now remains of a once numerous population does not exceed nine hundred souls.

But to return to the Falcon, which we left scudding along the northeastern side of the reef. The wind was fair, and continued so until we rounded the northern point, when we were compelled to haul aft the sheets as we stood to the southwest. The "Dos Amigos,"

from the south, had filled away on the larboard tack as we reached
the northern side of the passage; but as she was "square-rigged"
forward, while the Falcon was a "fore-and-after," we could hug
the wind closer, and the moment we had "'bout ship," we found to
our satisfaction that we could lay more than a point higher than our
rival. The length and breadth of the entrance are about a half and
a quarter of a mile, but unfortunately the winds that sweep down
from the ridges and through the valleys are almost always baffling, so
that beating into the harbor is a tedious task. With a fair wind, the
anchorage might be reached in half an hour. Sometimes in making
a good "board," we flattered ourselves that we would "fetch in" on
the next tack, but having "come about," had the mortification to
find that we were heading below our starting-point. Beating in is
sometimes a delicate affair, owing to the narrowness of the channel,
(which is fortunately deep and unobstructed,) for a vessel has barely
time to fill away on one tack before the order "Stations!" is given,
almost immediately succeeded by "Ready about!" for the next.

The Falcon worked admirably, and we could approach within ten
yards of the reef, without fear of "missing stays," for the moment
the helm was shoved "a-lee," she rounded-to as gracefully as a
swan, and without losing headway, came up shivering in the wind,
and immediately fell off before it on the other board. After we had
fairly fought our way into the harbor, the winds still continued baffling,
and it was dark before the pilot succeeded in conveying us to our
anchorage, which our consort reached soon after. The Falcon
mounted two brass swivels on pivots over the stern; one of them was
heavily loaded and fired by way of announcement; its reverberations
among the mountains were re-echoed by merry shouts from dark
groves, which in the obscurity seemed blended with the still water.

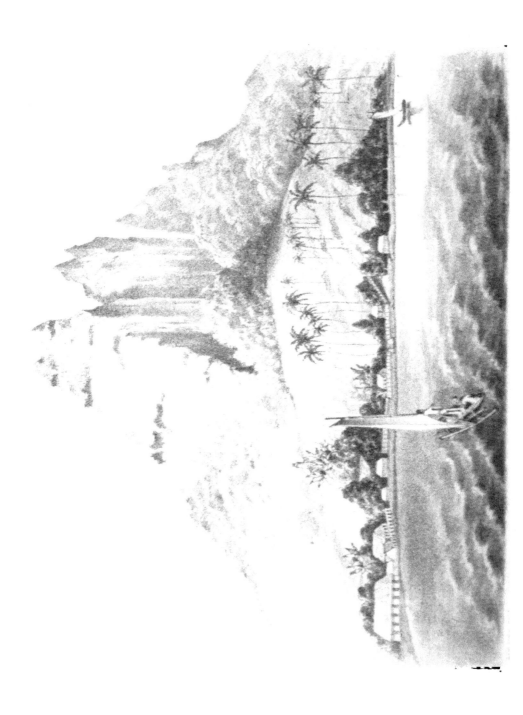

CHAPTER XIII.

B O R A B Ó R A .

MORNING dawned brightly behind the dark pinnacles of Mount Pahía, whose sharp outlines stood forth in bold relief against the background of a cloudless sky. Beyond the sweep of adjacent hills, a roseate tint was mantling the pure ether, while in the foreground a subdued light lingered upon the landscape, reposing in the shadow of the Titan rock. Suddenly the steep ridges of the distant islet, Tubuái, brightened as the sunbeams flashed across the hills of Waiáti, creeping downward to paint in glowing colors the orange and palm groves that border the still lagoon.

It was one of those bright, unclouded mornings that, wherever enjoyed, has a powerful influence in dissipating the vapid reveries of despondency, inspiring and invigorating by its freshness and purity. The very huts that nestled beneath the spreading boughs of the bread-fruit peeped smilingly from their leafy canopies, and the happy voices of children, sporting amid ripples upon the sand-beach, were boisterous chords in nature's harmony.

Presently, a breath of vapor, like a faint wreath of smoke, curled around the castle rock, whose turrets and bastions were flecked with the mantling evergreen. From invisible sources, light clouds were mustering; seemingly, they crept from hidden recesses in the dark cliff to float in the pure atmosphere, and commingling, to veil the mountain summit with a misty coronet. Then a sparkling shower fell upon the groves that clustered around the base, while beyond, the distant hills and islets were basking in the sunlight. These morning showers are peculiar to Borabóra ; but they are of brief duration, and are nature's choicest regalia with which to deck her emerald robes ; for, when the rain-cloud has melted, the sunbeams flash upon a sea of liquid diamonds.

An hour passed on, and a light breeze crept down from the steep ridges ; it seemed as fickle as were fantastic the peaks with which it sported. As if Æolus and his mythic sprites were revelling amid the labyrinths of the stern old rock, it scattered the already melting vapors, and received the obeisance of a host of nodding plumes and tossing branches. Gaudy robes fluttered upon the sand-beach, where loiterers were indulging a morning stroll, and two or three canoes with snowy sails glided from the dark headlands of Fanúi and came sweeping toward us. Ripples were already dancing upon the broad surface, and when we encountered the puff, the Falcon swung gracefully at her anchor, while the awning flapped and the cordage sang. Signal-halliards were rove, and our colors, loosely folded, bent on; having run them up to the main peak, we jerked the cord, and that type of liberty, the star-spangled banner, sprang forth anew, and waved a joyful welcome to the morning breeze.

After a substantial breakfast, we landed in the forenoon on the stone jetty in front of the native church, where Mr. Evans, both trading master of the Dos Amigos and merchant in Tahiti, was waiting to receive us. We were conducted by him to the house of Matehá, who acted as regent during the absence of King 'Tapóa, then in Tahiti. He was a man about forty-five or fifty years of age, with an intelligent countenance, and, as far as I could learn, bore an exemplary character; like all natives of this group, whether patrician or plebeian, he was innocent of pretensions to dignity, either in his intercourse with inferiors, or in the aspect of his household.

Having paid our respects, we walked out upon the grass-plot in front of the house, a sort of public square; this was ornamented by the only public edifices of the kingdom, a school-house, church, and court-house, specimens of architecture similar to those of Raiatéa. Near the shore were some half dozen carronades, mounted upon worm-eaten carriages; some of them had evidently performed their last offices, and like old pensioners, were now reposing on their laurels. Around their wheels the grass was creeping luxuriantly, while above them was a canopy of shady boughs. Evans desired us to accompany him to an adjoining yard, to look at a mammoth specimen of bread-fruit he had discovered. The tree was small, but the fruit suspended from its branches would have delighted the heart of a horticulturist, for it exceeded in size anything of the kind I ever beheld; each slender branch arched gracefully, as from its extremity a beautiful oval pendant swayed to and

fro in the breeze like an emerald jewel, beneath a crown of glossy sinuated leaves.

The bread-fruit tree, or Hawaiian *úlu*, Tahitian *maióle*, is one of the most beautiful specimens of vegetation in the South Sea Islands. Its height seldom exceeds fifty feet, and the average height of those on this island is perhaps thirty feet. Its symmetrical form and dark glossy foliage, with the light-green fruit suspended among its branches in beautiful contrast, render it an object of universal attraction; to its grace and elegance are united strength and utility, for its trunk furnishes beautiful and durable timber of a dark color resembling mahogany. Among some of the islands of this ocean, the natives fashion their garments from the inner bark of its branches, while its trunk is converted into canoes and other purposes. The fruit, which is about five or six inches in diameter, is never eaten in its natural state, but is roasted, and when broken open, exhibits a core in the centre; the food itself is of a delicate straw color, agreeable to the taste, and exceedingly nutritious. Of this tree there are many varieties, and as they produce two crops annually, the natives are provided to a certain extent with this description of sustenance throughout the year. I have frequently noticed among the islands the habit of inclosing the young trees with stakes, to protect them from the ravages of quadrupeds, especially horses, which are fond of feeding upon the leaves and tender shoots. These trees require a certain degree of attention; while the orange suffers no diminution in its golden harvest, when surrounded by the tangled guava, the bread-fruit similarly situated, like a deciduous plant, would shed its leafy covering, and stretch out its naked branches, as if upbraiding man for his neglect, craving only the removal of the parasites that deprive it of the moisture which lends vigor, to renew again the blessings for which it was bestowed.

The settlement is situate on the western side of the island, having a level site bounded in the rear by Mount Pahía, that rises perpendicularly above it. Here, in a narrow compass, we have beauty and majesty in their extremes, for the breadth of the level land between shore and mountain does not exceed half a mile, and above a luxuriant garden of bread-fruit, cocoanut, orange, lime, pápaw, (*Carica papaya*,) banana, and a variety of other trees and flowering shrubs, towers the dark-gray rock, frowning upon the waves of verdure that encircle its base in gentle undulations. Viewed from the northern portion of the settlement, this mountain assumes a different aspect: instead of a perpendicular wall, it descends at a steep angle, broken by four or five petrified terraces, the gray rock partially exposed or covered with vegetation. In the morning, light showers are of frequent occurrence, cooling the atmosphere, and imparting a freshness and purity to this tropical garden, the abode of perpetual spring. Beyond the still waters of the bay reposes the beautiful islet Tubuái, encircled by a fringe of palms, while on the right and left stretches the coral barrier, over which the waves roll incessantly in sheets of foam. The streams on this island are small, but pure and cool, and to one of these, in the rear of the town, I accompanied Evans to enjoy a bath, a luxury we indulged in every morning during our sojourn.

Following the footpath that led to the mountain, we crossed a sparkling stream in the rear of the village, spanned by a bridge of cocoanut logs, and tracing the bank beneath the shade of fruit-trees, we presently entered the forest from which it issued by a narrow dell. Down a gentle declivity it was gurgling and foaming in miniature cascades, sporting with the nodding boughs and plants that drooped in its clear waters. We had not proceeded far before the woodland solitudes re-echoed a merrier sound, and ascending a slight eminence by the stony pathway, we saw some half dozen girls sporting in a clear basin, plashing the water in each other's faces. They caught sight of us at the same moment, and some of them shouting, "*Papaá! papaá!*" (strangers, strangers,) all hastened to gather their garments, and with streaming tresses they skipped from rock to rock as lightly as wood-nymphs, and disappeared among the guavas.

Evans called after them, "*Tehéa tou hamá?*" (what are you ashamed of?) but the only reply was the faint echo of a laugh, and we saw no more of them.

Few foreigners reside on this island, and the only resident missionaries are Mr. and Mrs. Krause. The contrast between the social condition of the natives of Borabóra and those of Raiatéa was striking; without a breath of discord to disturb their domestic peace, everything wore an aspect of tranquillity and contentment. At the

school-house, we heard the pleasant voices of the children pursuing their studies, and after their dismissal, saw the juveniles playing upon the green-sward, and the pleasing countenances of the elder pupils, as they passed by, books in hand, and wishing us " *iauránа*." During the afternoon, by invitation, we visited Mr. Krause. His premises consist of a park bounded in the rear by a garden, in which his residence is situated. We entered the former, an area of between two and three acres, covered with a magnificent carpet of grass, free from underwood ; through its centre was an avenue shaded by orange-trees, and scattered around were noble specimens of the bread-fruit, cocoanut, and banana. We also noticed that beautiful shrub, the rose-tree, with its delicate pink flowers, together with that unique gem of vegetation, the *papáya*. This tree, a native of the tropics, has a soft, herbaceous trunk, usually straight and naked, rising to a height of twelve or fifteen feet. On the top is a crown of sinuated leaves, having long footstalks, and between and beneath these grow the flowers and fruit, the latter about the size of a small melon, which it resembles, and when ripe is of a rich yellow color, having a delicious flavor. It is seen adhering in clusters around the upper part of the stem. After strolling leisurely through the park, we entered the garden, elegantly ornamented with shrubs and flowers, both native and exotic ; among which we noticed the ginger plant, Chinese pomegranate, also roses and geraniums, bordering the path, or fringing the green embankment in front of the house.

From Mr. and Mrs. Krause we received a friendly welcome. By his accent, I at once recognized him to be a German ; Mrs. K. was a native of England. Mr. K. had been educated as a physician in Berlin, but subsequently accepted the position of chaplain to an English company established in Guatemala. The projects of this enterprise being afterwards abandoned, he visited these islands, and for nearly twelve years had been a resident, finally becoming a member of the London Missionary Society. When Mr. Krause informed us that the smiling evidences of industry everywhere apparent were the result of his personal labors, our credulity was severely taxed. He apologized for what he termed the partial neglect of the premises, as they were too extensive for his own unaided efforts. We accompanied him to the garden in the rear of the house, where were various culinary herbs growing, and several rows of cabbages evidenced a national propensity. On an eminence was a small octagonal building—a conspicuous object from the harbor. It is neatly plastered and whitewashed, having an observatory. This is but one of the many evidences of his mechanical ingenuity; it was erected for a school-house, where, during the evening, he has a class of a dozen young men, whose acquirements are above the elementary branches, and whom he instructs in geography and history. The view from the cupola is enchanting; the blossoming groves beneath, and the broad harbor, bounded by its islets and reefs, are spread out like a beautiful panorama.

The house of Mr. K. is encircled by a verandah, at one extremity of which he has a small apartment for a fine collection of rabbits. These innocent creatures may be seen at any time skipping over the lawn or among the flowers; and while watching their gambols, it occurred to me that, could the author of

> " O for a lodge in some vast wilderness !—
> Some boundless contiguity of shade !"

have dwelt in Borabóra, in its present condition, he might have favored us with a more detailed account of the domestic habits of " Pussy," and amid quiet groves realized some of his poetic conceptions.

After partaking of the refreshment prepared for us by Mrs. Krause, we took our departure; and the conviction intruded itself that, had other laborers in this group condescended to manifest equal zeal for the temporal advancement as well as spiritual welfare of their converts, encouraging industry by personal example, a different result would be witnessed among the natives. Yet Mr. Krause has not passed unscathed by the breath of calumny, and it might be added, neither has any other missionary residing in the group. Hardly a traveller can visit the South Sea Islands, and mingle with all classes of society, without being doomed to the recital of lengthy statements of nutshell importance, and wire-drawn disquisitions on the immorality and avarice of missionaries, besides a formal list of the concomitants of hypocrisy and intrigue; nearly all of which, when thrown into a proper receptacle and well shaken, disappear like chaff before the breath of truth.

CHAPTER XIV.

TUBUÁI AND ITS COCOANUT GROVES—INCIDENTS ABOARD.

DURING our sojourn at Borabóra, Evans and I slept ashore, at the house of Matchá. We were provided with musquito-nets and clean bedding. One evening, owing to the heat, I left the house and took up my quarters in a large canoe that for years had been reposing beneath its shed. But I had reason to repent of it, for the premises were infested by hordes of musquitoes ; besides, by lying in the bottom of the canoe, enveloped in the net, I effectually prevented a free circulation of air.

At this place resides Tafaáura, a high chief, and, excepting Pomaretáne, the consort of the queen at Tahiti, he is the handsomest and best-proportioned native I have seen among the islands. He is powerfully and symmetrically formed, yet his countenance lacks the dignity of expression observable among some of the Hawaiian nobles. With all his attractions, he proved recreant to his country in the hour of need, for, during the French war, he attached himself to the invaders, from whom he received testimonials of their esteem ; and I noticed suspended in his house the French sword and belt worn by him on that occasion. Recently, he attempted to revolutionize the island, during the absence of King 'Tapóa at Tahiti, but this was promptly checked by the interference of Mr. Krause. A fine-looking young man, I think his son, who resides with him, I hired to carry me in his canoe to the little island of Tubuái opposite. Having embarked, we had hardly left the shore before a sudden flaw of wind struck the sail with such violence as to throw the canoe on its side, breaking one of the sticks of the outrigger, and swamping it. The man instantly jumped overboard, while I remained in the canoe, which, though beneath the surface of the water, was sufficiently buoyant to support me. By his swimming and my paddling we reached the shore, where it was speedily repaired. After procuring dry garments we again embarked, and this time with better success, for after a pleasant sail of a mile we reached our destination, and hauled the canoe upon the beach.

19

This island, including the islet Tubuái-íti (little Tubuái) immediately adjoining, is a mile and a half in length and three-eighths
of a mile in breadth, having a ridge of high hills traversing its entire
length. The land between these hills and the shore is low, and
covered with a forest of cocoanut and occasionally other fruit trees ;
the hills in some places are scantily clothed with trees and bushes.
It was untenanted, unless by swarms of musquitoes. Mr. Krause
informed me that a single deer roamed wild upon the island, its mate
having died. Both were brought from South America.

Before strolling through this solitary forest of palms, my attendant ascended a tree and threw down three or four young cocoanuts,
by way of refreshing ourselves with their cooling beverage ; after
which he looked about upon the ground, and picked up an old
nut that had fallen from the tree, and from which a bright-green
sprout had protruded itself through the coarse, dry husk in two beautiful shoots. This he divested of its tough covering and broke open.
The centre was completely filled with a concrete substance, yellow-
ish externally, owing to the natural oil of the kernel that exudes
when old; but, upon being penetrated, it was white and spongy,
having a sweet, agreeable taste ; it is called by the natives *utu*.
In this way many of these forests are propagated. The ripe fruit
falls from the tree among the loose decomposing vegetation around
it, and, whether covered or not, in a short time two shoots burst
from it, one finding its way into the earth, while the other curves
upwards, and in a few years ranks with the other trees of the forest.
Like the date or other varieties of palm, it is *endogenous*, and its
coarse gray trunk may be hacked and mutilated with impunity, for
its stem increases by *internal growth*, deriving nourishment from
the bud that grows in the centre of its leafy crown. If this be
destroyed, its broad plumes wither and fall.

On all these trees the nuts were hanging in clusters, while the
ground was strewed with them in every stage of decomposition. At
a low estimate, this island and that adjoining contain perhaps five
thousand of these trees, and which, allowing for domestic consumption, should yield upwards of ten thousand gallons of oil annually, having a gross value of $2,500. It is a staple commodity, and is always
in demand ; but this source of wealth to the natives is suffered to pass

unheeded.   This is but one of the islets.   From this branch of commerce alone, upwards of twenty thousand dollars might be derived
annually ; but the income from this South Sea staple will probably
never be increased by the present race.   Traders among the islands
have offered the natives every inducement to manufacture oil, by advancing merchandise on credit, but they have failed to create new
wants for them ; and so long as the few they possess are supplied by
the spontaneous products of the soil, they prefer poverty and sloth to
industry and wealth.   The value of this article exported annually
from Borabóra amounts to only a few hundred dollars.   The process
of its manufacture is very simple.   A pile of old nuts having been
procured, they are deprived of their husks and broken in the middle.
The native sits astride of a rude bench, at one end of which is affixed
an iron—usually an old plane-iron, ground down to an oval and
armed with teeth like a saw.   He then takes one of these pieces,
and with both hands grates it over the iron, when the kernel falls
in light particles into a trough placed beneath for its reception.
This process is continued until the trough is half filled, when it is
placed on forked sticks about four feet from the ground, to rot in the
sun.   This requires but few days ; and after the oil has exuded, the
residue is subjected to pressure to remove any yet remaining, and
then thrown away.   During the rotting process the odor arising from
it is extremely offensive.   At the Hapái Islands, a Swedish company
have a steam-mill in operation for the manufacture of this commodity.
   We continued our walk along an almost obliterated path, through
the seemingly interminable forest ; on the left was the rippled surface of the bay, and on our right, beyond the belt of cocoanut-trees,
a heavy growth of forest and bushes, so that I abandoned my intention of ascending the hills.   Two or three rills crossed our path, and
after travelling about a fourth of a mile, we came upon the ruins of a
house and a huge oven, situated in an open space near the water,
from which many of the trees had been cut down or destroyed.
This place, my guide informed me, was the spot selected by the
French during the war for a detachment of their troops, sent down
to attack Borabóra, and the oven had been constructed by them for
domestic uses.   We continued on until we reached the southernmost point of the island, and here our progress was checked by huge

boulders that covered the precipitous ridge rising from the water, also by the dense growth of trees and underwood, so that I was reluctantly compelled to forego the pleasure of walking around the island. A narrow channel, about four feet in depth, separated us from Tubuái-íti. The water was flowing slowly out from the harbor, over a bed of white coral; and although the open grove on the opposite shore looked inviting, we did not cross over.

After retracing our steps, we gathered a quantity of young cocoanuts and oranges, and started for the Falcon, which I reached in time to witness a sad accident. While sitting beneath the awning, upon the quarter-deck, and conversing with the captain, one of the seamen aloft called out, "Stand from under!" and almost immediately a ponderous iron-bound block bounded upon the deck, striking in its fall a native boy, fourteen years of age, who was splitting wood near the galley. Knocking him senseless, it inflicted a ghastly wound on the back of his head, by cutting through the scalp to the bone. When we reached him, he was lying in a pool of blood. I dashed a basin of water in his face, which revived him; the bleeding was checked by cold water and pressure. The wound was dressed in the usual manner, by shaving the scalp in its immediate vicinity. stitching it together, and applying adhesive plaster. He was then removed to the quarter-deck, where he passed the night in great distress, a fever having ensued, attended with frequent vomiting of blood. His parents watched with him during the night, removing him in the morning to the shore in a canoe. At the time, I had my doubts as to his recovery, but on a subsequent visit, I found him as hearty as ever. Previous to the accident, our decks had swarmed with natives, but after its occurrence we had no further trouble with them.

A few mornings subsequent to this event, a circumstance occurred that completely destroyed my relish for fresh fish. The *table d'hôte* of the Falcon was unexceptionable, for we had an excellent cook, and our pork, poultry, and pastry were served without stint. If I happened to be on shore at dinner-time, the swivel was loaded and fired by way of intimation, and a boat sent off. On the morning in question, one of our dishes consisted of fried fish of delicious flavor, so that Mr. Taylor, the first officer, and I partook largely of it, while

Adams contented himself with a broiled fowl. Breakfast finished, we lighted our cheroots and seated ourselves upon deck. I soon felt an intense heat in my head, while my face was burning hot. I threw my cigar overboard and examined my pulse, which beating violently, I remarked to Adams that I had a sudden attack of fever, and should be compelled to retire. At this moment Taylor sprang up, with both hands clasped to his head, exclaiming that he was poisoned. His features were perfectly livid, and I felt alarmed. Approaching me, he said, " You are poisoned, too ; look at his face, Adams." " Gracious ! both of you *are*," was the reply, " and you had better do something for yourselves as quickly as possible." Taylor said he should take an emetic, which I knew was the proper remedy ; but at that moment I had a particular aversion for tartarized antimony, and jumping into a canoe, was paddled ashore, to place myself under the treatment of Matehá. The old women immediately held a hasty consultation, and the result was, that I was condemned to eat an indefinite number of lemons, seasoned with salt. I remonstrated, but they insisted, and to make sure, they proposed to lay me on my back and squeeze the juice into my mouth while I swallowed it. I negatived at once such infantine proceedings, and sat down to the bitter antidote.

For three days I experienced the effects of the poisoning, while Taylor, who took the emetic, reported himself in *statu quo* on the following morning. What made the circumstance remarkable was, that many of the natives partook of the same description of fish, (all of which were taken the evening previous,) and none of them complained of unfavorable symptoms.

CHAPTER XV.

TAHITI.

Occurrences at this island induced Mr. Adams to revisit Tahiti before consummating his proposed voyage, and the third morning after leaving Borabóra, the lofty peak of Urohená loomed before us,

while the mural spires of Mooréa were on our left.   We beat up
through the channel between the two islands, and by noon were
"hauled aback" abreast of the town, Papeéte.

As it was not the owner's intention to remain above an hour in
this place, the officer in charge was requested "to lay off and on,"
while we landed in a boat which was immediately lowered.   The
appearance of this island at the distance of a few miles is anything
but flattering to the glowing descriptions which travellers have concurred in giving, and the praise lavished upon it without stint has
been overwrought.   It is not decked in a robe of universal beauty
to be comprehended at a superficial glance ; its attractions consist of
a combination of pleasing scenes, blended or interwoven with each
other by sprinklings of the ideal.   These are only to be found amid
its groves, valleys, and within its amphitheatre of mountain peaks,
for, viewed at a distance, Tahiti has nothing to distinguish her from
sister isles in this ocean ; indeed, I have seen others more inviting.

The trade-winds were blowing strongly from the southeast as we
pulled off from the Falcon, making the sea unpleasantly rough.   The
mountains before us were in many places sterile, though their valleys
and summits were densely wooded.   Around the mountain's base
was a belt of verdure, and these groves, scattered upon the level
land between the mountain-spurs and the sea-shore, are the boast of
Tahiti.   The entrance to the harbor through the reef is narrow,
and as we approached it, there was a strong current setting to leeward upon the reef, and on both sides the sea was breaking violently.
Having pulled through into still water, the town was before us,
stretching around the bay in a semicircle.   Owing to the level nature of the land on which it is built, only the front row of white
houses is seen, bounded in the rear by a dark grove.   Directly
abreast of the passage, and commanding it, is Fort Uranie, where
troops are always stationed.

We landed nearly in front of the house of Dr. Johnstone, where,
in a shady verandah, the doctor, Wm. H. Kelly, Esq., U. S. Consul,
and an American gentleman were sitting, and after paying our respects to them, we walked up to Adams's residence on the Broom
Road.

In approaching the town from the sea, its most conspicuous ob-

jects are French improvements; these consist of government-house, barracks, arsenal, workshops, and neat stone jetties, with hydrants for watering ships, also lamp-posts placed at regular intervals around the semicircle of the bay. To give a general idea of the town and harbor of Papeéte, let the reader imagine a sheet of water a mile and a half in length and half a mile in breadth, bounded on one side by a reef of coral, and on the other by a semicircular shore a mile and three-quarters in extent, from Point Fareúte on the east, to Point Hotuanéa on the west. This level strip of land has an average breadth of half a mile from the shore to the mountain-spurs, although valleys extend from it towards the mountains to a much greater distance, and is covered with a continuous grove of majestic trees, chiefly lofty bread-fruit, orange, and banana. Beneath this grove, which is watered by six or eight small streams, are scattered the habitations of between two and three thousand persons, native and foreign. The buildings along the shore, bordering an excellent road, are chiefly wooden; two or three are occupied as foreign consulates, and the remainder are stores and restaurants; the public buildings of the French are usually two stories, and of stone. About one hundred yards from the shore runs the original Broom Road, which encircles the island; this, in the town, is perhaps twelve yards broad, and is intersected frequently by others of lesser breadth. The lofty trees on either side of this road frequently form a canopy over it, so that it resembles a shady avenue, and in several places along its border, from the lion mouths of hydrants, streams of pure water are perpetually gushing. On this road, and towards the west, are located the government-house and arsenal, before which guards are constantly patrolling.

The houses of some of the residents are delightfully located amid gardens of plants, native and exotic, and in the garden of Dr. Johnstone, I noticed the aloe, vanilla, ebony, and a variety of others, all of which seemed thriving in a congenial soil. Many of the native houses make greater pretensions than those of the Society islanders, but the rickety appearance of *some* of them detracts from the natural beauty of the scenery. The market, which occupies a central position between the Broom and Shore Roads, consists simply of two thatched sheds, open on all sides, and each about thirty feet

in length by ten in breadth, having a hydrant near them.   Its
transactions are very simple : when a native has any provision or
fruits to dispose of, he repairs to the market and awaits patiently the
arrival of a customer.   This the law requires ; in the morning are
usually found here old men, women, and children with bread-fruit,
feis, bananas, *vis*, (spondias,) oranges, bunches of cocoanuts deprived of their husks, and occasionally pigs and fish, the former living or roasted ; and it is sometimes amusing to witness the haggling
among natives and foreigners about prices.   Towards the western
portion of the town, and in the rear of the Bethel, is the cemetery,
where were buried many of those who fell during the war.   On the
east, the Broom Road has been reopened through an embankment
or old line of fortification, erected by the French about ten years
ago, which, conforming to the sinuosities of a small stream, extends
from the shore to the mountain.   A neat and appropriate residence
has been erected for Queen Po-má-re near the arsenal, and is occupied
alternately with her native residence at Papáoa, at the option of her
majesty.

The shirt and *paréu* constitute the universal costume ; even the
royal consort condescends to promenade the streets barefooted, his
loins girded with a fathom of Merrimack prints, over which is loosely
adjusted a fancy regatta shirt.   The garments of the females are in
accordance with the liberality of their admirers.   Some of them
make a costly display of silks, while sauntering along the Broom
Road, with their glossy black hair perfumed with the sweet-scented
manóe, and ornamented with the white flowers of the Cape jessamine fastened negligently among the braids.   During the evening a
motley assemblage is usually witnessed upon the shore, where the
street is promenaded by sailors, civilians, and soldiers wearing the
imperial uniform, hand-in-hand with naiads of questionable reputation.   At eight o'clock the bugle sounds, when natives are compelled
to retire to their homes, and strangers who are found without a
"*Permis de Sejour*" are liable to arrest.

With all its beauty, Papeéte cannot boast of a hotel, this description of public convenience being confined to the houses of entertainment frequented chiefly by seamen.   In consequence, it is customary for visitors to rent a small house, and either hire a cook or

effect an arrangement with the proprietor of a restaurant to have meals sent to their residences. The *table d'hôte* is at present of the most ordinary description ; and for two meals a day, including wines, thus served, at 9 A. M. and 4 P. M., the expense is twenty-eight dollars per month. Visitors have just reason to complain in this respect, and there is sometimes a scarcity of fresh provision, which is confined almost wholly to pork, fish, and poultry.

The chief attraction of Papeéte is its tranquil aspect and the rustic simplicity everywhere observable. Although there are spacious residences reposing beneath canopies that never fade, there are scenes equally attractive in the humbler walks of life, and the lattice hut, with its drooping thatch of pandanus, embowered amid groves of the broad-leafed plantain, merits a share of the admiration Nature's prodigality voluntarily calls forth. The Broom Road, shaded by umbrageous arms raised over it from venerable trunks that have scattered food to generations now forgotten, is the scene of many a pleasant meeting, at sunset or in the mellow twilight of evening. Here, the soldier or civilian who has sauntered through continental cities, and who, perhaps, longs again for the scenes of *la belle France*, strangers of various climes, and, above all, the happy groups of native lords, promenade its beaten centre, or repose on the green-sward of its margin.

The ominous blast of the war-conch and the expiring wail of the victim for the sacrificial altar are forever hushed. Though its quiet groves respond less frequently to the mellow notes of the bamboo flute or the soft harmony of the *uté*, in the still evening the stirring strains of the bugle-call, echoing over hills and through valleys, awaken their repose with the peans of a conqueror.

CHAPTER XVI.

LIFE IN TOWN.

I RENTED a snug little cottage on the Broom Road, shaded by bread-fruit trees ; and beneath the windows bloomed the jessamine, periwinkle, geranium, and other flowers, while from the hydrant opposite, a pure fountain was perpetually gushing. True, it was meagre in furniture, for what little I possessed remained at Raiatea. However, it was in this respect sufficiently embellished to answer the requirements of a temporary sojourn. It may be necessary to mention that the contemplated voyage of the Falcon was broken up, and I was compelled to abandon my visit for the present to the Paumotu Archipelago.

I was usually awakened at an early hour in the morning by the merry sound of voices proceeding from a group known as the " Broom Road Gang." It was certainly the most interesting " gang" assigned to this description of labor I ever witnessed, for it consisted· of fifteen or twenty females, from the silver-haired matron to the laughing child, who, for indulging too freely in the intoxicating beverage, had been condemned to sweep the road every morning for a certain number of weeks, but were permitted to return to their homes during the day. There were no taskmasters to interfere with them, and, as usual, there was more gossip than work. Sometimes the girls would dip their brooms in the clear water of the hydrant and sprinkle each other by way of pleasantry, and then there would be a chase among the guava bushes. None of them lost caste by performing this sanitary regulation, and there was at times as flaunting a display of fancy robes and *paréus,* as when hand-in-hand they promenaded the thoroughfares with their dusky beaux.

Unfortunately for them, but fortunately for me, two or three American captains " were thrown upon the beach," owing to accidents to their vessels, and rather than submit to the invalid diet of the restaurants, we clubbed together, and, through the kindness of W. H. Kelly, Esq., our consul, were favored with untenanted rooms in the consulate building, where we met to enjoy *three* meals a day. Without occupation, time hangs heavily on one's hands in Papeéte. You sit in the verandah to look out upon the harbor with its shipping, or watch the monotonous patrol of the sentinels, the careless lounging of the natives through the streets, or the foreigners passing in their neat light dresses with umbrellas. The arrival of a ship is an event, and any item of intelligence thus procured is gratuitously circulated through the little community with surpassing quickness. Sometimes the low, black steamer Phoque is seen getting up steam, and this occasions comment among the curious as to the object, for the government usually maintains a mysterious silence in this respect. Some surmise that she is destined for the Marquesas, to avenge an attack made by the natives; others, that she is going down to see how things look among the leeward islands; and, between the surmises of one and the conjectures of the other, she steams out of the harbor and disappears, no one knows where. Occasionally, a pearling schooner arrives with its valuable freight, and discharges it on the jetty, in front of the store of its owner. It is no uncommon sight to see tons of beautiful mother-of-pearl piled up in solid walls by the roadside.

This trade was formerly very extensive in this ocean; but it now appears to be engrossed by a few persons, and the nucleus of its operations is Tahiti. One of the principal dealers in this article of commerce is Mr. Branda, a native of Scotland, but for many years a resident of this island, and who has schooners continually engaged in the trade. In fact, the greater portion of it he monopolizes, or among the islands of the Paumotu or low Archipelago, he has persons continually stationed to look after his interests. The natives of these islands where shells are to be found, are indebted to him for merchandise advanced to them for diving, and he finds it politic to keep them constantly in his debt. In procuring these shells, the Paumotuan divers are very expert. Having discovered a " bed" in a lagoon, they are conveyed in a boat to the spot. They then descend to the bottom, carrying with them a bag, to which is attached a rope with one end of it secured in the boat. When this is filled, (the divers coming frequently to the surface for respiration,) it is drawn up and emptied, and the process repeated until the boat is ladened.

It is a life of fatigue and danger for the natives. On coming to the surface, the blood frequently streams from their noses, while their eyes are bloodshot. The true pearls are seldom found ; often a cargo of shell is procured, without discovering one. The natives are well acquainted with their value, and are seldom disposed to part with them without an equivalent. These islands are low, and of coral structure, inclosing at times extensive lagoons, their outer margins descending abruptly, and frequently the ocean in the immediate vicinity is unfathomable. They are covered with forests of cocoanut and pandanus, and sometimes low bushes. The food furnished by these trees, together with fish and swine, is all the natives have to subsist on. From the pandanus they obtain a sweet seed inclosed within a husk or drupe. The actual cost of the shells is trifling, compared with the price they bring in England, which is something like fifty pounds per ton.

In the vicinity of Papeéte are many pleasant walks, and the numerous streams afford admirable opportunities for bathing ; the A-ti-ri-a-éa on the east, and the Ti-pai-a-rúi on the west, are beautiful streams, both spanned by neat and substantial bridges, and where at any hour of the day may be seen natives of both sexes enjoying this cool luxury. I was standing upon the bridge of Tipaiarúi one day when sixteen or eighteen men, darker than the Tahitians, and under the guidance of a French overseer, divested themselves of their garments, and were permitted the privilege of a short bathe ; after which, they were hurried out and driven forward like a gang of felons. These, I was afterwards informed, were Christian martyrs ; they were natives of the Chain Islands, and had embraced the Protestant faith through native missionaries ; French priests were subsequently introduced, and acting under the protection of their government, their acts were deemed arbitrary by those whose faith they sought to subvert. On one occasion a family was engaged in evening devotions, when a Catholic priest knocked for admittance ; the Paumotuan gave him to understand that no one should enter his house until he had finished praying ; whoever did, would do so at his peril. The priest then retired and procured *mutóis* or constables ; these forced an entrance, and in the melée that ensued, one of them was killed. When the government at Papeéte was notified of the occurrence, a vessel was dispatched to the island, and the homicide, and such other persons as were obnoxious to the priest, were conveyed to Papeéte, where one or two of them were hung, protesting to the last their innocence of intentional murder ; the others were enslaved as we have seen. This is the story current at Papeéte. I frequently saw this gang of old and young men pass through the streets on their way to labor upon public works, and sincerely pitied them ; whether they were condemned or not to a lifetime of servitude, I have never learned.

Equestrian exercises are an agreeable diversion to the monotony of town life. I hired a horse of a cousin of Queen Pomare, which I usually kept tethered in the yard, with the gate closed, but twice he was missing in the morning, and each time my native attendant found him in the *pound*, where I was obliged to pay two dollars for his recovery. I have always believed that the animal was purposely removed, for the *mutói*, or native constable, who deposits him in limbo, is entitled to one half the fine, and I have been credibly informed that such transactions are of frequent occurrence.

A beautiful ride is upon the Broom Road towards Fatáoa ; having reached the Atiriaéa, the road diverges to the right, and following the bank of the river, winds through a beautiful valley, arched over in many places by a luxuriant growth of guava, covered with the yellow fruit, which is also strewed upon the ground. After riding about two miles, the valley grows narrower, until it finally becomes a deep mountain-pass, the road running beside a foaming torrent ; the *mape* and other lofty trees of the forest are now discovered, and on the opposite side of the river is witnessed one of the features that lend beauty to the landscapes of Tahiti. This is a narrow stream, that for several hundred feet has torn its way in a line of foam down the almost perpendicular side of the mountain ; too distant to be heard, it seems a thread of silver spanning a green mantle.

Fatáoa itself is situate among fantastic peaks, forming, as seen from the harbor of Taonóa, a mural crown, almost perfect in its resemblance to that description of regalia, and serves also as a conspicuous landmark in approaching that harbor. This spot is considered the key of the island ; it was the last fortress that held out against the French, and was only reduced by the treachery of a renegade native ; it is now occupied by the French as a post of defence, and is stocked with ammunition and provision. Though having forded the river and ascended the mountain a considerable distance, I never visited this interesting locality, procrastinating until it was too late. Its scenery is said to be the most wildly romantic to be met with throughout the group.

Another favorite ride is to Mataväi or Point Venus, four miles from Papeéte, over an excellent road, passing through the hamlets of Taonóa and Papáoa. Mataväi is a broad level space of land, covered with groves and beautifully watered by a large stream running parallel with the shore. The spot derives additional interest from its association with the names of early voyagers, including that of Wallis, its discoverer in 1767 ; Cook, who observed the transit of Venus on the point bearing that planet's name ; also, Bligh. of the ship Bounty, for it was here that his crew found the blandishments of the fair islanders irresistible.

I should have mentioned that among the sights of Papeéte I saw one that awakened old recollections ; it was all that remained of the beautiful yacht "Kamehaméha," now lying a dismantled hull upon the water, and unrecognizable but for the faded diadem upon her stern. She was taken by the French from Honolulu after their disgraceful foraging expedition in 1849, and used as a sort of convoy, or express schooner, and subsequently performed trips between Tahiti and the Marquesas Islands. But the days of her pride appear to have been numbered, and her hull now floats a faded relic of petty larceny.

CHAPTER XVII.

JOURNEYINGS ON THE BROOM ROAD

SEQUESTERED amid an amphitheatre of lofty summits, and twenty-five hundred feet above the sea, reposes a beautiful lake, receiving the tribute of a hundred gushing rills, and courting solitude among evergreen mountains. No canoe skims over its cold, green waters, no wreath of smoke curls above the forest that surrounds it ; precipitous ridges, clothed with a mantle of dark foliage, mottled by the lighter verdure of the broad-plumed *feí*, descend abruptly to ,its margin, and save the murmur of rills, or the distant waterfalls that leap from their sides into the basin beneath, no other sound disturbs the solemn stillness. Owing to unavoidable difficulties, but few ever visit this lake, and hundreds have probably rambled among the groves of Tahiti, and departed without knowing that such a mountain reservoir ever existed.

For lack of more agreeable occupation, I conceived the idea of visiting it. As such an enterprise was uncongenial to the tastes or habits of my nautical companions, I set out alone, simply providing myself with blankets and a few changes of apparel, which were secured in a roll behind the saddle. I started from town at six in the morning, leaving it by the road on the west. It ran parallel with the sea-shore, though a space perhaps of a quarter of a mile intervened. It was bounded on either side by the apparently interminable succession of groves. Several streams were passed, usually forded, and near one of them, half hidden by a grove of orange and bread-fruit trees, was a small *auberge ;* noticing my travelling equipment, the *aubergiste* came out and wished me " *un bon voyage.*" Occasionally I encountered a mounted gendarme cantering leisurely along ; but the most interesting spectacle was a comment on the sweets of matrimony. Coming along the road, I saw a man and woman engaged in loud debate, and as they approached nearer, I discovered that the right wrist of the man was fastened to the left wrist of the woman with a strip of bark, leaving the space of a foot intervening. They were followed by two native constables, from whom I learned they were man and wife who had had a disagreement with each other. These officials listened complacently to their bitter colloquy, occasionally shouting to them when their repugnance towards each other compelled them to monopolize the greater portion of the road by fruitless efforts to twist their bonds asunder.

Natives of both sexes, conveying their fruits to market in the cool of the morning, were frequently met, and from all I received a cordial *iaurana.* About six miles from town the road was crossed by a

narrow stream with abrupt banks and a muddy bottom, into which
the horse refused to venture; the more I spurred, the more he
pranced, until he shied bodily into the guavas. I dismounted, and
leading him by the bridle through the bushes, discovered a spot where
it was fordable by stepping upon the trunk of an old tree that lay in
the water. Having reached the opposite bank, by dint of coaxing
my beast made a plunge. It was the work of a moment; for, after
two or three nervous springs, he was out of the slough, throwing up
with his hoofs, as he landed upon the bank, a shower of black mud,
which in its descent made a conspicuous contrast on my white linen
attire. Saddle and baggage were completely bespattered, and for a
brief interval my thoughts were of the " earth, earthy ;" but I refrained
from changing my garments until after arriving at Aówa, where I
took breakfast at half-past nine. Before reaching it, I passed the
wide and deep valley of Punarú, where a broad stream foamed
over a rocky bed; and here were a number of females engaged in
fishing.

The Broom Road might be rendered one of the most agreeable
thoroughfares among the isles of the Pacific, for its course is among
the low level land of the shore, sometimes winding through a dense
forest of guava, or beneath a leafy canopy of bread-fruit and orange
and lime trees, and often skirting the sea-shore, amid extensive
groves of cocoa-palms. Its usual breadth is from eight to ten
yards; some portions of it are as clear as a garden-walk, the natives
being compelled by the government to remove the grass and other
obstructions from that portion of it in front of their premises. Its
greatest defect is the want of suitable bridges, the streams, which
are numerous, being frequently spanned by cocoanut logs, with a
few planks laid carelessly across. At short intervals, the habitations
of the natives are seen embowered amid groves, whose fruits supply
their wants; and some of these rustic domiciles, constructed of the
tender stems of the bamboo, and neatly thatched with the pandanus,
were exceedingly picturesque and in harmony with the landscape.
Occasionally a small hamlet is passed, and the merry shouts of
children are heard sporting among the groves, while groups of the
romance-loving of both sexes are frequently seen coquetting beneath
shady boughs by the road-side. All seem to possess open expres-

sion of countenance, and the cordial welcome extended to the traveller at once banishes formality or suspicion. The habitations of the natives are usually inclosed with low fences, constructed of *puráu*, or short cocoanut posts, placed uprightly in the ground, containing sometimes small cultivations of sweet potatoes and taro, and almost invariably groves of bananas, plantains and bread-fruit. The cocoanut-trees prefer the sandy soil of the shore, where they flourish vigorously, though the sea sometimes washes their roots.

I selected Aówa as a halting-place, because recommended to do so by Adams, who was acquainted with a family residing here. It is a small hamlet, scattered through a shady grove, and watered by a clear stream ; one of the young men removed the saddle from the horse and turned him out to browse, while my breakfast was being cooked, which consisted of roast fish, chicken and bread-fruit, and the unfailing beverage of the young cocoanut. After breakfast, I laid down upon the mats and enjoyed a comfortable nap ; it was half-past one before I was again in the saddle, galloping along the Broom Road.

Soon after leaving Aówa, I passed a row of about twenty large *aíto* trees, standing upon the shore in beautiful contrast to the denser foliage beyond, and about four o'clock reached the village of Pápara, the most considerable one to be met with on the western portion of the island. Here for the first time I saw native children sporting upon the reef with surf-boards, as at the Sandwich Islands.

At a French house of entertainment, I halted for a few moments to obtain refreshment, and a group of the young of both sexes soon gathered round to witness the new arrival, all making good-humored comments on my travel-stained appearance.

As soon as I had opened my mouth to reply, there was a general shout among the girls of, " *Taáta 'yheé ! taáta 'yheé !* " The truth is, such a similarity exists between the Hawaiian and Tahitian dialects, that in attempting to discourse in the latter, I invariably betrayed my acquaintance with the former, a knowledge of which is a valuable acquisition to persons travelling in the South Seas.

When preparing to leave, I was importuned by half a dozen of these laughing damsels for a ride, and, being indifferent as to the

20

duration of my journey, I gave them permission to mount the "*pua horo fenúa,*" which they did two at a time, galloping down the road for about a hundred yards, and then returning to give place to others. The delight they appeared to derive from their equestrian exercise was infinite, for their dark tresses streamed loosely behind them as they dashed on laughing and shouting, waving green boughs of guava. We presently came to a clear, shallow stream, with a pebbly bottom, when I requested them to dismount that I might cross it. This they refused to do, saying that I would ride away and leave them. They insisted on carrying me over ; but I told them that at home we would consider it a very unfeminine occupation. In reply they said, that America and Tahiti were two very different places, and that they could not see any impropriety in performing so humane an office. Suiting the action to the word, two of the strongest seized me, *nolens volens*, and carried me across, after which they mounted and galloped off.

Having indulged them for nearly an hour, I told them I could not possibly lose any more time. Shaking hands and exchanging *iaurá- nas* with each other, we parted mutually pleased, they at having ob- tained, and I at having conferred, a favor. I continued my journey more slowly, for the girls had given my horse a long race, and about half past five, began to look out for comfortable quarters in which to pass the night. These I found at Aurófa, at the house of a native named Apó. I was enticed to the spot by the odor of fish and bread-fruit that were roasting upon a fine bed of embers in front of the house, and around which were sitting a dozen persons, male and female. Upon inquiry, they told me I was welcome to such accommo- dations as they could provide ; one of the young men disposed of my horse, while the children carried the saddle, bridle, and baggage into the house. This was of ample dimensions, and had three bed- steads in one general apartment, besides chests, and the ordinary furniture of a Tahitian household. The supper being cooked, I joined them at the fire, and in addition to the articles before enume- rated I found they had pork and shrimps. But a brief interval was required to establish a familiar acquaintance. The two daughters or visitors of my host soon began to joke me about my adventures at Pápara. They called me a "*taáta 'yheé*" and sent for a Sandwich Islander who lived a short distance off to come and converse with me. Our colloquy was listened to by all with considerable interest, the affinity of the two dialects to each other frequently calling forth their remarks. About eight o'clock our neighbors dispersed, when the family were assembled for worship. The melody of their voices was charming, and after the hymn a chapter was read, followed by a prayer. Their sleeping arrangements occasioned them no inconvenience. Apo's wife showed me a bed with sheets of unquestionable purity. She and her husband occupied one a short distance off; while between my bed and that of the girls a space of but two or three feet intervened. There were no curtains in the house, and the juveniles were disposed of upon mats. A light breeze from the sea crept through the interstices of the *puráu*, rendering the apartment refreshingly cool, and a deep sonorous breathing, to which I probably contributed, soon disturbed the stillness, for, having once closed my eyes, I slept soundly until morning.

CHAPTER XVIII.

THE MOUNTAIN LAKE.

I ROSE early in the morning and went out to the bank of a clear rivulet to perform my ablutions; and after partaking of an early breakfast, set out for Papeuríri, from which place I had been instructed to ascend to the lake. Like other hamlets, it was scattered through the grove at convenient intervals. I found a temporary abode in the old mission residence, which had long been tenanted by Tahitians.

Being unable to obtain from the natives the information required respecting the lake, and having learned that a foreigner was residing in this district near the shore, I rode down to the place as directed. It proved to be a sort of Robinson Crusoe cottage, bounded by an almost impenetrable thicket of guava on one side, and the ocean on the other; its possessor, Mr. Skelton, was an

Englishman, and insisted on my dismounting and partaking of a second breakfast, or rather lunch, consisting of hot toast and butter and a cup of coffee, prepared by Mrs. S——.

He gave me such information as he could, but as he had never visited the lake, his directions were desultory; however, he looked out for a guide to accompany me, and the one selected was a young man named Ailíma, who had visited the place but once, when quite a boy. Mr. Skelton having furnished me with a few articles which, he said, I would need to complete our preparations for the ascent, I returned with the guide to the house—a spacious, dilapidated affair. As is usual on such occasions, there was a crowd of idlers looking on, some of them finding fault with Ailíma's arrangements, simply because his services had been preferred to theirs. As a Sandwich Islander would have done on a similar occasion, our baggage and provision were carried in two bundles, adjusted to each extremity of a dry *puráu* pole. It was now ten o'clock, and the guide and others advised me to remain where I was over night, and start early on the following morning, in order to return the same day, alleging that no foreigner who visited it slept there, on account of the humid atmosphere of the mountains. As I intended camping out, two additional boys were hired to assist in carrying the bedding, and at half past ten we commenced our journey, accompanied by an ugly little cur belonging to Ailíma.

On leaving the settlement, we crossed a low strip of land thickly covered with *puráu*, its interlacing branches frequently retarding our course, and after proceeding nearly half a mile, we heard the roaring of the river, whose bed was to be our principal pathway to the mountains.

Knowing that it was to be crossed frequently, I dashed into it without removing my boots; it was about twenty yards broad, and in depth to the knees; the bottom was covered with loose rolling stones. After fording its sinuosities four or five times within the space of fifteen minutes, I found that the task of sitting upon a log and elevating my feet for the escape of the water from my boot-tops, was becoming very inconvenient; accordingly, the boots were removed and suspended upon a branch until our return.

Our path lay through a forest of majestic *vis*, or Brazilian plum-trees, whose ripening fruit was studding the dark foliage like yellow gems; there were numerous other lofty "monarchs of the forest," whose thick branches wove a dark canopy overhead, and from Papeuríri to Lake Waihiría, our path was in the shade. I paid dearly for my experiment; walking through bushes and over loose rolling stones barefooted, requires an understanding more callous than one accustomed to leather. Ascending the valley, the river became more circumscribed and rapid, in crossing which, I was always compelled to lean upon the shoulders of Ailíma and one of the boys for support. Such torture to the feet soon became unendurable, and, fortunately, having with me a pair of coarse overalls, I tore them in two and swathed up each foot, lacing both with strips of cloth. Under other circumstances, I might have been mistaken for a patient suffering from gout. Though exceedingly cumbersome, they served their purpose tolerably, the greatest inconvenience being their weight and the trouble of readjusting the straps; a pair of thick trowsers lashed on to the feet and completely saturated with water could not be otherwise than an impediment to travelling.

The valley grew narrower, and large trees were jutting out from its precipitous sides. Growing in seemingly inaccessible places was the wild banana or broad-leaved *fei*, with the reddish fruit clustering around the stalk that arose perpendicularly from the leafy crown. The bottom was covered with an almost impenetrable growth of trees, underwood, clumps of bamboo, and cane-brakes, so that travelling through them was very fatiguing, as we were compelled to stoop continually to avoid the low branches above. Instead of pursuing a straight course, the river was more sinuous than ever, and we were compelled to ford it continually, though in some places it was exceedingly rapid. Ailíma's dog was a great source of inconvenience to him, for he would never plunge into the cold, rapid current until after he had seen us cross over and disappear among the bushes, when we were notified of his movements by a few premonitory yelps as he jumped into the water, to be borne downward some fifteen or twenty yards before reaching the opposite bank. Sometimes Ailíma would coax and scold before he could induce him to venture the torrent. In fording one of these rapid

passages, the boy who carried the coffee and a few other items in a
large tin pot found the current too deep and strong for him when he
had reached mid-channel, and he shouted lustily as he lost his footing and was swept downward.   This was a new feature in the pro-
gramme.   I anticipated nothing less than the complete destruction
of our small stores.   But the boy was a brave one ; while struggling
in the water, the hand that held the cup was raised above his
head, so that not a drop could enter.   He was borne into shallow
water, where he regained his footing.   Occasionally we sat down to
enjoy a smoke, and our fire was procured by rubbing together two
pieces of the *puráu*, which was an infallible resource.   Sometimes
the boys gathered the ripe *feis* and ate them, but to me they tasted
too raw without having undergone a culinary process.

Having ascended the valley to within a short distance of its com-
mencement, we had a beautiful sight on our left.   Down the almost
perpendicular side of the mountain, and more than a hundred feet in
height, a narrow stream tore its way through the verdure in a line of
foam and fell in a shower upon the groves beneath.   Several others
from a lesser height were pouring from rocky fountains, and all con-
tributing to swell the Waihiría.   The mountain bounding the head of
the vale rises abruptly, and from its base, in two serpentine streams,
bursts the river, several hundred feet below the surface of its reservoir.   The ascent is accomplished by a narrow rocky path, winding
frequently along the face of a cliff, and barely wide enough for one
person to pass at a time.   After attaining a safe eminence, we found
the ruins of an old fort erected by the natives during the war.   Its
position commanded the only route by which the eminence could be
gained.   The view from this spot was wildly romantic ; the narrowness of the valley, and the corresponding inequalities in its lofty
precipitous sides, appeared the result of some mighty convulsion
that had rent the earth asunder.   Every portion of it was now
clothed with a variegated mantle of living green, vegetating with the
profuse luxuriance of the tropics ; through openings in the grove
beneath, glimpses were caught of the rivulet foaming over its rocky
bed.   We now entered a vast forest of *feis*, and here was lost every
vestige of a path.   The thick leaves overhead completely shut out
every object from view, so that we had nothing by which to direct

our course. Ailíma was sadly puzzled to recognize localities ; and after roaming at random for half an hour, he told us to remain where we were, and he would go and look for the lake. After a short absence he returned, saying he could not find it, and that we must push on through the forest. Our progress was much obstructed by the herbaceous stems of *feí* trees that covered the ground, in every stage of decomposition ; and, after floundering over them for a considerable time, we began gradually to descend. Huge boulders were scattered around ; and at four o'clock, emerging from the bush, the beautiful lake was spread out before us.

This (the southern) is the most convenient and favorable side from which to view it, for here, to a considerable extent, the ground is level and comparatively unobstructed, while on the other side it is bounded by fantastic peaks and precipitous ridges that descend in abrupt spurs to the margin of the lake. The brows of some of these lofty summits appear to be a mass of rock across which vegetation creeps horizontally, and are frequently enveloped by the dense vapors floating around them.

Captain Beechy, in his voyage to the Pacific, estimates this lake to be but three-fourths of a mile in circumference, with an elevation of one thousand five hundred feet above the sea ; while Kotzebue has assigned to it an elevation of about two thousand five hundred feet. From my own superficial observation, supported by that of others, I should judge its extent to be more than double the estimate of the former voyager. Its temperature, as observed by Lieut. Belcher, of the expedition, was, " at 7 A. M., 72°, and that of the atmosphere 71° ; during a shower of rain it rose to 74° ; a thermometer at the level of the sea at the same time stood at 77°." On the eastern side Mr. Belcher found great quantities of vesicular shaggy lava, and also noticed other evidences of volcanic action, such as crystals of basaltic hornblende, and a few of olivine, upon the surface of the lava. The general contour of the mountains favors the supposition that the waters of the lake repose in a volcanic basin or crater. The water looked clear at a distance, as the sunlight was sparkling upon it ; but on examination, I found it to be of an opaque greenish color ; yet when poured from a cup, it had nothing to distinguish it from the clear river of which it was the reservoir. It is said to abound with huge eels, and of this I have not the slightest doubt, for they are numerous in the mountain streams. On my return to Papeuriri, some of the old natives informed me that, during the French war, when many of them had fled to the mountains for safe refuge, these eels, with *feis* and taro, were all they had to subsist upon. For conveyance across the lake, they usually lashed together *feí* trunks and made a raft. When I left Papeuríri, it was my intention to swim across it; but being fatigued with my jaunt, I abandoned the project. A memorandum which I have accidentally discovered in an old pocket-book that I carried with me on that occasion, will give an idea of our situation, and which I subjoin without the alteration or addition of a word.

Sunset.—" Encamped on the shore of Lake Waihiría at last; but what a penance I have undergone to gratify a whim! A jaunt to Kilauéa is positively a pleasure, compared with this pilgrimage. I have travelled nearly all day barefooted, and by count have forded the river Waihiría sixty-five times. Our road lay up a narrow valley, and when not in the river wound through brush and brake—in fact, there was nothing that could be dignified with that name. We arrived at the shore of the lake about four o'clock, when my guide and the two boys immediately set about constructing a hut. At this moment it is completed, though primitive enough—a shed, the frame of guava, and thatch of *feí* leaves. The interior is strewed with the dried leaves of the *feí* and wild sugar-cane. Our supper is well under way, consisting of roast fowl, ditto fish, *feís*, bread-fruit, and, thanks to the kindness of Mr. S——, a loaf of bread, coffee, and sugar. I'll wager that few have encamped upon the shores of this lake with prospects so inviting."

Our supper was excellent, and was eaten with a relish after the fatigues of the day. This necessary ceremony having been disposed of, we sat around the fire, and Ailíma entertained us with stories about the war, which terminated in a series of whoops, in imitation of an old custom among the natives; after which we spread our bedding upon the dry leaves in the hut, and Ailíma having offered up a short prayer, we laid down and slept soundly through the night.

CHAPTER XIX.

ETCHINGS AND INCIDENTS.

In the morning, my feet were so lame I could hardly stand. This was in some degree remedied by binding on a quantity of dried leaves, to render them less susceptible to the inequalities of the ground over which we were to travel. Without incident worthy of note, we reached Papeuríri about noon, and here I concluded to remain until the following morning.

This, like the other districts through which I had passed, was fertile, and covered with luxuriant groves ; but there was hardly an evidence of cultivation to be witnessed around the habitations of the natives. Bread-fruit and wild-bananas constituted their vegetable diet. To procure the latter, they encounter more actual trouble than they would to cultivate an acre of ground. On such occasions they sometimes travel miles, fording streams and ascending mountains, to return by the same difficult route encumbered with heavy loads. In every direction are to be met stout, athletic young men, too independent to work, and not ashamed to beg ; and it unfortunately happens that the hospitality of these natives encourages such idleness. Frequently a gang of young fellows, in want of a breakfast or lunch, will assemble to take measures for gratifying the cravings of an empty stomach ; and, instead of going out upon the reef to earn a meal, one of them ascends a lofty tree to make observations, while his companions sit patiently beneath. From his eyrie of leafy boughs, he looks over groves of bread-fruit, banana, orange, and other trees, not forgetting to take cognizance of the Broom Road and its pedestrians. This individual has ascended to his post for the purpose of making observations, not astronomic, but *gastronomic ;* for, being perfectly acquainted with localities, he watches until he sees a light breath of smoke curling above the foliage. Then he soliloquizes :—

"Let me see. That smoke must come from old Ohúri's (Baldpate's) oven, because it rises close by that clump of cocoanut-trees, near the shore, where his house stands. I wonder whether he has got any friends this morning. Should like to know what he's got cooking there. Smoke looks very black. Perhaps he is roasting a pig."

This discovery is announced to the expectants below, with the inquiry whether any of them were acquainted with the recent condition of Ohúri's larder. Perhaps one says he saw him mending his net yesterday; upon which another immediately suggests that they shall probably have roast albicore for breakfast; and all congratulate themselves on their good fortune. Meanwhile, the individual in the tree maintains his position, watching for any new phase that may come over the aspect of things. An additional wreath of smoke, the launching of a canoe, or even the squealing of a pig, are all jotted down as strong circumstantial evidences, and are treasured in his memory as events that must necessarily have a sequel. He can calculate to a nicety how long it is necessary for an oven to smoke before its contents are removed; and measuring with his eye the distance to the object from the point of observation, he seldom errs in judgment. These graceless young scamps then take their departure for Ohúri's domicil, which they enter, each with a salutation equivalent to " Peace be unto all within this house !" Old Ohúri has just " taken up his oven," consisting of a piece of fish and a few roast *feís*, just sufficient for a comfortable meal for himself, Mrs. Ohúri, and an only daughter. He yearns over the viands smoking before him, for they have been procured by his own exertions. Nevertheless, he must return the salutation and invite them to partake with him, because it is a custom held sacred, and was considered inviolable by their ancestors before them.

With reference to their Protectorate, the French are certainly lenient in some respects; if the proprietor of a habitation is compelled by law to improve the road that passes it, the requirement is both simple and just. A project has been entertained, compelling *landed proprietors* to cultivate an acre, or at least a half, of land; the theory is good, if it can be reasonably adopted, for arbitrary measures having a tendency to coerce industry cannot prove worse than the existing state of affairs.

A limited number of foreigners reside in this vicinity, but their residences are so scattered that there are but few opportunities for social intercourse. Occasionally a small place of entertainment, usually French, is seen, stocked principally with claret and inferior brandy ; as to sleeping accommodations, such an arrangement is never expected. Everything seems to lack vitality, and yet the absence of native industry cannot be for want of suitable encouragement ; all their surplus produce would find a ready market in Papeéte. Their principal resource are their orange-trees, which yield them a harvest without trouble, while some of the more industrious resort to the forest for *feis* and *vis*, which they convey to market in canoes, and for which they always receive an equivalent in cash.

The following morning I left Papeuríri for Papeéte, thirty miles distant, which I reached at five o'clock in the afternoon ; while passing his house, Adams came out to meet me, remarking that I had arrived just in time, as a party had been made up to visit the adjoining island of Mooréa the next day, an invitation I could not conveniently accept.

One morning while enjoying the sea-breeze in the verandah of Mr. Evans' store, Pomare-táne, the royal consort, walked into the main apartment, and reclining upon the counter, disposed of his head upon a pile of blue drills. Soon after, two females entered the store, one of them almost decrepit with age, the other young and pretty ; between Pomare-táne and the latter, suspicious glances of recognition were exchanged as they cordially shook hands with each other ; the former, however, deemed herself unworthy of such royal condescension, and taking hold of the king's great-toe, she gave it a gentle oscillation with her thumb and finger, to the great diversion of Pomare-táne and others present. Evans remarked that she was one of the ancient *régime*. The king is a finely-proportioned man, with handsome features, but careless and dissipated in his habits. At the time of my visit, Queen Pomáre was in ill health, and in consequence, I deferred waiting upon her. King Tapóa, of Borabóra, was here—a fat, portly, good-natured individual, who preferred playing the courtier to her majesty to superintending the administration of laws in his own kingdom.

A broad distinction is observable between the royalty of the Hawaiian and that of the Georgian and Society Islands. At the former group we find the nobility educated, familiar with court etiquette, and the usages of polite society ; also manifesting a preference for apparel suited to the position to which by birth and attainments they have been exalted. At the latter, on ordinary occasions, we hardly discover a characteristic distinction of royalty among the chiefs, notwithstanding the efforts that have been made in their behalf. Their acquirements, except those requisite for ordinary social intercourse, are chiefly limited to scriptural catechism ; from daily evidences, it would appear that the old leaven has not been thoroughly purged out, for there is hardly a noble who would not prefer girding his loins with the unfettered folds of the *paréu*, to incasing them with the fashions of civilization.

An anecdote illustrative of the administration of justice during the first years of the Protectorate, is too good to pass unnoticed : for the truth of it I can vouch. A native had presented an American, the proprietor of a restaurant in Papeéte, with a fine roaster worth two dollars, which was duly dressed and suspended in the cook-house. During the night it was stolen by a hungry Tahitian, and subsequently disposed of in the ordinary manner; without difficulty the perpetrator of the theft was detected, and a warrant or *procès verbal* issued accordingly, summoning the culprit to appear before the *grand tribunal*. He pleaded guilty, alleging, in extenuation, an irresistible hankering for fresh pork, which he innocently sought to appease. In accordance with the evidence, he was convicted, and sentenced to imprisonment. But the joke is to come : by the law, if the criminal is unable to pay his prison fees, the expense attending confinement must be defrayed by the prosecutor ; in the present instance, the native being destitute of either chattels or legal tender, the costs, together with those of the *procès verbal*, &c., fell upon our publican. The price of the document was five dollars, and the expense of imprisonment about twelve and a half cents per day.

At this time the American consul arrived, and the prosecutor having already expended something like ten dollars, with the prospect of indemnity for his wrong remote as ever, he applied to the representative of his country for redress. As this was not an international affair, the consul could simply advise, which was, to call upon his excellency the governor, and respectfully to make a plain statement of the case to him, when his grievances would probably be redressed. Accordingly, he started off with this intention. During the afternoon, when returning to his residence, the consul met the aggrieved party in his best attire coming down the Broom Road, with several neatly folded papers in his hand (documentary evidences) secured with red tape, and he very naturally inquired whether his excellency had favored his petition.

" No," said the plaintiff, " I reached the gate—raised the latch—thought a moment—then dropped it ; I concluded that if I went in, they'd manage to get ten dollars more out of me, so I thought I'd let well alone and come away."

At the present day, cases of this description are more summarily disposed of ; if a native steals a pig, he must pay ten in return, or become a public servant for a few months.

A few days subsequent to my return to Papeéte, the steamer " Monumental City" arrived with a large number of passengers *en route* for Australia. The vigilance of the police was brought into requisition, for a liberal proportion of these northern invaders would have made themselves conspicuous at a Vigilance Committee execution. As might be supposed, the fillibustering propensity that had been nurtured among the cañons of the Sierra Nevada, occasionally displayed itself amid the quiet scenes of the Broom Road ; but the police were always prompt to suppress these ebullitions of republicanism, and a night's lodging in the calaboose proved an admirable antidote for effervescing spirits. The tragedy connected with this unfortunate vessel is familiar to many : during a voyage from Melbourne to Sydney, she was wrecked off Ram's Head, by which sad occurrence thirty-two lives were lost, including the surgeon and the owner, Peter Strobel, Esq., of Baltimore.

It was my intention to visit Australia by this steamer, and learning from Captain Adams that she would be detained at this port nearly a week, I determined to proceed at once to Raiatéa to procure a few indispensable articles left there, and return immediately in season to take passage. As there was neither ship nor schooner up for the leeward islands, I was compelled to charter a native

sloop, bound for Maupíti, to deviate from her course and land me at
Raiatéa ; having effected an arrangement with the proprietor, I sailed
from Papeéte the following afternoon.

CHAPTER XX.

A TAHITIAN PACKET.

IT must have been nearly two o'clock P. M. before our preparations for departure were completed ; natives are proverbial for their
slowness, and in this instance I was in no wise disposed to question
the imputation, we having contemplated starting at early dawn.   I
accompanied Jack, a grizzly old Tahitian who officiated as master,
to our conveyance, which lay moored near one of the stone jetties,
and for the first time boarded it.   But a glance was requisite to anticipate misery in perspective.   The boat was about eighteen feet in
length and of proportionate breadth, sloop-rig, but built by natives in
the most clumsy manner.   The hold and cabin were one—the former
stowed full, and the latter in nearly the same condition, with barely
room sufficient for three or four persons to lie down upon the baggage, and that in a variety of postures.   My *compagnons de voyage*
consisted of Jack the master, and three men, including the cook,
Tuahíne, who was shockingly disfigured by the *féfe*, (elephantía-
sis ;) also a Paumotuan with his wife and three children, and her
two sisters—the latter being of the respective ages of eight and
fourteen.

With a light breeze we swept slowly out of the harbor, encountering a heavy swell at the entrance that rendered our situation
extremely unpleasant, owing to the smallness of the vessel.   A strong
current setting to leeward, compelled us to resort to sweeps to
avoid the dangerous proximity of the reef, where the sea was breaking in sheets of foam.   Having obtained a good offing, we were
favored with a fine breeze from the southeast, and our boat, clumsy
as an ark, by dint of rolling and staggering, moved slowly along.

As the white houses, groves, and more minute features of the land-scape were fading, the elder sister, after many a longing look, hid her face in her *paréu*, and wore away her grief by sobbing in silence. Not so the younger, whose features were good-natured and mirthful, and soon the other, whose sadness proved transient as a passing cloud, assumed her usual demeanor, and joined with her companions in the light conversation peculiarly their own. Observers of Poly-nesian character cannot fail to remark how readily these natives seize upon incidents of trifling moment, and in them find matter of interest and diversion, frequently under circumstances of difficulty and danger. And thus with my companions, whose volubility con-tinued without interruption, until the appearance of the sky, which had become gradually overcast, betokened a storm. It was now draw-ing towards night ; Tahiti was barely discernible, so enshrouded was it by the heavy black clouds rising from the southeast, but Mooréa, with its wild mountains and sharp pinnacles, loomed darkly be-fore us. The approach of the storm was made apparent by the in-creasing wind that swept us rapidly along. At my request, mother, sisters, and children went below, though with seeming reluctance, thinking that they had no right to monopolize the cabin, as I had chartered the vessel. The rain poured like a deluge, but as drowning seemed preferable to suffocation, I remained for awhile upon deck. A half-hour's meditation in this shower-bath induced a change of resolution ; I went below, leaving orders with Jack to " make any port in a storm," and take us into one of the harbors of Mooréa.

The inconveniences of a small Hawaiian coaster were nothing in comparison with these : mother, sisters, and children were sleeping upon the luggage, cramped up in an inconceivably small space, with the perspiration pouring from them in torrents. A lamp was burn-ing, secured to one of the beams, and the heat was almost stifling ; add to this a number of streams trickling through the ill-calked seams, and some idea may be formed of our cabin. My first care was to extinguish the light, and then to beg Jack to partially remove the hatch from the scuttle, for ventilating purposes ; but he was in-exorable, and declared that if he did so, the vessel would fill faster than his men could relieve it by pumping. In consequence, the hatch was replaced over the scuttle and covered with an old tarpaulin.

The mother having appropriated a portion of my bedding, and the remainder being inaccessible, I reclined in a sitting posture against the side of the vessel, and, for a wonder, slept. About eleven o'clock the cook came to arouse us. We were snugly anchored inside the reef, but the night was so dark that the shore was barely discernible at a few yards' distance. Though the storm had passed over, the sky was still obscured by heavy black clouds. Tuahíne swam ashore and procured a canoe, which was alongside, and Tuani, the elder sister, with the infant, and I, landed first, after which the canoe returned for the others, while we groped along the beach in search of a dormitory. The barking of dogs soon announced to us that a habitation of some kind was at hand, and, stumbling over an oven and two or three logs, we reached the door.

After beating it for a reasonable length of time, it was opened by a large surly-looking native, rubbing his eyes, whose manner was neither hospitable nor inviting. He might have mistaken me for a *pater familias*, for appearances would favor such a conclusion, being bareheaded and barefooted, with my blankets, and an interesting girl beside me holding an infant. He was a churlish fellow, and after a few words of dispute we left, to seek hospitality elsewhere, being in the midst of a small hamlet. The girl preferred awaiting the arrival of her friends, while I pushed on until I reached a large house with the door standing open. This I entered, and after making a headlong plunge over a bench, concluded it to be a church. Spreading my blankets upon the floor, and covering my head with them to avoid the musquitoes, whose name was legion, I was soon in a sound slumber.

Before morning I was awakened by a native standing over me with a light, and at his request, accompanied him to his house, where the Paumotu family had passed the night. If the musquitoes were troublesome in the church, they were frightful here, and their roaming alone was sufficient to banish sleep.

In the morning our host read a chapter in the Tahitian Bible, and made a prayer ; after which we decamped to the sea-shore. The *maître de cuisine* was dispatched forthwith to purchase a pig, bread-fruit, and taro ; but, being unable to procure the former, he returned with a brace of fowls instead. All were soon roasting in the native oven, and in due season we made a hearty breakfast.

Near this place is a lofty peak more than four thousand feet in height, which, by a singular freak of nature, is perforated through and through not far from its summit. The tradition connected with it is, that upon one occasion the great god Oro, being angry with the little god Tíi, of Mooréa, threw his spear at him, which the latter avoided by skilful dodging. The weapon passed through the mountain, leaving a remarkable hole to record the prowess of the great god Oro.

CHAPTER XXI.

IN WHICH THE READER WILL PROBABLY MEET AN OLD ACQUAINTANCE.

THE wind being insufficient for getting under way, I determined on a short ramble through the settlement, which consisted of some fifteen or twenty native houses scattered along the shore and among the trees. The road, as usual in these out-of-the-way places, was an indifferent foot-path, often obstructed by bush and branch, and, in several places where the land was low, by water-courses, where the tide flows for a considerable distance inland.

Emerging from the grove to an open space, the principal objects were a dilapidated house and a carpenter's shop ; also under a shed near by was a schooner of perhaps forty tons, reposing on its stocks and nearly completed. Certain sounds from the house indicated revelry of some description ; as I passed, a head with a very significant expression of countenance was protruded, and, after stammering some kind of an apology for the interruption, begged me to come in and make myself at home. A jug and bottle bore unequivocal testimony as to the cause of the merriment. The occupants consisted of the before-mentioned individual, the carpenter, a middle-aged man, and his partner, who was perfectly sober. Two

21

young girls, in high spirits, together with the carpenter's (native)
wife (minus the left visual organ), completed the company.

As is usual on such occasions, the bottle was at once brought forward, a civility I acknowledged by merely moistening my lips with
as pungent a compound as was ever concocted in a still.

" I hope you'll excuse my house," said the carpenter. " If those
I hired had done as they agreed to, I should have had a comfortable
place by this time. But there's no use talking ; you can't get the
natives to do anything, unless they are amind to. They've got their
orange rum agoin, and are on a bust now ; and the foreigners about
here don't seem to behave much better."

" I say, carpenter," said our first acquaintance, " hold your temper,
and don't expose yourself before strangers, for you know your failings." Then, to me—" There's no mistake about it ; the carpenter
is pretty well to do, for a person on these islands ; but, as he says,
you can't do anything with these lazy beggars—they will drink.
For my part, I'm going home as quick as I can settle my business
and arrange some little family matters." (Here he cast a knowing
look towards one of the girls, whose *deshabillé* bespoke an indifference to observation.) " I say, Matéa ! *hére mai !* and join your sweetheart in a glass—no, a bowl of Old Tom." She, " nothing loth,"
complied ; and, having drained it, twined her arms lovingly around
the waist of her partner. " I'm a down-east Yankee, bound home
to the land of steady habits." These and a few similar expressions
terminated with his whistling " The girl I left behind me."

The carpenter for some time had been bustling about with his
wife, to serve up a breakfast, of which he invited me to partake ;
but, having made a hearty meal an hour before, I necessarily declined. However, three or four hungry visages that for some time
had been peering through apertures in the thatch, at a signal, fell to
and commenced a sharp attack upon the portion prepared for them.
I would here mention that, throughout the group, the settler's hospitality is freely proffered to a stranger.

While sitting upon the bedstead, a thought suddenly occurred to
me, suggested by my host's occupation, the island, and his long
residence upon it ; I casually inquired whether he had ever heard
of Omoo.

At the sound of that word our down-east friend started, as if by magic, from his *téte-à-téte* with the native girl. " What !— Omoo! Ha, ha! I say, Chips, tell us all about the work-box and shavings, *old boy*. Well, now, didn't he give it to us ! Carpenter got his share. I don't know what the devil *has* become of Shorty. Perhaps, though, you are Herman Melville, come to spy us out."*

I assured him to the contrary.

" Are you really the person mentioned in that book ?" I inquired of the carpenter.

" I am that ; and I don't thank Mr. Omoo for saying I was up to my——knees in New-Zealand pine shavings, making a work-box ; nor insinuating that that scamp of a Long Ghost offered to do my courting for me."

" O, the girl ! Did you get her at last ?"

" Yes, indeed ; and a good one she's proved to me."

I turned to have a view of the woman, who, by some intuitive perception, thinking herself the subject of our conversation, was looking up with inquiring glances. Whatever she might have been, her present appearance afforded no criterion for judging. Add ten years to the existence of a young Tahitian woman, and time will leave its indelible trace upon her features. At my request her husband inquired whether she recollected either of the persons mentioned. She could call to mind Long Ghost, who lived upon Mr. Bell's plantation, but all recollection of the other had escaped her. Poor Mrs. Bell's fate was tragical ; the family having removed to the Navigator Islands, she was drowned in one of the streams of Upólu. Long Ghost led a free-and-easy life for some time, and afterwards took his departure. The carpenter was disposed to be vexed at the position he had been made to assume, but I soon convinced him that although Mr. Melville had handled his subject familiarly, he had said nothing to his disparagement, and he finally concluded it was " a good joke after all."

Being informed that the lake spoken of on Mooréa was about a mile distant, though almost inaccessible, owing to swamp and forest,

---

* His precise words.

I started for it as directed, following the beach for half a mile, then striking into the forest. After floundering through the bushes, creeping and climbing, I at length reached what appeared to be an interminable forest of *fála* or pandanus-trees; it was as gloomy a retreat as could be desired on a sunshiny day; the long, drooping leaves, unmoved by a breath of air, formed a canopy impenetrable alike to light and sound. No warbler, not even the ticking of an insect, nor even the distant beating of the surf, awakened these solitudes; the only sound was the echo of my footsteps upon the dry leaves, into which I sank ankle-deep at every step, pricked and scratched by the short barbs with which they are armed. Having wandered on until sure the distance mentioned had been passed, and being undesirous of continuing so useless a pilgrimage, I reluctantly abandoned the search; intending to return by a different route, I kept more to the right, towards the mountains. After travelling a short distance, the ground became swampy and the underwood as thick as ever, but pushing through, I had soon the gratification of standing upon the marshy shores of the lake. It was a small and pretty sheet of water, but from no single point can a complete view of it be obtained. From where I stood, a short distance off, it curved to the right, and the extreme portion was hidden by the intervening forest. No sign of life was visible, not even a bird upon its surface; the low forest sweeping down to the water's edge, seemed as solitary and deserted as that of primeval growth, while the precipitous mountains formed a picturesque background.

On my return, I found Jack making preparations for departure; the cook had already laid in a supply of green cocoanuts and bread-fruit, and was turning about on his huge pedestal, issuing orders with the officiousness of a *major-domo*. It was now about one o'clock P. M.; the sails were set and the Paumotu family aboard; the men had already commenced weighing anchor, when we received a visit from the man at whose house the family had lodged the preceding night. The old hypocrite and extortioner insisted that fifty cents should be paid by the Paumotuan for himself, and the same for each member of his family, as the price of his hospitality. The poor man looked blank enough, for it was not in his power to pay the sum of $3.50 at that time; but indignation soon got the better of his modesty, and then commenced a series of recriminations and abuse loud and long, in which the woman joined. Seeing there was no prospect of an amicable adjustment of the affair, it was compromised by my paying a portion of the sum demanded, and the woman in her thankfulness promised me a fine pig when we should arrive at Raiatéa. This uncharitable act is the only instance of the kind that ever came under my observation during my sojourn in the Pacific : with all their failings, Polynesians are proverbial for their hospitality, but when habits of intemperance are fastened upon them, the old Tahitian can no longer be recognized, and I think the present instance attributable to the poison that is decimating them.

CHAPTER XXII.

INCIDENTS BY THE WAY.

THE weather was far from being settled ; the heavy clouds creeping up the mountain-side and wreathing around their sharp pinnacles, wore a threatening look, while the sun was obscured by the thick scud rising rapidly from the southeast. I confess I had some misgivings at leaving a safe harbor to tempt the winds and waves, with a storm in perspective, but being anxious to reach the small island Máui, our only stopping-place between this and Raiatéa, the word was passed and we started. Having obtained a good offing, I spread a mat and laid down upon deck—the boat creeping slowly along with a light breeze—but after a short repose, was awakened by the flapping of sails and the roaring of breakers. Starting up, I thought it night, the sky was so darkened overhead. We had made about eight miles progress from our place of departure, and the natives were now sweeping the boat into a passage through the reef ; here the prospect looked forbidding enough, for the mountain ridges seemed shooting up from the water's edge, and save a diminutive shed, there were no other signs of habitation. Not a breath of

air was stirring where we were, but among the mountains a tempest
seemed raging.   We succeeded in gaining an anchorage before encountering the storm ; and were fortunately within hailing distance
of the house, where no one but a woman was visible.   At our request,
she paddled off in a canoe, but before reaching us, the rain began
to fall, so throwing the mats over the main-boom, we formed a
tolerable shelter, beneath which we sat shivering for half an hour,
until the storm had nearly, if not quite abated.   In answer to
our inquiry, whether we could find lodgings at her house for the
night, she laughingly replied, " *He fále atnihúru me te púa,*" (her
house was fit only for the pigs,) that it was not her permanent residence, which was around the other side of the island, and that she
and her husband temporarily occupied the shed while clearing a
piece of land.   However, she carried us ashore, with our bedding,
good-naturedly jumping out and shoving the canoe, when the water
was not deep enough.   The habitation was merely a shelter without sides, and what was worse, there was no house that we could
reach that night, on account of a high rocky hill that obstructed the
path along the beach.   But we were determined to sleep ashore,
and after exchanging " *iauranas,*" pushed ahead, Tuáni, as usual,
keeping close to me with the infant, and the younger children bringing up the rear with sundry articles of baggage and the relics of our
morning's repast.

After traversing the beach for about a quarter of a mile, we came
to a couple of conical huts similar to the wigwams I had seen
among the Digger Indians in Cálifornia, and of the same size and
appearance, with this exception, those were constructed of bark, and
these of cocoanut branches.   Here we halted for a consultation ;
there was yet half an hour's daylight.   I was in favor of moving on,
though my baggage, consisting of a pair of heavy blankets, a pair
of sheets, two counterpanes, and a musquito-net, had become somewhat cumbersome.   The Paumotuan thought a " bird in hand worth
two in the bush," and voted to remain, though he could not
very well see how eight persons were to accommodate themselves
in two huts, each six feet in diameter.   However, we arranged the
matter by depositing our luggage and sending the two girls off to
make observations.   They scampered lightly along the beach, and

soon disappeared behind a projecting point. It was not long before they returned, saying they could go no farther on account of the mountain. I could not believe it, and started off with the native, but as soon as we had passed the point, the sight was a damper : a ridge of the mountain ran directly to the sea, terminating in high, abrupt cliffs. Here I picked up a pair of shells, beautiful specimens of mother-of-pearl. We continued on to the base of the cliff. After entering the forest, we found with difficulty the path that led over the hill, and climbing the rocks for some distance among the wet guava bushes, and seeing no better prospect ahead, we concluded to return. A few guavas hastily gathered from the bushes afforded a trifling acquisition to our cheerless supper.

We all set to work to render our wigwams as comfortable as possible ; additional cocoanut branches were piled on to render them weather-proof, and trenches dug to carry off the water. Having more bedding than I required, I gave a portion of it to the mother, who sat shivering in her wet garments with her infant. My net completely lined the hut, and together with my remaining blanket and sheets, gave it quite a snug and tidy appearance. The next point to be settled was a division of the occupants, which was arranged by my taking three of the children into my apartment. Our shelters did their duty admirably, not a drop of water finding its way through the thatch, while the trenches carried it from our beds.

The morning broke gloomily as ever, and at an early hour I packed up and retraced my steps over the hill. After a short walk through the wet guava bushes, I began to descend on the opposite side, and at intervals, through forest openings, caught glimpses of a little hamlet beyond, bounded in the rear by a fertile valley. I do not recollect the name of this place, which was reached at seven o'clock. At the first house, I found preparations for a breakfast going forward : fish was being rolled up in leaves preparatory to baking, while one of the young men scraped the green rind from bread-fruit with a cowrie shell prepared for that purpose ; another had just been cutting the tops from several large heads of taro. On the arrival of a stranger, the villagers gathered around, all eager to ask questions and make comments. The young ladies also, some of them neatly attired, were not at all backward in making my travel-stained appearance a subject of derision, while one of the old men administered summary reproof to such of the Juveniles as were too forward in their demonstrations of curiosity.   I did not have an opportunity of receiving an invitation to breakfast at this house, for it appeared to be conceded by all that I should accompany a demure-looking young man, who proffered his services to relieve me of my bundles, to his dwelling.   He was the minister of the place, also the schoolmaster, and he anticipated my wants by serving up a substantial breakfast of roast fowls, bread-fruit, taro. squash, *feis*, and the never-failing young cocoanut, in which I was joined by the Páumotu family, who by this time had made their appearance, and who took up their abode with me.

After an interval of two hours, the boat arrived and anchored at the extreme end of the settlement.   I could now enjoy the luxury of a bath and clean garments.   Jack had determined to go no farther that day, and as the morrow was Sunday, (which he could not conscientiously violate,) I resigned myself to the necessary alternative of remaining until Monday.   Time hangs heavily without companions in such a place : you saunter up and down the beach, paddle about the bay in a canoe, or go visiting, when you are barked at by dogs, and perhaps stared at by owners.   A bridge that crossed a stream near my hotel deserves a passing notice, as being a sample of this description of viaduct to be met with throughout the group, with the exception that it was larger than any other I had seen. The stream might have been ten yards broad, but its depth I never fathomed ; the tide flowed in and out.   Upright cocoanut posts were driven down at convenient intervals in two parallel rows, and "capped" by long slender trunks of the same tree ; across these, a few old pieces of board for about one-third of the distance had been nailed.   This addition, however, appears to be optional with the judge of the district, the bridge being either improved or neglected according to his honor's partiality for wading.   The architect must have intended this as a *chef d'œuvre*, for he had given it a formidable curve, but had so far erred in calculation, that either extremity was several feet above the road with which it was intended to communicate.   Steady nerves are required to walk one of these round, elastic sleepers, with a stream twelve feet below, and I was at first undecided whether to venture on my hands and knees, or attempt it *à la Ravel.* Were a small sign tacked to a neighboring *puráu,* "One dollar fine for crossing this bridge faster than a walk," the requirement would certainly never be violated.

After dinner, I strolled along the well-trodden path leading up the valley, bounded on either side by guava bushes, and sheltered from the sun's rays by the thick foliage overhead. I had not gone far before the merry sound of juvenile voices was heard echoing through the grove, and I soon discovered the source whence it proceeded. A clear, cool stream was rippling over its stony bed, laving the green branches that, bending low, often entwined with each other from opposite banks, and the whole o'ercanopied by the dense foliage of the mape and wide-spreading *puráu.* A rude dam had been thrown across at a convenient point, and here in the cool shade some dozen children of both sexes were swimming and plashing about, sometimes climbing the trees and leaping from the branches into the water. Though in nature's own, they were in nowise abashed at my presence; they rather seemed emulous of excelling each other in their aquatic sports.

That evening a singing-school was held at the house, my host first inquiring whether it would be agreeable to me. A goodly number of both sexes, young and old, were assembled with their hymnbooks, and all sat promiscuously on the mats. A prayer was first offered up by one of the elders, after which the singing commenced. The songs were all of a sacred character, and the school continued until a late hour. In one respect, it differed not widely from our singing-schools at home, for some of the young ladies in the midst of their harmony were smiling and holding a sort of pantomimic converse with their dusky beaux—at times so openly as to merit rebuke from their seniors. During the intervals, some of the young men produced slates and amused themselves with their arithmetics, in which they did not appear to be very proficient, for several simple questions proposed to them, and which I doubt not would have been readily solved by an ordinary Hawaiian scholar, seemed to give them considerable trouble.

Sunday passed as is usual in such places: all went to church, Bibles in hand, the men with their best *paréus,* and the females with their unbecoming bonnets, which rob age of the respect its due and mock the charms of grace and beauty. After service, all return to partake of a cold repast, for no oven is permitted to smoke on the Sabbath, and the improvident must either suffer or crave a neighbor's hospitality.

It was nearly nine o'clock on Monday before we were under way; with a light breeze, we swept slowly along the channel inside the reef. The water was clear as crystal, and we could see the finny tribe playing hide-and-seek among the coral groves. Once a large turtle was observed floating upon the water, but on our approach it dove, and swimming rapidly, was soon lost among the coral branches shooting up in every direction. When fairly at sea, we steered w. n. w. for the little island of Maiáu, which was too far distant to be seen. Fortunately the weather was fine, and our prospects for a speedy and pleasant termination to our trip looked more promising than ever, and seeking protection from the sun's rays by the main-sail, we made ourselves as comfortable as our resources would permit. At noon, the cook's defection set us all at fault, he having neglected to lay in a supply of provision, save a few heads of taro, which were nearly exhausted that day; owing to the absence of cocoa-nuts, we were compelled to resort to a small keg of water rendered almost unpalatable by the heat of the sun.

At daylight, the low conical hill rising imperceptibly from the water was Maiáu, but we were still a long way off, and two hours had elapsed before the trees and low-lands fairly appeared. We ran before the wind along the shore, where the surf was dashing furiously upon a dazzling sand-beach, but neither hut nor canoe was in sight, and we made a considerable circuit before signs of inhabitants were visible. Around a low point the sea broke less violently, and hauled upon the beach were three or four canoes, and not far off, was a native fishing. There were no houses in sight, but as soon as we had made our appearance off the point, some half dozen natives emerged from the bush, and launching their canoes, were soon alongside. They wore nothing but the *máro*. The news they brought was sad for Tuahíne. He anticipated much pleasure in meeting his child, and we had deviated from a direct course for the purpose of gratifying him in this respect, but to his grief he learned it was dead.

He went ashore, and I gave him the means of purchasing fish, flesh, and fruit of every description. Not thinking it worth while to risk a drenching in the surf, I contented myself with simply looking at the uninviting spot : a small island without harbor, low and sandy, except in the middle, or thereabout, where rose a wooded hill. Tired of laying " off and on" for the cook's return, we bore away, and continued our circuit until we had reached the leeward side, where the wind headed us off on the other tack.   After a few " boards," Tuahíne made his appearance, accompanied by one person, each holding a bundle of some kind.   Coming close to the edge of the reef, and watching an opportunity, they plunged into the surf, and were soon buffeting their way among the rollers, no easy task, encumbered as they were with bunches of what proved to be green cocoanuts. The cook returned the money ; according to his account, pigs and fowls had all given up the ghost, and neither fruit nor vegetables of any description were to be obtained.   The young cocoanuts he offered as a present. His visit to his son's grave overcame his resolution, and he concluded to remain.   More than thirty hours had elapsed since I had eaten anything, save a small allowance of taro and cocoanut, and feeling half famished by his neglecting to provide for us as he ought to have done at Mooréa, I was almost tempted to throw his gift into the sea and bid him follow ; but sympathy mastered inclination, and after we had all shaken hands with them and exchanged *iauránas*, they once more jumped overboard and struck out for the shore.

It was now about the middle of the afternoon, and with hungry stomachs we bade farewell to a spot that denied us the means of existence, and shaped our course for Huahíne, steering N. N. W. by compass.   That night the wind came out ahead, blowing in squalls, and sometimes sending a shower of spray over us.   Notwithstanding, I preferred sleeping on deck, where the two sisters, at their request, shared my blankets.

Huahíne was barely discernible at daylight, but we were heading for it, with a fair wind.   Having already lost so much time since leaving Tabiti, I had abandoned all hope of returning to take passage in the steamer; and, fearful lest the brig at Raiatéa, also bound for Melbourne, should take her departure before my arrival, I concluded to forego visiting Huahíne and proceed at once to Raiatéa, which was now just making its appearance.

At four o'clock we were becalmed off the Opoa passage, and lending a hand, we swept into the harbor. I thought at first it might be necessary to remain at this rendezvous of loyalty for the night, and trespass upon the hospitality of old King Tamatóa; but at this juncture, being in mid-channel, a favoring breeze sprung up, hardly perceptible at first, and soon covering the broad lake with ripples, we were only sensible of our progress by watching the ever-varying features of the landscape as we glided along.

I had never before seen so many canoes under sail at Raiatéa, and was at a loss to account for it, until bearing away for a heavily ladened one, we hailed, and found they were carrying oranges for the brig, from the other side of the island. To see this tiny fleet sweeping along with its juicy freight, was truly picturesque : the heavy canoe, with its projecting bow, uncouth outrigger, and snowy sail, harmonized well with the landscape ; a small schooner that was beating its way up, gave an animated effect to the scene. It was dark before we reached the settlement, which we recognized by the lights glimmering along the shore ; and, " rounding-to" under the stern of the brig that lay alongside of the jetty, we let go our anchor. I was almost famished, and, at the captain's invitation, jumped aboard and enjoyed a hearty supper.

CHAPTER XXIII.

THE CAVE TAMEHÁNE—A FEAST.

DURING my absence, H. B. M. steamer Virago had arrived from Valparaiso, bringing the British consul, B. Toup Nicholas, Esq., appointed for the Society Islands. To a certain extent his position is unenviable : to act as arbiter between two contending factions, whose veneration for England leads them to solicit advice, but whose stubborn resolution urges them on to acts of open warfare, is a position requiring at once firmness and forbearance. During the outbreaks that have subsequently occurred, he has not devoted himself exclusively to British interests, but his offices have been manifestly for all ; so far as I have observed, he has been indefatigable in his efforts to bring order out of chaos.

I found the settlement as when I left it, filled with rumors, but no war. Eelspring was still tenanted by Merton and Jasper, but Howard had taken up his abode with 'Teó, to oblige the consul, as our house was said to be the best finished one in the settlement. The British brig " Maid of Julpha," Captain R. N. Beauvais, had nearly completed her cargo of oranges for Australia, and was to sail in a few days. My companions had already entered their names as passengers, delighted at an opportunity of escaping from the island.

One day I proposed to Howard a visit to the Cave Tamehâne, of which the Raiatéans boast so much and know so little, magnifying a trifling freak of nature into a subject of awe and reverence. They said there was a cave among the mountains, both dark and deep, no one having ever ventured into it, and which rumor gave out, was the abode of large gray dogs with marvellously long ears and tails. The legend connected with the spot is, that many years ago a native and his wife, while engaged fishing in a canoe, observed one day a bird flying up the mountain-side with a huge eel in its beak, and which suddenly paused in its flight—descended and disappeared. Thinking there was something remarkable in the circumstance, they forsook their occupation, and climbing up the mountain in the direction taken by the bird, discovered the cave. The bird was never afterward seen, but his eelship lay coiled up at the bottom of the cavern, looking to them as formidable as the dragon of St. George. Nothing daunted, and supported by his courageous spouse, the man boldly cast his line of sennit, with a hook of mother-of-pearl attached, into the deep gulf ; this was quickly seized by the eel, who was drawn forth in triumph, but not until, in their superhuman efforts, a foot of one of them sank deep into the black rock, where its impress is shown to wondering visitors at the present day.

Such was the tradition connected with the locality we were about to visit, and thinking it more formidable than it afterwards proved, we provided ourselves with thirty fathoms of ropes and an iron crow-bar, for the purpose of effecting a descent.

Having hired an islander to accompany us, we set out on our journey at eight in the morning. The place is accessible from several points ; our guide chose the path along the shore to the east of the settlement, as being the route most frequently taken. After traversing the beach for half a mile, we turned into the forest on our right, not, however, until we had called at a native house and engaged the proprietor to have a dinner provided for us on our return. Our path was twice interrupted by a stream in its windings, and to avoid the trouble of divesting ourselves of shoes and socks, our conductor carried us over on his back. We soon reached one of the mountain spurs, which we commenced climbing, frequently on our hands and knees, to avoid the low branches that, shooting out hori-zontally and entwining with each other, seemed to hem us in like the meshes of a net. Until now our path had been in the shade, but emerging from the forest to the open ridge, the rays of the sun were almost overpowering, for the regular breeze had not yet sprung up. We continued ascending through the coarse grass that reached to our knees, and after half an hour's plodding, welcomed the wind that swept in gusts over the mountain ridges. As if anticipating our wants, the guide descended to a spring a short distance below, and brought up some pure cool water in a kind of basket hastily formed of wild taro leaves. The ocean on the opposite side soon appeared, and from this point it was interesting to notice the course of valleys and ridges, which, with some irregularity, seemed radiating from a common centre like the spokes of a wheel. A very beautiful sight was the barrier reef, whose position was indicated by a narrow fringe of foam upon a sea of blue, as it encircled the island, inclosing Taháa and a chain of islets in its capacious fold. Owing to the peculiar texture or formation of its corals, and the yellow sand-beds of zoophytic branches, the quiet surface of the lagoon seemed a com-bination of mellow tints imperceptibly blending and glowing in the bright sunlight. A span of delicate green was bordering a broad surface of milky whiteness, and beyond, a light azure deepened to an ultra-marine ; thus revealing at a glance either hidden shoals or tranquil depths. On the right were the misty mountains of

Huahíne, and in front, the dim rock of Borabóra loomed in the horizon. At this elevation we crossed a mountain valley, if I may hazard the expression, which in some respects resembled those of the low-lands, though far above them ; it had a slight inclination seaward, and I should judge, terminated abruptly, from the appearance of the broader valley beyond. The soil was good, and the course of a clear stream rippling over gentle declivities was indicated by clumps of the drooping pandanus. Its elevation above the sea might not have been more than twelve or fifteen hundred feet, but I fancied the atmosphere cooler with the breeze blowing fresh from the higher ridges.

A short distance beyond, our guide called our attention to a small shrub growing beside the path, with the leaves of which the natives make a perfume called *manói*, to scent their oil for cosmetic uses. Here we first saw a remarkable flower, the simplest description of which would be, to carefully divide a blossom of Cape jessamine longitudinally, leaving half the petals and pistils on one side, and half on the other, and you will have two of the former. The shrub is somewhat lower than that of the other, though it resembles it in its general appearance. On our return we gathered a number of these, together with several other varieties of wild flowers, and, though between the time of gathering and our arrival at the seashore hardly an hour elapsed, they had withered and lost every appearance of beauty and freshness. Numerous attempts have been made by the missionaries to introduce them into their gardens, but without success. The only soil congenial to their habits appears to be among the elevated regions, where they are nourished by the clouds and mountain breezes.

After passing several small streams, some of which had worn deep channels in the rock, we reached the vicinity of the cave. The side of the mountain seemed one mass of dark, porous rock (volcanic), scantily covered with creeping vegetation ; but there was neither tree nor bush within a wide circuit. Numerous little rills trickling over its surface, rendered the path slippery and difficult.

Our guide was the first to announce the termination of our journey. When we joined him immediately after, my first impulse was to laugh at the trouble we had taken for so trifling a reward. The famous cave was apparently nothing more than a deep fissure in the rock, about thirty feet long by fifteen broad, and eighty feet deep by measurement. A small stream that had worn a deep channel, shot over the ledge at its upper extremity, and fell in a shower upon the loose shingle at the bottom. The most favorable point for observation is from the lower side, or towards the sea; but owing to its depth and jutting points, a small portion only of the bed is discernible.

The crow-bar was thrust into a crevice of the rock, and the rope being long enough, was doubled around it, and both parts thrown over the mouth of the cavern. It was strong, but means were taken to prevent its chafing on the edge of the rock; and a man on whom I could depend was stationed at the bar to steady it. Having divested myself of everything but a pair of coarse duck trowsers, I commenced the descent, sliding rapidly down. The atmosphere grew damp and chilly, and care was requisite to avoid jutting rocks. Having reached the lowest depth, I hailed to those above to announce my safe arrival, and immediately after, saw two heads peering cautiously over the cliff. The area of the bottom was considerably greater than that of the mouth, owing to the receding of the sides. These were basaltic, and for about thirty feet, consisted of massive boulders piled up in curvilinear rows, and partaking of the trappean formation.

At the upper extremity, and almost concealed by a rank growth of fern, I discovered a dark passage to depths beneath. Howard was requested to throw down the oil bamboo that had been provided for such a contingency, and a fine torch was soon blazing; with it I commenced the descent.

No stronger evidence of the volcanic origin of the island would be required than the appearance of this fissure, which was in every respect similar to those noticed in the immediate vicinity of Kilauéa, with the exception that the others bore traces of more recent igneous action. The cavern consisted of a number of low irregular passages, branching out in various directions, and inclining seaward, with a rapid and abrupt descent. I took the principal one, sometimes walking, and again crouching almost to the earth, until it terminated in a chasm as dark as Erebus, and I was half disposed to watch for the Cerberus that guarded this gate to the realms of Pluto. Throwing down a blazing piece of bamboo, I found it was but little more than ten feet deep, after which, there was a continuation of the gloomy vault; the descent was easy by the irregularities of the sides, but here the path was obstructed by masses of rock. With no object in view other than curiosity, I groped along, making another descent similar to the first. Since entering this subterranean vault, I had heard a faint sound as of water percolating among loose rocks, which, as I advanced, gradually increased, until now it seemed rushing above and around, while its roaring through the narrow passages was almost deafening. The atmosphere was damp and chilling, and beads of moisture that covered the dark rocks sparkled in the flickering torchlight. The half-consumed bamboo burnt dimly, but the bare thought of its extinguishment was sickening, and having already gone too far without a clue to my exit, I turned to retrograde. It was too late—the blaze flashed up for an instant, then disappeared; I stared for a moment at the useless brands I grasped, until they too smouldered, and the last lingering spark vanished.

Amid pitchy darkness I sat down, hardly daring to move, lest I should stumble into some pit before unseen. I extended my arms above and around on every side, but they only met the wet rock; it seemed as if I were immured in the bowels of the earth in a stone vault, and though perfectly collected, I could not repress a sense of suffocation that came over me. My first impulse was to wait patiently for assistance, but recollecting there was a full box of matches in my pocket, I took them out and struck a light, and with the assistance of these, after a quarter of an hour's groping, discovered an opening upward. Although the match-light was insufficient to show its termination, by crowding and squeezing I forced my way up until a glimmering light relieved the sepulchral gloom. Henceforward my progress was comparatively easy, and after being entombed for nearly an hour, I once more emerged from the entrance of the cavern. The most disagreeable task was yet to be performed—climbing a height of eighty feet by a rope swinging loosely —and after the fatigue undergone in the vaults below, I would gladly have relinquished it. This was accomplished, and Howard informed me that more than an hour had elapsed since the de-

22

scent.   Our guide inquired about the dogs, concerning which I had
an appalling account to give.   After partaking of the lunch we had
provided, and picking our initials into the rock with the crow-bar, we
took our departure, not, however, until the native had called our attention to the marvellous footprint, but which we were incredulous
enough to believe had been formed by the action of water.

Soon after leaving the cave, the native pointed out the relics of a
hut that had been built by the Sandwich Island deserters ; the situation was well chosen for observation, and a short distance below, a
small stream of water fell into a rocky basin, forming an admirable
reservoir for bathing.

We reached the house where we had engaged our dinner about
one o'clock, and as the oven had not yet been " taken up," we spread
a mat under a shady bread-fruit and reclined upon it to enjoy a short
nap before dinner.   At two we were awakened, and in the house
found our repast spread out upon leaves.   It consisted of two nicely
roasted fowls, emitting a savory steam, and done to a turn ; spheres
of bread-fruit, with the burnt rind peeled off, looking rich and mealy,
with the faintest possible shade of yellow, were served up on plantain leaves.   The taro was not forgotten, and a pile of baked *feís*,
that seemed anything but inviting externally, required but the removal
of the skin to show a rich yellow pulp both sweet and nourishing.
A bunch of ripe China bananas (a favorite species) made a tempting display ; and a kind of jelly pudding, composed of arrow-root
and grated cocoanut, mixed up with the milk and baked, was served in
a small gourd.   The never-failing *miti*, made of the expressed milk
of the old cocoanut and sea-water, and white as the nourishing beverage itself, was brought to us in two plates.   A couple of young
cocoanuts, fresh from the tree and divested of their husks, were both
perforated sufficiently to show the clear, cool liquid within, looking at
that moment more inviting than goblets of ambrosial nectar.

We ate in primitive style, sitting upon the ground and using our
fingers, Howard facetiously remarking that they were " made before
forks."

Having appropriated half of one of the fowls, with a sheath-
knife he cut two or three thick slices of bread-fruit, his eyes meanwhile resting affectionately on the favorite *feís*.

An exclamation of "*Ehóa !*" from the door-way, startled us from our epicurean reveries, and in the "*iaurána*" that followed, Howard recognized an acquaintance who, with a profusion of flowers in her hair, came smilingly towards him. Being something of a gallant, he arose to escort his fair visitor to a seat beside him ; but, alas for his courtesy ! Two or three lean, famished-looking dogs had been sitting upon their haunches and staring at the viands with glazed eyes and moistened lips, and one of them, thinking the moment opportune, like the prowling cur in the " Distressed Poet" of Hogarth, deliberately seized Howard's selection, and disappeared through a small aperture in the thatch.

A general hue-and-cry announced the theft. Howard comprehended in a moment, and, forgetting alike politeness and dinner, started off in pursuit of the robber, not with a hope of recovering stolen meat, but to punish a species of quadruped to which he bore a strong antipathy. His only satisfaction was a chase through the guavas, and pelting the animal with bits of coral and cocoanut husks.

Nothing further occurred to interrupt our meal. After we had finished, a smoking addition of baked fruit was brought in, upon which old and young commenced a simultaneous attack. I noticed an acquisition to our company of three or four old women, who made their appearance just before dinner, and who as a class are happily gifted with a strong scent. They had probably some important communication to disclose, and " accidentally happened in" as the oven was about being opened.

I would again beg leave of absence from the reader, while cruising among islands and lands to the westward, promising that our next interview shall be brief and final.

CHAPTER XXIV.

" A HUNDRED SWORDS IN THE AIR."

It was early dawn in July, '53, when we were dashing along before the strong trade-winds, for the Ohélau passage, to the settlement of Raiatéa. It was too dark to distinguish objects upon the shore, and our only landmarks were the outline of the mountains, more especially the conspicuous cone whose apex seemed to have been broken off. Through the gloom we could distinguish an apparently unbroken line of foaming breakers, whose roaring as we bounded towards them was appalling. But Captain Beauvais was an experienced navigator, and had calculated his distance and position, to a nicety ; instead of waiting for daylight to show him the narrow passage, he kept boldly on, trusting to find it by close proximity. * I cannot refrain from a slight tribute to his merits as a seaman—one of the real English stamp, nurtured among the typhoons of the China seas. I have seen him in instances of great emergency display a commendable coolness ; and have stood by him at the wheel when a tempest of breakers, rolling in like avalanches, threatened every moment to ingulf us ; deserted by his crew, who had fled to the rigging, and by his mate, who was upon his knees at paternosters, (a true incident ;) and in this, as in every other instance, his conduct was such as would characterize a man of judgment and decision.

We soon saw the two islets that bounded the passage, and gliding rapidly through, were in still water, sweeping forward with undiminished speed. From behind a point covered with cocoanut-trees that intercepted our view of the settlement, a well-manned whale-boat shot out and pulled towards us, and this was the only sign of animation observable. Its occupants shouted to us as we passed ; without altering our course for them, we continued on towards the settlement. After rounding the point, we saw the white house of Messrs. Jordan and Lassiter ; and immediately beyond, an embankment thrown up, extending from the shore to the mountain. Near by was the flagstaff and

flag of King Tamatóa. About half a mile distant another intrench-
ment, similar to the former, had been raised immediately adjoining
the premises of the British consul. Here we dropped anchor, and
were soon after boarded by the boat, which was headed by the
native pilot of the king, who had come to demand the harbor dues.
From him we learned that the war had just been renewed, and that
a decisive battle was anticipated. Our captain was a strong Liberal,
and withheld the tribute until the result of the battle should be ascertained. Presently, a boat was seen approaching from Tamáre's
camp, upon which the royal barge immediately took its departure.
Approaching us, we found it to be commanded by our old friend
Dr. Doan, with a stout crew, their muskets and spears being carefully laid in the bottom of the boat, for it was their intention to
capture the other, which had given them the slip. From the
doctor we learned that affairs were approaching a crisis ; that old
Tamatóa, determined to carry the war into Africa, had come
down from Opoa, the stronghold of royalty, and fortified himself
in the eastern portion of the settlement ; upon which Tamáre had
immediately checkmated him in an opposite direction. Among
the parties occupying the intermediate space, natives and foreigners,
a general stampede had taken place. The British consul alone remained at his post. Tamáre's breastwork had been thrown up
within fifteen yards of his house, formed of earth and cocoanut logs
of sufficient strength to resist a cannon-ball ; and, owing to the close
proximity of the consulate, his guns could be trained to avoid it ;
but, on the other hand, it would be a conspicuous object for the
royal cannon. Accordingly, he had been notified by the belligerent
parties that, as hostilities were about to commence, his safety would
be endangered by occupying his present exposed situation, and that
it would be necessary for him to remove as others had done, for they
would not be responsible for the consequences. In reply, Mr.
Nicholas gave the deputation to understand that he should continue
to occupy the premises assigned him, and that for any injury he
might sustain his government would hold them responsible. The
propriety of his remarks somewhat staggered them, and before active
hostilities were commenced, he prevailed upon both parties to send a
deputation to his office to conclude peace, or, at least, negotiate an

armistice, as in the present state of affairs their orange trade would be cut off, for vessels would be forced to depart without their cargoes.   These deputies were to meet on the day of our arrival. .

After breakfast, we accompanied the doctor in our boat to the camp of Tamáre.   It grounded upon the coral, but some stout natives waded in and carried us ashore on their shoulders.   Tamáre himself was surrounded by a group of warriors, haranguing them most eloquently ; temporary sheds had been constructed, and beneath them were stout, athletic men reposing upon the mats in inglorious ease, while around them was scattered the offensive panoply of war. Muskets and spears were suspended from the rafters or lying upon the ground, and occasionally a young man might be seen brandishing a cutlass.   In the camp were also the wives and sisters of the warriors ; and I saw a stout woman patrolling with a musket on each shoulder.   The girls, many of them, were arrayed in their best apparel ; some of them wore beautiful wreaths fashioned from the delicate fibre of the arrow-root into rosettes that completely encircled the head, and from the left side a thick plume, formed of the tender sprout of the cocoanut, of a delicate straw color, floated gracefully in the breeze.   They all recognized, and gave us a cordial welcome, as did also Tamáre, when he had finished his speech.

After paying our respects to the consul, and receiving confirmation of what the doctor had communicated, we returned to the camp. The Broom Road, where we had strolled so often, was completely barricaded, the only passage through the embankment being a narrow embrasure, obstructed by a mounted cannon, with a sentry on either side. Messrs. Jordan and Lassiter were in trouble ; they had been compelled to abandon their store and residence to occupy a larger house recently purchased by the latter, within the limits of Tamáre's camp.   Their shop had proved valuable to the Royalists, for a stout foreigner, who had recently come upon the island, had appropriated the loose iron for the manufacture of slugs, and had also remounted such of the guns as required it.   Independent of this, Lassiter had his domestic afflictions ; the family of Mrs. Lassiter, it appears, were adherents of the king, and as might be supposed, her sympathies were with the Royalists, and as she was compelled to reside in the camp with her husband, she had commenced a regular system of espionage. This being detected, she was prevented egress from the fort, and held as a prisoner on parole; from last accounts, she was leading her spouse an interesting life. A Jamaica negro, who had been "beach-combing" among the islands, a mischief-making fellow, was similarly situated, and instead of being shot, he was suffered to roam about the camp unmolested, Tamáre having ordered him to be fired upon the moment he attempted to escape. The doctor called my attention to some herculean fellows from Taháa, (this island having espoused the cause of the chief;) they had come over to fight, and were determined, too, before returning home.

About eleven o'clock, both deputations waited upon the consul, who was attended by the resident missionary, Mr. Chisholm, but they were only able to negotiate an armistice of ten days, and that each party should withdraw half a mile beyond the opposite extremes of the settlement. When this was announced by the messengers on their return to Tamáre's camp, considerable indignation was manifested by some of those assembled to hear it beneath a large open shed, and I noticed that the countenance of Tamáre himself underwent a considerable elongation, while the Taháa men expressed their disappointment in unmeasured terms. All the spare room was occupied by females, and to judge from the interest they appeared to manifest in the negotiations that were pending, one would suppose himself attending a woman's rights convention. At Raiatéa, as is often the case at home, females make themselves very officious concerning the affairs of their husbands; it was formerly their custom to accompany them to battle, something after the manner of esquires, to supply them with new weapons when required, or with refreshment when wounded or fatigued; they are occasionally serviceable in making cartridges, and that day I saw the wife of Tamáre, after her return from the vessel, with an old log-book under her arm, which, she told me, she intended to devote to that purpose.

The wind blew strongly across the lagoon, and about noon we saw a white speck beneath the mountains of Taháa, which the natives said was Teo's boat. He carried an enormous sail, and beat up to the settlement in a very short time. We were invited

over to his house, where a lunch was served up for us.   He said he
expected a siege, and was prepared for it ; and so appearances would
indicate, for he had a profusion of swine and vegetables on his
premises.   During the afternoon, while passing the house of Tamáre, his wife came out and invited me in, insisting that I should
remain until she could have a dinner cooked, which was served up
by her daughter, whose manifestations of sympathy during my
illness had not been forgotten.   On this visit to Raiatéa, I found a
young New-Yorker, whom I had taken from the Bónin Islands, off
Japan, more than a year previous, while on a voyage from Hong
Kong to San Francisco.   Instead of returning, as intended, he had
visited this island in a trading vessel, became enamored of one of
its beauties, married, and " settled down."

Captain Beauvais found it impossible to procure a cargo here,
owing to existing hostilities ; both parties were fearful of weakening
their respective camps by disbanding to pluck oranges, and in consequence he was compelled to proceed to Borabóra, which we did after
remaining here two days, taking Doctor Doan with us, to act as
trading master.   My last reminiscences of Raiatéa are associated
with recollections of Tamáre's wife, who came to bid me good-bye as
I was stepping into the boat, accompanied by a boy leading a nice
fat pig, which she bestowed as a testimonial of friendship.

CHAPTER XXV.

WHICH TREATS ON DOMESTIC ECONOMY.

With a fair wind we weighed anchor and stood across the harbor towards Taháa, intending to pass out by the passage through the
reef on the western side of that island, a distance of nearly ten
miles from the settlement.   After reaching the southern point, the
channel lay close along the shore, which was exceedingly irregular,
and sparsely inhabited.   Near the head of one of its deep bays, the
doctor pointed out a small hamlet, where he said he had an adopted

mother, or rather, he had been adopted as a son by an old woman, which entitled her and her family to the privilege of crossing over to the settlement and making his residence a home; besides appropriating to herself whatever she thought needful, as a manifestation of maternal affection, inviting in return filial love by conceding like privileges.

We reached our anchorage during the afternoon, opposite the church. After landing and visiting old acquaintances, a commodious house was hired by the doctor, in which he installed himself and family, together with the trade provided for purchasing cargo. During our absence, Mr. Krause had formally renounced his allopathic principles for those of hydropathy, and on one corner of the verandah had erected a neat bathing-house, where he was prepared to administer the prescriptions of Priessnitz in every form, from the douche to the tepid sitz-bath.

To my gratification, I learned that both Monsieur Augúste and Captain Flores were here from Raiatéa—a circumstance that in itself would banish apprehensions of *ennui.* Their little trading schooner was anchored off the southern portion of the settlement, where they were temporarily located in a native domicil. I went down to pay them a visit, and discovered the premises by inquiring of the natives for the " *fále Fráne*," (French house.) Like most others in the settlement, it was almost hidden by the shade of fruit-trees, the whole inclosed by a scraggy fence of *puráu* and surmounted by a stile.

Both gave me a cordial reception, and the captain ordered an attendant to place glasses upon the table, while he drew a cork to cement acquaintance. He had brought his native wife with him, who, like her sex in Hawaii, had no lack of relatives and acquaintances. These thronged to offer congratulations to the *vahíne no Raiatéa*, (woman of Raiatéa.) The Hawaiians are a migratory race, roving from island to island; for, should a coaster drop anchor at either Hawaii or Kauái, the extremes of the group, there would be a general mustering of dogs, calabashes, and dried fish, by perhaps a dozen of them, who would be simultaneously reminded that they had some pressing business on hand at either Lahaina or Honolulu. The Tahitians, on the contrary, are less aspiring or versatile in their

dispositions ; from age to infancy, there are many who would be content to pass their dreamy round of existence reposing beneath boughs
that shed perennial harvests, and would " crave alliance with no
wider scenes" than the tranquil groves of their island-home, or the
boundless ocean that limits their ambition.

To return to our entertainers : Monsieur Augúste had brought
with him a small hand-organ, of Paris manufacture, that executed
exclusively the airs in vogue during the days of Louis Quatorze. It
was ornamented with a graceful little automaton, attired in the costume of the most elegant court of the seventeenth century. He was
seated upon an antique specimen of furniture, supporting in his
ruffled hands a mandolin ; and when, at my request, Mrs. F——
commenced turning the crank, he fingered his instrument as lightly,
and bowed to her perhaps as gracefully, as the original would have
done to Madame de Maintenon. The airs were simple, and their
gentler modulations would be easily retained by a musical ear. The
young ladies present looked on admiringly ; some of them, with a
delicate perception of harmony, chimed in with the air, while others
evinced their appreciation of foreign courtesy or politeness by exclamations of " *Méa nehenéhe !*" (superb.)

Not wishing to trespass too frequently on the hospitality of Mr.
Krause, I took up my abode with an old native named ——— 'Táne,
whose habitation was pleasantly located near the shore, about the
centre of the settlement. The family consisted of himself, wife,
a married daughter with her husband and infant, and another daughter fourteen or fifteen years of age, who was, without exception, the
belle of Borabóra. There were also a couple of young urchins, but
whether his children or not I never learned. Táne bore no resemblance to the fat, sleek-looking specimens so frequently met with.
On the contrary, he was one of the lank sort, with a famished-looking
visage, lowering brows, and a net-work of wrinkles. He sported a
chip hat and a fancy calico shirt, rakishly adjusted over a navy-
blue *paréu*, bestudded with white figures which at a short distance
bore a strong resemblance to diminutive Cupids. To this latter garment he gave a peculiar hitch, so that it hung awkwardly around his
ankles. Had she worn one, I should fancy that he had borrowed
one of Mrs. Táne's undergarments. He had a hobbling gait, and

upon inquiry I learned that it had been occasioned by his indiscretion. Many years before, while in a state of intoxication, he had killed his former wife by repeated blows. When thoroughly sober he contemplated with horror the deed he had perpetrated, and, meditating suicide, climbed a lofty cocoanut-tree, and threw himself from its branches. The result of the collision was a temporary suspension of the intellectual faculties, a dislocation, a number of severe bruises, and the subsequent conviction that banishment to an uninhabited island was preferable to a duplicate crime. After turning hermit for a few years, his majesty King Tapóa was graciously pleased to extend to the culprit his royal clemency, and he once more returned to resume his position in society.

He always moved about with a deacon-like solemnity, and to turn from him to his blooming daughters, one would almost feel uncharitable enough to question their paternity. I have sometimes detected him staring gloomily at me, when he would inquire in an impressive manner, " *Támate ! heá tou manáo ?   Hinaáro oc e ámu te má ?*" (Thomas ! what is your thought ?   Do you want anything to eat ?)

Mrs. Táne, from a casual observation, was an ornament to her sex. As a laundress, I can testify to her scrupulous neatness. Whether or not according to her standard of human growth and decline, she recognized in my physical contour evidences of antiquity, I fancied that she craved at least a share of the attention I endeavored to bestow upon the daughter. It is frequently the case that these South Sea Hesperides are guarded by a phalanx of duennas.

The elder daughter had recently become a mother, and manifested all a mother's fondness for her offspring. She seemed never to weary with nursing the dusky little innocent, and chanting lullabies to soothe its slumber. She had prepared a neat little bed for it upon the mats, over which was suspended a tiny musquito-net of white gauze ; this was sometimes removed, that she might have the pleasure of bending over it to watch its gentle respirations, while fanning it with a bread-fruit leaf. These manifestations of maternal fondness were mutually shared between mother, sister, and husband.

The conduct of the latter was enough to make one nervous. He was a handsome, athletic young fellow, and sported a slight moustache, but day after day he would sit cross-legged among the women, tending baby, and making himself generally useful. His only garment was a *paréu* thrown over his shoulders for modesty's sake ; during the entire period of my sojourn in the family, I do not recollect having ever seen him beyond the premises. He was evidently in good health, for his appetite would have been a serious consideration in the event of a dearth of provision. Out of all patience, I frequently tried to shame him from his hen-pecked occupation, but his only reply would be an innocent laugh. What old Táne's sentiments were respecting his aspiring son-in-law, I never ventured to inquire ; although he sometimes looked sulkily at him, he apparently took it as a " matter of course."

But the pride of the household was the younger daughter, whom I shall call Matéa. A more graceful child of the ocean it would have been difficult to find in the Pacific. Possessing in no ordinary degree the peculiar beauty of these islanders, (which becomes a sickly exotic when removed from parent soil,) she was destitute of the levity of manner that characterizes too many of these syrens ; at the time, I thought the principal defect in disposition was her reservedness in social intercourse.

Like most other natives, she was an early riser, and after cooing a while with the baby, she would step out to perform her ablutions at a clear spring in the rear of the house ; then she would come in, seat herself upon the mats, and placing a little Dutch looking-glass upon a pillow before her, comb back her wavy tresses, afterwards anointing them with the sweet-scented *manóc* and gathering them tastefully into a knot behind. When making an elaborate toilet, she would array herself in a white robe, with a diminutive collar turned down at the neck, and display the graceful contour of her figure by girding a fancy *paréu* around her waist ; then, with the snowy flowers of the Cape jessamine in her hair, and adjusted like little cornucopiæ in the lobes of her ears, she was prepared to make and receive her morning calls. She never wore beads ; while the Hawaiian girls are passionately fond of this description of ornament, it is almost entirely discarded by Tahitian belles. Matéa was the fairest of a merry group of *improvisatrices* that assembled around the "watering-place" every evening, and more than one stranger were victims of their sarcastic pleasantry.

Having arranged matters with Táne, I sent off to the brig the same evening for my curtains and bedding. Nothing could exceed old Táne's officiousness; he cuffed one of the boys and slapped the other for doing as he had directed. The office of chambermaid was admirably performed by him, for the sheets and spread were adjusted without a wrinkle; the net was suspended over the bed by attaching strips of bark to the corners and recuring them to the rafters. The house was small, having a single door on the seaward side; the bed, a chest, table and chair monopolized nearly one-half of it; the family, with their chests of apparel, chattels, &c., accommodated themselves in the other portion. The apartment was innocent of both curtains and partition; through the interstices of the *paréu* sides could be witnessed all that was passing without, while the sea-breeze that stole through gave to the whole an air of refreshing coolness.

In the morning, preparations were made for breakfast. Táne killed a fowl, plucked it, then, wrapping it in leaves, placed it under ground to roast, and at the proper moment put some bread-fruit on the fire. The lazy son-in-law went out, broke open a ripe cocoanut, and grated the kernel into a saucer, after which he separated finely some of the fibre of a green husk until it resembled hemp, and removing the prepared kernel to it from the saucer, he wrung it with his hands until a thick cream-like substance streamed from it into a dish placed for its reception. This was deliciously sweet, and an excellent substitute for butter, by dipping into it the mealy bread-fruit. Foreigners who sometimes wish to be exceedingly nice with its preparation, drop hot stones into the dish containing it, and in a short time the watery portion evaporates, leaving only the sweet and pure oil. There were no *feis*, for this island, like Huahíne, produces none.

After one of the boys had climbed a tree and thrown down some young cocoanuts for the sake of their cooling beverage, old Táne arranged the dishes and food upon the table for breakfast. In doing this, he panted laboriously, and drove away Matéa, who had proffered her services. His crockery had been culled from various sources, and, for a wonder, he provided me with a knife and fork. The latter was a fair specimen of Sheffield cutlery, but the palmiest days of the other had evidently been passed amid scenes of salt junk and rigging ; it was a worn-out sheath-knife, and its wooden handle, polished by age, bore the impress of a " foul anchor" and two or three initials. None of the family could ever be persuaded to join me at my meals. Sometimes, after I had devoured the better half of a fowl, besides two or three hemispheres of bread-fruit, a complete surfeit, my landlord would inquire commiseratingly whether I was troubled with dyspepsia, deducing the inference from what he really considered my delicate appetite.

It should have been previously remarked that Táne occupied the enviable post among his neighbors of "commercial agent" for a German trader residing in Huahíne, who had intrusted him with a few varieties of unsaleable prints that had grown musty upon his shelves, also a small assortment of haberdashery. These evidences of prosperity the " agent" kept carefully concealed in one of his green chests, lest they should become too commonplace by the vulgar gaze of outsiders. When a customer called to examine his stock, he would unlock one of his private chests to obtain the key of that containing his goods. In expatiating upon the merits of some of his styles, his eloquence was never exhausted. To convince a customer that a *paréu* pattern was becoming, he would wrap one end of the calico around his waist, and, with head erect, step off like a militia colonel, while the remainder of the print was trailing after him upon the mats and dried grass of the *floor*. Had he received a proper schooling at the period of imbibing " first principles," he would have made a capital "drummer." But his arguments failed to convince, and a loss of commissions was painfully obtruded as he gathered up his piece-goods and replaced them in the chest without reference to original fold. I do not believe he sold a fathom of cloth during my sojourn in his family.

Táne had one specimen of personal property that hung near my bed, which I could never look at without laughing ; it was a tricornered pasteboard *chapeau*, fashioned much like those of juvenile " trainers" at home, though more elaborately decorated. Its sides were ornamented with red cotton fringe, and crowning its apex was a tuft of poultry feathers ; at either extremity hung a yellow tassel. But the grand effect produced was by the frontispiece ; this was a square green ticket (probably purloined from his dry goods) pasted on the hat, emblazoned with the American eagle, who bore in his beak the somewhat mercenary announcement of " Merrimac Prints— Warranted Fast Colors." Whether this emblem of warfare had been borrowed from Raiatéa, or had been prepared in anticipation of a French invasion, I never learned, but am certain that the paper cone was never sported in my presence.

CHAPTER XXVI.

THE "COBBLER'S DAUGHTER."

SEVERAL days had been passed in the family of Táne, when one morning a little schooner was seen off the entrance to the harbor. With a " foul" wind, it tacked incessantly in the narrow passage, until " catching a slant," she shot in on the larboard tack, stretching away towards Fanúi, and with every stitch of canvas spread, she came dashing across the bay " with a bone in her teeth." The next board brought her nearly opposite the premises of Táne, where she let go her anchor. It was a dingy-looking little craft of twenty or thirty tons. Defect in proportion and other deformities were the result of domestic manufacture, for naval architecture has not yet reached the acme of perfection among the Pacific Isles. She bore the singular name of " Cobbler's Daughter," having been built in Huahíne by a shoemaker and his daughter.

In many respects it was an evil hour for Táne when the " Cobbler's Daughter" furled her sails in Borabóra harbor, for she was owned, and at the time commanded, by the German trader who had exalted him to the post he then occupied, and who, among other purposes, had come to receive an account of his stewardship.

Captain Harry was a loud-spoken, hard-working man, who, in

many respects, by his long residence in the group, had become Táhitianized. His first request to Táne was to construct a small inclosure for the purpose of containing a number of porkers he had picked up during a trading cruise among the islands. Táne bustled about, shouting to his attendants as they brought the light stakes, thinking that delinquencies *to be* discovered would be cancelled by present officiousness. In due season the pen was completed, and the work of disembarking commenced, canoes being used for lighters; and such a medley of discordant grunts and squeals perhaps never before echoed through the quiet groves of Tarapíti.

The indulgent reader may, perhaps, sneer at the intrusion of such trifling occurrences, and call them *swinish ;* but, as every historified subject contains events both trivial and momentous, to avoid a charge of remissness has been sought in the present narration. Borabóra has its commerce, which in its way is as much entitled to consideration as the income of a Rothschild or the Hebrew mothers who wove linen girdles for the merchants. The arrival of the "Cobbler's Daughter" perhaps deserved and received the same attention in the archives of Borabóra that would have been claimed for H. B. M. —— seventy-four, ——, Rear-Admiral of the Blue ; for she floated the independent flag of Huahíne. Matehá made a note of it in his records, and compared it with the entry in the pilot's book. In future years this cargo of live stock may figure largely in statistics of foreign imports.

Captain Harry had visited the place more especially to settle an account of long standing. It appears that, about six months previous, a person familiarly called "Bill," an old resident of Borabóra, had visited Huahíne, and by largely representing the quantity of cocoanut oil and swine he could procure among the leeward islands, for such merchandise as he should select, Harry was induced to furnish him with a snug little invoice. The merchandise he carried with him to Borabóra, but removed a portion of it to the little island Motuíti, ten miles distant, where he went to superintend the manufacture of cocoanut oil. According to Bill's statement, the casks furnished him by Harry proved worthless, and the oil leaked out. As he had written him to have them removed, he could not conscientiously consider himself responsible for the loss.   In the meantime he had disposed of the goods to remunerate natives for their services.

Harry's story differed vastly ; he said Bill had by fraudulent pretences obtained goods to the amount of —— hundred dollars, which he had disposed of and retained the proceeds for his own benefit ; and further, that the casks containing the said oil were of his own selection, and that instead of attending to his business as he ought to have done, he had been imbibing pale brandy among the cocoanut groves of Motuíti.

This was an international affair, for, as before stated, Huahíne and Borabóra were independent kingdoms ; the judiciary of the latter considered itself unauthorized to act without official notification from the authorities of the neighboring State, and then the evidence was so conflicting, that even the regent Matehá frankly admitted his incompetency to give a decision.   Harry proposed submitting the whole affair to the arbitration of disinterested foreigners and non-residents, but to this the other would not consent.   Bill was an American, with a liberal endowment of general information, especially in figures, and his account-current was drafted as neatly as would have been that of a San Francisco commission merchant, showing a balance in his favor.

Harry said it looked very well on paper, but it reminded him of the old story of the Yankee and Indian who went out hunting on shares, resulting in two items of game, a turkey and a hawk, to be divided between them.   Said the Yankee to the Indian, " You take the hawk and I'll take the turkey, or I'll take the turkey and you take the hawk."   The Indian said it sounded fair enough, but somehow or other he always got the hawk.

During my stay in Borabóra, the two parties never met face to face, for both breathed chivalrous deeds towards each other.   Bill had been hired by the doctor to superintend the native women while packing oranges, which was done in the large court-house upon the common.   Now and then Harry would pass by bareheaded, in full Tahitian costume, beating the air with his fists, and howling threats in Teutonic.   On these occasions, Bill turned a shade browner, and hitching up his trowsers uneasily, stared savagely at him through the *puráu* slats, and giving his head two or three serious shakes, re-

23

marked, " I shall have to take hold of that man yet." I sailed before the adjustment of the affair, but the last threat of Harry was that he should carry off a beautiful boat belonging to Bill. According to this gentleman's sentiments, its execution would involve the delicate question of physical ability.

A day of reckoning had come for Mr. Táne. One morning Captain Harry came over to examine his account-current, and take an inventory. The purification of the Augean stables was a trifling affair in comparison with this tax upon Táne's ability ; the occupation of fifteen minutes consumed a day, and a vocabulary of invectives was expended upon those who assisted him. His sales had been registered upon two or three greasy-looking papers, covered with characters that bore a stronger resemblance to Ethiopic symbols than Arabic figures, and in deciphering which he had recourse to a neighbor's assistance. To augment his perplexity, his statement exhibited a deficit of two pongée handkerchiefs ; this discrepancy was very promptly attributed to his wife's neglect, and he questioned both her and his daughters somewhat severely as to what they had been about in not looking after the store during his absence. All protested their innocence of having had anything to do with the sales, upon which Táne bundled them into the yard, including son-in-law and infant, and then commenced a rigid search, in which mats were pulled up, grass scattered, chests researched, and the interstices between the thatch and rafters carefully examined. But all to no purpose ; the missing property was never recovered, and that night poor Táne sat down disconsolately upon one of his chests, and with chin in his hands, supported by the joint assistance of elbows and knees, he stared gloomily out upon the water, crushed——annihilated by a moral conviction that with all his assiduity to please, he was only a *mene tekel* " agent" after all. The culminating point of his troubles was yet in perspective. That evening Captain Harry came in to pay me a visit ; and to moisten the link of friendship, one of the boys was sent off to the " Cobbler's Daughter" with a written order, and presently returned with a huge bottle of cherry bounce. Though of superior flavor, it contained a liberal per centage of alcohol, and was accordingly sipped with caution. Harry was evidently sensible of a " genial glow," and lest the company should understand here

and there a word while discussing family topics, we spoke German.
He sung several songs, and among them those somewhat equivocal
stanzas, familiar alike to Saxons and Wurtembergers—

"Als ich an einem Somer-Tag, &c."

Soon after, he returned to the premises occupied by himself and
wife, almost adjoining ; but, unfortunately, he forgot to carry the
bottle with him, and I to remind him to do so. The consequence was
that, after I had retired, I saw Táne look wistfully at it for a short
time, then deliberately pour out a tumblerful, which he drained
without stopping to breathe. Placing the glass upon the table,
he gave two or three audible respirations, as brandy-drinkers are
wont to do, and, half soliloquizing, remarked :—" *E ! méa maitái
teia.*" (Really, this is excellent!)

Mrs. Táne remonstrated ; but the old man replied, good-humoredly, " *Areána oe vahíne.*" (Woman, have patience.) This
only made her more importunate in her request that he would forsake immediately the dangerous proximity of the bottle, which called
forth another exclamation of " *Titála tou paráu !*" (Have done with
your talk.)

After a brief interval, another glass disappeared ; and Táne began
to feel on excellent terms with himself. At this juncture I took the
liberty of remonstrating, when Táne discovered for the first time
that I was awake. He came to the bed, and deliberately raising
the curtain, drew up a chair and sat down beside me. I knew
what was coming, and braced myself to endure with fortitude the
infliction ; for the climax of colloquial annoyance is to be doomed to
the incoherences of a person who is " three sheets in the wind, and
the other shivering."

He commenced, in a silken voice :—

" Thomas, what do you call that stuff in the bottle ?"

" Cherry bounce."

" *M—te—erry bout—y,*" was his ludicrous attempt to repeat the
name. He then continued—

" Thomas, you my friend ; this is my thought. I want you to
live in Borabóra. We'll keep store and get rich. Plenty hogs and

cocoanuts in Borabóra. This my yard, and all these fruit-trees. I'll build a house, and you shall marry Matéa. My thought is she likes you, (literally, has a passion.) If she don't, I'll make her. You can have——"

"*Aíta oe hamá?*" (Are you not ashamed of yourself?) interrupted Matéa.

Táne continued :—" You can have the benefit of all my property, and I won't charge you anything for the use of it." He then fell into a fit of musing ; but presently resumed :—" *Raatíra* (the captain) thinks I've stolen his handkerchiefs, but he's mistaken. I've built a nice pen for his pigs, and bought cocoanuts to feed them with ; but he don't thank me for it."

He continued his nonsense until I grew sleepy and vexed, when I told him to drop the curtain and be gone. He obeyed very promptly, but had hardly taken five steps from the bed before he returned, and gently raising the curtain, inquired, as softly as an infant :

" Thomas, what did you call that stuff in the bottle ?"

"*Cherry bounce*, sir !" was the reply, with all the sternness I could muster.

" *E ! M—te—erry* BOU—*ty, tir?*" replied Táne, with a strong emphasis on the penultimate, and counting the syllables on his fingers. He then retired, apparently satisfied.

I slept until midnight, when I was awakened by a bellowing and howling that might have distracted the lunatics of Bedlam. Táne had drained the bottle. Looking through the gauze net, I beheld a sight that would have made a rumseller blush. The two daughters in *deshabille*, by their united efforts, were holding their frantic father, who sometimes struggled and shouted like a maniac. When the paroxysm had passed, he would cry and laugh as if in a fit of hysterics ; then again, with his powerful arm, he would draw his youngest daughter to him with indelicate fondness, and the utmost efforts of the poor girl, who was sobbing ready to break her heart, were exerted to disengage herself from his embrace. Had Shelley witnessed it, he might have realized his conception of " The Cenci."

The mother, who held the infant, sat trembling in one corner of the apartment, perhaps apprehensive of the Bluebeard propensity of her husband, while the son-in-law occasionally assisted the girls. The pretty little musquito-net had been torn down, and with the infant's bed was trampled under foot. The general confusion of the apartment evidenced a drunken struggle.

I bore it as long as I could, then jumped up, dressed myself, and with my bedding sought refuge in the house of a neighbor. When Táne saw that I was in earnest, he set up a series of howls, such as : *"Aué ! Tamate aita paráu i te metúa ! Farúe te vahíne ! Iaurána oe, Tamate ! Aué, aue-e-e !"* (Alas ! Thomas won't speak to the father ; he is forsaking the daughter ! Farewell, Thomas ! Oh dear ! oh dear !)

That night the *mutóis* (constables) took Táne in charge, and the next day he was fined for drunkenness. This was not the worst : on the following morning the report went abroad that he had turned a stranger out of his house, thereby violating the sacred laws of hospitality ; but the climax of misery was the loss of the enviable post of " commercial agent for Huahíne."

Matéa never spoke to me afterward ; if we chanced to meet on the Broom Road, she carried her head as stately as a queen, without even deigning me a look. This loss of favor I attributed solely to the cherry bounce of the " Cobbler's Daughter."

CHAPTER XXVII.

THE ORANGE GROVES OF FANÚI.

It having been ascertained that a cargo of oranges could be procured here, chiefly at Fanúi Bay, where they were still upon the trees, Captain Beauvais and the doctor visited that locality, and on their return the former gave a glowing description of the scenery. On the following morning I accompanied them in the boat, it being a more expeditious route than following the irregularities of the shore, and after a pull of nearly two miles, we fairly opened the beautiful bay, which is a mile in length by half a mile in breadth ; a short distance from the entrance it curves toward the southeast, thus forming a commodious harbor independent of the reef that encircles the island. The land on both sides was high and densely wooded, but no houses were seen until we had reached the head of the bay, where they were scattered beneath the grove that extended to the water's edge. A group of both sexes were standing on the beach to welcome us to Fanúi ; as it was ebb tide, our boat grounded a short distance from the shore, when several natives waded in and transported us on their shoulders.

Leaving Dr. Doan to attend to financial matters, the captain and I indulged in a short ramble. Although not given to the " melting mood," he declared it to be the loveliest spot he had ever visited, and I should envy not the fastidiousness of Rasselas, had he looked with indifference upon the orange groves of Fanúi. This happy valley is bounded on the north by gently receding hills, covered with luxuriant vegetation ; at its southeastern extremity the gray castellated rock of Mount Pahia rises perpendicularly to the clouds. Through its centre winds a small stream, gradually increasing by the tributary rills that ripple down gentle declivities, until it empties into the sea. In every direction are groves of orange and bread-fruit trees ; from the former the fruit was unplucked, and hung temptingly in golden clusters. Wherever we strayed, it was beneath the shade of a leafy canopy ; and the perfume and freshness of the atmosphere were invigorating. Occasionally we came upon a small inclosure, with its rustic hut half hidden by the broad leaves of the banana or plantain ; and as we passed, *iaurana* came pleasantly from within. Toward the head of the valley the land is more rolling, and standing as it were upon terraces are groves of bread-fruit. This portion is unoccupied ; and the scenery, often wildly romantic, is solitary. in the extreme ; for, save the voice of nature in the rippling brook and the whispering leaves, no other sounds are heard. I noticed a row of huge gray boulders beneath a dark canopy of boughs, a gloomy relic of darkness and superstition. Like the forest of ancient oaks, where the sacred mistletoe hallowed the Druid altar, these solemn shades were a fitting spot for the celebration of impious rites, and the phantoms of those who had bled upon the sacrificial stone seemed to haunt their awe-inspiring solitudes.

From the hills in the rear a charming view is obtained ; the eye wanders over a sea of foliage and mottled plumes, undulating in waves of verdure. On the left are precipitous ridges, where evergreen surges are mantling cliffs—flinging upward their emerald spray to encircle sharp pinnacles with leafy chaplets. The azure of the still lagoon mirrors the shadows of forest headlands. Palm-covered islets repose on the reef, girdled by the snowy fringe of breakers, and stretching away to the horizon is the broad sweep of ocean.

On our return to the landing we found the doctor surrounded by quite a crowd, chiefly the owners of the oranges, from whom he was endeavoring to purchase a cargo. The bell suspended to a tree had been rung, and the natives were assembled to consult with each other as to the price they should demand. Numerous speeches were made by the old men, setting forth the disadvantages under which the agriculturists of Borabóra labored in suffering their fruits to grow spontaneously, only to be disposed of to the *papaás* (foreigners) at prices ruinous to their own interests ; as, for instance, fifty cents per hundred for cocoanuts, and only four dollars per thousand for oranges, and that, too, in part trade. Some insisted on holding out for four dollars in cash ; but the doctor shook his head seriously, and made a movement toward the boat, telling them that their oranges would soon drop from the trees, and that they would afterward regret having let so good an opportunity for disposing of them pass unimproved.

The bargain was accordingly made, and afterward for the crates ; all to be conveyed to the court-house in the settlement, which had been hired for the purpose of packing.

I noticed many pretty faces among the females, to whom our arrival was an advent. Some of them, adorned with the choice ornaments of nature, and surrounded by the luscious fruits they had brought to dispose of, suggested thoughts of Pomona, or a corresponding divinity in Polynesia.

We remained at Borabóra for two days, then visited Tahiti ; returning after an absence of twelve days. Almost the first object that attracted my attention on entering the harbor was the little sloop which I had chartered several months previous ; it had arrived from Maupíti that morning, and in passing it on my way to the shore I saw the Paumotu girl, who gave a shout of recognition. During our absence the doctor had not been idle. We found him comfortably installed in the house of Matehá, which he had rented for the occasion; the spacious court-house was nearly filled with crates and boxes, and some forty or fifty females, from the sexagenarian to the laughing girl, were engaged wrapping oranges in the *fála* leaves, preparatory to packing. On these occasions there appears to be a tacit understanding among the old gossips, that every subject that can afford matter for comment shall be raked up and discussed; and between this and smoking cigaritos, made of fine tobacco wrapped in a small piece of *fála* leaf, they manage to pass their time very agreeably. The girls, too, appeared to enjoy a lively conversation among themselves, and were modest in their demeanor toward strangers, the extent of their temerity being to beg the favor of a puff or two from a cigar. At sunset all repair to the house to receive their pay, usually fifty cents per day; after which, the young ladies decorate themselves with the *tiáre*, and saunter along the Broom Road, to enjoy a *téte-à-téte* with their sweethearts.

I was conversing with the doctor one afternoon in Matehá's yard; near by were several natives, and leaning against the house was an interesting little girl about ten years of age, who wore on either side of her head a single flower of the Cape jessamine; soon after, Mr. Krause, the missionary, was seen walking toward the court-house, and although at a considerable distance from us, such was the fear his presence inspired, that several of the elder girls said immediately to the child, with decisive gestures, " *Farúi te tiáre; hapépe !*" (throw away the flowers; be quick!) Reluctantly the innocent creature plucked the fresh ornaments from her hair, threw them upon the ground, and trampled them under her feet. To me this required no explanation, for throughout Polynesia, I have noticed that although filling their own gardens with exotics, the missionaries look with pious horror upon this description of ornament when worn by natives, and would instil a prejudice to the indulgence of this innocent taste, irreversible as the extremes of the magnetic pole. That was wrong, Mr. Krause, and the pleasing evidences of your horticultural taste are diametrically opposed to it; if you permit them to indulge with impunity their fancy for tinsel finery, introduced by foreigners, you should never instruct the innocent child that the snowy petals exhaling a sweet perfume amid its raven tresses are symbols of subjects unmentionable. The doctor merely shrugged his shoulders and said it was " characteristic of the faith in this section of the country."

We were frequently the recipients of Mr. Krause's hospitality, and, though perhaps too ultra in some of his views, I consider him one of the most practical men of his calling in the group. From the consul who visited this island during our sojourn, we learned that at Raiatéa the armistice between Tamatóa and Tamáre having been concluded, the former had retired toward Opóa, pursued by the rebel chief, and that the two parties were cannonading each other at the time he left.

CHAPTER XXVIII.

A WORD CONCERNING MISSIONS.

WITHOUT designing to enter upon the topic of missionary duties and privileges, which is not comprised within these limits, I cannot forbear giving a few desultory thoughts or reflections upon the subject, as they occur at a moment of retrospection. Without aspiring to the championship of either sect or party, I esteem it a privilege to contribute my mite to the scale of public opinion toward counteracting the influence of evil reports that have gone abroad, dictated perhaps by guilty consciousness, and propagated by kindred fellowship. It has been said, " Let him who is without sin cast the first stone"—a just rebuke to officious meddlers who groan without accomplishing, while preferring their wire-drawn charges. But it is conceded to be hardly applicable in the present instance ; for, were our right to judge based upon our own merits, how few would attain to that eminence! It is a privilege we possess, and perhaps a duty, to examine the constituent principles of any charitable institution that claims our sympathies in its behalf, and it is not to be supposed that a society so comprehensive in its views, so world-wide in its enterprises as that of Foreign Missions, should escape the censure of those whose tenets are perhaps as heterodox as the superstitions of less-favored brethren. It is believed that all will concur in admitting that efforts having a tendency to elevate a fellow-being from corrupting influences to a higher grade in the social scale, and pointing out the way to intellectual enjoyment, are praiseworthy ; and this conceded, it can hardly be denied that the system of evangelizing in connection with them can be otherwise than beneficial in its results.

In confirmation of the preceding, it might be shown that the increased facilities for commercial intercourse among the groups of the Pacific where the words of truth have been sown in prolific soil, are paramount to those of the isles that still sit in the shadow of darkness ; this may perhaps engage a future remark. But the pivot on which turns the equipoise of public opinion, and which has proved a most fruitful source of animadversion, is the " undue influence acquired by the mission over the minds of its proselytes," and to this are ascribed the obstacles that have arisen in the way of private advancement where the spiritual and secular conflict ; but the whole tissue of obloquy is usually so slightly woven that it disappears at the first breath of truth. Their object was to acquire an influence over the minds of those they sought to instruct ; they have succeeded, and should be proud of it. They found vice and ignorance ; they have endeavored to inculcate virtue and knowledge. It would be accounted strange if a guardian who had watched the dawn of the first germ of intellect, carefully tending its progressive development, should, after simply instructing it in its spiritual duties, send it abroad to combat superior intelligence with its selfish interests. Thus with the natives of Oceanica less gifted than those whom commerce and adventure have thrown among them, and in every instance where an isle or group has been reclaimed, the rightful lords of the soil have voluntarily solicited the advice of their spiritual teachers, to enable them to meet on more equal footing the advances of those who claim their hospitality or intercourse.

No brighter example of the success of missionary labors need be adduced than that of Hawaii in its present condition. Since the battle of Kuamú, fought in the autumn of 1819, sealing forever the fate of idolatry upon her shores, and the subsequent establishment of Christianity in 1820, she has steadily progressed, building up institutions for learning, which have disseminated the blessings of truth and knowledge ; and at the present day she stands forth without a parallel in the annals of heathen regeneration. A casual observer would perhaps require stronger evidences of radical reform than present themselves at a superficial glance ; but when it is considered that teachers have labored among a race vicious from its origin, whose language expresses no symbol for either virtue or gratitude, an index to disposition, an unprejudiced mind will admit that much has been accomplished. Who will doubt the sincerity of the Hawaiian queen, reclaimed from idolatry, who sat composedly within the appalling domains of her fabled deity, and, renouncing her allegiance, sang praises to Jehovah, while fiery surges were rolling at her feet ? Or who would not admire the harmonizing influences of Christianity on the imperious disposition of the haughty Kaahumánu ?

These are not solitary instances. A liberal mind would refer the hospitality and friendly intercourse that characterize native converts to their true source, the successful introduction of the Gospel. The trader whose pursuits are amid the vast archipelago of Oceanica, and who encounters the two extremes of existence, can answer for this. There are those whose abilities and acquirements would lead us to hope for more liberal views on this subject, who have uncharitably attributed the numerical decline of the inhabitants of evangelized groups to causes nearly or remotely allied to missions. Such arguments are almost too absurd for refutation. I will merely refer the holders of such opinions to those two once populous islands of Micronesia, Strong's and Ascension, which, when first discovered, were inhabited by thousands, holding frequent communication with trading vessels ; but the mission established in 1852 is welcomed by a few hundred natives, physically and morally deteriorated by their intercourse with foreigners. Again, there are others who would exhaust reams of letter-press to convince the public generally that " charity begins at home," and adduce a standard of moral precedents from the theories of Socrates or Plato. Let us simply inquire of these *exclusive* champions of domestic regeneration, whether, during the five thousand years that have recently elapsed, or since the building of the first city by Cain, such a quality as benevolence really existed ; and if so, whether during this period it lacked objects on which to bestow its sympathies, before the project of foreign missions was in embryo. Were the spirit of such an argument literally adopted, it would imply a selfishness inconsistent with the moral sentiment that characterizes the march of intellect at the present day ; and from the pinnacle of our own conceit we would look down upon the masses revolving around us as necessary appendages, subservient to our interests. There is another class of writers upon this subject who enchant us by their fascinating style, and whose productions would be better appreciated if upon subjects of vital interest they would forbear to condemn where, through prejudice, they cannot approve. Like birds of the night, they delight in ruins, erecting the fabric of their greatness over the fancied wreck of the hopes and reputation of those who have never done them an injury, and who with becoming charity would extend the arm of support to such as deservedly need it. But the castle they attack is built upon a rock, and the winds of contempt and waves of reproach will forever blow and beat in vain, for its foundation " is not of earth."

With reference to the social condition of the missionaries in Polynesia, in many respects there is little to envy : their responsibilities are great, their duties fatiguing, frequently precluding them from domestic enjoyment, and their existence dependent on the caprice of savages. Instances might be adduced of years of toil with almost inadequate means for support, and premature decline engendered by an enervating climate on peculiarly susceptible temperaments. But on the other hand, we have evidences of worldly prosperity among those who court prospective enjoyment by secular pursuits, and whose acquisitiveness has induced comment among the observing as to the sincerity of the tenets by which they profess to be guided. Although instances occur that clash discordantly with the constituent principle of evangelization, they are too isolated to affect comprehensive results. Such have a refuge and defence in that applicable proverb, " There is none perfect—no, not one."

It is unpleasant to draw distinctions where the benevolent of two great nations are engaged in the same object ; in doing so, reference should be had to natural facilities or advantages, and affecting causes, with charitable regard for the feelings of each. It would appear that by tacit consent the English have occupied the groups south, and the American missionaries those north of the equator, for their respective fields of labor. In the year 1797, Tahiti was fixed upon by the London Missionary Society as the basis for its operations in the South Seas, and in that year a ship was sent out with twenty-five teachers for the Society, Marquesas and Friendly Islands. During subsequent years the number was greatly augmented, but this enterprise failed to realize the anticipations of its projectors ; for various reasons post after post was abandoned, and in many instances missionary efforts proved futile. The station at Tahiti was alone preserved, and after years of toil and perseverance, the labors bestowed upon it were crowned with success, for it stood forth the shining nucleus of the isles around it. Later results may be witnessed in the conversion to Christianity of the inhabitants of that group ; also, of New-Zealand, the Austral, Hervey, Friendly, and portions of the Fiji, Samoan and Paumotu Islands, aided by the Wesleyan Mission. It is not of the extent or sincerity of their conversions that I wish to speak, but of the results that have attended them pertaining to education and industry. It will be conceded that the moral deportment that characterizes the converts of less frequented groups is in strict accordance with the faith they profess, and in this respect, superior to that exhibited at the Sandwich or Society Islands. Their limited education may be adapted to their wants, but the examples, for comparison of intellectual advancement, should be the Sandwich and Tahitian Islands ; for to these have the respective efforts of each been mainly directed, and from both radiate light and knowledge to surrounding groups.

In both instances we have the complete abolition of idolatry ; by the English Mission this was found in all its deformity, and after years of persevering zeal, successfully combated ; whereas, the American missionaries found the field clear, and a nation without a creed waiting to receive the Word. The former have labored more than fifty, the latter more than thirty years ; for beneficial results, we have only to examine the present condition of the two groups. At the Society Islands we find, with bold exceptions, the natives prone to be ignorant, vicious and warlike, deriving their subsistence chiefly from the spontaneous products of the soil, without possessing the ambition even to clothe themselves with the habiliments of civilization ; exhibiting but few evidences of industry, and their intellectual acquirements confined to the simple branches taught in the primary and only class of schools in this group. But at the Sandwich Islands, whose population quintuples that of the former group, we have a nation of more industrious habits, exhibiting at least the outward attributes of civilization, and devoted to the cultivation of the peaceful arts ; possessing in an eminent degree the desire and capacity to appreciate and comprehend the instructions of their teachers. They have four hundred and twenty-three primary and common schools with native teachers, the number of whose scholars nearly equals the entire population of the former group ; besides having nine seminaries, or private schools, where English and the more complex branches are pursued. The annual outlay for educational purposes, by contributions, but chiefly by government appropriations, is not far from $25,000. The Rev. Henry T. Cheever, who has visited this group, furnishes the following interesting summary of missionary statistics :—

" We have spent some time at all of the nineteen missionary stations but one where there are resident missionaries, except on the island of Kauai. We have surveyed missionary and native life under various aspects, and have become somewhat acquainted with the modes and means of operation upon the native mind, and their results ; and with the trials and difficulties which the missionary has to contend with.

" We have mingled with the people in the house and by the way, in the field and the school, at their work and their play, in the meeting for religious inquiry and at the public sanctuary. We have seen by observation what they now are, and we have heard from others what they once were. And in instituting our final comparison between the Heart of the Pacific as it was and is, or between times now and times that were, when the first missionaries landed at Kailua, we will take the state of progress found at the lapse of just one quarter of a century, as indicated by a careful survey and comparison of statistics derived on the spot.

" In the first place, there labored at the Sandwich Islands from

1820 to 1844, at different times, sixty-one male and sixty-seven female missionaries, who performed in all ten hundred and eighty-eight years of missionary service. By these there were expended $608,865 in their outfit, support, and missionary work. After twenty-five years from the first settling of missionaries among a race of the very lowest savages, there were to be seen erected forty permanent dwelling-houses, two printing offices and binderies, with which were connected four printing-presses ; four commodious seminary and school buildings, all which, together with large and valuable lands attached to them, were the property of the American Board of Commissioners for Foreign Missions.

" Besides these results of Christian industry and perseverance, permanent stone meeting-houses were found erected at almost every station, by the united skill and resources of missionary and people, giving and laboring voluntarily ; and about three hundred and seventy-five school-houses. The Hawaiian tongue had been mastered, we might almost say created, and reduced to writing, and one half the adult population taught to read. There had been established four hundred and three public schools, in which seventeen thousand four hundred and forty children and youth were being instructed.

" The entire Bible had been translated from the original tongues, and there had been printed fifty-two thousand copies of the New Testament, and twenty thousand of the Old, besides several editions of one and ten thousand copies of fragmentary portions of the Scriptures, before the entire translation was completed. Upwards of seventy other different works, large and small, had been compiled and issued from the press, and the total number of pages printed at the missionary presses up to 1844, were twenty-two million sixty-one thousand seven hundred and fifty.

" There had been organized twenty-five independent native churches, and there had been received to them, on examination, thirty-one thousand four hundred and nine persons, of whom there were then living in regular standing twenty-two thousand six hundred and fifty-two, being more than one-fifth of the entire population of the islands.

" Besides these educational results that can be condensed into statistics, it should be added as a part of their education as a people, that the institutions of the Sabbath and of Christian marriage had been firmly established; government had been rendered comparatively just and stable; a good written constitution and laws had been enacted; life and property were rendered secure; the country's industry and resources were beginning to be developed. The Hawaiian nation's independence had been acknowledged by other nations, and it was admitted into the fraternity of Christian States. The commerce of the islands, that is, the value of its commercial exchanges, or bills negotiated there for the supply of ships, had grown from little or nothing to two hundred thousand dollars, while the yearly net revenue of the kingdom had reached to seventy thousand dollars, and the annual consumption of foreign goods was one hundred and seventy-five thousand dollars."

It will thus be seen that the conquest of the American missionaries has been morally greater; and although it may be urged that the present condition of the Society Islands affords no just criterion for comparison, since the conquest of Tahiti and Eimeo by the French has occasioned a moral retrogression, the American missionaries have also reason to complain of the pernicious examples and influences that have been greatly augmented by increased foreign intercourse, owing to recent developments on neighboring shores.

The Roman Catholic Mission has made but little progress in Polynesia. From Tahiti, as a starting-point, they have extended their sway over the Gambier Islands, an insignificant group, constituting the southeastern extremity of the Paumotu Archipelago; at Wallis Island; also in a few instances at the Paumotus, where some of the natives have endured martyrdom, while the creed was forced upon them by French bayonets. At the Sandwich Islands, their faith was earlier established; and the actual number of converts in this group probably exceeds that of all the South Pacific Isles. These, however, are chiefly drawn from the lower classes, on whom the creed and doctrines sit as lightly as their rosaries and amulets. Tahiti is their stronghold; but even here their converts are comparatively few, so deep-rooted is the aversion of the natives toward the French, since the deprivation of their liberties. Several Sisters of Charity have found their way to these far-off isles, to lead their erring sisters by the hand, to breathe an atmosphere of moral purity. Their humane and benevolent efforts, in every clime where they have been established, call forth encomiums from the liberal-minded, irrespective of schismatic prejudices, who bid them God-speed in their pious labors.

Certain tenets of the Romish missionary, diametrically opposed to those of the Protestant, admit of no examples of domestic enjoyment which, by imitation, would tend to the elevation of their converts. Whereas, the Protestant missionary, by drawing around him the refined associations of a home, encourages the native to seek a more exalted position in the social scale, while instructing him in his spiritual duty. The former, a true zealot of the faith he professes, wanders through valley and over mountain, enduring hardship and privation, with no domestic ties to engage his attention, but with his whole soul devoted to the cause he professes, to extend the temporal dominion of his god, the Church. Though wielding their power with arbitrary sway, where they have obtained a footing, I have not observed that the natives influenced by Catholic control were more circumspect or fettered in their intercourse with foreigners than those professing the Protestant faith at the Friendly and Austral Islands, where the spiritual dominion of their teachers is absolute. The animosity exhibited by both sects toward each other is bitter and uncharitable.

But to all who in truth and sincerity have conveyed the glad tidings of "peace, good-will toward men," carrying forward the great work of evangelization throughout the earth, is due the gratitude of the civilized world. This wide field for the display of Christian benevolence will repay a hundred-fold the labors bestowed upon it—temporally, in its commercial developments; spiritually, in the creation of a new link to the chain that shall ultimately unite the human race in one common bond of fellowship, hallowed by reverence for a Supreme Creator. From the isles of the South, the "still, small voice" sends back a cheering response; for, in many a bright glade that re-echoed the sound of heathen orgies, the Lily of the Valley lifts its unsullied head, sheltered by the vine of Love, and nourished by the still waters of Truth. Nor does the bread-fruit yield less abundantly, nor the cocoa-palm rustle less joyfully where buds

24

and blooms the Rose of Sharon, for " the earth is the Lord's, and the fulness thereof."

The reader and I, who have so long rambled together, must now bid each other farewell.

For several days the sky has been overcast, and the thick fog and greenish tinge of the water indicate our proximity to colder scenes ; but at parting let us, in fancy, once more stand together upon deck, in the bright moonlight of a summer evening, and, while watching the misty outline of Borabóra looming dimly in the horizon, feel that—

> " As slow our ship her foamy track
>   Against the wind is cleaving,
> Her trembling pennant still looks back
>   To that dear isle 'tis leaving.
> So loth we part from all we love—
>   From all the links that bind us ;
> So turn our hearts, where'er we rove,
>   To *scenes* we've left behind us."

PART IV.

APPENDIX.

and blooms
the fulness

The read
bid each oth
For sever
and greenish
scenes ; but
upon deck, in
watching the
feel that—

A'PPENDIX I.

A GLANCE AT THE PRESENT CONDITION OF POLYNESIA.

In venturing a remark on the present condition of Polynesia, or the groups of the Pacific, we do not propose entering into idle speculations on their formation, nor exhibiting in detail their productions or history ; the field has been too often gleaned by abler writers, to render a recapitulation interesting to the reader. But at the present day, when golden discoveries have opened new fields for commercial enterprise amid this vast archipelago, and when important events are transpiring in the political drama of nations, which, to a certain extent, must influence its condition, it may not be uninteresting to bestow a superficial glance upon these clustering groups or detached islets, which, like nebulæ or solitary stars, besprinkle the Western Ocean. Though comparatively unimportant, they are becoming interwoven, incorporated as resting-points, by the lines that commerce is drawing through and around them.

Not many years ago, the broad Pacific rolled its waves from shore to shore, seldom disturbed save by the keels of whalers and occasional traders among the islands. Now, it is traversed in every direction ; and no islet is too insignificant to be visited that can suggest an avenue to wealth, or furnish acquisitions to science. The improvements in naval architecture, and the appliance to navigation of principles carefully deduced from meteorologic observation, have greatly promoted the maritime branch of commerce, and voyages that were heretofore contemplated as formidable from their duration are now regarded with indifference.

But few years will have rolled by, ere the bands of commerce that are fast uniting its remotest shores will introduce the blessings and vices of civilization to nearly every isle of Oceanica, and the realities of romance will be as tales forgotten. Already do the Society, Tonga, and Samoan Islands receive the adventurous Californian who pauses for a moment on his way to the more recently discovered gold fields of Australia; and it is to be hoped that the two rising empires now so cordially extending the hand to each other from opposite shores may continue to advance in the mutual enjoyment of peace, and build up life-giving beacons which shall scatter the rays of enterprise and benevolence among the dark isles of ocean.

Oceanica comprises all the groups of the Pacific Ocean, having an extent of 11,000 miles from east to west, and more than 6,000 from north to south, and although impossible to ascertain its precise population, it has been computed at upward of 18,000,000. It is recognized by geographers as comprising three grand divisions : *Malaysia, Australasia,* and *Polynesia*—though by others it has been more definitely classified, as suggested by ethnographic distinctions and geographic position. These subdivisions are *Malaysia,* comprising Sumatra, Java, Borneo, Celebes, Timor, the Philipine and numerous islands in the Soloo Sea. *Australia* is confined to New Holland and Van Dieman's Land. *Melanesia* comprises the islands adjoining, peopled by natives nearly allied to the African race, having black or dark skins and woolly or frizzled hair. The principal islands of this division are Papua or New Guinea, lying north of New Holland ; also, New Ireland, New Britain, New Georgia, the Soloman and Fiji archipelagoes. *Micronesia* includes the central groups, together with the Ladrones, Pelew, and Caroline Islands. *Polynesia* proper, with which we have at present to do, may be comprised in one vast triangle, drawn from the Sandwich Islands on the north, southeast to Easter Island, 4,000 miles ; thence southwest to New Zealand, constituting its southern leg, 4,700 miles ; then nearly northeast again to the point of starting, a distance of 3,700 miles. The four volcanic or principal groups within these imaginary lines are the Hawaiian or Sandwich, Georgian and Society, Samoan or Navigator, and the Washington or Marquesas Islands. The second class, or those between the volcanic and coral islands, or commercially insignificant, are the Hervey and Austral, together with a few other islands of lesser note ; the others, of which the Paumotu or Dangerous Archipelago is the principal, are mostly low coral islands, scantily covered with vegetation. In point of number, extent of territory, population, and natural resources, the Hawaiian Islands rank first, being eight in number, with an aggregate area of more than 6,000 square miles. Next in order are the Samoan, Georgian and Society and Marquesas Islands, all being, by a singular coincidence, like the first eight in number. Although a single island about ninety miles in circumference, Tongatabu, in point of geographic advantage, might take precedence of the Marquesas. The Hervey and Austral Islands are respectively five and seven in number, while the Paumotu Archipelago comprises upward of eighty islands.

With reference to the structure of these principal groups, there can exist no doubt; their igneous masses and crateriform outline bespeak them of volcanic origin, and they probably constitute the culminating points of lofty ranges which for ages have been submerged beneath the ocean. The fiery craters of Kilauea and Tofua, also the boiling springs of Vanua Levu, which act as escape-valves for pent-up vapors, and the ebullition of molten masses, are strong evidence that their constituting element has only slumbered. Unlike most other volcanic countries, they are characterized by the peculiar, almost unique formation of their mountains, most of which attain an elevation above the clouds, and some of them are capped with snow. The gradual slopes of the Andes or Sierra Nevada, or the symmetrical cones of Fogo and Pico, are seldom noticed here; peaks have fantastically shot up like spires into a colder zone, as at Mooréa or the Marquesas. These are at times linked together by precipitous, irregular ridges; and in Borabóra we have an island consisting of a curved ridge with projecting spurs at almost regular intervals, while in the centre rises a perpendicular and almost inaccessible rock of basalt to an elevation of one thousand five hundred feet above the sea.

Many of these summits are crowned with craters, which for ages beyond tradition have been quiescent, and some of them, as that of Haleakalá, more than thirty miles in circumference, are almost unparalleled in their dimensions. Smaller ones are sometimes discovered in the midst of forests, clothed with luxuriant foliage, or they frequently occur as isolated cones with flattened apex, or irregular hills near the shore, serving as conspicuous landmarks from the sea. An idea of the rugged character of these islands may be formed by comparing the bases of some of them with the altitude of their mountains. The island of Hawaii, whose greatest length and breadth are ninety and eighty miles, has three lofty mountains, the sum of whose heights is about 38,000 feet; or Tahiti, whose culminating point is Orohená, 6,993 feet high, having for a base a circumference of only sixty miles, excluding the peninsula.

Easter Island, or Vaihoa, upon which rests the southeastern leg of this triangle, lies in lat. 27° 8' S., lon. 109° 17' W., and is about 2,200 miles from the South American coast. It is very small, being but twenty miles in circuit, having a bold shore and no harbors. Its structure is volcanic; within its limits have been observed several small extinct craters, now covered with vegetation, and into one of them, four miles in circuit, near the centre of the island, M. De Langle, who accompanied the expedition of La Perouse, and was subsequently massacred at the Navigator Islands, descended to a depth of near eight hundred feet. The island is moderately elevated; but there are neither cocoanut nor bread-fruit trees upon it, the natives subsisting chiefly upon yams, potatoes, and other esculents, which they cultivate to a great extent, giving their island-home the appearance of a terraced garden. They have no canoes, and in supplying vessels that occasionally touch there, chiefly whalers, they swim off with their produce, for being hostile in disposition, no unarmed boat has the temerity to land. Captain Beechy describes the natives as handsome; and he also noticed several relics of huge stone idols much marred and defaced by the present race, who have no tradition of their origin. This island was discovered in 1722 by the Dutch navigator, Roggewine.

In natural productions, the first-class islands are almost uniformly prolific, the upper stratum of earth being usually composed of vegetable matter, which for ages has been accumulating and undergoing decomposition, and of decomposed lava or volcanic rock, furnishing a rich trachyte soil. This, including the deep alluvial bottoms formed like deltas by the *debris* of the mountains, is of unsurpassed fertility, as is sufficiently proved by the luxuriant vegetation that covers it. Situate between the tropics, these groups are not exposed to the alternations of heat and cold incident to climates of the temperate zone. The lofty mountains catch the trade clouds in their flight, which in turn discharge perennial showers over the land. The observations of Dr. T. B. C. Rooke, of Honolulu, show the mean temperature of the atmosphere of that place for one year to be 75.8° Fah., also rainy days 41, and the amount of rain during that time 46.8 in.; the remaining days were fine. This town is situate on the leeward side of the island; on the opposite portion, more rain and a lower temperature would have been observed; the inter-tropical groups south of the equator are several degrees warmer. During the summer months the leeward portions of the Hawaiian Islands wear a sterile aspect, and only recover their natural freshness during the rainy season, from November to March.

Their natural salubrity of climate is unsurpassed; most of the diseases that have tended to depopulate these groups are not indigenous, but the result of foreign innovation. Among the catalogue of ills entailed, and confined chiefly to the Hawaiian Islands, are croup, cutaneous eruptions, fevers, influenza, ulcers, scrofula, syphilis, &c., and recently the small-pox has made its appearance in this group, and already carried off about 3,000 of its inhabitants. *Elephantiasis*, though not peculiar to the Pacific Islands, as some have supposed, prevails to a considerable extent among the Society and Samoan Islands, manifesting itself in swollen limbs, at times hideously disproportioned, or in a corrugated, *leprous* appearance of the skin, (though from that disease it is quite distinct,) and foreigners as well as natives are sometimes affected by it. Without investigating its cause, which is still a subject of controversy, it may be simply added, that by a proper resort to febrile remedies, in its incipient stage, relief will be experienced, or a change of climate will immediately check its progress.

It may be again remarked, that the temperature of the atmosphere is not so high as might be inferred from their situation as inter-tropical lands, owing chiefly to their isolated position and prevailing winds. More especially is this the case on the windward portion of these islands, and during the nearest approximation of the sun to the zenith, the heat will not be found so oppressive as in the cañons of the Sierra Nevada, or during the summer months in our Eastern cities. However, from some of the sterile tracts on the leeward portion of the Hawaiian Islands, the rays of the sun seem to radiate with an intensity almost unendurable; yet, were a preference ventured for the climate of either group, it would be for this. It has to recommend it a close proximity to the temperate zone, and lofty mountains more uniform in their character than those of the southern groups, and by ascending which the temperature of the atmosphere may be varied at pleasure; their gradual and almost imperceptible ascents, elevated plateaux, diversified by valleys and gentle declivities, possess a climate cool and invigorating.

The second-class islands present but few indications of volcanic phenomena; their rocks are chiefly a carbonate of lime, apparently solidified and rendered firm by exposure to the atmosphere, and the spacious caverns of some of them bear a strong resemblance to those of limestone countries elsewhere; their mountains and hills are usually rolling, and their elevation above the sea from 100 to 500 feet. The vegetation with which they are clothed embraces nearly every variety of that of the first-class islands, having a soil equally fertile, but usually they are destitute of harbors or convenient anchorage, and being of limited extent and somewhat isolated from the channels of commerce, they are merely visited for supplies by vessels that pass near them.

Of the third class or coral islands in this ocean, Tongatabu ranks first, being more than ninety miles in circumference, having a rich soil and a great variety of luxuriant vegetation; it possesses a good harbor, and its geographic position is such as to secure for it a transient commerce. The nebulæ of islands designated Paumotu, constituting the southeastern bound of Polynesia, are scattered over an extent of ocean about 1,000 miles from east to west and 600 from north to south ; they are chiefly low coral and lagoon islands, having a thin soil, with a vegetation restricted principally to the cocoanut and pandanus, which constitute the vegetable diet of the inhabitants. Eminent geologists have regarded them as the crests of submerged volcanoes, to which saxigenous polypes, or coral insects, have cemented their structures. These have continued to augment, until reaching the surface of the ocean, they are clothed with vegetation, as before described. The crater constitutes the tranquil basin or lagoon where the pearl-diver seeks his treasure. Some of these islands, when viewed at a distance, are exceedingly beautiful ; a quiet lake of varied tints is encircled by a belt of emerald green, bordered by a fringe of snowy breakers, where the waves are perpetually surging. Being generally destitute of harbors, navigation among them would be dangerous were it not for the steady easterly winds which prevail throughout the greater portion of the year, these islands being too low to influence them, as is the case with those of the first class, where there are alternations of land and sea breeze. The shores of most of them are singularly bold, and Mr. Dana, the geologist of the U. S. Exploring Expedition, makes the following remark relative to one of them :—

" These garlands of verdure seem to stand on the brims of cups, whose bases rest in unfathomable depths. Seven miles east of Clermont Tonnere, the lead ran out to 1,145 fathoms (6,870 feet) without reaching bottom. Within three-quarters of a mile of the southern point of this island, the lead, at another throw, after running out for a while, brought up in an instant at three hundred and fifty fathoms, and then dropped off again and descended to six hundred fathoms, without reaching bottom. The lagoons are generally shallow, though in the larger islands, soundings gave twenty to thirty-five, and even fifty and sixty fathoms."

Mr. Dana computes the entire area of coral islands or formations in this ocean to be 19,000 miles, though but one-eighth of this area is dry or habitable land.

Their commerce, together with that of similar islands within these imaginary limits, is confined chiefly to pearls, mother-of-pearl, and cocoanut oil, and thousands of tons of shells that have been gathered from them, prove it to be a lucrative enterprise to those who, with the requisite capital, have embarked in it. The depot for this fishery is Tahiti ; it is now completely monopolized by two or three merchants of that island, who have trading stations scattered throughout the group, and small vessels to convey the shells to Papeéte, whence they are shipped to Valparaiso, Australia, or England.

North and west of the Society Islands, and south of the equator, are numerous solitary islets, some of them sandy and uninhabited, but chiefly similar to those just described ; concerning some of them little is known, further than that they are inhabited by a race of hostile savages, as at Pennryhn and Savage Islands, in habit and language resembling the other tribes of Polynesia.

In the natural productions of the first-class islands there is a similarity, though some of them possess certain indigenous varieties. The bread-fruit, cocoanut, banana, plantain, yams, sweet potatoes, sugar-cane, and a variety of esculents, are common to all. For luscious fruits, the Georgian and Society Islands are noted ; in addition to those of other groups, they have the Brazilian plum and the delicious cherimoya, together with a profusion of the choicest oranges in the Pacific. The Sandwich Islands, however, enjoy the greatest variety and quantity of vegetable productions conducive to the wants of civilization, cultivating to a considerable extent the staples of other tropical countries. Among the forests of these groups are noticed a variety of trees, valuable for commercial purposes, as, the *koa*, or mahogany of the Hawaiian Islands, and the *tománu* (calophyllum) of the South Pacific, which sometimes attains an extraordinary growth ; it is solid and durable, and for strength, would be well adapted to ship-building ; from the tenacity with which it retains a nail or iron imbedded in it, it resembles the teak of the East Indies. These woods, together with several other varieties, are susceptible of a high polish, and are valuable for building purposes, or articles of furniture.

But few specimens of the animal kingdom were noticed by early voyagers ; these were confined chiefly to swine, dogs, and a few ornithological varieties. The waters of all abound in excellent fish, which are easily taken. A small species of lizard and centipedes appear to be common to all the groups ; and at the Samoan Islands are several species of snakes, also of vampire bats ; none of these, however, are venomous. The Samoan Islands possess a greater variety of game than any other island of this division. Here are several varieties of the turtle-dove, with exquisite plumage ; also water-hens, wood pigeons, wild ducks, paraquets, and a few other varieties of the feathered tribe. Vessels lying in the harbor of Apia may be abundantly supplied with wild pigeons by merely loaning a native a fowling-piece with ammunition. It is worthy of notice that at the Hawaiian and Samoan Islands alone are found owls.

The cattle, goats, and sheep, landed by Vancouver at the Sandwich Islands during the years 1793 and 1794, were *tabooed* for the ten years following ; the former propagated wonderfully, and for a considerable period their hides were an article of export. At the present day there are numerous herds and flocks roaming among the hills and mountains, and, to a limited extent, at the Tahitian Islands.

The following casual estimate of the population of these groups will approximate nearly to the truth :—Hawaiian Islands, 73,000 ; Samoan, 60,000 ; Georgian and Society, 14,000 ; Marquesas, 10,000 ; Tongatabu, 6,000, and the Hapai and Vavao groups adjoining, 5,000 ; Austral and Hervey Islands, 10,000 ; and the Paumotu and other low islands of this division, 5,000. The entire foreign or European population of Polynesia (excluding New Zealand) would not probably exceed 4,000, including French military and transient sojourners, and the grand total would only be equivalent to about one half the estimated population of the Sandwich Islands by Captain Cook, in 1778, seventy-six years ago. The causes that have tended towards this wholesale depopulation have been their wars, infanticide, sacrifices attending their idolatrous system of worship, and, above all, the contaminating influence of foreigners.

These natives, by their appearance, affinity of language, and rites and ceremonies, are indubitably of Malay origin. In complexion they are of a light copper color or olive brown, hair straight, curling, or wavy, and glossy black, with pleasing features and graceful in their physical contour. Males are often met with upward of six feet in height, in every respect models of symmetry, and with the bold, fearless gait that should characterize lords of the soil. The females are frequently graceful and delicate, but in applying to them the quality of beauty, the Caucasian standard of perfection must be disregarded. Our estimate of their attractions is associated with natural scenery, climate, their vivacity, inherent wit and hospitality—a combination of pleasing realities that bias a critical judgment, while lending favorable impressions. The Hawaiians perhaps make less pretension to superior charms than any other branch of the Polynesian family, while the Marquesans in personal attractions are unrivalled in the Pacific. A laxity of morals appears to be inherent, and is only partially restrained by the strong arm of the law among those groups that have the benefit of a Christian form of government; to the persevering efforts of English and American missionaries can alone be ascribed the preservation of the relic of a once numerous race. Possessing a fair intellectual capacity, they are quick to comprehend, but having naturally habits of indolence, the majority of South Sea Islanders are seldom inclined to profit by their instructions.

Many of the Hawaiians possess the advantage of a liberal education in the higher branches ; but with all their attainments, we look in vain for a literary production, a really intellectual labor, if we except the fragmentary evidences of poetic talent, and sound, almost logical argument. Of shrewd and quick perceptive faculties, many are qualified for the responsible stations they occupy in offices of State; but from existing evidences, we may infer that an era of national literature is vaguely in perspective.

For domestic economy and industry, the Hawaiians rank first, next the natives of Tongatabu, the Hervey and Austral Islands; while for the Samoans, Tahitians, and Marquesans, nature has been so prodigal of her bounties, that, instead of cultivating through necessity, as at the other groups, they derive an easy subsistence from the spontaneous products of the soil.

In noticing the language of the Polynesian family, reference must necessarily be had to New Zealand, although that extensive country has, for the sake of geographic, and perhaps political convenience, been recognized as one of the constituents of Australasia. It is remarkable that the dialects spoken at New Zealand, Hawaii, and the Marquesas, though respectively distant from each other 3,700, 2,200, and 3,200 miles, have so strong an affinity for each other, that the natives of one country find but little difficulty in holding verbal communication with those of the other, while the Samoans, situated nearly midway between New Zealand and Hawaii, speak a dialect quite distinct. It may seem a singular coincidence that the Samoan Islands, though distant 2,400 miles from the Hawaiian Islands, are the same in number, lie in the same direction, about w. n. w. and e. s. e., having the largest island at the extremity, which, like that of the Sandwich Islands, is called Savaii, the Samoans using the *s* instead of the *h*, and the *v* instead of the *w* of the Hawaiian dialect. Their language, by the frequent recurrence of the *l* and *s*, and the adoption of a soft nasal sound, the *ng* instead of the *k*, is more euphonious than any other spoken in the Pacific, and is to Polynesia what the Italian is to Europe, or the Malayan to the East Indies; it has also the peculiarity of being the only one that expresses an equivalent for *thank you*, (Taa fetai.)

The original language, or the one from which the dialects of the Polynesians is derived, is probably the Malaysian; that of the Hervey Islanders is more extensively spoken than any other, being used at a small group a long distance to the westward of those islands, and is also spoken throughout the Paumotu Archipelago as far as the Gambiers. Each group has usually a dialect of its own, but by their affinity for each other, all may be traced to a common origin.

The peculiarity of these dialects is their limited number of consonants, which do not exceed ten, while every word or syllable terminates with a vowel. Another remarkable feature is the absence of the auxiliary verbs *to be* and *to have*. In pronouns they are exceedingly rich, and which, together with their verbs, possess many nice distinctions. Their sentences are constructed with a grammatical precision that would hardly be supposed to exist in a savage dialect.

Having a better acquaintance with the Hawaiian than any other, though our knowledge of it is necessarily limited, a few examples of this dialect are offered; but owing to the absence of a vocabulary, or any work of reference whatever, it has been found necessary to draw from memory such items as are thought to be too forcibly impressed to admit of error. For even this slight insight into its structure, acknowledgments are due to an article from the pen of the Rev. Lorin Andrews, of Honolulu, that appeared in the "Hawaiian Spectator" many years since; also to the attentions of several members of the mission.*

The letters of the Hawaiian alphabet are twelve: A, E, I, O, U, H, K, L, M, N, P, and W, the vowels having the sound peculiar to the Spanish or Italian languages, while the consonants retain the English accent.

Two classes of nouns have been recognized, having reference, for the sake of euphony, to the definite article *the*, which, according to the nature of the case, is signified by *ke* or *ka*. The indefinite article *a* or *an*, is *he* before nouns of both classes, while *na* precedes and indicates the plural number. The nouns are indeclinable, their condition being signified by simply prefixing the requisite prepositions.

The same distinction is also observable among some of the pronouns preceding nouns; as, *kau* before those of the first class, and *kou* before those of the second class, both signifying *thine*. A singular feature of some of them is, that when the first letter or syllable is strongly aspirated, the signification of the word becomes the reverse of that of its root: as, *kau*, thine; *ka'u*, mine; *nau*, for thee; *na'u*, for me; *au*, of thee; *a'u*, of me, &c.

The following will exhibit the declension of the personal pronoun *au*, I, and the dual *máua*, we two:—

SINGULAR.		DUAL.	
Nom. Au,	*I.*	Nom. Máua,	*we two.*
Gen. O'u,	*of me.*	Gen. 6 Máua,	*of us two.*

* Since writing the above, the "Polynesian" has advertised the publication of a complete Grammar of the Hawaiian Language, from the pen of the Rev. Lorin Andrews. No person in the kingdom is better qualified for the delicate and erudite task of reducing a barbarous dialect to a written system of speech, and establishing the rules of syntax, thereby exhibiting at a glance its beauty and deformity. The reputation of the author will secure its worth as a literary production, and being the only concise and careful analysis of this dialect of Polynesia, it merits the attention of every philologist.

SINGULAR.			DUAL.		
DAT.	Ia'u,	*to me.*	DAT.	Ia máua,	*to us two.*
	No'u,	*for me.*		No máua,	*for us two.*
ACCU.	Au,	*me.*	ACCU.	Máua,	*we two.*
VOC.	——			&c.,	&c.
ABL.	Me'au,	*with me.*			
	Mai ou,	*from me.*			
	Eau,	*by me.*			

A possessive adjective pronoun may be formed from the above by pre-fixing the noun ; thus, instead of

Ko káua.móku, our ship, they say with equal propriety,

Ka móku o káua, the ship of us.

There are several forms of the demonstrative adjective pronoun, the most expressive of which are *ua—néi,* and *ua—la,* to which the Hawaiians give peculiar emphasis. A native might simply say,

Maikái no kéia kamalíi, this boy is good. But if he should express himself,

Maikái no UA *kamalíi* NEI, it would be equivalent to, this boy *here* is good.

The interrogative pronouns *owái,* who? *áha,* what? and *hea,* where? may be declined by simply applying the prefixes as in the preceding examples.

Adjectives are compared by affixing the diminutives *íki* and *ae,* and the augmentative *lóa :* as,

POSITIVE.	Maikái,	*good.*
	Maikái íki,	*a little better*
COMPARATIVE.	Maikái ae,	*better.*
	Maikái íki ae,	*better still.*
SUPERLATIVE.	Maikái lóa,	*best.*

The forms of the dual are four, and are as follows, with the plural to correspond :—

Káua, *we two.*

Máua, *we two,* (person addressed excluded.)

Olúa, *you two.*

Láua, *they two.*

PLURAL.

Kakóu, *we.*

Mákou, *we,* (person or persons addressed excluded.)

Okóu, *ye or you.*

Lákou, *they.*

Máua is equivalent to *he* and *I*, or the speaker and another person represented.

Káua is the person speaking and the single person addressed, or *thou* and *I*.

Mákou is equivalent to *they* and *I:* it is the person and those represented, amounting together to more than two, and excluding the person or persons addressed.

Kakóu, we, the person speaking and person or persons addressed, and whoever may be represented.

The people petitioning the king, or their Maker, would speak of themselves as "*Mákou;*" but if they intended the king should engage with them in some national enterprise or reform, they would say "*kakóu.*" The minister of religion, prefatory to a public prayer, says for "Let us pray," "*E vúle* KAKOU;" then looking heavenward, and including his auditory or fellow-worshippers as before, says, "*Ke púle nei* MAKOU."

Foreigners who can make themselves intelligibly understood in this language, are often ignorant of these nice distinctions, but with ready tact the Hawaiians easily comprehend them. They never ridicule an error of speech when it occurs in a stranger, and a natural delicacy prevents their correcting a mistake, unless requested to do so.

Officially, the kingdom is called *Hawaii nei*, or *Ko Hawaii nei Pae Aina;* but it would hardly be proper to use these designations abroad, as *nei* involves the idea of *present* as to *time* or *place*—as *here*, or *this* or *there*, applied to *things*, and *now* as applied to active feeling and state of being.

The Tahitians have no equivalent for the Hawaiian *alóha* (love), and it is not a little remarkable that a language containing a word applicable to either spiritual or sensual emotion, should be totally devoid of expressions implying either virtue or gratitude. This circumstance alone is a comment on national morality. When persons meet, the salutation is *alóha*, and when departing the same is exchanged. The phrase, or exclamation, *alóha ino !* is used by way of sympathy or commiseration ; *alóha maikái* is expressive of satisfaction or approval. In the interchange of salutations, strict reference is had to the requisite form of the personal pronouns.

Aúwe ! or *auwé !* is an exclamation of frequent recurrence ; according to emphasis, it is expressive of either joy, surprise, contempt, sorrow, or the most poignant grief.

The following paradigm of the verb *láwe*, to carry, in the indicative mode and active voice, may convey an idea of the nice distinctions observed in this part of speech, which are susceptible of ramification almost to infinity :—

ACTIVE VOICE, INDICATIVE MODE.

INFIN. Láwe, to carry.—PRES. PART. Láwe ana, carrying.—PAST PART. Ua láwe, carried.

	Singular		Dual		Plural	
PRESENT TENSE.						
1.	Ke lawe nei au,	I carry.	Ke lawe nei kaua,	we two carry.	Ke lawe nei kakou,	we carry.
2.	Ke lawe nei oe,	thou carriest.	Ke lawe nei maua,	we two carry.	Ke lawe nei makou,	we carry.
3.	Ke lawe nei ia,	he carries.	Ke lawe nei olua,	you two carry.	Ke lawe nei okou,	you carry.
			Ke lawe nei laua,	they two carried.	Ke lawe nei lakou,	they carry.
IMPERFECT.						
1.	I lawe au,	I did carry.	I lawe kaua,	we two did carry.	I lawe kakou,	we did carry.
PRESENT PERFECT.						
1.	Ua lawe, nei au,	I have just carried.	Ua lawe nei kaua,	we two have just carried.	Ua lawe nei kakou,	we have just carried.
PERFECT.						
1.	Ua lawe au,	I have carried.	Ua lawe kaua,	we two have carried.	Ua lawe kakou,	we have carried.
PLUPERFECT.						
1.	Ua lawe e au mamua,	I had carried.	Ua lawe e kaua mamua,	we two had carried.	Ua lawe e kakou mamua,	we had carried.
FIRST FUTURE.						
1.	E lawe au,	I will carry.	E lawe kaua,	we two will carry.	E lawe kakou,	we will carry.
SECOND FUTURE.						
1.	I lawe auanei au,	I will soon carry.	I lawe auanei kaua,	we two will soon carry.	E lawe auanei kakou,	we will soon carry.
THIRD FUTURE.						
1.	E lawe ana au,	I will carry now.	E lawe ana kaua,	we two will carry now.	E lawe ana kakou,	we will carry now.

25

The conditional mode is formed by prefixing *ina*, if, and rejecting certain particles, as the case may require ; as,

Ina láwe au, *if I carry.*

The passive voice is formed by adding the syllable *ia* to the root or verb ; as,

Ke láwe*ia*, nei au, *I am carried.*

Like the Hebrew, the Hawaiian has also a causative form of the verb, which is signified by *ho'o* : as,

Akaáka au, *I laugh.*
Hooakaáka au, *I am caused to laugh.*

In the Tahitian dialect this is denoted by haa ; as, *hére*, to go ; ʜᴀᴀ*hére*, to cause to go.

The syntax or construction of this language would involve too much prolixity for further digression ; a sentence from *Ka Elele Hawaii* is merely appended, with a literal translation :—

I ka la 29 o Iánu. ího nei, ma ke kulánakauhále o Wasinetóna, ma America
On the day 29 of Jan. came here, at the   city   of Washington, at America
Huipúia, ua máke he kanáka núi ma ia áina; O Henry Clay kóna inóa.—
United, (has) died a man great at that land ; — Henry Clay his name.—
Noláila, kaumáha na naáu o na kanáka a pau o kéla áina no kána (máke ána.)
Therefore, heavy the bowels of the men — all of that land for his dying.
(sorrowful)

Though by no means copious, this dialect is sufficiently comprehensive for Hawaiians to express their ideas, and even sentiments of a poetic character. The enunciation is rapid, which sometimes renders its acquisition difficult to foreigners ; the peculiar manner of emphasizing often renders it very expressive.

From the following specimens of Hawaiian poetry, it is not to be inferred that this people are more gifted than other branches of this great family ; they evidence the refining influence that civilization and mental culture may exert upon minds whose conceptions were the mere promptings or vagaries of ignorance and superstition. They are furnished by the Rev. Hiram Bingham. The first was pencilled as uttered by Kapioláni, a female of high rank ; and though wanting in metrical harmony, the circumstance in nowise detracts from the originality of sentiment or beauty of expression. It was suggested by the illiberal policy of Governor Adams with reference to the introduction or propagation of Christianity during the early years of the mission.

" Love to thee, my sister Waahila,
My sister Waahila, rain of Kona ;
In the days of Kanaloa, descending, gentle, and fine,

Enlarging the opening blossom of the *ohia*.
 Thou didst crown thyself with a rainbow coronet.
Richly adorned was the interior of Naniuapo,
Then flourished the shrubbery of Waiakekua.
 Thou playest a god to trample down without cause ;
Recklessly to confound the right policy.
The bud, the tender shoot, the stem is broken by thee ;
The shoot of that which is excellent and holy."

The following beautiful elegy was written in Hawaiian by a medical student named Hoohano, an intimate friend of the deceased. He died soon after. Mr. Bingham furnishes the following prefatory remarks :—

" Hawaiian poetry is not accurately measured, either in respect to the succession of feet, or the length of the lines ; nor did it exhibit prior to the introduction of sacred hymns by the missionaries any chiming at the end of the lines. As the Hawaiian songs were unwritten, and adapted to chanting rather than metrical music, a line was measured by the breath. Their *kopúna*, answering to our line, was as many words as could be easily cantillated at one breath.

" Though this piece has no more measure or chime than the compositions of the ancients or of Ossian, yet every line of it is *poetry*, and of no inferior order, compared with the ancient Greek or Latin odes. It is one of the many respectable specimens of poetic composition, among the instructed Hawaiians, of a Christian character and salutary tendency."

" Farewell to the beautiful flower of the Doctor's garden !
It has fallen and vanished away.
The flower that budded first did blossom fair ;
Its splendor was seen ; its fragrance exhaled ;
But the burning sun came, and it withered,
And that beautiful blossom has fallen !

The occupant of the garden then wondered
That a single flower should have fallen ;
He sought it, but found it not again ; it was gone ;
It had perished ; it had mingled with the dust.
Alas ! What a pity for the flower-plants,
Which grow up well, and lo ! they are withered.
All the flowers bowed their heads, smelling the fragrance ;
They stood around in great sorrow.
Alas ! alas ! O my blossom that has fallen !

The chief tenant inquired of his landlord,
' What thinkest thou concerning this flower
Which thou didst plant in my border ?'
The Lord replied,
' I have taken away the image of all its glory ;
Its bud has fallen, and is mingled with the dust.'

How beautifully did the plants flourish !
Compassion great for the tenant resident,
Mourning and searching with great lamentation !
' Whither, O Gérrita, hast thou gone ?

When wilt thou return to thy birthmates!
Alone hast thou gone in the way that is lonely;
Thou hast gone a stranger by an unknown path.'

O Gérrita! Gérrita! Behold we all
Are falling flowers, and soon shall fall;
Where art thou! Go thou, and be a kind welcomer for us all.
O Gérrita! Gérrita! thou goest at the pleasure of thy Lord,
And none can forbid thy design. Go thou,
Travel on, until thou art wholly gone, along the lonesome pathway;
Then ascend the ladder of God,
And pass within the glorious walls of Jerusalem;
And enter into the peace of God's kingdom.

Thou art singing hymns with good angels;
A never-ceasing employment is thy employment there.
O Gérrita! Gérrita!
Deeply we mourn that we cannot behold thee;
Forever hast thou gone from our sight,
And wilt return hither no more."

The government and social condition of the inhabitants of these groups remain next to be noticed. Again Hawaii stands pre-eminent; and as a free and independent kingdom, has taken her place among nations. In this comparatively insignificant state, the advantages and benefits of civil and religious institutions accord more fully with our views of national worth than the boasted privileges of more pretending principalities. Industry and commerce have been encouraged. the customs of the old despotic system abolished, and with spiritual instruction for guidance and the secular arm for support, a nation has emerged from obscurity to enjoy the blessings of civilization and freedom.

France controls the destinies of the Georgian Islands, Tahiti and Mooréa, under the name of Protectorate. Pomare is nominally the queen, but without a shadow of power; and the assumption of regal pageantry, to which humiliation she is occasionally subjected, is merely a dumb show or political farce, for the gratuitous entertainment of her former subjects. It is to be regretted that so powerful a nation as France, having assumed the specious title of "Protectorate" over the vestige of a once numerous people, should deem the establishment of a military conscription paramount to the advantages of civil institutions which would tend to improve its condition. The natives are prone to indolence, and to a certain extent its attendant evils, though a more hospitable and friendly race are not to be found in Polynesia.

Of the social condition and domestic habits of the Society Islanders, hints have already been given. Their days of prosperity have gone by; many of those who once cultivated the small plantations scattered throughout the group, have either perished in repelling French aggression, wandered abroad, or passed away. The evidences of their industry may be witnessed in the dilapidated mills and tenements, and once culti- vated fields, now covered by the spreading guava. The worst feature of that conflict is the warlike propensity bequeathed to, or awakened in the natives, who are frequently distracted by domestic dissension, and whose only arbiters are their muskets. Raiatéa and Borabóra have kings, and Huahíne and Maupíti queens ; the chiefs of all possess but little authority. Each island is independent of the other, having a simple code of written laws adapted to its wants.

The sway of France is also claimed for the Paumotu Archipelago and the Marquesas Islands, but it is mere assumption : at the former, many of the islands are inhabited by savages that defy any attempts of foreigners towards friendly intercourse. The Marquesas are of less extent and geographic importance than any of the first-class groups. They possess but few harbors ; their mountainous and almost inaccessible ridges are shaded by groves of sandal-wood, and their narrow valleys, bounded by precipitous hills and spire-like mountains, are peopled by a race of savages, the fairest and most graceful in their physical contour, and at once the most vicious and warlike in their propensities of any in Polynesia. In some of their secluded valleys, the abode of superstition, cannibal orgies are celebrated. Their intercourse with vessels that have occasionally touched there for supplies has been attended with few beneficial results, and hardly a day passes without a conflict between two opposing tribes in some portion of the group. Each valley possesses its king and chiefs ; the superstitions of the *taboo* are in full force—the chief weapons, muskets and spears.

It will be recollected that the occupation of these islands by the French was abandoned a few years since, but for political reasons has been sub- sequently resumed. Their actual possession amounts simply to a cir- cumscribed fortification on Nuheva, the principal island, and beyond the reach of its guns it would be unsafe for a person wearing the imperial uniform to venture ; nor can they exhibit a shadow of power in any other portion of the group, unless among a limited number of con- verts of Romish priests. Their nervousness is extreme at the appear- ance of a vessel designing to trade with the natives ; and their restrictions, when they can enforce them, amount to a prohibition, for the only ar- ticles of traffic desired by the Marquesans are those by law made con- traband, muskets and ammunition. Usually, a frigate and a land-force of fifty or a hundred men are stationed there.

The Marquesans are a shade lighter in complexion than the Tahitians, and the fairest and most comely of any natives in the Pacific—the men strong and athletic, their faces disfigured by tattooing, a practice common at these islands. The females are fascinating, being delicate and of symmetrical form, their features animated with seductive smiles. Their hands are often fantastically tattooed, and frequently four or five delicate lines are traced upon the under lip, which in nowise detract from their beauty.

At the Samoan Islands there is no acknowledged king or supreme power, each chief ruling in his own district. An inconsiderable portion of these islands only have been converted to Christianity; and, as at Savaii, many of the inhabitants in their habits and customs approximate to their former heathenism, and are frequently harassed by a predatory warfare. Upólu is the principal island, on account of its excellent harbors, one of which, Apía, is the chief station or nucleus of missionary efforts. A monthly paper is published here, called the *Samoan Reporter,* containing chiefly notices of the mission, and local intelligence. The natives in appearance resemble the Tahitians, but are more modest in their deportment; and those professing Christianity are the most exemplary in the Pacific, for here the marriage rite is respected.

At Tongatabu the natives have been converted to Christianity by the Wesleyan missionaries; through necessity industrious, they are, like the Samoans, more exemplary in their morals than the natives of the Hawaiian or Tahitian Islands. The chiefs are elected, and their power limited, while the government of the Hapai and Vavao groups adjoining is despotic.

The Hervey Islands have their kings or chiefs of districts; these natives have also been reclaimed from idolatry by the London Missionary Society, and no happier picture of domestic comfort and tranquillity can be witnessed than that exhibited in their present social condition.

These islands are seven in number, and their aggregate extent of surface is about 200 square miles; by judicious instruction, aided by their somewhat isolated position, being 500 miles west of the Society Islands, and absence of harbors for commercial convenience, their inhabitants, for habits of industry and correctness of moral deportment, are, like the Tongatabuans, equally exemplary. Being of the second-class islands, (according to the distinction given,) their gradually sloping hills and fertile valleys are well adapted to agricultural pursuits, and their fruitful groves are frequently relieved by smiling cultivations tastefully laid out. It is remarkable that at this insignificant group more small coasting vessels are built and launched than at the Tahitian Islands.

The Austral Islands, of nearly equal extent, are the southernmost of Central Polynesia, some of them extending beyond the tropic of Capricorn. With reference to social condition, the observations on the Hervey Islands will apply to these, though the natives are less advanced in civilization.

The final and most important considerations relative to these islands, groups or archipelagoes, are their natural advantages and resources, trade or commerce, and their geographic and political worth. Not the least important feature are their facilities for intercommunication afforded by the almost uniform winds and excellent harbors; the prevailing winds within the southern tropic vary from east to southeast, while north of the equator, and within the tropic of Cancer, they are from east to northeast; within these ranges the current sets slowly to the westward. The harbors consist of indentations or bays in the land, but are often formed by massive barriers of coral, with safe and easy entrances; and many maritime nations might envy these atoms of earth their havens of safety. A fertile soil watered by numerous streams, having suitable mill sites, a salubrious and almost uniform climate, and the absence of venomous reptiles, are a combination of advantages seldom met with in other lands. If for resources we look simply to their spontaneous productions, they will be limited indeed; for groves of sandal-wood and choice varieties of timber can exist only for a season, should convenience and necessity render them articles of commerce. With reference to the former, the Marquesas Islands alone yield sandal-wood to any extent, and these groves will probably long continue to flourish undisturbed, on account of their remoteness from the Chinese market, about 6,000 miles, and the difficulty of inducing natives to procure it, as it grows on elevated and almost inaccessible ridges. This staple commodity for China is usually procured from the New Hebrides and islands adjacent, also from the northern and western coasts of Australia. It exists in considerable quantities in the vicinity of Swan River, on the southwest coast, as far south as latitude 32°, and was by the early settlers frequently consumed as fuel, being ignorant of its properties or value. From this point these groves, with various intervals, extend towards the north; and we have been informed by an American shipmaster, for many years a resident at Swan River, and who on his own account has visited many unexplored points on this coast, and has been engaged in the trade between China, Singapore and Australia, that a cargo of this wood procured from the vicinity of Swan River brings a less price in Hong Kong than that obtained farther north, so expert are the Chinese dealers, who have no knowledge of its locality; and this circumstance, among others, shows that this tree requires a tropical climate to attain perfection.

The valuable timber of their forests may in future years prove far more profitable, but at the present time the expense and difficulty of procuring it, and the want of a suitable market, where the manufacture of furniture will be found cheaper than its importation, are obstacles in the way of its becoming an article of commerce—at least for the present. It unfortunately happens that the most valued specimens are frequently found growing in almost inaccessible localities, and those familiar with the general aspect of volcanic countries may form an idea of the difficulty of obtaining it. Logs are usually converted into boards by means of pitsaws; and to a limited extent, and for ordinary purposes, beautifully variegated and substantial specimens may be procured at reasonable rates, susceptible of a high polish, and which, if fashioned into ornamental furniture, would gratify the most fastidious taste of the boudoir.

Since these islands possess no available mineral wealth, it is obvious that their prosperity is to be found in agricultural developments; this applies chiefly to the Hawaiian, Georgian, Society, and Samoan Islands. The principal varieties of the indigenous fruits of Polynesia are common to all, but in addition to these, various other tropical fruits, and vegetables of the temperate zone, have been introduced, and thrive as if in parent soil. Among these are the orange, lemon, lime, fig, grape, pineapple, cherimoya, guava, coffee, cotton, tobacco, indigo, mandioca, &c., together with a variety of esculents, and at the Hawaiian Islands, the Irish potato, the only group of Polynesia where it can be procured. Of domestic animals, horses, asses, cattle, goats, sheep, (swine are indigenous,) and numerous varieties of poultry, have been introduced, and which in some of the islands have extensively propagated.

At present, the staple exports of the Hawaiian kingdom are, sugar, coffee, syrup, hides, potatoes and vegetables, and, to a limited extent, fruits, together with an annual surplus of imported merchandise. Those of the Georgian and Society Islands are, oranges, lime-juice, cocoanuts, pearls, mother-of-pearl from the Paumotu fishery, and, in small quantities, arrow-root and cocoanut oil; while the Samoan, Marquesas, Hervey, and Austral Islands, are visited only for recruits, or cargoes of swine and poultry, and smaller items of trade. With the exception of the pearl-shell and cocoanut oil, which are shipped to England and Sydney, the other exports are conveyed chiefly by American traders to the California market.

For the growth of coffee and sugar-cane, those staple products of intertropical countries, the soil of all these islands is well adapted, as results have shown. Thousands of acres are lying uncultivated, which, with proper attention bestowed upon them, would yield ample and profitable returns, and the peculiar richness of the soil obviates the necessity of annual manuring for years to come. At the Hawaiian Islands, an estate may be purchased in fee-simple, but at the Tahitian Islands the natives are averse to selling their lands, though, what is equivalent, they will furnish a transferable lease for any term of years, with the privilege of renewal *ad libitum*, and that for a sum comparatively trifling.

The thought of parting with their lands forever is unpleasant to them; but taking into account the present decrease of population and their short-sightedness, a lease may be so drawn that at the period of its expiration both heirs and assigns will have ceased to exist.

It may be safely asserted that these groups will never be reclaimed from their present condition by the race that now inhabits them. The experiment has been fairly and thoroughly tested, backed by plausible theories, and the most favorable results are witnessed at Hawaii. To inherent indolence and lack of energy, noticeable throughout the entire Polynesian family, must be added its rapid numerical decrease—a circumstance alone that confirms the assertion. But a remedy is happily at hand; the tens of thousands of poverty-stricken laborers that throng the Asiatic shores, known as Chinese and Lascar coolies, furnish the desired substitute. Together with African slaves, they have developed the resources of the Isles of France and Bourbon in the Indian Ocean, and are indispensable to the prosperity of the English, Spanish, and Dutch East India possessions. The Lascars are milder in disposition, tractable, and more easily managed than the Chinese. Recourse has been had to this experiment at the Sandwich Islands in 1851, and subsequently. Those imported were from Amoy. Parties contracting for them pay from fifty to sixty dollars for the passage of each, after engaging them for a term of years at the nominal sum of two or three dollars per month. To a considerable extent, they have been exported to Peru, to labor amid the guano fields of the Chincha Islands, where mercenary speculators have reduced them to a worse than Egyptian bondage. It has been surmised that the French have entertained this project of introducing them at Tahiti, and which, if put into execution, will be the first creditable enterprise that will have attended their conquests in this ocean. For the cultivation of their chief article of food, rice, the Tahitian and Society Islands possess better natural facilities than any others; broad tracts of low and swampy land frequently occur near the shore, and the formation of their valleys admit of irrigation to any extent. Rice planted at Raiatéa by way of experiment, thrived remarkably, though unaided in its growth by the systematic attention which the Chinese are accustomed to bestow upon its cultivation. For present purposes this commodity may be procured from the island of Bali, off the eastern coast of Java, one of the East Indian magazines, for the trifling sum of one half cent to two cents per pound.

The commerce of the Hawaiian and Tahitian Islands is greater than would at first be supposed from their comparatively limited extent and partially developed resources. This is derived chiefly from the immense whaling fleet in this ocean, trading vessels, and those sailing between

California and Australia, and are resorted to by them as convenient resting-points.

In alluding to the principal tracks of commerce across the Pacific Ocean, it may be necessary to premise, for the convenience of those unacquainted with the nautical phenomena influencing navigation, that although the direct distance from point to point is given, it is necessarily increased by reference to prevailing winds and currents. For example, the port of San Francisco is in lat. 37° 48′ N., lon. 122° 21′ W., and Shanghai is in lat. 30° 1′ N., lon. 122° 6′ E., and the shortest distance between them is 5,400 miles, but owing to the westerly winds prevailing without the tropics, vessels sailing from the former to the latter port would proceed in a southwest direction towards the Sandwich Islands, and sail westward within the tropics, in a course from eight to twelve hundred miles south of the direct line of distance, and when within about 2,000 miles of the China coast, steer gradually to the northward. The distance from San Francisco to the Sandwich Islands is about 2,100 miles, and from thence to Shanghai 4,400 miles, and allowing for necessary deviations, a distance of more than 7,000 miles is traversed in sailing from one port to the other. On their return, an opposite course is pursued, vessels steering to the northeast; those from Hong Kong through the Formosa Channel, and along the coast towards Chusan, if the monsoon will permit, or south of Formosa and between the Ladrone and Bonin Islands. A circular course of sailing is found to be the most expeditious in abridging space, and for the benefit of strong westerly winds, vessels sometimes sail as far as lat. 44° N. on the return voyage.

Honolulu, with comparatively slight deviation, is situated in the track of many important routes, besides being in itself a depot of considerable importance; it lies in lat. 21° 19′ N., and lon. 157° 52′ W. From San Francisco to China, from the former port to Australia, no great deviation is required, and it is directly in the proposed route of steamers from Panama to Shanghai, being distant from the former port 4,500 miles. Its distance from Valparaiso is 5,760 miles, and from Sydney, 4,440 miles. The ports of the kingdom of which it is the capital, constitute the nucleus of our whaling fleet in this ocean. Independent of their regular intercourse with America, England, and the various maritime countries bordering on the Pacific, they are frequently visited by transient trading vessels.

Since the discovery of the Tahitian Islands by Captain Wallis, in 1767, they have continued up to the period of their conquest by the French without any important commercial or political change; but the golden discoveries in California and Australia, attended by the impetus given to commercial enterprise and its almost incredible results, will have a tendency to render this heretofore isolated group of greater importance. The harbor of Papeéte, in lat. 17° 31′ S., lon. 149° 34′ W., is situated in a direct line between Panama, that thoroughfare of nations, and South Australia, and is about midway between the two. Persons designing to visit Australia by the Isthmus, are ordinarily compelled to reach it by the way of San Francisco, distant from Panama 3,240 miles, which being 6,500 miles from Sydney, occasions a detour from the direct route of about 2,000 miles, attended by additional expense and delay. The "Australian Direct Steam Navigation Company," with a capital of £1,000,000 in 40,000 shares of £25 each, have established a route from England to that colony, and which it is contemplated will soon be in operation. The route proposed is from Milford Haven to Aspinwall, distance 4,500 miles ; transit of Isthmus, 46 miles ; from Panama to Tahiti, 4,488 miles, and from thence to Sydney 3,351 miles, making an aggregate distance of 12,385 miles, which it is proposed to accomplish with steamers of 3,000 tons burden in 55 days, giving an average rate of speed, including stoppages, of about 225 miles per day.

As a coaling depot for this route, no better than Tahiti could be selected : its safe and spacious harbor, convenience for obtaining supplies, and facilities unsurpassed by any other port in the Pacific for procuring pure fresh water from the mountains, are its chief recommendations. A few days, the necessary interval required for recruiting, passed among its groves and shady walks, could not fail to be agreeable to passengers, and a charm would be imparted to the otherwise monotonous voyage.

The only objection that could possibly arise as to adopting this island for a depot would be the anticipation of political discord between England and France, a contingency which it is hoped may continue invisibly remote. In this event, the island of Raiatéa, next in extent, and one hundred miles west, having the most extensive and accessible harbor in Polynesia, may offer equal facilities. Owing to its numerous passages or channels through the reef, vessels may enter and depart with a leading wind. It has been suggested that steamers may possibly touch at the Gambier group instead, constituting the southeastern extremity of the Dangerous Archipelago, but this group has nothing to recommend it for such a depot, unless steamers should deem it expedient to deviate from a straight course for the convenience of westerly winds. They are under French dominion, about 800 miles s. e. of the direct route, and are circumscribed in extent, being comparatively low islands ; excepting a good harbor, they have nothing further to recommend them.

The coals for these island stations will be procured chiefly from Australia. Previous to the discovery of gold in that country, they could be

purchased for about $8.00 per ton ; but subsequently, since the laborers
in the copper and coal mines, together with the majority of the laboring
classes, have turned their attention to the accumulation of wealth among
the auriferous lands, the price of labor has been greatly enhanced, and
has had a corresponding effect upon the price of coal, so that for the last
two years it could not be delivered from the port of Papeéte for less than
$28.00 or $30.00 per ton.   A steamer that sailed from California for Melbourne during the early part of last year, by the way of Tahiti and
Sydney, was compelled to disburse, including outfit, $27,000 before reach-
ing her port of destination, while her receipts for passage money did not
exceed $18,000. We noticed in May last an agent of the French Protec-
torate in Melbourne, contracting for coals in anticipation of the arrival
of steamers.   If purchased at that time, the original cost, together with
freighting to Tahiti, will render them too expensive to entertain a hope
for profitable steam voyaging, if companies are to depend on the French
Government for supplies.   A company should have its own depot,
purchase its own coals, and either own or charter vessels for carrying
them.

Tahiti is frequently visited by vessels from California to Australia,
and *vice versa*, the wind being favorable both ways.   To the latter port,
they are favored by easterly winds until after crossing the southern
tropic ; on their return, it is found expedient to sail almost due east,
near the 30th parallel of south latitude, and to cross the tropic either
in the vicinity of the Austral Islands, or farther east towards Pit-
cairn's Island.   Between Valparaiso and Tahiti there is considerable intercourse, the distance being about 4,200 miles.   The distance from
Papeéte to Honolulu is 2,350 miles, and between the two there is a transient trade in surplus merchandise.

In position and natural advantages, the Navigator Islands have much
to recommend them, lying almost in a direct line from San Francisco to
Sydney.   The distance from the former port to the harbor of Apía, in lat
13° 49' S., lon. 171° 41' W., is 4,140 miles, and thence to Sydney, 2,400
miles.   These islands, 1,200 miles west of Tahiti, are independent,
the policy of European governments having as yet deemed them unworthy of notice.   Should a line of steamers be established between
the two ports above mentioned, a depot at these islands would tend
greatly towards bringing into notice the thousands of acres of valuable
land now lying unimproved, and which must ultimately prove the basis
of their future worth.   Since the emigration from California to Australia
has increased so rapidly, they have been frequently visited by passenger
vessels, and, as heretofore, by American whalers.

In noticing the regular channels of commerce, we must not overlook the small trading vessels that cruise among the groups of this ocean for pearl and tortoise shell, sandal-wood, *biche de mer*, cocoanut oil, stock, &c., all combining to link together this island-world.

Since the preceding was written, no movement on the part of either established or projected companies would imply that the enterprise of Pacific Steam Navigation between the East and Western Continents is at present deemed practically feasible. The immense emigration from Australia to California and *vice versa*, also from China to the latter port, has in a measure subsided. Our clipper ships, of remarkable speed, aided by scientific discoveries which materially abridge time and space, testify their adequacy to commercial necessities, and the expense attending the transportation of either freight or passengers is trifling in comparison when applied to steamers. However, the recent discovery of coal mines on the Pacific coast may change the aspect of affairs. In the vicinity of Valparaiso, a valuable bed of this indispensable has been found, and contractors have offered to furnish it at the almost unprecedented low price of six dollars per ton. The recent opening of Japan, where coal is said to exist in abundance, may alter materially the present means of intercommunication.

The following paragraph from a foreign paper appears to be a scientific embodiment of facts upon this subject; showing that the present overland route to China is the most expeditious, until the construction of a railroad across our continent, which is destined to revolutionize the present channels of commerce :—

"At a meeting of the members of the British Association for the Advancement of Science, held at Hull, on the 14th September, the Rev. C. G. Nicolay discoursed, in the geographical and ethnological section, upon the importance of certain places in the Pacific with reference to great circle routes across that ocean.

"The general want of appreciation of great circle sailing is evidenced by the routes selected by steam packet companies, both to the east and to the west. This has arisen from the habitual disk of Mercator's projection. To facilitate the consideration of the subject, a stereographic chart of the Pacific, showing the lineal concentricity of its shores, has been constructed ; great circles have been laid down on a Mercator's chart, between many of the most important places in the world, and tables of distances have been completely calculated. From these the distances involved in the Pacific route to Australia, *via* the Isthmus of Panama, appear to be, from Land's-End to Panama, 4,369 geographical miles ; from Panama to Sydney, 7,680 miles ;—making altogether 12,049 miles. But from the Land's-End to Hobart Town, *via* the Cape of Good Hope, is only 11,200 miles— 849 miles shorter. The facilities afforded on the route from Panama are, however, great. The Galapagos Islands, where the existence of coal is reported, afford a refuge from the horrible climate of the Isthmus, and they offer every advantage for a depot. The steam company formed for the purpose of effecting communication by this route, proposes Tahiti as the intermediate depot, but Tahiti lies far out of the shortest track, and is dangerous of access from the east. Easter Island lies nearest the direct line, and, if its harbor be sufficient, is well suited in other respects.

"The Sandwich Islands present themselves as the most important insular position in the North Pacific. They are distant respectively from Vancouver's Island, 2,293 miles; San Francisco, 2,083; Central America, 4,023; Callao, 5,060; Valparaiso, 5,905; Japan, 3,853; Chusan, 5,301; Singapore, 5,832; Sydney, 3,500; Auckland, 3,817.

"The conclusions come to by Mr. Nicolay are, that what is now called the overland route to China ought to be the most rapid, until one is opened across North America. That by the Cape has the next preference, while the advantages of that by Panama are almost exclusively confined to the Southern States of the Union and the West Indies; and with respect to them, it will be superseded by the overland route. British Northwest America, Mr. Nicolay considers more favorably situated than any other part of the coast in the Pacific for commanding the trade of that ocean; and the establishment of rapid communication with it, and the development of its resources, are, therefore, objects of the first importance."

APPENDIX II.

THE ISLAND KINGDOM OF THE NORTH PACIFIC.

Territorial Extent—Comparison with Cuba instituted—Natural Conformation—Soil and Pro-
ductions — Climate and attendant Phenomena—Chief Towns — Inter-Communication—
Steam Navigation—Statistics for 1853—National Legislature—Imports—Exports—Rev-
enue, &c. —Whale Fishery — Department of Interior — Public Instruction—Finance—
Foreign Relations—Census—Agriculture—Value of Staple Commodities—Sugar Planting
—Retrospective View of Statistics—Annexation Considered—Comparison of Results—
Capability of Hawaiians—American Politics and Interests Predominant — Prospective
National Decrease—Policy of European Nations—The Independence or Possession of
these Islands Important to the United States—Conclusion.

HAWAII, as a kingdom, merits a greater degree of attention than the
casual and imperfect remarks of the preceding chapter. But having already trespassed beyond original limits, a brief allusion only is proposed
to its geography, resources, and commercial relations, and offer perhaps, a remark on the contingency of its ultimately becoming an integral
portion of our confederacy. No other nation exists whose laws, interests,
and to a certain extent social relations, have so strong an affinity for our
own. Already have the varied classes of society, and even opposing
factions, manifested a unity of sentiment on the absorbing topic of political union with the State that has guided their own to maturity. There
is no other nation in whose behalf American sympathies have been so
strongly and deservedly enlisted. Yet, so long as the sacred obligations
of international law are respected, no fostering aid is requisite; possessing in itself the elements of prosperity, Hawaii needs only the enactments of a liberal government to move like a sphere in its orbit through
the system of nations.

Hawaii nei, or the kingdom of Hawaii, consists of eight habitable
islands : Hawaii, (the largest, and from which its name is derived,) Máui,
Oáhu, Kauái, Molokái, Lanái, Niiháu, and Kahuláwe. In addition to
these are the rocky and insignificant islets, Lehúa, Molokíni, and Kaúla.
These islands lie in the North Pacific Ocean, in an E. S. E. and W. N. W.
direction, between the parallels of 18° 50' and 22° 20' N. lat., and between

the meridians of 154° 55′ and 160° 15′ lon. W. from Greenwich. Combining agricultural with commercial importance, they rank as follows: Oáhu, Máui, Hawaii, and Kauái, all of which have foreign ports of entry. Though portions of Molokái are unsurpassed in fertility, a broad and desolate tract stretches away on the north and west. Lanái, except in some of its valleys and upon its summit, which is densely wooded, is adapted only to grazing. Niiháu, though smaller, is more fertile. Kahuláwe is barren, and tenanted almost exclusively by wild goats. It has been used as a penal abode. The altitude of the summits of these islands (save the two latter) ranges from not less than 1,500 to 14,000 feet. Their superficial area, &c., has been estimated as follows :—

Name.	Length. Miles.	Breadth. Miles.	Height in ft.	Square miles.
Hawaii	88	90	14,000	4,000
Máui.	48	29	10,000	600
Oáhu..............	46	23	4,000	520
Kauái	33	28	5,000	520
Molokái..............	40	9	2,800	170
Lanái	20	12	1,600	100
Niiháu..............	7	7	800	80
Kahuláwe..............	11	8	200	60

This exhibits an aggregate area of about 6,000 square miles.

As Hawaii and Cuba, at the present day, furnish topics of political interest, a very brief comparison is instituted ; though geographically important, the entire group is inferior to Cuba in extent and resources. Were these islands joined to each other in a direct line, their aggregate length would be less than 300 miles, and their greatest breadth, 90 miles ; the same estimate applied to the other would be 800 and 130 miles. As the group exists, the extremes of Hawaii and Kauái are distant from each other about 350 miles. The superficial area of Cuba is more than seven times greater than that of Hawaii ; the former country favors the construction of railroads, while the natural formation and commerce of the latter will neither admit nor require them. To institute a comparison between the exports and imports of Hawaii and that of a country whose revenue is nearly $10,000,000 per annum, is deemed superfluous, for while the one has had an economic existence for centuries, the other has barely emerged from infancy.

Comparatively a small proportion of the 6,000 square miles of this kingdom is arable land, though its extent can be greatly augmented, owing to facilities for irrigation and other advantages. Except that of Honolulu, these islands possess no harbors where safe anchorage may be obtained for-vessels during all winds, though at nearly every important point the material exists, aided by the natural conformation of the shore, to construct artificial ones. Eligible mill sites are abundant throughout the group, but there are no streams navigable for other than boats, and this for only a short distance.

At times, the shores are singularly bold, and again they recede gradually from the sea, with an almost imperceptible ascent, for thousands of feet. Nowhere do they exhibit the low swampy lands, liable to overflow from the sea, that are witnessed among other islands in this ocean. By artificial means, valleys and level tracts are irrigated for the cultivation of the staple article of native diet, *taro ;* these localities are equally adapted to the cultivation of rice. The soil is of every variety, from unsurpassed fertility to that of the most barren and worthless description ; perhaps no group in the Pacific, proportionably to extent of territory, will display so broad an area of waste land.

The soil, having reference to locality, will yield every description of tropical products, as is sufficiently proved by a large family of exotics, which would almost be regarded as indigenous. As observed elsewhere, this group possesses natural advantages for rearing plants of the temperate zone, where they can be easily accessible. This is owing to the conformation of the elevated lands, which are either inclined planes, or a rolling surface of gentle slopes. Fruit-trees, grains, and a variety of esculents have been introduced, and in these upland districts thrive as if in parent soil. This applies almost exclusively to Hawaii and Máui.

The climate, if equalled, is certainly unsurpassed by that of any other portion of the globe, for it exists in every variety—dry, moist, and with every gradation of heat and cold, from the torrid to the frigid zones. In explanation of the first, it will be necessary to state that the principal islands would present two broad distinctions in a summary of meteorological observations : these are the natural phenomena peculiar to their " windward" and " leeward" portions. By the former are meant those districts exposed to the full sweep of the N. E. trade-winds ; and by the latter, such as are sheltered from them. Condensed vapors of the ocean are borne along as clouds, that gather around lofty summits like a vast reservoir, and, bursting, shed perennial showers over the land, which clothe it with dense forests and a mantle of perpetual verdure ; from the mountains gurgle innumerable rills, and larger streams, sometimes swelling to torrents, rush foaming and leaping from crag to crag, or in eddying floods, roar through the dark ravines. Thus, while the windward portions have a surfeit of moisture, the leeward districts are frequently parched with drought, and only recover their natural freshness during the winter months or rainy season, which, with frequent intermission, continues for about four months, while during the remaining

26

eight months the weather is almost uniformly fine. The average temperature of the eastern sides is about 72° Fah.; and for the western, at least four degrees should be added. During the winter months the thermometer sometimes indicates 60°, and continues so for several days. This applies to lands bordering the sea-shore; by ascending the mountains, almost any degree of temperature may be obtained.

The principal towns of this kingdom are as follows: Honolulu, the capital, island of Oáhu; Lahaina, Máui; Hilo, Hawaii; and Hanalei and Waimea on Kauai. Though Kawaíhaé and Kealakekúa are ports of entry, they merit no consideration as towns, being merely channels for the surplus produce of Hawaii. The mountain villages, such as Waimea, Ulupalakúa, Makawáo, &c., are few; they consist usually of a limited number of native families residing in the immediate vicinity of a foreigner's estate. As our States are divided into counties, these islands are portioned into districts, whose bounds (frequently with great irregularity) radiate chiefly from the centre to the sea; subdivisions are native hamlets or villages; every *land* or locality, however insignificant, possesses its name. Communication between these towns or districts of an island is by sea and land; recourse is frequently had to the former, when bad roads and natural obstructions render a land journey fatiguing. Except by water, there are no public conveyances; unless in the vicinity of Honolulu, travelling is performed almost exclusively on horseback. Honolulu is the nucleus of these inter-island routes; a foreigner or native speaks of going from a distant portion of the kingdom to the capital, as a citizen of the United States would of visiting New-York. Between Honolulu and Lahaina (seventy-five miles) packets perform trips regularly, while numerous coasters are constantly visiting other portions of the group, as freight or passage may offer. Recently, December 19th, 1853, a company of five persons have received a charter under the name of "The Hawaiian Steam Navigation Company." Liberal privileges have been granted, and with certain restrictions, (including the provision that another steamer of at least 350 tons burden, in addition to the one already employed, shall navigate Hawaiian waters within twelve months from the date of charter,) the company receives the exclusive monopoly of steam navigation among these islands for ten years. This new feature of commercial enterprise is regarded with interest by all, as another evidence of national prosperity. In addition to the regular packets plying between San Francisco and Honolulu, and the annual visits of the whaling fleet, the islands have commercial relations with the principal maritime cities of Europe and America.

Without comment upon the growth of Hawaiian commerce, the following summary of statistics, compiled from official reports, pubished by the *Polynesian*, will exhibit at a glance the commercial and financial condition of these islands. It may be premised, that the sudden increase of imports and domestic exports during the year 1850, beyond those of preceding years, was owing to the unprecedented immigration into California that followed the discovery of the gold-placers.

The National Legislature assembled on the 5th of April, 1854. The House of Nobles has 25 members, including the king, queen, and four ministers, of whom three are foreigners ; the remaining members are native. The Lower House has 27 members, including 8 foreigners.

STATISTICS FOR THE YEAR 1853.

The value of foreign imports is $1,281,951.18 ; value of foreign goods re-exported, $191,397.66 ; value of domestic exports, $281,599.17; revenue, $326,620 ; disbursements, $265,795.

Total dutiable imports, $1,160,355.13 ; duty free, $79,402.80 ; entered in bond, $16,284.35 ; withdrawn from bond for consumption, $25,908.90, giving the total value as above.

Of the dutiable goods, $587,770.29 were from the Atlantic States ; and $367,149.64 from the Pacific side, or California and Oregon. From China the imports were $42,056.36 ; from Chili, $38,090.30 ; Great Britain, $20,471.74 ; Bremen, $12,225.91 ; Philipine Islands, or Spanish Possessions, $12,038.57 ; and from France, $30.

The domestic exports consisted chiefly of sugar, 634,955 lbs. ; syrup, 18,244 gals.; molasses, 58,448 gals. ; coffee, 50,506 lbs.; salt, 3,509 bbls. ; Irish potatoes, 15,464 bbls. ; sweet potatoes, 8,979 bbls. ; swine, 3,724 ; sheep, 733 ; goat skins, 5,600 ; hides, 1,741 ; tallow, 16,452 lbs. ; fresh beef, 38,000 lbs. ; salt beef, 13,260 lbs. ; wool, 10,824 lbs. ; cocoanuts, 2,000 ; melons, 2,500 ; together with numerous other articles.

The total of custom-house receipts during this year were $155,640.17. Of this amount, $146,964.52 were received at Honolulu, and $8,128.37 at Lahaina ; the remaining $537.38 was received at the ports on the islands of Hawaii and Kauái.

Of these receipts, $58,114.86 were for duties on goods ; $70,209.68 on spirits, and $8,261.75 for harbor dues.

The amount of oil and bone transhipped, free of duty, was as follows :—

SPRING SEASON.	*Sperm Oil.* Galls.	*Whale Oil.* Galls.	*Bone.* Lbs.
To United States	132,251	1,897,116	435,846
" Havre	476	37,038	22,000
FALL SEASON.			
To United States	42,669	1,853,194	1,520,559
" Cowes, England	—	—	21,040

FALL SEASON.	Sperm Oil. Galls.	Whale Oil. Galls.	Bone. Lbs.
To Bremen	—	—	14,819
" Havre...............	—	—	6,000
Total .... 175,396 ....3,787,348 2,020,264			

The number of merchant vessels that visited these islands during this year was 211, of which 154 arrived at Honolulu, 29 at Lahaina, 10 at Kawaihae, 8 at Waimea, 9 at Kealakekua, and 1 at Hilo. Of these vessels 137 were American, with an aggregate tonnage of 45,234 tons ; 17 Hawaiian—tonnage, 2,072 ; 32 British—tonnage, 6,185 ; 5 Danish—tonnage, 866 ; 5 French—tonnage, 1,034 ; 3 Russian—tonnage, 1,223.

Of 535 whalers, 246 visited Honolulu ; 177 Lahaina ; 66 Hilo; 12 Kealakekua ; 20 Kawaihae ; and 12 Waimea. Of these, 500 were American, 19 French, 12 Bremen, and 4 Russian.

The total number of native coasters is 32, with a tonnage of 1,338 tons.

From the Interior Department we learn that out of 119 foreigners naturalized during this year, 53 were Americans.

Sales of public land were made for $15,065.

Licenses for stores, hotels, coasting, peddling, &c., amounted to $26,769.

By the report of the Minister of Public Instruction, there are 423 public free schools, with native teachers, who instruct in the Hawaiian tongue: of these 344 are Protestant, and 79 Catholic. The number of scholars is 12,205, on an average about 35 to a school. The expense of maintaining these schools was $21,256 for the year. In addition to these, there are 9 select schools or seminaries, where English and the higher branches are pursued. In his report he makes the following observation :—

" Of the whole number of pupils in our free schools, the average for their terms last year was 12,205, and 517 for those in the select schools, and we have 12,722. The ages of our pupils are generally from four to sixteen years. No account is made here for the numerous Sunday schools for both adults and children."

The number of marriages licensed was 1,954.

The Minister of Finance recommends that the ports be freed from all restrictions on commerce, and that no specific exemption be made of duty on imports ; also the extension of the city upon the vacant water lots of Honolulu, a project the estimated cost of which by others, is $130,000, probably underrated.

The report of the Minister of Foreign Relations exhibits at length the diplomatic affairs of the kingdom. Though an amicable understanding exists with all nations, it would appear that relations with France are still a source of national interest, if not apprehension. It contains the following retrospective view of financial affairs :—

" For the financial years 1842 and 1843, our whole revenues were calculated at $48,842.77 ; in only eight years, with all our inexperience and defective administration, chiefly through the impulse of foreign commerce, they amounted to $315,735.84 for the years 1850 and 1851, at which rate of increase in twenty years hence, our yearly revenues, going on as we are, and on our present basis of taxation, ought to be $1,200,000."

Referring to the introduction of the " Maine Liquor Law" into the kingdom, which Mr. Wyllie has always steadily opposed, he remarks :—
"As for the adoption of the Maine Law in this kingdom, in the present state of our revenue, which I shall show hereafter, no man of practical sound sense would recommend it."

The official returns for the census of the group for 1853 will be read with painful interest, since they exhibit the annual decrease of population, which neither legislative enactments nor individual philanthropy can avert.

	NATIVES.			FOREIGNERS.	TOTAL.
	Males.	Females.	Total.		
Hawaii	12,443	11,750	24,193	259	24,452
Maui	8,905	8,425	17,330	244	17,574
Molokai	1,799	1,766	3,565	42	3,607
Oahu	9,551	8,264	17,815	1,311	19,126
Lanai	317	283	600		
Kauai	3,672	3,054	6,726	262	8,378
Niihau	392	398	790		
Total	37,079	33,940	71,019	2,118	73,137

Population in 1849............80,641

Decrease............ 7,504

On this subject the *Polynesian* contains the following :—

" The immense labor of footing up, analyzing and putting the statistics into a tangible shape, can only be appreciated by those who have examined the piles of returns in the office of the Minister of Public Instruction. That labor is progressing with all possible dispatch, but some considerable period will yet elapse before it is completed. We are enabled to present our readers with the following details in regard to the foreign population of the first district of Oahu, which includes Honolulu and vicinity, and is believed to be accurate. This census was taken the last week in December, 1853 :—

Native Countries.	No.	Males.	Females.
United States	371	291	80
Great Britain and Ireland	259	189	70
Australia	*26	16	10
British North America	4	3	1
Germany (including Belgium, Holland and Prussia)	66	62	4
France	36	32	4
Switzerland	3	3	—

* Chiefly children of English parents.

Native Countries.	No.	Males.	Females.
Denmark	7	5	2
Sweden	5	5	—
Portugal, Spain, and Spanish America	23	21	2
Turkey	1	1	—
Western Islands and Cape de Verds	9	9	—
West Indies	3	3	—
Sierra Leone (Africa)	1	1	—
St. Helena	2	2	—
Isle of France	1	1	—
East Indies	6	6	—
China	124	124	—
Malaysia	1	1	—
Philipines	3	3	—
Ladrone Islands	1	1	—
Society Islands	4	2	—
Marquesas Islands	*1	1	—
Born on the Hawaiian Islands	†202	103	99
Native countries unreported	21	21	—
Total	1,180	906	274

Of the above about 20 are negroes.

Married to natives, (11 Chinese) 98 ; to half-castes, (1 Chinese) 20 ; to resident foreigners, 214. Total married, 332. Over 50 years of age, (4 Chinese) 64 ; from 20 years to 50, (74 Chinese) 716 ; from 10 years to 20, (26 Chinese) 173 ; under 10 years, 160 ; age unreported, (20 Chinese) 67. Total, 1,180. The oldest person in this district is 88 years. The oldest resident has been here 49 years ; residents over 20• years, 52 ; from 10 to 20 years, 82 ; from 5 to 10 years, 143 ; from 1 to 5 years, 441 ; under 1 year, 88 ; time of residence unreported, 172 ; of Hawaiian birth, 202. Total, 1,180.

In the remaining four districts of the island of Oahu the total number of foreigners is only 131, of whom 121 are males and 10 females. Their nativity is as follows :—

	No.	Males.	Females.
United States	40	37	3
Great Britain	18	18	—
France	6	6	—
Germany	2	2	—
Sweden	1	1	—
Portugal, Spain and Spanish America	3	1	2
West and Cape de Verd Islands	27	27	—
Africa	1	1	—
East Indies	3	2	1
China	22	22	—
Hawaiian Islands	8	4	4
Total	131	121	10

* Of American parents.
† 137 of American parents ; 51 of British and Irish ; 5 of German ; 5 of Danish ; 3 of French : 1 of Spanish. Total, 202. Only 5 are over 20 years of age.

DIMINUTION OF THE POPULATION.

The official returns of James W. Marsh, Esq., to his Excellency the Governor of Oahu, of births, deaths, and marriages, for the year 1853, show the following results for the First District, in which Honolulu is situated :—

Births	191
Deaths	3,759
Marriages of natives	458
Do. of foreigners	61

This district is comprised between Maunalua on the east and Moanalua on the west, a distance of some fourteen miles, and containing a population, it is supposed, of about 10,000 souls. The deaths from small-pox, included in the above, are supposed to be about 2,800—the balance from other diseases.

In this same district during the year 1852, there were,

Births	337
Deaths	906
Marriages	418

It is to be remarked that it was in this district that the small-pox first broke out, and was more fatal, perhaps, than in any other portion of the islands.

By the appended extract from the report of the Minister of Public Instruction, will appear the seemingly anomalous fact, that with the decrease of population crime is on the increase, while it also exhibits in a favorable light the intellectual progress of the nation.

"I am much indebted to the several District Attorneys, F. Baker, Esq., of Hawaii, J. W. Austin, Esq, of Máui, A. B. Bates, Esq., of Oáhu, and G. Rhodes, Esq., of Kauái, for their valuable statistics of criminal convictions in the courts of their several districts, and for the valuable letters of two of the above-named gentlemen accompanying the same. Such statistics do not form a perfect criterion, it is true, of the state of public morals on the islands, as many offences against the law doubtless escape detection. Yet they enable us to form a tolerably correct judgment on the subject. By these returns, it appears that the whole number of convictions for crime in 1853, in all the courts, was 3,173, or one to about every twenty-three of the whole population, and 130 more than were reported for the year 1852.

"Of the above convictions, 1,059 were for drunkenness—55 less than were reported for the previous year ; 860 were for fornication and adultery—that is, 40 more than were reported during the previous year ; 109 were for disturbing the peace ; 199 for thefts and larceny ; and the remainder for gambling, violating the Sabbath, and minor offences.

"Let it be observed that, of the 3,173 convictions for crime, on the whole islands, 1,369, or nearly one half, were in the police courts of Honolulu ; and, as near as I can ascertain, about 692 occurred in the police courts of Lahaina ;—

making in all 2,061, or nearly two-thirds of the criminal convictions on the islands in these two seaports, confirming what has been often stated, that these are the great hot-beds of vice on the islands. Purify the populous towns, and you purify the nation. How can it be done? Where is the wise man who will devise the proper means?

"One of my respected colleagues has introduced a bill during several successive meetings of the Legislature for discouraging prostitution, by preventing young females of the more remote districts from visiting the seaports without a pass. The bill has been rejected as often as presented, on the ground of its unadaptedness to meet the case, and also of its impracticability; but the subject was referred by the House of Nobles to the undersigned for further consideration. It is a subject on which I have bestowed much reflection for years, and I confess myself very much of the opinion of Chief Justice Lee, as expressed in his report of last year, that no law can be framed on this subject that will be practicable and efficient, and not interfere too much with the liberty of the subject. If any remedy is ever found for this tremendous evil, that is fast consuming the native race, it will be in the general moral health of the body politic, resulting from the progress of Christian education and civilization, rather than in legislation, which at best can only lop off the branches, while the root remains.

"I have endeavored to ascertain by circulars addressed to all the School Inspectors throughout the islands, what proportion of the natives use intoxicating drinks and tobacco. The returns are by no means satisfactory, and therefore I will not attempt to give the results in full. The following will be read with interest:

"On the Island of Molokái, with a native population of 3,565, only two persons, one native and one foreigner, are reported as having been intoxicated during the year 1853; and no habitual drinkers of spirits. 563 only are reported as using tobacco on that island. In the fourth and fifth School District on Kauái, with a population of 2,013, not a case of drunkenness is reported in 1853, and no habitual drinkers. There are 72 foreigners in the district. In the second or Kolóa district on Kauái, with a population of about 1,200 natives, only four are reported as given to strong drink, and five foreigners.

"On the Island of Niihau, population 790, all natives, not one person is reported as using intoxicating drinks; 377 use tobacco. In the first district of Máui, the Lahaina district, with a population of 4,684 natives, 181 are reported as habitual beer drinkers to excess, and 1,560 use tobacco. In a part of the second district on Máui—that is, from Waihee to Waikapu, 303 natives and foreigners are reported as using intoxicating drinks, and 1,011 use tobacco.

"The above statistics are not wholly reliable, and can only be regarded as an approximation to the truth. Of the other districts I have not received reports on these subjects.

"The total amount of intoxicating drinks consumed on the islands in 1853 was 14,669 gallons, or 4,066 gallons more than were consumed during the year 1852.

"By those most acquainted with the natives, their inveterate habits of indolence are still regarded as the source of a vast deal of their immorality. Being unwilling to work, they are apt to resort to any means, however reprehensible, for obtaining a livelihood.

"I have heard, also, judges of courts complain much of the practice of false swearing among natives. Some very marked instances have come to my own knowledge.

"But on the whole, the state of public morals, as reported by the school inspectors and district attorneys, cannot be said to be bad on the islands. Life, property, and reputation are as secure as in most Christian lands; and we are almost entirely free from the more aggravated species of crimes, such as robberies, murders, incendiaries, and the like.

"I beg the attention of the Legislature to the valuable suggestions of Attorneys Austin and Baker, in regard to public morals, in their letters herewith submitted, particularly to the common practice of married persons forsaking their partners on the most trifling grounds, thus breaking up domestic relations, and exposing the parties to great temptation.

"I have made an effort, by addressing circulars to all the school inspectors of the twenty-five districts, to ascertain what proportion of the adult native population, or those say over sixteen years of age, are able to read their own language; but the returns on this subject are yet too imperfect to furnish the basis of a very accurate calculation. The nearest approximation to the truth, and I think it is not far from it, is three-fourths."

After instituting comparisons disparaging to educational results in America and European kingdoms, as manifested by statistic returns, and the concurrent testimony of writers, his Excellency continues:—

"Nothing invidious is intended by this comparison of our school statistics with those of other countries; much less is it introduced by way of boasting of our success. The undersigned is too painfully sensible of the wretched condition of many of our schools, kept, as they too often are, in cheerless and unfurnished grass huts, without floors, and many of them without even a bench to sit upon; without a sufficient number of books and apparatus; with bad government, and but poorly qualified teachers, to indulge such a thought for a moment.

"The object is simply to show what provision has been made by other governments, and some of the most enlightened and Christian, for the instruction of the whole people; what it has cost; what degree of popular education has been attained, and what has been the result where the State has made little or no provision for the education of all the people, with a view to afford encouragement and hope, and to show that poor as our schools are, our success has been great, considering the time and the efforts made; to drive away despondency, and to lead to greater and more wisely directed effort in the cause on the islands. It is less than sixteen years since the King's government, as such, made any attempt at supporting a system of free schools, and this department has not been organized eight years; yet the proportion of our islanders who can read their own language is already, as we have seen, greater than in some old and enlightened States. In the Sandwich Islands only about one adult in four cannot read his Bible, his newspaper, the constitution and laws under which he lives, and the ballot he throws into the box, while in North Carolina one out of every three is unable to do so. This result is more worthy of notice since here the State has done almost the entire work of educating the masses, while there the State has done little or nothing.

"But you are told that the knowledge acquired in our native schools is of no practical value; that the pupils learn merely by rote, and do not comprehend what they are taught, or make any use of it. Such assertions are not founded in reason, or supported by facts. True, our islanders who read their own language may exercise less the power of independent thought, and possess really less practical knowledge and good judgment than those people of North Carolina who cannot read at all; and this is not strange. All knowledge is not to be derived from books. A people surrounded by intelligence and active enterprise, keeping all minds and all hands in motion, and, what is perhaps more than all, disciplined from infancy by the use of a language rich in the accumulated thought of ages, will necessarily acquire much mental strength, habits of industry, and, perhaps, elevation of general character, which a people situated as these islanders are cannot so readily obtain, even with a considerable knowledge of books. But this does not prove that such knowledge is valueless. It only shows the vastness and difficulty of the work it has to do.

"Knowledge is power here as well as elsewhere ; and if combined with virtue, it is power for good, and good only, to its possessor and to the community. This is as well established as the laws of cause and effect ; but time is required for general education to work out its legitimate results here or anywhere else.

"Several of the honorable members of the House of Representatives being school inspectors, have had a practical knowledge of the working of our free school system for years, and need no argument to convince them that the common school has been one of the most potent instruments in preparing the people for a constitutional government, for exercising the elective franchise, for introducing trial by jury, placing natives in offices of high trust and power, securing public tranquillity ; in short, for sustaining the whole machinery of a regular government made to supersede a despotism of the worst form, without revolution or shedding one drop of blood.

"Without free schools diffusing intelligence among the entire people, it would be next to impossible for the king to govern his people by a constitution and laws. But being brought into the common school at four or five years of age, and kept there until they are fourteen or sixteen, they not only acquire valuable elementary knowledge, but are early trained to habits of subordination, learn subjection to law, and when arrived at years of maturity, they are easily governed. Who ever heard of a native, whether of high rank or low, rising up against the law ? Such a thing is unknown. Why ? Because they have been accustomed from youth to bow to the majesty of law.

"In short, the tendency of a diffusion of knowledge among the entire people here is the same as in other countries, that is, to dissipate the evils of ignorance, increase industry and the productiveness of labor, diminish pauperism and crime, support good government, and diffuse general happiness. In proportion to the value of these, then, let efforts be made constantly and increasingly to sustain and perfect our free schools.".

AGRICULTURAL.

Sales of 12,011 acres of the public lands were made for $15,065, averaging about $1.25 per acre.

The annexed table will exhibit the extent of sugar-cultivations in these islands :—

	ACRES CULTIVATED.	
	1852.	1853.
Lihue (Oahu)	200	580
Koloa (Kauai)	240	650
Honuaula (Ulupalakua)	250	300
Makawao (Maui)	325	500
Hana (Maui)	45	130
Waimea (Hawaii)	50	50
Hilo (Hawaii)	540	540
Total	1,650	2,750

The average yield per acre is 2,000 lbs. ; average value, 5 cents per pound.

The yield of Irish potatoes, of excellent quality, still continues prolific in the Kula district. In Makawao, from 1,200 to 1,500 acres of wheat have been sown, and the crop promises to be a fair one.

The *Polynesian* of January 14th, 1854, furnishes the following rates of the city retail market :—

"We confess to a feeling of shame while recording and publishing to the world the rates of some of the following articles, as paid for by housekeepers in Honolulu. Many of them are exorbitant, to say the least, while others are far too high for a country like this, where gold is not produced, nor business very brisk. Some of the articles, however, are reasonable.

Beef, per lb.	7 to 9 c.	Bananas, per bunch		75 to $2
Pork, fresh, lb	12½	Squashes, each		25 to 50
Mutton, lb.	15 to 18	Onions, per bushel		$5
Sausages	25	Tea, lb.		75 to $1 25
Hams, lb.	25	Sugar, brown		8 to 12
Butter, lb.	50 to 62½	do. refined		16
Lard, lb.	25	Coffee		16
Flour, bbl.	$15 to $18	Dried Apples, lb.		12½
Meal, per half bbl.	$6	Potatoes, Irish, per bbl.		$3 50
Fowls, each	50 to 75	do. Sweet, "		$2 50
Ducks "	75 to $1	Syrup, gall.		75
Turkeys "	$1 to $2	Radishes, per bunch		25
Eggs, per doz.	75 to $1	Carrots "		25
Milk, per quart	12½	Tomatoes, a small mess		25 to 50
Charcoal, per bbl.	$3 to $5	Oranges, per 100		$2 50 to $3
Wood, per cord	$16	Limes, per doz.		10
Melons, each.	12½ to 25	Cucumbers, per doz.		25 to 37½

Under date of January 21st, the same paper contains a lengthy article on the subject of "Sugar Planting at the Islands," a portion of which is subjoined :—

"A shrewd and candid observer of matters and things at the islands cannot but be impressed with the fact that our staple articles of export are by a thousand-fold too limited for either individual or national prosperity. We are poor because we have so little to sell. We have but little to sell, because but little capital and effort are bestowed upon the production of staple articles, which are always in demand, and not dependent upon a prosperous or adverse whaling season.

"It cannot be denied that the supply of the whaling fleet, and the shipping connected with it, is the life of the agricultural interest, in its present condition. By far the larger proportion of the labor bestowed upon the soil has immediate reference to the demand thus created. And this is right and natural. That demand should be promptly and fully supplied, in every particular, so far as the islands have the ability to produce what is wanted. We would go farther and say, that the whaling fleet should not only be provided for, to the fullest extent of its demands, but many articles of their greatest necessity should be furnished them at a rate considerably lower than the now current prices of the market ; and this could be done, were there more system in the matter, and still leave a profit to the producer. But this is not the point of our remarks ; we would supply the whaling fleet, and thus secure that important business to the islands, and in addition, strongly urge the increased production of such staples as will bear exportation and yield a profit to the producer.

"It is a palpable fact that forces itself upon the observation of every business man in the community, that with the whaling fleet departs the active business of the islands. Not only are the principal ports where they touch affected ; the stagnation is felt also in every corner of the land, and every branch of business languishes alike. The demand being cut off, the supply, of course, ceases, and with it the means of keeping business in a state of activity.

" Under such a state of depression, a multitude of opinions are broached in regard to the cause of the dulness of the times. One is of opinion that it is occasioned by the tonnage dues on merchant vessels ; another, that 5 per cent. duties on merchandise is the cause. Another thinks that a property tax would remedy the evil, and make money plenty ; while another still attributes it all to the Legislature, which fails to do something that would act as a specific against ' hard times.' Without attempting to discuss these various opinions, we assert it as our belief, that they have very little to do with the matter. The causes lie deeper, and are scarcely affected by the ripples upon the surface. Ships bringing cargoes, or coming for them, will not be deterred by the tonnage dues. As much merchandise is, and will be imported, as we can pay for, even with 5 per cent. duties upon it. A tax upon property would not bring an additional dollar into the country, and it is the lack of dollars that makes the times hard. If the Legislature could force men to become industrious, or could they compel capitalists and laborers to cultivate our waste soil, and produce from it some staple article that would *sell*, then indeed could they reach the cause, and apply the remedy. But this may be beyond their province. If we are ever to expect an increase of business at the islands, it must be brought about, as we apprehend, by a greatly increased development of our agricultural resources. We see no other possible way for its accomplishment. We already supply the demand for recruits and supplies of a perishable nature ; and when the demand for these ceases, by the departure of the whaling fleet, we have nothing to fall back upon. Coffee, sugar, syrup and molasses may be in demand, at a remunerating price, but unfortunately there is nothing of the kind to be had. Indigo, arrow-root, cotton and wool may be produced to a large extent, but they are not. The simple fact stands out boldly before us, that we have very little to export, the sale of which would bring money into the country. And as a consequence, the business of the islands is limited to the necessities of the whaling fleet, which will never exceed its amount for the few past years.

" In view of these facts—and we deem them such—the inquiry is apposite and of vital consequence, How can the business of the islands be increased ? In what way can an export be produced, that will bring money into the country ?

" Without for a moment overlooking the importance of our present business, based upon the wants of the whaling fleet ; or that coffee, salt, arrow-root, fruits, &c., are all-important articles of export that should not be neglected, it is still our opinion that the production of sugar, syrup and molasses must become the great staple of the islands, and be relied upon chiefly to increase our business.

* * * * * * *

" To establish sugar or coffee plantations in any country, successfully, requires a large capital, as experience and common sense would dictate ; and this is just what is wanted here to render the business profitable, and of the highest benefit to the islands. Without it, we must be content to see our business confined to its present limits, and raise potatoes and squashes for the whaling fleet, while thousands of acres of good soil lie uncultivated and unproductive."

A correspondent of the *Polynesian*, writing under date of January 2d, 1854, in speaking of the agricultural districts of East Maui, makes the following complimentary allusion to the estate at Ulupalakua :—

" Mr. Torbert's plantation at Ulupalakua (it is a musical name) has suffered some from drought of late, but not so much as some of the plantations. It is in a flourishing condition. The cane looks well, and there is more of it than can be ground with the existing machinery. The sugar and syrup recently made there are certainly of a superior quality, and cannot fail to command a high price. This Ulupalakua is a choice spot. We think more of it on every successive visit. For climate, soil, prospect, peaceful retirement, as a place to live, and with the requisite means to make money, where is its superior ? The pleasure of a visit there, too, is not a little enhanced by the generous, farmer-like hospitality of the noble-hearted 'laird' who conducts the establishment. The half or the whole of this plantation of over 4,000 acres is for sale, and fortunate will be the man who will purchase it at a fair price. The climate alone is a fortune."

A retrospective glance at the commerce of this kingdom will prove interesting, as it exhibits up to the year 1852 a steady increase of imports and revenue :—

	Value of Imports.	Gross Duties.	Re-exported.	Return Duties.
1843	$223,383 38	$6,701 84	$66,618 17	$1,670 41
1844	350,357 12	10,326 13	60,054 06	1,501 34
1845	546,941 72	21,536 94	67,010 93	2,098 82
1846	598,382 24	53,447 78	62,325 74	21,667 02
1847	710,138 52	101,512 25	55,208 07	56,991 17
1848	605,618 73	142,357 73	33,551 55	90,148 27
1849	729,739 44	222,118 99	107,102 07	156,098 16
1850	1,035,058 70	202,603 61	46,529 72	110,687 12
1851	1,751,671 93	189,090 19	82,273 27	63 102 81
1852	715,295 27	135,423 77	63,661 18	52,929 70
Total	$7,265,587 05	$1,085,119 23	$644,334 76	$556,894 82

	Net Amount.	Net Duties.	Transit Duties.	Harbor Dues.	Net Receipts.
1843	$156,565 21	$5,270 74	$239 31	$2,958 83	$8,468 34
1844	289,969 77	8,970 13	411 60	4,881 33	14,263 58
1845	471,319 78	19,465 12	734 01	4,890 83	25,189 96
1846	536,056 50	31,780 76	220 56	4,705 32	36,506 66
1847	653,930 45	44,521 08	184 93	4,095 24	48,801 25
1848	572,067 18	52,209 46	264 52	3,094 96	55,568 94
1849	622,637 37	66,020 83	235 13	5,687 53	71,934 49
1850	989,528 98	91,916 49	443 42	12,644 54	116,190 68
1851	1,751,771 93	125,987 38	1,043 45	12,905 71	148,936 54
1952	651,634 09	135,423 77	991 56	7,711 90	144,127 23

The average amount of imports during the last four years is $1,225,175.02; and the excess of imports above the average of the four years past is $56,776.16.

DOMESTIC EXPORTS.

1850.	1851.	1852.	1853.
$596,522 63	$309,896 94	$257,251 59	$275,374 17

REVENUE FOR THE LAST FOUR YEARS.

1850.	1851.	1852.	1853.
$121,506 73	$160,602 19	$113,091 93	$155,640 17

ARRIVALS FOR THE LAST FOUR YEARS.

	1850.	1851.	1852.	1853.
Merchant,	469	446	235	211
Whale-ships,	237	135	519	535

The following censual review will exhibit the rapid decrease of population. In 1779 Cook's estimate was 400,000, but this was probably overrated by more than 100,000 ; his inference was drawn from the immense number of natives that flocked to every locality visited by his ships. A loose estimate for 1823 gives 142,050 for the entire group. The following are official returns :—

	1832.	1836.	1849.	1853.
Native	129,814	108,002	—	71,019
Total	130,313	108,579	80,641	73,137

Dr. Fisher, in his " *Statistical Annual for* 1854," makes the following observation upon this subject :—

" The excess of deaths over births in 1848 had been 6,465, or 8 per cent. About 10,000 died of measles and hooping-cough in 1847–8. At this rate of mortality the population in 1860 would be 32,224 ; in 1870, 14,073 ; in 1880, 6,134 ; in 1890, 2,667, and in 1900 only 1,162. In 1950 the Hawaiian race would be extinct. Such is the influence of civilization on aboriginal races—the same throughout America and throughout the world."

It must be remembered, however, that these deductions are based on the statistics of what has been emphatically called " the year of death," and are intended only to show the prospective decrease under special circumstances ; yet when it is shown by official returns that nearly 60,000 out of a population of less than 130,000, or nearly one-half, have died off in 20 years, the extinction of the whole race at no distant period would seem to be realized.

The subject of annexing this kingdom to the United States will require but a brief consideration. The acquisition of property is to individuals a welcome event, and an increase of territory is salad for national cupidity ; but when the whirlwind of enthusiasm has passed, let us deliberately consider what many are seeking. Neither a Texas, California, nor a Cuba, would be the result of such a consummation. As a territorial acquisition, it hardly merits a consideration. But, on the other hand, a most important point would be secured for our rapidly-increasing commerce in the Pacific—a resting-point that we can call our own ; also a tropical garden adequate to the requirements of that portion of our republic bordering the Western Ocean. Another result would be a diminution in price of the staple products of that country among those regions or districts for which San Francisco or Columbia River are entrepots, and the advantages of an increased commerce would be mutually shared between Oregon and California and a sister State.

On the other hand, Hawaii would in every respect be benefited. The apprehension that necessarily arises where a weaker power is exposed to and experiences the intimidations of a greater would no longer exist. The simple fact of its being an integral portion of our country would insure the speedy occupation of waste lands, enhance the value of every description of real estate, and immeasurably develop its resources, (which are strictly agricultural,) to the profit of the merchant, the planter, and to every industrial class of society. With the absence of the thirty per cent. *ad valorem* duty on Hawaiian exports, a host of cane and coffee plantations would besprinkle the mountains and valleys; harbors would exist in place of open roadsteads, and the construction of docks, *roads*, together with other local improvements, would be the immediate evidences of future prosperity. The confidence inspired by this consolidation of power would be deemed ample security for the investment of capital in the lucrative fields of this archipelago, which even now exist, and an era of commercial enterprise would dawn for Hawaii, which, as an independent sovereignty, she can hardly hope to attain. While the one has nothing to lose, the other has everything to gain.

Another point to be considered would be the incorporation of a distinct race with our own. It is hoped that preceding remarks and extracts have sufficiently exhibited the habits and intellectual capacity of this branch of the great Polynesian family. Their education, associations, and political bias, are purely American; religion, laws, and democratic ideas, implanted by a liberal form of government adapted to their wants, are results of American commerce and philanthropy. At the present day, the natives, independent of foreign residents or denizens, are better educated, have clearer conceptions of rectitude in moral principle, than the hundreds of thousands of emigrants with which we are annually inundated from European shores, who infect us not only with physical, but even moral pestilence. Almost every Hawaiian can read his vote, while, at the same time, he possesses liberal ideas of the principles he endeavors to sustain, besides fully appreciating the inestimable privilege of free suffrage. This is more than can be said for those whose views from infancy have been anti-republican, whose religion, more than anything, has retarded the healthy growth of knowledge. Such are they who at present land upon our soil, the passive tools of others whose ambition and cupidity would curtail the liberties of its rightful possessors. There would be no immigration into this country of Hawaiians; the relic of a once numerous race would still continue sparsely scattered among native hills.

Invidious comparisons are not sought in a spirit of national prejudice. For absolute notions of republicanism as evidenced by religious fanaticism, so at variance with the sentiment of more conservative society, a weight of responsibility devolves upon our statesmen. The annexation of territory is of trifling consideration in comparison with the annexation of principle; and this we are daily incorporating with our free institutions, until the bulwark of our confederacy is breasting an element of conflicting creeds, theories, and abstract principles, unavoidably entailed. Its subsidence will only be insured by careful analysis based upon moral conviction, and bold and determined action to secure the triumph of American supremacy. A union with the worshippers of Fo or Boodha would involve less controversy than the precocity of republicans of a day, the early aspirants for political honors, the class that profits by the industry of others. A skilful masking of sentiment, a cloaking of principle, are at present prerequisites to political fame; but posterity will cherish the memory of the patriot-statesman who sacrifices the bauble—transient renown, for the nobler achievement—national prosperity.

The majority of State officers, planters, merchants, and foreign residents, who give character to society, are Americans, and manifest as deep an interest in American politics as their neighbors upon adjacent shores. The press is essentially American, and in its moral tendencies encourages and promotes those time-hallowed observances that link us to the past by cherished associations. Hawaii would still continue to legislate for herself, and a new bond, established on a broader basis, would unite us to our countrymen who have conferred upon these islands their present political importance. If she come to us, it will be as a free State; in principle, there will be no constitutional deformity to remodel, no monarchical sentiments to be combated; existing institutions are a sufficient guaranty for harmony of union.

The rapidity of the numerical decrease of the inhabitants of this group, and in a disproportionate ratio the foreign increase, have already awakened the attention of the far-seeing. The present subject may be indefinitely postponed, but the problem will sooner or later require solution. It is absurd to argue that the present race by intermarriage will become merged into a distinct nation that shall retain its present code and system of government. Existing evidences and growing prejudices are opposed to such a result. The Anglo-Polynesians bear but a small proportion to the number of resident foreigners; nor do we discover in them, save in few instances, an increase of intellectual capacity. The alarming decrease of population is exhibited by official returns, and a nation must either be enriched or impoverished in accordance with its growth or decline.

American conquests have been peacefully achieved; but there is another power less fastidious in its moral scruples, (if political economy will sanction the application to national policy,) that has long yearned parentally for this interesting group. France, not content with the assumed monopoly of the South Pacific, has sought every pretext for inflicting her unjust aggressions to goad an infant nation to open opposition, that a plea might be afforded for crushing it out by her own weight. But in every instance her ambitious machinations have been baffled by skilful diplomacy, creditable alike to the kingdom and its Minister of Foreign Relations. Except the unauthorized proceedings of Lord George Paulet, and the disgraceful acts of a former British Consul, occurrences which had well nigh weaned Hawaiian gratitude from a cherished benefactor, there has always been a higher tone—a dignity of feeling on the part of England in her official intercourse with this group, which in a measure have confirmed early impressions as to her zeal and interest in its welfare. Though a strong remonstrance would be urged against the abdication of Hawaiian sovereignty in behalf of another power, it is equally certain that she would never tarnish her national dignity, nor violate the sanctity of treaties, by political aggression with a view to conquest.

If those interested will examine the subject, unbiased by national prejudice, they will discover that no country is more interested in the possession or independence of these islands than the United States. The first has already been shown; their geographic position will explain the latter. The growing commerce of San Francisco with China, the East Indies, Australia, and in future with Japan, owing to prevailing winds, must necessarily pass by this group, or at most within a few degrees of it, in its egress; so that, notwithstanding their comparatively isolated position, they may be regarded as the key of the North Pacific. Within a circuit of thousands of miles north of the equator, there exists neither group nor island to checkmate this absolutism of natural advantage. Once in possession of a hostile power, and properly fortified, their conformation would oppose almost insurmountable obstacles to an invading force. American interests are to be regarded, since (native excepted) they are paramount to all others in the group. Were Hawaii to become a colony of Great Britain, the commercial privileges of our countrymen might in nowise be curtailed, while, on the other hand, they would not be in the slightest degree improved. California is the vortex that absorbs Hawaiian produce. The merchant who exports his surplus wares, and the planter his coffee and sugar, would have the same international restrictions to encounter that are at present a serious impediment to more extended enterprise. The contingency of a French monopoly should never for a moment be entertained; such an event would be disastrous to the interests of all. Tahiti furnishes a precedent that needs no comment.

Whether Hawaii shall still continue an independent kingdom, become incorporated with our republic, or exist as a foreign colony, remains to be seen.   Its annexation to this country would not be the result of a necessity.   Her present revenues are adequate to immediate requirements, and she is politically capable of sustaining her position among nations, though the zenith of prosperity be vaguely remote.   It is not for Americans to agitate.   This kingdom possesses the requisite elements for guiding the helm of State, and with these rests the decision. If the sequel be annexation, and consonant with American interests, no foreign intervention will prevent our country from pursuing a course that may be deemed mutually beneficial and politically just.

APPENDIX III.

THE FRENCH IN THE PACIFIC.

THE political horizon of the Old World is at present obscured by gathering clouds; however we may speculate or surmise, it is only when the pall shall have risen that we can comprehend the sequel. The three great powers now drawn up in hostile array have extensive possessions in this ocean; but such is the position of their mutual and opposing interests, that the arena of strife must evidently be confined to continental fields, unless there occur a new phase in national policy, which none would wish to anticipate, to sever the bond of amity between two great maritime nations at present so cordially fraternizing. We cannot suppose that the Russian bear, so long dormant, has awakened from his lethargy to snuff up delectable odors amid the palm groves of the Southern Ocean, nor that the eagles of France will seek for prey or more genial eyries amid the inhospitable snows of Kamtschatka; to bombard the fishing huts of Petropaulski would furnish but sorry gratification. However fiercely the conflict may rage in Europe, the present combination of powers will insure the tranquillity of the Pacific, if we except the possible rencontre of a national vessel with a struggling privateer; and whatever may be the anxiety respecting neutrals in the Atlantic, the guardians of the Black and Baltic Seas relieve from anticipated contingencies the commerce of the Western Ocean. Since the treasure of the old Spanish galleons was scattered by the cannon-shot of Drake and Anson, and in later years the reverberation of the Essex's guns carried consternation to British whalers, the broad Pacific has slumbered undisturbed. The peaceful developments of nearly half a century had prepared the civilized nations of the east and western hemispheres for the dawn of a new era, and the glitter of El Dorado was the mighty lever that set in motion an avalanche of cupidity, enterprise and ambition Since the Crusades, there was never such a mustering of nations and tribes as have marched steadily on to the shores of the great Western Ocean ; and the obscurity of ages, that like an incubus brooded upon its clear waters, has been dissipated forever by the surging and reflux of human waves.

The possessions of Russia, England, our own great Republic, and the oligarchies or military despotisms of degenerate Castile, bound the Pacific on the east ; on the west are the bleak mountains of Siberia, the magnificent empire of the east—and again, in the Southern Ocean, the cross of St. George waves over a continent nearly as broad as our Republic from ocean to ocean. Over a watery area of 50,000,000 square miles is scattered the almost countless archipelago ; and here, in the Southern Ocean, amid the groves of an emerald cordon three thousand five hundred miles in extent, flutters the tri-color of an empire. It will be found that nations, like individuals, have their distinguishing characteristics ; and whatever may be their manifest policy, history records true qualities ; either human achievements, political prowess, or military renown, emblazon their escutcheons. In the French, we have a people refined, enthusiastic and warlike, whose courtesies have enchanted courts, and whose thunder startled cabinets, who for nearly two centuries have been pursuing a shadow—that master intellect, whose power was felt from the pillars of Hercules to the Pyramids, and from the dykes of Holland to Moscow, failed to accomplish his cherished project, the establishment and maintenance of colonies. From the days of Colbert to Guizot, through a political atmosphere of intrigue and diplomacy, France has made but a sorry exhibition in the way of foreign conquest ; and yet, there is hardly a Parisian in his native city who sips his coffee with the columns of the *Moniteur* before him, whose vanity does not suggest self-gratulation at the vast acquisitions of " *la grand France.*"

It is unnecessary to recapitulate the rise and decline of French colonies in the East and Western Oceans, since, with the success of the Dutch and Spanish for a precedent, Colbert established in 1664 his first colony by purchasing settlements already formed among the West India Isles. The success and reverses of France upon the American continent are alike familiar to readers of history. Algiers was a wide field for the display of military enthusiasm ; but aside from principles of right ostensibly paraded, its conquest was the result of a national effervescence.

While scheming for the coffee and sugar of the West, the spices and precious stones of the East were not forgotten, and in 1664, Colbert founded an East India Company, which, with various reverses, existed until 1769, when it was dissolved ; while the West India Company, established about the same time, expired within ten years after it was created. In 1670, Pondicherry was founded on the coast of Coromandel, after a fruitless attempt had been made to establish a colony on Madagascar, and this at present constitutes the capital of the French East India possessions, which, with the exception of the Isle de Bourbon in the Indian Ocean, and the most profitable colony France possesses, exist only in name.

It would appear that during the years 1841 and 1842, three great powers were animated by the desire of territorial acquisition in the Pacific Ocean. This was evinced by the seizure of the Hawaiian Islands by Lord George Paulet, the Marquesas by Du Petit Thouars, and the occupation of Monterey by Commodore Jones. The former and latter proceedings being unsanctioned by the respective governments, the posts were quietly restored ; but the French still retain Nuheva, and with this for a starting-point, they have continued to augment their territory by force or fraud, until at the present day their possessions extend from the Gambier Islands in the East, lon. 134° 55′ W., in an almost uninterrupted line for 57 degress, to New Caledonia in the West, lon. 168° E., a distance of nearly 3,500 miles, including the Marquesas, Tahitian, Paumotu, Gambier, and some of the Austral Islands, Wallis Island, and New Caledonia, thus giving her apparently the command of the great commercial routes from the North to the South Pacific.

La Perouse, Bougainville, D'Entrecastreaux, and other French voyagers cotemporaneous with Cook and Wallis, traversed this ocean during the last century, to the credit of France and the advancement of science ; but to Rear-Admiral Du Petit Thouars, about the middle of the nineteenth century, was reserved the honor of territorial conquest in the Pacific. During the year 1841, a squadron, under the command of that officer, sailed from France, under secret orders, and its *denouement* was the seizure of the Marquesas Islands, on the first of May, 1842.

These islands, eight in number, were discovered by the Spanish navigator Alvaro Mendana, in 1596, who called them after the Marquis of Mendoza, then viceroy of Peru. After remaining long unnoticed, they were again visited by Cook, and in 1791 by Captain Ingraham, an American, who gave them the name of Washington Islands. Commodore Porter found them a convenient rendezvous for his operations in the Pacific during the late war with Great Britain, and, it is said, claimed them in behalf of the United States. From Nuheva Bay, he carried destruction to the British whaling fleet then cruising in this ocean, until his vessel, the Essex, was subsequently captured by two English cruisers at Valparaiso, under the guns of a neutral port.

The account of Du Petit Thouars is worth transcribing, on account of its ingenuousness. Though plausible to French credulity, an American or an Englishman would at once detect the artifice, for it is more than probable that the plan for obtaining possession of these islands, and of subsequent conquests in this ocean, had been matured by M. Guizot long prior to the sailing of the fleet.

"On the 28th we got to the western coast of the island Tahuata, (the Christina,) but were prevented by calms from coming to anchor in the Bay of Valtahu before three in the afternoon. Scarcely had we arrived before we received a visit from M. François de Paula, head of the mission establishment in this island ; and the next day the king Yotété came on board, accompanied by the Rev. gentleman, who was to act as interpreter. The king appeared delighted to see me again, and said that he would have come to visit me the evening before, but that he thought we were Americans. He then informed me, that, about four months before, a whaling boat belonging to an American vessel had arrived, after several days suffering for want of provision, at the island of Fatuhiva. The crew were received with musket-shots when they were about to land, and lost a man by the unexpected attack. Being thus prevented from landing, they proceeded to Tahuata, where the king scarcely received them better, for he stripped them of their clothes, and took away the boat in which they came on shore. Some time after, a whaler having put in, they were received on board, but protested, before embarking, against the acts of piracy practised against them, and threatened Yotété with the vengeance of their government. The king being since then enlightened on this point by the missionaries, and by some captains who had put into the Bay of Vaitatu, got alarmed as to the consequences of the affair, and was still in a state of great anxiety when he saw me. He requested my protection, and besought me to leave on my departure a portion of the crew and some of the cannon of the vessel. I replied that I should do so, provided he agreed to acknowledge the sovereignty of his Majesty Louis Philippe, and hoist the French flag. He eagerly accepted these propositions, and we agreed that the declaration of possession having been taken should be made on the 1st May, his Majesty's fête day. On that day, at ten in the morning, I landed with the officers of the vessel. A guard of sixty men had preceded me, and had drawn up in line near the flag-staff, to pay due honor to the national colors. When I arrived at the spot, I declared that I took possession of the island of Tahuata and the rest of the islands of this group, in the name of his Majesty Louis Philippe. The flag was immediately displayed, and we saluted it with cries of ' *Vive le roi!*' which was followed by three rounds of musketry and by martial music executed by the band. My ship, the 'Reine Blanche,' also fired a salute of twenty-one guns. The inhabitants testified the greatest delight, and besought me to land the cannons at once. We proceeded to the king's habitation, where the act of recognizing the sovereignty of his Majesty was signed."

By the preceding, it will be perceived that M. Du Petit Thouars humanely interfered to protect the Marquesans from any collision with America on account of an alleged insult to its flag, although he must have known that the United States would never permit a rear-admiral to interfere with the requirements of a national obligation. M. Du Petit Thouars probably formed his estimate of the character of American whaling captains from that of his own countrymen in some portions of this ocean, who, for the trespassing of a goat, or for the privilege of imbibing choice brandy for something less than a livre per glass, petition their consuls to make a national affair of their complaints, and forthwith a frigate is summoned, a diplomatic correspondence ensues, and the honor of France is maintained. Our whaling masters, whose pursuits are abroad, seldom yearn for maternal protection—an affair with a hostile tribe is usually adjusted by them on their own account. M. Du Petit Thouars must also have known that each island, as well as each valley of this group, is in itself independent; and whatever may be the concessions of the chief of one district, they are in nowise binding upon those of the lands adjoining.

The policy of M. Guizot in seizing this group may be inferred from his remarks in the Chamber of Deputies on the 31st of March, 1843, suggested by a claim set up by the French government to renew an attempted sovereignty over the island of Madagascar, on which occasion he said that, " in endeavoring to form colonial establishments, it was not the policy of France in any way to compromise herself by hostile collision with the natives of those countries, or foreign powers generally. No, that which is advantageous to France and indispensable for her, is to possess points on the globe destined to become great commercial centres of trade and navigation, and which will prove secure and strong maritime stations, which would at once serve in aid of our commerce by affording harbors and shelter for our shipping, with means of repair, without our being compelled to resort for those objects to foreign ports." It would also appear that similar sentiments were entertained by Louis Philippe, for at the opening of the French Chambers on the 9th of January of the same year, in his speech was made the following allusion to the then recent conquest : " By the occupation of the Marquesas, I have secured to our navigation in those distant seas a protection and refuge of which the necessity had long been felt."

The position of the French at these islands has been maintained at comparatively great expense, and unattended with beneficial results. The requirements of their commerce in this ocean, which do not exceed the necessity of a few dozen ships, can well dispense with the isolated assistance immured in the Bay of Nuheva. It was found that the sovereignty conceded by King " Yotété" pertained to himself alone, for to this day the Marquesans maintain a haughty independence. A few years since this port was abandoned, but for political reasons has been again resumed. It is said that several State prisoners who had rendered themselves politically obnoxious to Louis Napoleon, are now dwelling amid the groves of Nuheva.

The fortifications at this place consist of barracks erected upon a projecting rock, near the head of the bay ; these are defended in front by breastwork and glacis ; in the rear the former has been perforated for the convenience of musketry. A large stone mansion has been erected for the officers ; it is two stories high, and the upper is pleasantly relieved by a balcony extending around it. The governor's residence is neatly built of wood and stone. The general effect of these structures is that of relief to the natural wildness of the scenery.

Leaving this bay, the fleet, consisting of the " Reine Blanche" and " La Diane" of 50 guns each, and " L'Uraine" of 64 guns, proceeded to the Tahitian Islands ; and the second grand act in the drama was the dethronement of Queen Pomare on the 6th November, 1843, and the formal occupation of her possessions on the 9th day of the same month, on which occasion 300 men were landed in the town to erect fortifications, and about 100 men, consisting of mechanics and general laborers. It cannot be denied that this consummation was hastened by the uncharitable course pursued by the Tahitian government towards the two Roman Catholic missionaries that had recently arrived at that island, probably instigated by the counsels of Mr. Pritchard, a Protestant missionary and acting British consul. Previous to this, redress had been demanded by Captain La Place of the " Artemise" for alleged indignities towards French subjects. Having made the island, his vessel accidentally touched upon the reef on the north shore, and but for the timely assistance of the natives, would have been lost—they at least rendered essential service. Considerable damage was sustained by the vessel, which was detained in the harbor for a considerable length of time undergoing repairs, in which Captain La Place was aided by the subjects of Queen Pomare. These having been completed, he showed his true colors and demanded the payment of a certain amount within a specified time, otherwise he would discharge his broadsides indiscriminately upon the town. The sum of $2,000 was collected by Mr. Pritchard from the foreign merchants, and the honor of France nobly maintained.

The banishing of two unoffending persons, simply on account of ecclesiastical dogmas, to Wallis Island, more than 1,500 miles distant, where from savages they found a more hospitable reception than among those professing to worship the same God, was an act only equalled by the mistaken zeal of the American missionaries at the Hawaiian Islands, who, in 1831, expelled from the jurisdiction of their hierarchy Messrs. Bachelot and Short. Both suffered their schismatic prejudices to obtain the ascendency and tempt them to extremes ; subsequent embarrassments have been the atonement for their unchristian conduct. In both instances the act was premature and censurable. On the simple ground of international rights or privileges, it merited the prompt interference of France in behalf of her subjects, though undeserving the presumption with which that nation has subsequently asserted her unjust demands.

It is unnecessary to recapitulate the events connected with the conquest of the Tahitian Islands, or to notice the efforts of British officials and residents to ward off this consummation of French *annexation* policy. It need only be said that the claims of Du Petit Thouars were purposely estimated beyond the ability of either the queen's government or the foreign residents to meet them, and the consequence was the formal occupation of Tahiti and Moorea.

The conquest was by no means bloodless, and together with the numerous lives sacrificed, hundreds of thousands of lives have been expended on this as yet useless acquisition. The natives were brave and jealous of their liberty, and in many a hard-fought battle among their wild ravines they came off conquerors. It was only when betrayed at Fatáoa by a renegade countryman that they were forced to surrender. This important post, the Constantine of Tahiti, is the key of the island, and is situate among the lofty mountains in the rear of the town, and about five miles distant from it. Its scenery is said to be the most wildly romantic among the South Sea Islands ; it is at present occupied by a French garrison, and is considered impregnable. During this war, several attempts were made by the French upon the leeward or Society Islands, at Huahíne, Raiatéa, and Borabóra, but their efforts were unattended by advantageous results, and at the former island the troops under Bonard were signally repulsed. On this occasion their chagrin was manifested in cutting down bread-fruit, orange and fruit trees ; but the natives declared that rather than yield, they would live in the mountains upon yams and roots. British interference at a later period confined them to the Georgian Islands, leaving the Society Islanders free to act for themselves in the absence of French protection.

The Protectorate once established has continued with various modifications or changes to the present day, conforming to the two great political phases that have opened a new chapter in French history. The soldiers that charged through these mountain wilds with shouts of "*Vive le roi !*" were quietly reposing from their fatigues when the stirring strains of the Marseillaise, chanted beneath shady groves, announced the dawn of a new era in the destinies of France—the birth of a republic, the embryo of an empire. But the eagle of liberty had hardly soared aloft, before a nation's homage was rendered up in one enthusiastic cry of "*Vive l'Empereur !*" re-echoed from the shores of the South Pacific.

The extent of the naval armament stationed in this ocean, including steamer, frigate, corvette, schooner. &c., would not probably exceed half a dozen vessels of every class ; and the estimated force, including artillery and marine, now occupying the Georgian and Marquesas Islands, is considerably less than a thousand men. Opposite the entrance to the harbor of Papéete is Fort Uranie, which commands it, and the yard of the arsenal makes a prodigal display of guns of heavy calibre and projectiles. On fête days, companies in full uniform are said to make an imposing appearance in the streets of the town.

The policy adopted in the administration of affairs by the Protectorate is arbitrary in the extreme for a government professing to encourage commerce, and in its present condition partakes more of the military outpost than the commercial colony. The governors have been usually naval officers, above interesting themselves in theories that might tend to the advancement of commerce or agriculture, and the confirmation of this will be found by comparing the former condition of these islands with the present manifest results. The natives have been completely subdued; no offensive weapons of any description being allowed in their possession, their humiliation is complete. No institutions for their improvement, that formerly existed, have been encouraged, and subsequent arbitrary legislation has in a measure suppressed them. A sort of conscription has been adopted instead, and young men are made acquainted with the manual exercise. After a certain term of service, they retire, and are succeeded by others. Thus, their instructors are forging a formidable weapon against themselves, in the event of future troubles. The Code Napoleon is that at present in use ; and to suit the emergency, the judges of their tribunals are either drawn from the military or civilians, while his Excellency (at present Gov. Páge) professes to be, in his own words, "the law." An instance or two will suffice to show that the policy pursued by this government is detrimental to its own interests, if, as it professes, it seeks to encourage commerce ; and with reference to this suicidal course, the hackneyed proverb of " penny wise and pound foolish" might not be inappropriately applied. The following extract of a letter from an American ship-master, of Massachusetts, is an abridged statement of facts pertaining to his case, as they actually occurred. Its impartial tenor is its best feature :—

"On the first of January, 1853, my vessel, the ' E——e,' of Mystic, sailed from Honolulu, with about 300 tons whalebone and about $20,000 worth of furs, bound for New-Bedford. On the 22d of January, being then about 500 miles N. W. of Tahiti, my vessel sprung aleak, and I thought it prudent to put into Papéete and prevent it before attempting to double Cape Horn. I arrived there on the 25th, and immediately applied to the government (through our consul) for leave to discharge and store my cargo. It was very promptly granted, and I was allowed to place it in a building belonging to the government. After discharging, and waiting several days for a vessel then undergoing repairs to be launched from the railway, the government officials took charge of my vessel, and attempted to haul her upon the railway, but the cradle in which the vessel sits when drawn up was very improperly constructed, and it would not fit her bottom ; so, after hauling her up, they were obliged to launch her again. A day or two afterwards, they made a second attempt, but after getting her 'fore foot' about a foot out of water, they found it necessary to launch her again, and in doing this the 'rail' broke, and the cradle brought up with such a jerk that it threw the vessel from it, her heel falling down upon the coral bottom and her bow rising up in the air. In this position she was allowed to remain for *eight* days, and had she not been a very strong vessel, she would have broke in two. As it was, she was so badly 'hogged' (bent or twisted) and strained, that I formally abandoned her to the French government, and claimed as damages the value of the vessel, freight, money, and stores.

"About three weeks afterwards, our consul, Wm. H. Kelly, Esq., received notice from the Government that my vessel was a nuisance in the harbor, and that if I did not resume possession of her, *I should be imprisoned.* Being in daily expectation of the arrival of a vessel in which to ship my cargo, I thought it best to receive her back again under a formal protest, being compelled so to do—but the next day I advertised her to be sold at auction as she then lay, and on the fourth day after taking possession, she was sold for the benefit of whom it might concern. She brought about $2,500, and the stores about $400 more. After waiting until July 6th, I was enabled to get to sea again, with my cargo, on board the 'James Edward.' The Government declined receiving any pay for the storage of my cargo.

"The facilities for repairing vessels at Tahiti are tolerably good, but are all paralyzed by want of sober mechanics; the Government is at all times willing to afford all the assistance in its power—and although in my case *I think* they behaved dishonorably, yet, had not the railway broken, my vessel would probably have been repaired by them with dispatch, and at a moderate expense. As to refreshments and supplies for shipping, I have no doubt that if the natives could feel assured of finding a sale for their fruits, yams, potatoes, &c., they would furnish almost any quantity. During the year previous to my arrival at Papeéte, under the prospect of a large number of whalers arriving to refit there, they raised great quantities of vegetables, but the ships visiting the port were too few to purchase them, and the consequence was loss of produce by decay, as remuneration for their industry; and the following year, owing to their disappointment, they barely raised enough for the consumption of the inhabitants, hence the scarcity we experienced.

"The harbor is very safe and commodious, of easy access, having two entrances; a vessel should not attempt to enter without a steady breeze, however, as the current sets out of the passage through the reef."   *   *   *

The writer has modestly omitted to mention that a survey was held upon his vessel by competent ship-masters then in port, who were unanimous in pronouncing upon the damages sustained; also that a survey for a similar purpose was held by a committee of French officers, especially appointed, who concurred in certifying that the vessel had sustained *no injury* whatever, although when she was re-launched it was found necessary to man the pumps day and night to keep her afloat. A correct idea of the commercial and municipal regulations of the capital of French possessions in the Pacific cannot be formed without introducing the "Port Regulations for Tahiti," a copy of which is appended.

[Translation.]

PORT REGULATIONS,

TAHITI.

PORTS OPEN TO FOREIGN-GOING SHIPS.

Art. I.

No foreign-going vessel can, without special permission, or urgent necessity, anchor in any of the ports of the islands subject to the French Protectorate, other than the following, viz. : :

Papeete and Taunoa, at Tahiti.
Papetoai, at Moorea.

Offenders will be liable to a fine of from one hundred to five hundred francs.

REGULATIONS FOR THE COASTING TRADE.

Art. II.

The coasting trade of the islands, subject to the Protectorate, is reserved exclusively to vessels carrying the French or Protectorate flag.

All persons infringing the provisions of this article, will be liable to a fine of from one thousand to two thousand francs for the first offence, and to a double fine in case of repetition.

PILOTAGE.

Art. III.

The pilots licensed by the Commissioner of the Republic shall alone have the right of exercising the office of pilot.

They are to be paid according to the following tariff :—

	Francs.	Centimes.
Foreign line of battle ships and frigates	120	00
Foreign corvettes with upper decks	90	00
Foreign single-decked corvettes, and vessels of war of inferior class	60	00
All merchant vessels, per metre draught of water	11	70

In giving notice of their intended departure at the Port Office, captains will be required to present a receipt for the pilotage dues.

Art. IV.

Vessels entering or leaving without a pilot, shall pay one half of the pilotage dues established by the preceding Article.

Art. V.

When the pilot arrives in the offing for the purpose of bringing in a vessel, he is to inquire, before boarding her, if any contagious disease exists on board. On receiving a reply in the negative from the captain, the pilot will bring the vessel in. Should, however, a contrary answer be given, he will not go on board, but, without leaving his boat, and having first caused the quarantine flag to be hoisted in place of the pilot flag, he will conduct the vessel to a separate anchorage.

In all cases the pilot, or in his absence, the boat of the Port Office, or of the guard ship, will inform the captains, and also masters of coasters, that they must not communicate with any one, before being admitted to Pratique.

ADMISSION TO PRATIQUE.

Art. VI.

When the vessel is anchored, the pilot will communicate a copy of these regulations ; in cases where neither the guard ship nor the port office intervenes, the pilot will himself address the requisite questions to the captain, and after having taken note of his declarations, he will, according to the circumstances of the case, grant or refuse Pratique.

Art. VII.

Vessels from foreign voyages shall keep their pilot flag, and coasters their national flag flying, until they have been admitted to pratique ; and so long as these flags shall be flying, no one can go on board without exposing the captain to a fine of from fifty to two hundred francs.

Art. VIII.

The pilot, after having questioned vessels that do not enter, will grant or refuse them pratique, according to the nature of their declarations.

SANITARY MEASURES.

Art. IX.

Captains who make incomplete, inexact, or false declarations, and those who, being in quarantine, communicate either with the shore or harbor, will be liable to a fine of from 200 to 10,000 francs.

They will also be liable to the penalties prescribed by the French Sanitary Regulations, if, in consequence of false declarations, or culpable proceedings on their part, a contagious disease should make its appearance in the country.

Art. X.

Vessels in quarantine, as well as letters and packets coming from such vessels, will be subjected to such purifying and sanitary measures as may be directed by the Chief of the Medical Department.

DELIVERY OF LETTERS AND PACKETS, AND OF MANIFEST.

Art. XI.

As soon as a vessel is anchored, if she has been admitted to pratique, the captain or master of a coaster will proceed to the Port Office, and there deliver such letters and packets as may have been given into his charge, and also his general Manifest.

Extract from the Customs' Regulations.

"*Art.* 13. Every captain must, within twenty-four hours after his arrival, present to the Director of Customs his Manifest, with a detailed statement of the ammunition and arms of every kind, and also of the liquors, which, being subject to import duties, cannot be landed without the authorization of the Director of Customs. Those who shall infringe any of these regulations will be liable to a fine of from 50 to 400 francs.

"Any captain making a false declaration respecting prohibited goods, or those the sale of which is restricted, will be fined from 1,000 to 5,000 francs.

"*Art.* 15. When vessels have on board prohibited goods, spirits, arms or ammunition, intended alone for their own consumption or for the defence of the ship, captains must present to the Director of Customs a detailed declaration of such kinds of stores within twenty-four hours after their arrival. * * *

"*Art.* 16. Captains are required to inform the Director of Customs when the landing of the goods destined for the place has been completed.　＊　＊　＊

"*Art.* 18. The sale of munitions of war, powder, saltpetre, projectiles, muskets, arms of any kind, is prohibited, except under special permission from the Commissioner of the Republic.　All goods of this kind which may be attempted to be fraudulently landed, shall be *confiscated*, over and above the fine imposed by the Police Regulations.

"All spirits or liquors which may be attempted to be fraudulently landed, shall be *confiscated*, as well as the boat conveying them ; and the captain, who is held responsible for all goods which may be on board, under whatever conditions, shall be liable to a fine of from 1,000 to 5,000 francs.　In case of a repetition of the offence, the fine will be from 5,000 to 10,000 francs.

"*Art.* 21. Captains of merchant vessels, supercargoes, or traders, may themselves sell their goods under the following conditions.

"*Art.* 22. All goods admitted to entry in the French establishments of Oceania may be sold on board, provided that they be not sold by retail.

"Captains, supercargoes, or traders, must, however, in selling on board by wholesale, previously obtain a license of the first class, payable in advance, and for the period of three months.

"*Art.* 23. Captains, supercargoes, or traders, who may be desirous of landing their goods and opening a store on shore, must take out a license of the first class, payable in advance, and for the period of three months.

"*Art.* 24. The sale of wines and spirits is prohibited on board ship.　The liquors which parties may be desirous of selling must be sold on shore, either through the medium of a consignee, or directly by the captain or his agent, who will, however, have to comply with the regulations respecting licenses, and also with those respecting liquors."

EMBARKING AND DISEMBARKING CREW AND PASSENGERS.

Art. XII.

The captain or master or a coaster is required to report the number of his crew, that also of the passengers, and from whence they come ; and he must neither embark nor disembark any one whatever without a permit from the European Police, which must be presented either at the office of Maritime Inscription, or at the Consulate where the ship's papers are deposited.

Offenders will be condemned to a fine of from 200 to 400 francs for each person illegally disembarked or embarked.

Extract from the Police Regulations.

"*Art.* 44. No stranger is at liberty to establish his domicil at Tahiti, or to reside there for any period of time, without having first obtained permission so to do, and made known his domicil.　Every infringement will be punished with a fine of from 20 to 50 francs."　　　　•

CREW LIST.

Art. XIII.

French vessels, and foreign vessels having no Consul here, will deposit their crew lists at the office of Maritime Inscription, and shall receive them again on the eve of their departure.

The changes and notations shall be inscribed by the Commissary, who must be informed two days before the sailing of the vessel.

REGULATIONS RELATING TO THE MOORING OF VESSELS.

Art. IV.

Captains will have to change their anchorage when required to do so by the Director of the Port.

Art. XV.

No vessel is allowed to carry out warps in such a manner as to impede the public passage.

REGULATIONS CONCERNING THE CREWS.

Art. XVI.

The crews must be on board half an hour after gun-fire in the evening, and cannot return on shore before morning gun-fire.

Offenders will be subjected to the penalties prescribed by the Police Regulations.

REGULATIONS CONCERNING BOATS.

Art. XVII.

After evening gun-fire, no boat is allowed to land except at the Port Office wharf, under a penalty of from 10 to 50 francs.

Art. XVIII.

Boats may only remain alongside the public wharfs during the time necessary for loading or unloading.

PROHIBITION TO RECEIVE NATIVE WOMEN ON BOARD WITHOUT PERMISSION.

Art. XIX.

It is forbidden to receive native women on board vessels without permission from the Police.

BALLASTING AND DISCHARGING BALLAST.

Art. XX.

Vessels are not permitted either to take or to deposit ballast, except in conformity with the directions of the Port Office.

It is expressly forbidden to throw ballast into the harbor, under penalty of from one hundred to one thousand francs, which fine will be doubled in case of repetition of the offence.

DESERTERS.

Art. XXI.

Captains are required to make known the absence of deserters within forty-eight hours, under a penalty of from 200 to 500 francs.

They cannot leave the port before their deserters have been found, unless they deposit for each deserter the sum of fifty francs, for reward to the captors and prison expenses, nor unless an accepted surety engages to pay these expenses for them.

If the deserters are not found within three months after the sailing of the vessel, this money will be returned to the Consul, or to the person appointed by the captain to receive it, for nations that have no consuls here.

All other expenses occasioned by deserters after the sailing of their vessels will be arranged with the Consul, upon the production of the requisite administrative vouchers.

Extract from the Police Regulations.

"*Art.* 70. * ~ * * If deserters are captured after three days' absence, while the vessel is in port, the captain will have to pay 40 francs for each man for reward for capture if they be taken between Bunaauía and Haapape, and 75 francs for each man when deserters are arrested beyond those limits.

"After an absence of two days, the amount to be paid for capture will be 20 francs for the first locality, and 40 francs for the second.

"After twenty-four hours' absence, the amount to be paid will be 10 francs for the first locality, and 20 francs for the second.

"If the deserters are not captured until after the departure of the vessel, the reward to the captors will be reduced one half.

"In every case, it will be necessary to pay, in addition, to the Treasury, a fee of 10 francs for each arrest, and also the charge for food, at the rate of sixty-two and a half centimes per day.

"*Art.* 71. Whenever the gendarmerie shall be legally required by the captain of a vessel to proceed on board, and as a measure of discipline arrest one or more of his seamen, such arrest will entitle the gendarmerie to receive a compensation of 10 francs for each man, in like manner as for any other arrest effected by them."

ADMISSION OF MARINERS TO THE GOVERNMENT HOSPITAL.

Art. XXII.

Captains, officers, and seamen of merchant vessels will, in case of sickness, be admitted into the Government Hospital for treatment, upon the proposal of the Chief of the Medical Department to the Commissioner of the Republic.

In case of admission, the charge for treatment and residence will be, for all parties, 5 francs per day.

In case of the departure of a vessel leaving men at the hospital, the captain will be required to pay into the Treasury the amount of forty days' treatment, counting from the day upon which the ship's papers shall have been obtained from the office of Maritime Inscription, or the consul.

This payment shall be made upon vouchers prepared by the Commissary, in accordance with the regulations of the hospital service.

ASSISTANCE OFFERED BY THE GOVERNMENT.

Art. XXIII.

Upon the proposal of the Director of the Port, if private industry cannot afford the means, the Government will place at the disposal of ships of war and merchant vessels tackling for mooring and heaving down, and convenient buildings for receiving their crews and materials.

NOTICE OF DEPARTURE.

Art. XXIV.

Captains of vessels, whenever the length of their stay permits, must give notice of their departure at the port office forty-eight hours beforehand, and masters of coasters twenty-four hours before sailing; in case of their departure being postponed, fresh notice is required.

When it is desired that a vessel should remain less than forty-eight hours in port, the notice of departure should be given on the day of arrival.

CLEARANCE TO BE PRESENTED ON BOARD THE GUARD SHIP.

Art. XXV.

Before getting under way, the captains or masters of coasters will deliver up at the Port Office the copy of the Port Regulations communicated to them on their arrival ; they will also there receive letters, packets, and a clearance, certifying that they have complied with all the formalities prescribed by these regulations, which clearance they will present on board the guard ship.

Art. XXVI.

The crews, whenever they go on shore, will be subject to the police regulations of the country, as well as to the customs' regulations, of which captains can inform themselves at the Custom House.

Extract from the Police Regulations.

"*Art.* 36. Drunken people, either foreigners or natives, who shall be disorderly, or render themselves an object of scandal, will be put into prison until their drunkenness has passed off, without prejudice of the fine.

"*Art.* 42. All disputes in public, contrary to good order, will be punished with a fine of from 50 to 200 francs, and also from 1 to 3 days' imprisonment ; in case of a renewal of the offence, the fine will be from 200 to 500 francs, and the imprisonment from 3 to 5 days.

"*Art.* 14. All persons are forbidden to ride at a gallop within the limits of Papeete, in the space comprised between the Uranie Fort and the bridge over the river Pape-ava, on the Papaoa road. Offenders will be punished with a fine of 10 francs, without prejudice of damages, should there be ground for any.

"*Art.* 65. Every person arrested for a violation of the police or other regulations, when such violation shall not involve the prosecution of the party, shall pay 10 francs for fees of arrest, and 62½ centimes for food."

Art. XXVII.

Fines imposed on vessels must be paid within five days, at the furthest, from the date of condemnation.

In default of payment within the time specified, or of the acceptance of security by the Government in cases of inability to pay, a part or the whole of the cargo will be sold ; the vessel itself can be retained to liquidate the debt.

Art. XXVIII.

The Port Regulations, dated the 5th of April, 1847, and all the provisions of previous regulations and orders, in so far as they are contrary to the present regulations, are hereby abrogated.

Done at Papeete, the 6th of September, 1850.

The Commissioner of the French Republic, &c.

(Signed)

BONARD.

An instance of the arbitrary enforcement of Article 13th of "The Customs' Regulations" occurred a short time since. An English brig, the "Maid of Julpha," owned and commanded by Capt. R. N. Beauvais, arrived from the Marquesas, where it had been trading with the natives.

28

having on board the usual trinkets acceptable to savages, also a few condemned muskets in the lower hold.   The anchor was let go by the pilot on Saturday, who furnished no copy of the Port Regulations ; on going ashore the captain obtained them, when, to his surprise, he learned that he had committed a serious error in omitting to include his useless weapons in the manifest already handed in.   With his consignee, he proceeded forthwith to the office of the Director of Customs, but that official was absent ; time was flying, and he hastened to the British consul to state the case to him.   Again the Director was sought, but the search proved fruitless ; the hour for closing the office passed, and it would only be opened on the Monday following, when nearly forty-eight hours would have elapsed.   He was subsequently summoned to appear before the *tribunal*, and notwithstanding the evidence adduced in his favor by his consul, he was fined to the full extent of the law.   This outrage on an English subject was ostensibly for the violation of the 13th Article, but it was alleged behind the curtain that he had traded with the Marquesans in contraband goods, muskets and ammunition, but of this they had not a shadow of proof.

It was attempted, after the promulgation of this law, to adopt a similar course of proceeding with American whalers who were occasionally guilty of this " sin of omission ;" but by the prompt interference of our consul, who represented that the adoption of such an illiberal measure would be virtually to exclude American commerce from their ports, the accident has been subsequently overlooked.   The landing of either pistol or fowling-piece without a " permit" subjects the offender to an exorbitant fine, besides the confiscation of the weapon.   It is the enforcement of such petty restrictions as these that tend more than anything to frighten commerce from French colonial ports.

The facilities for apprehending deserters are unsurpassed by those of any other port in the Pacific, and vessels may visit Tahiti without fearing trouble in this respect.

It is not to be inferred from Article 44th of Police Regulations, that a stranger is to be in any way embarrassed by unwarranted prohibitions during a residence within the jurisdiction of the Protectorate, or from the subsequent articles under this head included in the Port Regulations. Any person whose propensities are not such as to outrage decency, or to subvert the requirements essential to the social tranquillity and law and order of a community, need apprehend no impertinence from the *gendarmerie*, a well-disciplined body, but may seek every rational enjoyment in a manner consistent with either taste or pursuits.   The following is the form of the permit referred to in Article 44th, and which every person is required to obtain on landing, after having made known his domicil :—

No.

PERMIS DE SÉJOUR.

Le Sieur   est autorisé à séjourner

provisoirement à Papeéte, sous la caution de

Papeéte le   185

L'officier chargé des affaires Européenes.

NOTA.—*Les cautions repondront moralement de l'individu, elles devront déclarer qu'il est a leur connaissance que l'homme qu'elles cautionnent, jouit d'une bonne réputation, et a les moyens de pourvoir a sa subsistance pendant son séjour Taiti.*

Signature des personnes qui cautionnent.   (Prix 2 francs.)

[Translation.]

PERMIT OF RESIDENCE.

Mr. ———— is authorized to reside provisionally in Papeéte, under the surety of ————.

PAPEETE, ———— —, 185 .

———————————————, Chargé of European Affairs.

N. B.—Sureties are responsible for the moral character of the individual ; they must declare that, according to their belief, the person for whom they are answerable enjoys a good reputation, and has the means of subsistence during his sojourn in Tahiti.

Signature of surety.   (Price 2 francs.)

Apparent results since the establishment of the Protectorate, are the moral retrogression of the natives, a lack of commercial vitality, and the fetters placed upon religious freedom. Let us at present briefly notice the last of these, which must necessarily involve the former.

The London Missionary Society, in selecting teachers as instruments for prosecuting their laudable enterprise, have always endeavored to engage only those of approved worth and ability, and these have been sent forth unfettered by any sectarianism whatever, simply to instil into the minds of their converts the consoling assurances of salvation, by faith in revealed Christianity, leaving with the natives the privilege of adopting whatever mode of worship might be congenial to their views. The teachers sent out by the London Board arrived at Tahiti in 1797, but it was not until 1819 that success attended their efforts, and the Church was firmly established. This has continued up to the period of the conquest of Tahiti by the French, and its attendant results were the abolition of idolatry, and numerous stills for the manufacture of intoxicating drinks, the social and moral improvement of the race, and the general diffusion of knowledge by the press.

The occupation of Tahiti by the French was looked upon by the English nation as a moral, if not political encroachment, for these islands were considered, and undoubtedly were, a monument of its philanthropy; it was probably from the conviction of similar sentiments that Commodore B. Toup Nicholas, of H. B. M. ship "Vindictive," issued his bold circular to the British residents of Tahiti and Moorea, on the 20th of June, 1843. On the 20th of March, during the same year, when the Marquis of Lansdowne, in the House of Lords, inquired of the Earl of Aberdeen, then Premier, whether the government had received any information respecting the French occupation of Tahiti ; also suggesting the necessity of an assurance from that government that "their authority should be exercised in a manner consistent with the rights of British subjects, and especially the missionaries," he was informed by the Earl that he had "no precise information on the subject ; but he was not of opinion that the commercial or political interests would be at all interfered with, but, on the contrary, he thought there was reason to look to it with satisfaction, and to anticipate advantageous results from it. He had caused representations to be made at Paris, and they were met by the most unqualified assurance that every degree of protection and encouragement would be afforded to the British ministers settled in those parts. In fact, there was an article in the convention between the French commander and the native authorities, by which it was stipulated that protection should be extended to all places of religious worship, and to the missionaries established in those islands."

The sentiments of Du Petit Thouars on the subject of religious belief, if sincere, do him more credit than any glory he may have acquired by his conquests ; for, among the provisional articles concluded upon between Queen Pomare and himself, he concedes on the part of France, "That the churches at present established shall continue to exist, and the English missionaries shall continue in the prosecution of their labors without molestation. The same shall apply to every other form of worship; no one shall be molested or constrained in his belief." In a letter to the missionaries upon the same subject, he again remarks, "That no person shall be constrained in his religious opinions or practices. Liberty of conscience is a good so precious that we ought not to desire it for ourselves only, but for all." The policy of M. Guizot on these points was conciliatory, as was manifest from his dispatch to the British ambassador then residing in Paris; and comparative tranquillity was enjoyed by the mission until the days of *liberté, égalité, fraternité*. From that time it dates the encroachments upon its privileges, and the bonds of intolerance have been drawn closer and closer, until at the present day every member of the board is virtually prohibited from exercising the functions of his sacred calling.

Under Gov. Lavaud, the native chapels were converted into national property, thus uniting Church and State, and the lands on which they stand have been declared confiscate, and some of the private dwellings of the missionaries have been either sequestered or become a government appropriation, to the sacrifice of the sums that, for enhancing their comfort and convenience, have from time to time been expended upon them. The next stone knocked from the foundation of religious liberty was the act passed by the Legislative Assembly in March, 1851, prohibiting a missionary from preaching in any other district than his own, unless he shall have received a written invitation. The following law, instituted at that time, pertaining to the election of ministers, will exhibit an unqualified veto power vested in the Governor, which was displayed in the case of Mr. A. W. Lind, who was sent out by the directors of the London Missionary Society; though according to law this gentleman was elected pastor for the district of Atimaouo, without a dissenting voice, the election was nullified by his Excellency, who alleged that the " English missionaries were enemies to the government, and that he could not allow Mr. Lind to settle there " The law is as follows :—

" These are the officers to be chosen by the chiefs (*hui raatira*) in the Protectorate Government : The district governors, the district minister of religion, and the members of Parliament.

" The whole of the chiefs (*hui raatira*) in a district shall have a right to vote in these elections.

" Any one may be elected to the office of district minister who may be agreeable to the electors, and approved of by the majority. *If a foreigner be chosen, the election must be submitted to the Governor, the Commissioner of the Republic, for his approval, because the foreign department is with him.*"

Nothing can be more absurd than a charge implicating the mission either directly or indirectly with the established order of things. Though suffering from the effects of the political change, and with their ordinary labors greatly augmented by having to combat a new faith, and the moral discord naturally resulting from a protracted warfare, they have patiently performed the duties of their calling, simply relying upon the indulgence of their new rulers. The act of depriving a minister of the privilege of being elected by his own church, and placing, instead, his election at the caprice of an entire district, whether dissenters from his creed or not, is virtually depriving him of his office, unless he consents to become an annunciator of the government.

The proclamation of Governor Bonard to district governors on the first of May, 1852, with special reference to the subject of ministerial election, will exhibit the style of an official *ukase.*

"PROCLAMATION
"TO ALL THE DISTRICT GOVERNORS.

" *Friends :—*

" There is to be only one minister in each district ; that minister is to be chosen by the chiefs of the district. If the minister chosen be a foreigner, his election shall be submitted to the Commissioner of the Republic for his approval, as the decision with regard to foreigners rests with him alone.

" That is what the law declares, and it is proper that this law be strictly enforced ; and it is your business to see well to it, that the law be neither disregarded nor evaded by means of little hidden stratagems.

" Therefore, as you are the representatives of the government in your respective districts, it is for you to prevent any foreigners (who call themselves missionaries, but who have not been chosen by the electors in the districts, and whose election has not been approved of by the French government,) from preaching in any of the chapels, under pretence that they have been requested—that request being only from a few insignificant people of the district.

" Those who may go and preach in any of the district chapels, when requested to do so in writing, are those only who have been chosen by a district according to law, and whose election has been agreed to by the Protectorate Government, if they be foreigners, and who hold the office of minister in some district within the limits of the Protectorate Government. That privilege is granted to *them,* since they are required to reside in the district where they were chosen ; but it is by no means right or agreeable to the spirit of the law, that either foreigners who casually visit Tahiti, or those who have their fixed residence here, describing themselves as missionaries, should, placing themselves beyond the law, and not submitting to the regular election and recognition of the Protectorate Government, enter the district chapels and set themselves up as if they were properly elected ministers.

" If such an evil as this should be permitted to pass, and as it has been attempted at Mahaena and Papeuriri, the law would thus be set aside, which declares that there is to be but one missionary in each district, and that it is necessary, in order to a foreigner holding the office, that he be approved of by the French government. It would also be a denial of the power of the chiefs and electors, for if a person be sent for as minister from another district, they ought to have a voice in that election, for this is what the law requires.

" The request in writing required by law, and according to which it is proper for a minister to go and preach in another chapel, must be from natives only, and the ministers who have been properly chosen according to law.

" If this be attended to, then the law will be properly enforced, which declares that there shall be only one missionary in each district ; the power also of the chiefs will be fully established, and it will not be possible for foreigners to place themselves beyond the control of the Protectorate Government which has been set over them ; and thus, also, liberty of conscience will be secured, and a complete separation of all the ministers, so that one may not be under another.

" In conclusion, I also make known to you my wish. That it be clearly made known to all the ministers who have been properly chosen by the several districts, that they will be carefully protected in their rights by the Protectorate Government, and that without any difference whatever being made between foreigners and natives ; and it will be by no means right for any foreign missionary to place himself above the others, either to command them or to find fault with them.

" It is right, notwithstanding this, that young ministers should treat with some respect the aged and the inexperienced amongst them, and those who have instructed them ; but that respect is one thing, and the improper subordination which is required by a certain party from the native ministers, is another, and a very different thing. Make it clearly known to them that they are perfectly free, but it is necessary that they continue to respect the laws.

" Do you also make known to them that they have perfect liberty in regard to matters of religion in their own districts, but let them also well respect the liberty of the ministers in the neighboring districts, and by no means let them interfere in the affairs of other districts than their own, as that is a cause of trouble, and it is necessary that it be completely put a stop to.

" Make known this letter to the proper minister of your district, and also the chiefs, and carefully attend to all the matters made known to you by this proclamation.

" PAPEETE, 1*st May*, 1852.

" The Governor, the Commissioner of the Republic.

(" Signed,)

" BONARD."

Such a Jesuitical production is worthy of its author, and such a complexity of absurd restrictions can only be supposed to emanate from one who lacks the moral courage to step boldly forth and at once shut down the safety-valve of religious freedom. Its paternal tenor is absolutely farcical, and may be instanced as an illustration of French protection. His Excellency's alleged violation of the law at Mahaena and Papeuriri is unfounded. In the first instance, his personal investigation could detect nothing approximating to illegality of procedure on the part of the resident minister ; and in the other, the case was prejudged, and the minister condemned to six months' confinement within the limits of his district, without being allowed a hearing. An invitation for this minister to preach in the chapel of Papeuriri had been tendered him, formally signed by the residents of that district, according to law ; this document was placed in the hands of his Excellency by H. B. M. consul, Wm. Miller, Esq., residing at Papeete, and by Governor Bonard's inability to offer anything in justification of his arbitrary conduct, and in lacking the manliness to redress a wrong, he has still further augmented the unenviable reputation acquired by his official proceedings at this island.

With these obstacles to encounter, the efforts of the resident missionaries, until lately, have not been relaxed ; more than 450,000 pages were printed by them during the last two years alone, and other scriptural publications received from England have been gratuitously supplied to the natives ; in short, they are the only persons to whom the natives are indebted for school-books. But lately the press has been silenced, and the field, through necessity, almost deserted. Only three foreign ministers are allowed to preside in native churches ; these have seceded from the London Missionary Society, and for reasons of their own have voluntarily rendered themselves subservient to the French Government. With these exceptions, the entire native population is supplied by native teachers, whose acquirements are inadequate to administer to its wants, temporal or spiritual. The Rev. Wm. Howe, resident chaplain at Papeéte, has passed more than eighteen years of his life upon this island ; and through all the vicissitudes of the mission during that period has maintained an unshaken confidence in his reliance upon Divine assistance, and has manifested a praiseworthy zeal in performing the duties of his sacred calling.

That a moral blight has been making steady progress throughout the land, is sufficiently apparent from the evidences daily transpiring. Dissipation walks unblushingly in the face of day ; and when more than fifty persons, from the age of fourteen and upwards, are seen at one time perambulating the streets in a state of intoxication, it seriously behooves a "great nation" exercising (or professing to do so) the prerogatives of protection, to give the subject at least a superficial attention, unless speedy decimation be the object sought. It has lately been discovered that those natives who, through all the turmoil of foreign warfare and its attendant evils, had been looked upon as the bulwark or supporters of the Church, have occasionally yielded to the allurements of dissipation to which they are daily exposed ; and it is feared that Queen Pomare herself, in whose behalf so much sympathy has been manifested by the Christian world, is becoming remiss in the performance of her spiritual duties.

Thus has "this splendid embassy of Christian mercy to the South Seas" been shattered—dissevered ; and the monument, of which it was the architect, built up by the free charities of true English benevolence, is left tottering upon its foundation, undermined by the secret approaches of the Seven Hills. Though justly aggrieved by the premature rashness of Protestant missionaries towards the propagators of her own established faith, it would redound far more to the honor of so great a nation as France to adopt a more liberal, rational policy towards those who acknowledge her supremacy, irrespective of sectarian feeling ; thereby promoting the best interests of her colony, and raising its elements from

moral degradation to the enjoyment of the greatest of earthly blessings
—civil and religious freedom.

Pleasanter evidences resulting from this conquest are local changes
everywhere observable. Roads have been improved, and, in some
instances, streams are spanned by beautiful and substantial bridges.
The thoroughfare designated the Broom Road, extending around the
island, if not the best, is certainly the pleasantest to be found on any
shore of the Pacific. Spacious public buildings erected in the town of
Papeéte, including the government house, arsenal, storehouses, barracks,
steam mill, &c., have an imposing effect ; and, as external evidences
of prosperity, enhance the natural beauty of the scenery amid which
they are situate. From numerous hydrants, pure streams of mountain water are perpetually gushing beneath the shade of orange and
bread-fruit trees, also from the substantial and commodious stone
jetties this element is forever mingling with the quiet waters of the
lagoon. The construction of a marine cradle or railway, for the
purpose of facilitating the repairs of vessels, although unequal to its
object, is a commendable undertaking. The absence of port charges,
and the facility with which deserters may be recovered, are strong recommendations for vessels to visit this port ; in point of extent and
natural conveniences, the harbor of Honolulu will hardly bear a comparison with this. Though every feature bespeaks the military instead of
the commercial colony, including the incessant patrolling of sentries
before the government works, and the white, isolated watch-towers,
which, like tombstones of liberty, are placed upon commanding emi-
nences and form a continuous chain around the island, Tahiti possesses
many attractions for the tourist, or others whose pursuits extend to the
Southern Sea. From M. Chappe, the present Captain-Director of European Affairs, visitors may obtain every indulgence compatible with
the established laws of the Protectorate for rendering their sojourn
agreeable. It is presumed that no visitor has had reason to complain
of want of civility, or lack of the ordinary courtesies of social in-
ercourse from foreign residents. More obliging and honorable merchants
than many of those resident at Papeéte, French, English and American,
are not to be met with on the shores of this ocean. Americans, whose
interests lie in this quarter, have reason to congratulate themselves that
they possess an efficient representative in Wm. H. Kelly, Esq., whose
official duties are no impediment in the way of hospitable observances
or polite attention, trifling in themselves, but whose appreciation is enhanced by their bestowal in a foreign land.

The Protectorate having been securely established, it is to be supposed
that the attention of the French government would have been directed

towards developing the agricultural resources of their newly acquired territory. Unfortunately, this has not been the case, and the thousands of acres of rich arable land that by judicious management might yield an ample revenue, are suffered to remain uncultivated—neglected. The remarks of Commodore Wilkes on the productions of this group during the visit of the U. S. Exploring Squadron to Tahiti in 1839, from information derived from residents, though brief, are worth transcribing, and are as follows :—

" The commercial resources of these islands are very limited. Most of the vessels that visit Tahiti belong to our whaling fleet ; these average less than a hundred annually. From them the natives are enabled to dispose of some of the supplies they raise, and in return obtain such articles as will promote their comfort and add to their pleasure. The whale ships have for the most part articles of trade which they barter with the natives, so that little money is required to carry on their business. The natives, particularly the chiefs, are well acquainted with the value of money. An estimate has been made that each of these vessels introduces goods into the island to the amount of $500 each, making a total of $50,000 ; but I very much question whether it can reach this extent.

* * * * * * * *

" The pearl-shell fishery of the Paumotu group centres here. I was told that it was principally in the hands of the French consul. For a few years before our arrival, from 1832 to '38, it had been very productive. The amount obtained was about 900 tons, which was estimated to be valued at $45,000 to $50,000 ; the greater part of this was sent to France.

* * * * * * * *

" The three chief articles of production are sugar, cocoanut oil, and arrow-root. The following statement was furnished me of the quantities produced :—

SUGAR.

	Tons.	Estimated Value.
Tahiti	105	$8,000
Eimeo	32	2,000
Raiatéa	15	1,300
Total	152	$11,300

COCOANUT OIL.

	Tons.	Estimated Value.
Tahiti	55	$3,500
Eimeo	20	1,500
Huahine	60	4,500
Borabóra and Raiatéa	50	3,800
Total	185	$13,300

Total value of produce....................$24,600

" Of arrow-root there are about 50 tons produced, valued at nearly $4,000, which, included with the above, will make the sum of nearly $28,000 as the value derived from the agricultural products of these islands. If they were under proper cultivation, this amount would be greatly increased ; and from the estimate of a competent person, it was believed that the productions might yield, if properly attended to, a revenue of $300,000, as coffee, cotton, and indigo, might be added to the above articles. But this is an estimate one half too great, and would require an amount of labor that the present population are inadequate to perform, and which their climate, wants, and desires, will never probably excite them to, or render necessary."

At the present day, instead of the cultivation of cane, the sugar required for domestic consumption is imported, and the trade in arrowroot and cocoanut oil is hardly worth noticing. These elements of prosperity still exist, but the moral lethargy, which, like an incubus, has brooded over the natives since their deprivation of liberty, seems to have paralyzed every effort towards re-developing this branch of commercial enterprise. Since the discovery of gold in California, and the rapid increase of population in that State, the numerous orange groves of this group furnish a new article of commerce, and the surplus fruit exported from the entire group amounts to about 1,000,000 oranges annually, at a cost of $5,000 or $6,000; and allowing one-third loss, and an average price of $50.00 per thousand, as they sell in San Francisco at $30.00 to $100.00 per thousand by the cargo, they yield a gross profit to the shippers of $300,000 to $400,000. The pearl fishery still continues profitable to those engaged in it, owing to the increased commerce that has sprung up in this ocean since the new phases exhibited by California and Australia. These islands receive their share of transient vessels, and their floating capital is greater than would at first be supposed.

The circumference of Tahiti is 84 miles; that of Moorea, 25 miles—both together equivalent to the Isle of France or Mauritius in the Indian Ocean, formerly a French colony, but which since 1810 has been in the possession of the English. If this island can support a population of 90,000 white and black, and export 68,000,000 lbs. of sugar in one year, what might not Tahiti do with a climate and soil equally favorable, and situate midway between the two great marts of the Western Ocean? While adding to her conquests in the Pacific, France should at least possess the ambition to enter the lists with the only colony that Spain possesses in the East Indies yielding a revenue. From the Asiatic shores, for comparatively trifling expense, may be procured the requisite material for promoting the interests of her newly-acquired territory, and Manilla, with her exports of sugar and tobacco, might find a rival in the Queen of the Pacific.

But recently, during the last year, the French have taken possession of the island New Caledonia, of the division Melanesia, and distant from the coast of Australia but 700 miles. This island is 250 miles in length, having an average breadth of near 60 miles, and has a range of high mountains extending throughout its whole length. On the western side is an extensive barrier reef, forming a broad sea or lagoon nearly the entire length of the island. A great portion of the country is rocky and sandy, but in other places the soil is fertile, being covered with luxuriant vegetation. Among the productions are noticed many of the fruits and esculents common to Polynesia. But little is known respecting its inhabitants, farther than that the island is comparatively thinly inhabited by natives, who, like those of the islands adjoining, are Papuans, or Oriental negroes, in every respect inferior to the Polynesians, warlike and barbarous. The alleged object for the occupation of this island by the French, is the establishment of a penal colony, and such an announcement has occasioned no little consternation among the Australians, on account of the proximity of that island to their shores, and from the possibility of their being contaminated by the escaped felons of France.

The establishment of a safe and convenient depot in this quarter of the Pacific for commercial purposes, if such be the intention of France, cannot in any way prove detrimental to the interests of the numerous trading vessels whose traffic is among the savage tribes of Melanesia, where, in case of emergency, assistance may be obtained. There is now but one link wanting to complete the chain of conquest across the Pacific, and this is the Island of Tongatabu. It cannot be denied that the emissaries of the Romish Church are in some degree instrumental in promoting these acquisitions. No later than last summer, a French frigate looked into the harbor of this island to investigate an alleged affront received by some Romish priests from the natives, they having, uninvited, established themselves among a professedly Protestant people. Upon investigation, the affair proved to be simply the decided stand made by the natives against any innovation upon their moral convictions, and, in one or two instances, incivility towards those who had zealously attempted to enforce it. On this occasion, the ordinary threats of vengeance were not resorted to, and the commander of the ship gave the disciples of the Church to understand that it was an affair in which he could not interfere. It will be recollected that an occurrence in some degree similar, furnished sufficient pretext for the enslavement of a race which, like the Tongatabuans, speak a dialect different from the Tahitians. However, it is but last September that the French steamer "Phoque" sailed for Tongatabu to adjust differences that have again arisen at this island. Should an attack be made upon the liberties of the people, they will never be surrendered without a struggle. They have good forts, capable of sustaining a siege, and in more than one conflict, have proved themselves as bold warriors as are to be found in the South Pacific. It is evident that they could not sustain a protracted struggle with so great a power as France, and it will occasion no surprise to those who have watched her proceedings in this ocean to learn that the tri-color waves over a new conquest. It would appear that Louis Napoleon in the Pacific is adopting the system of the *Grand Monarque*, who, in the seventeenth century, attempted the establishment of a chain of military posts from the mouth of the St. Lawrence to the mouth of the Mississippi. However feasible the project may appear, save the temporary derangement to commerce, there would be but little to apprehend in the event of a rupture between France and any of the great maritime powers of the Old or New World, remote as she is from these island colonies, and hemmed in as they are by American, English, and Russian possessions, comprising thousands of miles of sea-board, with excellent harbors, and each country possessing in itself the elements or means of equipping a naval armament. There yet remains one important post, situate nearly midway between her conquests, the occupation of which would checkmate her power among the isles, and this is the Navigator Islands. To their advantages as a commercial depot, allusion has already been made; and if they cannot, like the Hawaiian Islands, be permitted to remain an independent state, it would not be regretted if England, under whose fostering care the inhabitants have partially emerged from barbarism, deemed it not unworthy of her to take them under her protection. We have already a precedent on which to base a conjecture as to future results : the rapid growth of the only colony she possesses in Polynesia, New Zealand— the towns and villages that have sprung up—the encouragement given to agriculture and commerce—confirm the assertion that, in extending her dominions, England seeks not the enslavement of those she conquers.

A broad distinction between French and English colonies at once impresses an observer : with the latter, less of military, but more of commercial, evidences are apparent ; or should political necessity require the presence of an army, it is usually confined to its own sphere, without prescribing the duties and privileges of civilians, or fettering commerce with petty restrictions. An American who treads upon British soil, divested of arrogant preconceptions of national superiority, may feel, though in a foreign clime, that he breathes an atmosphere of political freedom, and is amenable only to the laws of a civil tribunal, while enjoying the refinements and associations of his native land. Conservative philanthropists view with pious regret the almost incredible conquests of England in the Indian empire, sympathizing with such invaders as Tippoo-Saib or Hyder Ali, forgetting that in many respects the victory of Plassey was the corner-stone of *native* freedom from Moslem bondage. But this field is too broad to admit of present argument. While charging upon that nation the human misery unavoidably apparent, we must not overlook the evidences of political shame or error that exist in our own land. We should not forget that the result of these conquests are no longer the selfish monopolies of the preceding century, but reflect that our present commercial prosperity is greatly indebted to the gratuitous gift of English blood and treasure. While regarding with indifference the progress of empire—the annihilation of primitive independence—the absorption of kingdoms—we may well smile at the happy unity of sentiment pervading the powers of the Old World, who nervously protest against the extension of American territory, though peacefully consummated by mutual concession. However, let us seek not to draw harrowing distinctions between our illustrious progenitor and ourselves. If we descend for a moment from the pinnacle of our egotism and examine facts as they truly exist, having reference to philanthropy and the peculiar results of Anglo-Saxon influence, we will say—God speed the cross of St. George! whether it waves on the banks of the Ganges, or flutters amid the the jungles of Sarawack.

It is hoped the preceding remarks will not be regarded as animadversions of national prejudice; France at home and France abroad, or a people individually and politically, are very different subjects. For intellectual refinement, encouragement of literature, the arts and sciences, hers is a proud position among nations. While proffering acknowledgments for disinterested courtesy, the writer would sincerely regret having trespassed upon this subject, if the truthful results of personal observation receive other than their intended application, exclusively to political economy.

APPENDIX IV.

AMERICAN WHALING INTERESTS IN THE PACIFIC.*

Prominent Features of Whaling—Cruising-Grounds of Sperm Whalers; of Right Whalers—Traffic and Exchange—Estimated Capital employed—Our present Fleet compared with that of 1844; with that of Europe—Imports of 1844; of 1853—Increased Value of Products —Relation to our Merchant Marine—Ports frequented—Petty Exactions—Micronesian Ports—Honolulu—Seamen, their Condition and Wants; Relations to Consuls—Foreigners as Commercial Agents; Ludicrous Incident—Our Consular System—Conclusive Glance at the Profession.

THERE is perhaps no branch of the marine service more arduous than that of whaling. Independent of the hardship to which every seaman is exposed, the whaleman is compelled to launch his boat upon the ocean in storm or calm, to "beard the lion in his den." Chilled among icebergs and scorched in a burning zone, he becomes inured to privations at the bare recital of which a landsman would shudder; and any young man who has passed the ordeal of a three or four years' cruise, if he be willing and of ordinary capacity, will have acquired a fair knowledge of practical seamanship, and will have seen more hard service than if he had served double that time on an ordinary merchantman.

Erroneous impressions are usually entertained respecting whalers, it being the custom to associate with them everything that is superlatively disagreeable. Whaling as it was fifteen or twenty years ago, affords but a poor criterion for judging the profession as it now exists. At the present day, greater reference is had to the comfort of those who man the vessels, both as pertains to their rations and convenience of abode. The former practice of employing cast-off liners of ancient model is being gradually superseded by vessels better adapted for this object, and some

---

* For statistical information pertaining to this subject, acknowledgments are due the attentions of James Taylor, Esq., Deputy Collector for the port of New Bedford; also to Dennis Wood, Esq., of the same city.

of them are model clippers, elegant in their proportions, and bidding fair to rival our merchantmen in speed. Another feature to be noticed is the frequent custom of masters being accompanied by their families, which would imply a greater reference to the comfort and condition of those under their command. From this it is not to be inferred that families' are necessarily confined to the vessel during its sinuous cruisings in the Pacific, for the various ports among the groups offer conveniences for a sojourn of any duration while the vessel is pursuing the objects of the voyage.

This profession has been divided into two branches—*sperm* and *right* whaling—the latter capturing several of the remaining varieties of cetacea; and though the former branch is confined to a single species, the right whaler attacks the sperm whale wherever it can be found. Formerly, when this profession was in its infancy, the Atlantic was the ordinary cruising-ground of whalers, and the Falkland Islands off Patagonia were its farthest southern limit, and the vessels employed being of inferior capacity, the duration of a voyage was from six to twelve months. But of late years, since the fleet launched against them has continued so rapidly to augment, the whales have become timid, and in schools resort to new feeding-grounds, so that the occupation of capturing them, heretofore confined to the Atlantic, has extended to the entire watery area of the globe.

The cruising-grounds of the sperm whaler are in the Indian Ocean, in the vicinity of the St. Paul's and Mauritius, near Madagascar and along the eastern coast of Africa; also about New Zealand, in the Australian seas, and among the islands within the tropics of the Pacific Ocean. Right whalers, on leaving the Atlantic ports, visit either the Azores or Cape de Verde Islands for supplies, and it is generally so timed that they double Cape Horn during the summer months of those latitudes, and reach the Sandwich Islands after a passage (cruising by the way) of from three to five months. From here, after a brief recruit, they start away for the "northwest" cruising-ground, (so called from its being originally confined to the northwestern coast of America,) extending through Behring's Straits to the Arctic Ocean and the seas of Kamtschatka, Ochotsk and Japan, the second being formed by the peninsula just mentioned, on the east, and China and Siberia on the west; while the latter is bounded by the Chinese and Japanese empires. Here they cruise during the months of June, July, and August, until in September increasing gales warn them to depart, when they usually return to the Hawaiian ports of Honolulu, Lahaina, and Hilo. Having remained at these stations as long as their several necessities may require, from one to three months, they renew their cruise during the "between seasons," so called, within the tropics, ranging among the southern and central archipelagoes for sperm whales, frequently holding intercourse with the natives of these islands, and gradually working their way towards Guam or Hong Kong, where they refit, and improve the season in the Japan Sea.   The average duration of a sperm whaler's voyage, or from the time it leaves home until its return, is forty-three months, while that of a right whaler is thirty-two months.

For trade or barter, whalers carry with them muskets and ammunition, cutlery, tobacco and domestic goods—American productions and manufactures—and these are scattered throughout the vast oceans they traverse.   For necessary repairs and the payment of discharged seamen, whose term of service has expired, cash is advanced in foreign ports at a premium of from 5 to 25 per cent., when drafts on their owners are given in return.   These bills of exchange are always negotiable abroad, and are never dishonored at home, which would be disastrous to whaling interests : so that whatever may be the nature of the expense incurred by their factors or agents, the owners, through policy, endorse them, and consequently in selecting masters for their vessels, judicious reference is had to economy as well as qualification.

The cost and outfit (including advance to crew) of a whaler on leaving port, that will stow from 3,000 to 4,000 bbls. of oil, is at least $40,000 ; to this is to be added insurance, which for the cruise is about 12 per cent., and we have more than $25,000,000 embarked in this branch of commerce.   During the last ten years the increase of our whaling fleet has been but slight : in 1844 it numbered 595 ships and barks, 41 brigs, 11 schooners, and 1 sloop; while on the 1st January, 1854, we find it to consist of 602 ships and barks, 28 brigs and 38 schooners, having an aggregate tonnage of 208,399 tons, and which is about twelve times greater than that of the combined whaling fleets of Europe that cruise in the Pacific.   The tonnage of the English fleet is about 7,000 tons, that of France the same, while the fleet of Bremen is less than 3,000 tons ; the number of colonial whalers that formerly sailed from Australian ports has gradually fallen off, until of late years it hardly deserves a consideration.

In quantity, there is comparatively little difference to notice between the imports of the whale fishery into the United States for each consecutive year during the last ten years.

In 1844 they amounted to 139,594 bbls. sperm oil, 262,047 bbls. whale oil, and 2,532,445 lbs. bone.   During the preceding year, 1853, the importations were, 103,077 bbls. sperm oil, 260,114 bbls. whale oil, and 5,652,300 lbs. bone, having an aggregate value of $5,442,441.

During the last two years no oil has been exported, though for several
29

years previous it was shipped abroad to a considerable extent; in 1846, the quantity amounted to 1,004,661 gallons of oil. Although the imports during the last ten years exhibit no decided decrease, the average price during each consecutive year has continued gradually to augment: in 1844, sperm oil was worth 63 cents per gall.; whale, 34½; and bone, 35¾ cents per lb.; while during the past year it has averaged about $1.25 for sperm, 85 cents for whale, and 34½ cents per lb. for bone.

Of late years, this branch of commerce has become somewhat interwoven with our merchant marine, owners deeming it to their interest to have the oil and bone taken by their vessels discharged at Honolulu or other convenient port, and reshipped as freight on board such merchantmen as receive it at reasonable rates. The result of this system, when fairly established in 1851–52, was for speculators in San Francisco to purchase old hulks for a nominal sum that had been lying in that port and were considered almost useless, and after a temporary refit, send them to Honolulu for a freight home, which would yield them more than a hundred per cent. on their investment. This was in many instances prejudicial to their interests—for some of these vessels proving unseaworthy, were, after a brief absence, compelled to put back, discharge their cargoes, and refit; or upon survey, were sometimes condemned, as at Honolulu and Papeéte. It has now become politic for carriers to offer none but approved and substantial vessels for this purpose, and at present it bids fair to become a lucrative branch of commerce to those who engage in it: until by over competition, as invariably happens in this ocean, it relapses to a lower basis. These freights are usually worth from 8 to 10 cents per gallon for oil, and a vessel of sufficient capacity to carry 4,000 bbls. realizes something like $10,000 by the transaction.

The sums annually disbursed by this fleet are large, and the amount of bills drawn at the Sandwich Islands on owners during the fall of the year 1852 could not fall far short of $500,000. The ports frequented are chiefly Honolulu, Talcahuano, Paita, Papeéte, Guam, Hong Kong, and sometimes San Francisco. It may sound strange to state, that the most expensive port in this ocean for a vessel, with respect to government charges and outlay necessary for repairs or recruits, is an American, while the cheapest is an English one: these are respectively San Francisco and Hong Kong.

The system of unwarranted exactions upon whalers that visit many of the out-of-the-way ports in this ocean, is detrimental to the interests of those who make them. An instance occurred recently at Raiatea: a New London whaler visited that port for supplies, but, save fire-wood, there was nothing else to be obtained; during the visit, eleven men deserted; and although a reward of $5.00 was offered for the apprehension of each man, such was the inefficiency of the government that not one of them was recovered. In addition to paying $8.00 for pilotage, other charges for harbor dues, &c., were preferred, swelling the amount to $16 —in itself an inconsiderable item, but the frequency of such charges during an interval of three years amounts to a sum worth noticing. Although the government was destitute of the means of enforcing payment, the amount was paid over, under verbal protest, to some one on the beach who professed himself authorized to receive it. On leaving the port, the master of the vessel expressed a determination never to visit it again, and to do all in his power to prevent similar imposition upon others. When a semi-civilized island, with a provisional government, can offer inducements for vessels to visit its harbors, then, and only then, should it venture a system of port charges, otherwise it drives commerce from its doors.

The two principal islands of Micronesia, Strong's and Ascension, are becoming more generally known since the establishment of the Mission there in 1852. From the 12th October, 1852, to April 7th, 1853, 56 vessels touched at their harbors : of these 1 was an English brig, 1 a Sydney trader, 1 a London whaler, 2 Sydney whalers, 2 Bremen whalers, and the remainder American whalers. The following table of exports and imports of the harbor of Bonabe, island of Ascension, copied from the *Polynesian* (Honolulu) of November 19th, 1853, will be found interesting, as exhibiting the manner in which trade is conducted among the islands of this ocean, where there is an absence of a circulating medium :—

TABLE OF THE EXPORTS AND IMPORTS OF BONABE,

For the Year ending April 1st, 1853.

1.—EXPORTS.

2.—IMPORTS.

Muskets—150 may have been imported during the year, price about 20 lbs. tobacco each. Sheath-knives, 1 lb. tobacco each. Powder, 1 lb. tobacco per lb. Shot. Calicoes, common, 2 yds. for 1 lb. tobacco. Turkey Red, 3 yards for 2 lbs. tobacco. Handkerchiefs, from ¼ to 1 lb. each. Red Flannel Shirts, 4 to 5 lbs. tobacco each. Red Flannel. Red Yarn. Beads. Iron pots, at an average of 1½ lb. per gallon. Hatchets and Axes. Tobacco.

With all its advantages, it cannot be denied that Honolulu is an expensive port for whalers, not so much on account of the port charges, which are subjoined, as the incidental expenses attending a sojourn of any duration there. The following is the list of

PORT CHARGES, &c., FOR WHALERS.

Buoys..	$2 00
Health Certificate	1 00
Pilotage, in and out, each way (per foot)........	1 00
Harbor Master's fees.............................	3 00
Clearance..	1 00

Whalers can land goods to the value of $200 free of duty ; $1,000 worth additional at 5 per cent., without being liable to tonnage dues ; but if they land more than $1,200, (including the $200 free of duty,) they are subject to the same liabilities as merchant vessels.

Products of the whale fishery transhipped free, except cost of entry and permit.

The increased advances demanded by seamen, and the cost of obtaining repairs, are at present the principal cause of complaint, and the following brief extract of a letter from an extensive shipping merchant in one of our Eastern cities will express the sentiments of this intelligent class of community on the subject :—

"Should things continue at the Sandwich Islands as they have for a year or two past, we shall be compelled to instruct our captains not to visit them, unless compelled to do so by stress of weather. The high price of recruits, with the chances of losing their crews, and large amounts demanded as advances to men shipped there, and advocated by the consul and others, will cause it to be ruinous to the interests of owners, if their vessels stop there."

Whaling vessels, on leaving home ports, are manned chiefly by raw recruits, though their insurance policies require that a sufficient number of able seamen be shipped on board of each, otherwise they become invalid. These recruits are sometimes allured on board by a dazzling perspective, but oftener they assume their vocation through choice, and it is to be regretted that an enterprise usually so remunerative to owners offers little or no pecuniary inducement to those of the forecastle, who, by their unwearied efforts abroad, heap up riches for their employers.

On the other hand, it will be adduced that the trouble of initiating them into the profession should be considered an equivalent for their services, and that this, together with a few dollars for liberty money advanced in foreign ports, is a liberal compensation. But the value of their services is lightly estimated. An intelligent and industrious man may in two or three "seasons" become as useful in his calling as those who have passed the term of their apprenticeship; but almost invariably they are shuffled off with the hundred and ninety-second share, or thereabout, and after an absence of two or three years, frequently return indebted to their employers. Certainly there are instances of successful voyages, where the returns have been as remunerating as could be expected, to the apprentices; however, it is reasonable to suppose that were more liberal inducements extended at the outset, (with certain restrictions,) the owners would profit by it in the end, for in all probability their vessels would be spared the delay and expense attending the desertion and providing of new seamen, or if so disposed, in this ocean a deserter can pecuniarily better his condition by reshipping on board other vessels for increased wages. It frequently happens that through sickness, accident, or desertion, these men are thrown upon the hands of our consuls in foreign ports, where hospitals and physicians are, if circumstances permit, provided for them. Having recovered, they reship on other vessels, and if whalers, usually by the season; thus, throughout most ports of the Pacific, will be found a class of half-disciplined seamen.

It is not uncommon to see at such ports seamen lounging about and indulging in the multiplied facilities offered for dissipation, while many of them are ostensibly invalids and reside in their hospitals. The number of protections furnished during the preceding year to *American* seamen engaged in the whaling service was 2,359, and this may suggest an idea of the number that is scattered over the Pacific in our numerous fleet. Many of these are young recruits, who, through recklessness or novelty, venture to sea for the first time, and with unsettled habits, they are at once thrown into the vortex of dissipation, a foreign port. On shore, they perambulate the streets amid strange sights and stranger faces, meeting none who possess with them a sympathy in common, save certain board-and-lodging-house harpies, who blind them by their assiduities until their every resource is exhausted, when they are turned adrift to shift for themselves, or are reshipped by them after having appropriated the lion's share of their advance.

Although our merchant fleet in this ocean is manned by thousands of American seamen, the present subject has reference more especially to our countrymen engaged in the occupation of whaling, and as their number is by no means inconsiderable, it deserves the attention of the benevolent at home with reference to improving their condition. The cause is equally praiseworthy, and would require but a moiety of the charities annually bestowed upon Foreign Missions. The first step towards accomplishing this object would be the permanent establishment of a *Home* which should be for the seamen of *all nations*, at a port most frequented by the whaling fleet ; and with this object in view, no better than Honolulu could be selected in the Pacific Ocean, where, after the return of our vessels from the Northwest cruising-grounds, more than one thousand of our seamen wander through the streets daily. Many of these, who have shipped only for the "season," are discharged, and in company with those whose sojourn is transient, frequent the low haunts of dissipation that abound in that city, where the fruit of their toil is scattered for the gratifications of a moment.

Such an institution should be ample, and conducted by those who have more the *welfare* of the sailor at heart than the acquisition of his earnings, which should be properly cared for, seamen being of all classes the most improvident. Independent of the temporal advantages resulting from its proper management, the moral benefits necessarily conferred could not be otherwise than gratifying to its founders. Amid a well-selected library would be passed many of the hours now worse than squandered, and the proceeds of their labors, instead of pandering to sensuality, would gladden many an honest hearth made desolate by the absence of a son or a brother. Had such an institution, or its equivalent, existed, the disgraceful occurrences of the fall of 1852 would probably not have been witnessed in Honolulu, nor would Americans have had occasion to blush at the conduct of their countrymen. When the "seasons" have been favorable, the amounts paid out to seamen are comparatively large, the greater portion of which go to enrich the vendors of liquors, and, as fines, the national treasury. On one occasion, the Sheriff of Oahu removed from the pocket of a drunken petty officer, who was staggering through the streets, one thousand dollars in Californian ingots, which were afterwards returned to him when sober.

It has been surmised by some that at certain ports in this ocean a mutual understanding has existed between consul and hospital physician. If such be the case, a trifling derangement of the system is construed into the incipient stage of some serious disorder, and half astonished, half pleased at the change, the seaman, despite the protestations of his captain, is transferred from the ship to the hospital, where he is dosed with boluses, while the Secretary of the Treasury subsequently foots the exorbitant, and in many instances, useless charges of the bill. The custom of employing the subjects of foreign nations to officiate as American consuls is rarely if ever satisfactory to either master or seaman, and it is useless to expect a manifestation of the same interest in their affairs that would characterize the offices of an American substitute occupying the same position; at least, let judicious reference be had to character or habits, so that personal remissness may not compromise or mock the dignity of the nation represented.

An instance of this nature occurred less than a year ago at one of the ports in this ocean, on which occasion a foreigner acting as American consul, having received a complaint from a passenger concerning alleged injuries received from the captain, proceeded, full of the importance of his mission, to the ship, at anchor in the harbor, and after reaching the deck, he was a spectacle of mirth for the crew. He wore the cocked hat, blue coat, buttons and epaulettes; in short, he was in full uniform, with one exception—he was *barefooted !* Having inquired whether the captain was on board, and receiving an affirmative answer, he assumed an oratorical position, and alternately poising himself on his toes and heels, to give emphasis to his sentiments, he commenced with : " Sir!—I have the honor—to be—the American consul." Such instances are ludicrous ; and the trappings of rank or station prostituted in this manner, savor more of the Fiji drummer than of the insignia of a great nation.

Our system of remunerating consular services by fees, in many instances works badly. While at such ports as Honolulu, Melbourne, &c., moderate fortunes are realized, the compensation received by our agents in less frequented situations is hardly deserving of consideration. For instance, while the British consul at the Society Islands receives a salary of £500 per annum, without a moiety of the national business to transact that devolves on the American consul at the Georgian Islands, the perquisites of the latter are so insignificant that they are freely tendered as remuneration for services to an assistant. Consuls so situated must necessarily engage in commercial pursuits, and are consequently regarded in an inferior light by those who grant them their *exequaturs.* To this paltry remuneration may be referred the unpleasant recriminations that have frequently transpired between them and those whose interests they represent, owing to their onerous charges for trivial services, and to which they are compelled to resort to glean a hasty harvest during the brief existence of their constituent administration.

There is another feature connected with this branch of enterprise that is worthy of consideration. As insignificant means are sometimes precursors of great events, we have evidences that the attainment of an object does not necessarily imply exclusive associations, equivalent or paramount to the principles it professes, but that from obscure beginnings we may often obtain the happiest results. No brighter example need be instanced than that of Hawaii, where those who have aided in framing her laws, together with those pre-eminent in developing her agricultural resources, have brooded their ambition in a whaler's forecastle. Without resorting to individual instances, we cast a comprehensive glance over this broad field, and discover that a great proportion of the original pioneers among the groups, pursuing the vocations of husbandry, trading, and mechanics, have at some period contributed their labors to this branch of American commerce. Daily do our whalers display the flag of their Republic to civilized nations and savage tribes, and in connection with American and English merchantmen, they are creating new wants for, and giving a new language to, the natives of the Pacific Isles. Though, as a general rule, the commanders of this fleet are skilful and intelligent men, they do not, except in a few instances, possess those scientific acquirements for observation which would enable them to profit by the numerous opportunities afforded for the investigation of nautical phenomena. An uniform system of hydrographic or meteorologic observations by them for one year would fill volumes, and comprehensive books, carefully prepared, for the latter purpose, are furnished them by Lieut. Maury, of the Observatory at Washington.

I cannot close this subject without expressing a sense of obligation for the uniform courtesy and attention experienced from those masters of whalers whom I have occasionally met during the last six years. It is sincerely hoped that nothing that has been written will be construed to the disparagement of themselves or their profession, for no unprejudiced observer can witness their efforts abroad without awarding the praise their energy and perseverance merit. To one and all, I return my warmest thanks for their attention, humbly offering my best wishes for their continued prosperity.

13

Check Out More Titles From HardPress Classics Series In this collection we are offering thousands of classic and hard to find books. This series spans a vast array of subjects — so you are bound to find something of interest to enjoy reading and learning about.

Subjects:
Architecture
Art
Biography & Autobiography
Body, Mind &Spirit
Children & Young Adult
Dramas
Education
Fiction
History
Language Arts & Disciplines
Law
Literary Collections
Music
Poetry
Psychology
Science
…and many more.

Visit us at www.hardpress.net

Im The Story

personalised classic books

"Beautiful gift, lovely finish.
My Niece loves it, so precious!"

Helen R Brumfielden

★★★★★

UNIQUE GIFT

FOR KIDS, PARTNERS
AND FRIENDS

Timeless books such as:

Kids

Alice in Wonderland · The Jungle Book · The Wonderful Wizard of Oz
Peter and Wendy · Robin Hood · The Prince and The Pauper
The Railway Children · Treasure Island · A Christmas Carol

Adults

Romeo and Juliet · Dracula

Highly Customize size   **Change** Book's Title   **Replace** Character's Names with yours   **Upload** Fluffo (not inside page)   **Add** Inscriptions

Visit
Im The Story.com

and order yours today!